John and Sally McKenna's .... *Irish Food Guide* is a unique exploration of Ireland's exciting food culture. The only objective the McKennas pursue is excellence, whether in examining the food of the best known restaurants or in assessing a farmhouse cheese sold only in its locality, describing country markets or artisan crafts people, visiting a salmon smoker or discovering the best places to eat when you are travelling the main roads of Ireland.

No other guide to Ireland encompasses such a broad range of subjects and describes them in such vivid and humorous detail, and no other guide book introduces you to the men and women who have become such a vital and enjoyable part of Ireland's food renaissance. With full details of the finest restaurants, shops and markets, the best places to stay and the most charismatic pubs, this is the essential guide and the essential travelling companion.

John and Sally McKenna won the first-ever André Simon Special Commendation Award for the second edition of the Bridgestone Irish Food Guide.

'An indispensable companion. Every possible food source...is described in memorable prose'. *Frances Bissell, The Times*

'An invaluable volume for proper eating in Ireland'. *Matthew Fort, The Guardian*

'Well written, independent — and utterly indispensable'. *Cara*

First published in 1993 by Estragon Press Ltd, Durrus, Co Cork
© Estragon Press

Text copyright © John McKenna and Sally McKenna 1993
Illustrations and maps copyright © Ken Buggy 1993
Cover photo © Lucy Johnston 1993

The moral right of the authors has been asserted

ISBN 1 874076 08 1

Designed by Karl Tsigdinos for Gold Star Media Ltd, Montrose, Dublin 4.
Tel: (01) 260-0899
Printed by Colour Books Ltd, Baldoyle, Co Dublin Tel: (01) 325812
Cover Photo by Lucy Johnston, Garville Lane Studios, Rathgar, Dublin 6.
Tel: (01) 960584

*Cover photograph features Hazel Bourke, chef at Assolas Country House, Kanturk, County
Cork, gathering herbs in the garden at Assolas. Organic vegetables grown by Paul Schultz,
near Bantry, County Cork.*

THE BRIDGESTONE
IRISH FOOD GUIDE

JOHN MCKENNA

SALLY MCKENNA

With illustrations and maps by Ken Buggy

ESTRAGON PRESS

FOR DES COLLINS

With thanks to:
Connie for sleeping nights, Colm Conyngham, Karl, Lucy, Eddie, Sarah Bates for her hard work, Benedict, Almut Schlepper and Kevin Connolly, Mary Hallissey and Des Rainey, Cynthia Harrison, Cathleen Buggy, Malachy Keenan, Patsey Murphy, Harry Browne, Mary Dowey, Ray Buckley and John Harold, James O'Shea, Tom Owens, Robin Gourlay, Roger Lascelles, Ethna McKiernan, and Pat Ruane

JOHN McKENNA was born in Belfast and educated both there and in Dublin, where he practised as a barrister before turning to writing in 1989. His work appears in newspapers and magazines in Ireland and the U.K. In 1993 he won the Glenfiddich Regional Writer of the Year Award for journalism.

SALLY McKENNA was born in Kenya, and brought up on the Pacific island of Fiji before coming to Ireland in 1982. She cooked professionally before turning to writing about food and restaurants. She is a member of the accreditation panel of the Bio-dynamic Agricultural Association in Ireland.

Ken Buggy was born in Dublin in 1947 and has spent most of his working life abroad. He now lives in Kinsale with his wife Cathleen and their four children.

Karl Tsigdinos was born in Boston, Massachusetts in 1954, and has lived in Dublin since 1977. He is a publisher and journalist, as well as an international award-winning graphic designer.

Lucy Johnston has been running her own studio in Dublin for the last fifteen years. In 1989 her photographic book on the capital, 'Dublin Then and Now', was published, and she has also contributed to the book 'Women in Focus'. She works regularly for Bord Failté publications as well as for a number of magazines and newspapers.

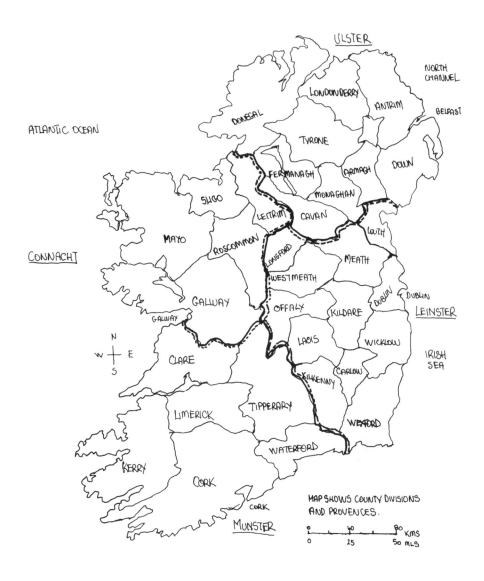

ULSTER

NORTH CHANNEL

LONDONDERRY

ANTRIM

BELFAST

ATLANTIC OCEAN

DONEGAL

TYRONE

DOWN

FERMANAGH

ARMAGH

SLIGO

MONAGHAN

LETTRIM

CAVAN

LOUTH

CONNACHT

MAYO

ROSCOMMON

LONGFORD

MEATH

WESTMEATH

DUBLIN

DUBLIN

GALWAY

OFFALY

KILDARE

LEINSTER

GALWAY

LAOIS

WICKLOW

IRISH SEA

CLARE

CARLOW

KILKENNY

TIPPERARY

LIMERICK

WEXFORD

WATERFORD

KERRY

CORK

MUNSTER

CORK

MAP SHOWS COUNTY DIVISIONS AND PROVENCES.

0   40   80 KMS
0   25   50 MLS

N
W + E
S

BRIDGESTONE

CONTENTS

⚡BRIDGESTONE

BRIDGESTONE IS JAPAN'S LARGEST TYRE MANUFACTURER and one of the top three in the world. Founded in 1931, the company has striven to maintain an emphasis on technological advancement and service while expanding the scale and scope of its operations. As a result the company is recognised as a leader in tyre manufacturing and technology.

Bridgestone Tyres are presently sold in more than 150 countries. There are twelve manufacturing plants in Japan with others throughout the world including the U.S.A. and Australia. Bridgestone now also manufactures its tyres in Europe following the acquisition in 1988 of the Firestone Tyre and Rubber Company.

They manufacture tyres for many different vehicles, from trucks and buses to passenger cars and motor-cycles. Its commercial vehicle tyres enjoy a worldwide reputation for superior cost-per-kilometre performance, and its aircraft tyres are used by more than 100 international airlines. Many Japanese cars imported to Ireland arrive with Bridgestone Tyres and a host of exotic sports cars including Ferrari, Lamborghini, Porsche, Jaguar and TVR are now fitted with Bridgestone tyres as original equipment.

Bridgestone is at the forefront of tyre research and development. Its proving ground in Kuroiso City, Japan covers 400,000 square metres and consists of a 3.5 kilometre banked test track and skid pan which together contain more than 40 different road surfaces. Bridgestone also operate an advanced R&D facility in Kodaira, Japan. Testing focuses on a wide range of features including directional stability, skid resistance, durability, abrasion resistance, riding comfort and noise reduction. All this data is then put to valuable use in the development of new and better tyres. Bridgestone is now the most technologically advanced tyre manufacturer in the world.

In June 1990 Bridgestone (Ireland) Ltd was established as a subsidiary of the multinational Bridgestone Corporation to take over the distribution of its tyres in Ireland. The company operates from its offices and warehouse in Tallaght in Dublin where it stocks a wide range of passenger car, commercial vehicle and earthmover tyres. Bridgestone staff also provide sales, technical and delivery services all over the country.

Bridgestone tyres are available from tyre dealers throughout Ireland. For further information contact Bridgestone (Ireland) Ltd., Unit A30, Greenhills Industrial Estate, Tallaght, Dublin 24. Tel: (01) 527766 Fax: (01) 527478

HOW TO USE THIS BOOK

THIS BOOK IS ARRANGED ALPHABETICALLY, firstly into the four provinces of Ireland — Connaught, Leinster, Munster and Ulster — and then into the individual counties within the provinces.

Within the counties, the arrangement of the book again follows alphabetically, so Galway city, for example, will follow after Clarinbridge, both of them in the chapter on County Galway, which is in the province of Connaught. The maps include the names of the major towns and villages which are described, but they should be used only as a general guide to location and in conjunction with an accurate Ordnance Survey map.

All visits to the restaurants, hotels, country houses and bed and breakfasts included in this book were made anonymously. All meals and accommodation were paid for and any offers of discounts or gifts were refused. Any food products bought from shops or growers were paid for.

Inclusion in 'The Bridgestone Irish Food Guide' is an implicit recommendation for every particular entry. Where producers, growers, shops, hotels or restaurants have been visited and found to be of an insufficiently high standard, or where they have recently changed hands, they have simply been excluded.

However, in certain cities we have included a restaurant directory in order to give as much useful information as possible. You will enjoy a good meal in these places but, obviously, they are not recommended to the same extent as those establishments which have been considered worthy of an individual entry.

In a number of cases, where we have encountered a producer, cheesemaker, grower, restaurateur, shopkeeper or hotelier whose work represents a special and unique effort in terms of Irish food and Ireland's food culture, we have awarded these people a star and marked these entries thus: ★. These people are, simply, the very best at what they do.

In other cases where we felt the food was of special interest we have marked the entry with a ➡, meaning that the entry is worthy of making a special detour to enjoy the food.

The farming community covered by the Guide is that body of growers who farm according to Organic or Bio-Dynamic principles and hold either the symbol of The Irish Organic Farmers and Growers Association or The Organic Trust, or the Demeter Symbol.

Many Irish restaurants and country houses, particularly those in the south and west of the country, are seasonal. Many others change their opening times during the winter. Even though opening times are given for restaurants it is always advisable in Ireland to telephone in advance and check opening times when booking a meal.

KEY:

PRICES: £ means a meal should cost less than £5, ££ under £10, £££ under £20, ££££ under £30 and £££££ over £30. Again, it is wise to confirm prices, which change frequently, when booking.

DIRECTIONS: wherever possible these have been given but, if in doubt, then do remember that asking a passing local will not only help you find your way, it will likely delay you for a further twenty minutes as you collect valuable and unrepeatable gossip about the people who run the place where you are headed.

THE BRIDGESTONE AWARDS

CERTAIN OBVIOUS AND EASILY ASSESSABLE FACTORS allow you to distinguish one cook from another, allow you to say that one baker, grower, shopkeeper, hotelier or Country House keeper is superior at what they do than their counterparts. They will, inevitably, demonstrate greater skill and competence, greater confidence, a more finely tuned vision of what they want to achieve with their work.

But, when one discusses those people in Ireland who are the very best at what they do, other factors become involved, other considerations come into play which then allow you to set these people apart, to consider their work as the very pinnacle of just what someone in a food culture can achieve. These factors can be more difficult to grasp, it may indeed take a considerable time before you appreciate just how important they are, but over time you realise that the contribution which these restaurateurs and growers and cheesemakers and fish smokers make to Ireland's food culture is a vital and important thing in itself.

This is one of the considerations which we have applied when deciding who should be awarded the following series of Stars and Detours. Certain individuals, over the course of time, can be seen to have contributed a significant and vital presence to our food culture, and this has allowed us to make the agonizingly awkward distinctions which separate those awarded a Star from those whose work we consider merits a Detour.

Another consideration which has weighed heavily has been the presence, amongst these people, of an instinctive capacity for self-criticism. Nothing is more disappointing than to see an individual achieve a peak of recognition, and for them to then believe that they can progress no further. The people we have distinguished from the major body of entries in this book have, we believe, an instinctual capacity for self-criticism which means that they insist on progress and improvement as an integral part of their work.

Entries in The Bridgestone Irish Food Guide Awarded a Star (★)

Restaurants

BALLYMALOE HOUSE, Shanagarry, Co Cork
CLIFFORD'S, Cork City, Co Cork
DRIMCONG HOUSE, Moycullen, Co Galway
LONGUEVILLE HOUSE, Mallow, Co Cork
ROSCOFF, Belfast, Co Antrim
TRUFFLES, Sligo, Co Sligo

Shops

CONTINENTAL SAUSAGES, Fossa, Co Kerry
COUNTRY CHOICE, Nenagh, Co Tipperary
COURTYARD, Schull, Co Cork
GALLIC KITCHEN, Dublin, Co Dublin
GOYA'S, Galway, Co Galway
HICK'S BUTCHERS, Sallynoggin, Co Dublin
JAMES NICHOLSON, Crossgar, Co Down
MANNING'S EMPORIUM, Ballylickey, Co Cork
NICKY'S PLAICE, Howth, Co Dublin
SEA VIEW HOUSE FARM SHOP, Inniscrone, Co Sligo
TIR NA NOG, Sligo, Co Sligo

Food Producers

COOLEA FARMHOUSE CHEESE, Coolea, Co Cork
CORLEGGY FARMHOUSE CHEESE, Cavan, Co Cavan
CROGHAN FARMHOUSE CHEESE, Blackwater, Co Wexford
DURRUS FARMHOUSE CHEESE, Durrus, Co Cork
EDEN PLANTS, Rosinver, Co Leitrim
GUBBEEN FARMHOUSE CHEESE, Schull, Co Cork
INAGH FARMHOUSE CHEESE, Inagh, Co Clare
LANGE, Udo & Penny, Kiltegan, Co Wicklow
MACROOM OATMEAL, Macroom, Co Cork
MAUCNACLEA CHEESES, Cork, Co Cork
UMMERA SMOKED SALMON, Timoleague, Co Cork
WEST CORK NATURAL CHEESES, Schull, Co Cork

Entries in The Bridgestone Irish Food Guide Awarded Worth a Detour (➥)

Restaurants

ASSOLAS HOUSE, Kanturk, Co Cork
BEECH HILL COUNTRY HOTEL, Derry, Co Londonderry
DESTRY RIDES AGAIN, Clifden, Co Galway
DUNWORLEY COTTAGE, Butlerstown, Co Cork
EUGENE'S RESTAURANT, Ballyedmond, Co Wexford
HEIR ISLAND RESTAURANT, Heir Island, Co Cork
LACKEN HOUSE, Kilkenny, Co Kilkenny
LETTERCOLLUM HOUSE, Timoleague, Co Cork
NICK'S WAREHOUSE, Belfast, Co Antrim
PACKIES, Kenmare, Co Kerry
SHIRO JAPANESE DINNER HOUSE, Ahakista, Co Cork
STRAWBERRY TREE, Killarney, Co Kerry
THE OYSTERCATCHER RESTAURANT, Oysterhaven, Co Cork

Shops

ADELE'S, Schull, Co Cork
ASIA SUPERMARKET, Belfast, Co Antrim
DAVID BURNS, Bangor, Co Down
LOUGHNANE, Sean, Galway, Co Galway
MCCAMBRIDGE'S, Galway, Co Galway
MCCARTNEY'S, Moira, Co Antrim
MCGEOUGH, Eamonn, Oughterard, Co Galway
WHAT ON EARTH, Dublin, Co Dublin

Food Producers

CHRIS JEPSON, Schull, Co Cork
CLONAKILTY BLACK PUDDING, Twomey's, Co Cork
COOLEENEY CAMEMBERT, Thurles, Co Tipperary
LAVISTOWN FOODS, Lavistown, Co Kilkenny
LIR CHOCOLATES, Dublin, Co Dublin
ORGANIC LIFE, Kilpedder, Co Wicklow
PAUL SCHULTZ, Bantry, Co Cork
SALMON & SEAFOOD, Clifden, Co Galway

INTRODUCTION

GOOD FOOD EXPRESSES AND REVEALS PERSONALITY just as readily, and just as wittily, as a person. Often, the wit and the personality one finds in good food — and by good food we mean real, handmade, individual food — is the personality of the person who makes it. What the food also likely shares with its owner is a sense of passion.

It is never easy to decide to make and create and prepare real food. There are more lucrative and more stable careers one could choose, easier lifestyles to follow than those of the organic farmer, the farmhouse cheesemaker, the discriminating wine merchant, the inspired and ever-learning chef. The attractions of the commercial marketplace are many, and yet, year in and year out, people in Ireland decide that their vocation — and it is necessary to use that term — is to grow or produce or make or create real food.

They do this, of course, because the making of real food is no less of an artistic yearning and the expression of an artistic need than is the desire to make music, pen poetry or paint pictures, maybe even direct movies. Making real food answers the need in the person to discover an instinctive, organic, pleasurable way of working. For, whilst few other métiers demand just so much of the individual — the necessity to appreciate all the aesthetics of taste, smell, appearance, intrinsic value, balance, satisfaction, sensual appeal — few other jobs of work give back such a sense of simple, untrammelled joy.

The secret of this pleasure, and it is often the root of the passion also, is the wondrous sense of transformation which making and cooking food involves. We might say, then, that cheesemakers are the poets of the food world, taking the base matter of their language, in this case milk, and by means of their skill and their sophistication and their sensuality, turning the base matter into something with all the pleasure-giving potential of an ode, an object that may be simple and may seem easy to take for granted, but one which is, in effect, fit for us to rhapsody.

Chefs and cooks are, surely, the musicians of this artistic world, their creations and inventions striving towards the mellifluity of Mozart, the perfect balance of Sinatra, the hungry famishment of John Coltrane. For the bakers and patissiers we must think of painters: the precise line of a risen loaf, the severe execution demanded of the pastry maker, the broad vista of taste which a good baker will give to each part of their work is no less than the panoramic canvas, which underhangs the forefront doodles and sketches and reiterations of the work.

It would be possible to draw these sorts of analogies endlessly, but what unifies them all is the fact that for the makers of real food, good food, simply churning out a product is not enough. Their work must evoke not only themselves — their personality, their passion — it must also evoke something greater than themselves.

What this is, we think, is a basic sense of optimism, the optimism which is expressed in the care, concern and skill they use to make their food. This optimism further manifests itself in their hope that their food will give pleasure, that it will be enjoyed in communion with family and friends, that it will give to our lives those very qualities of care and concern, and thereby enrich our days with the tactile enjoyment of their skills. This is the goal of artists everywhere, and whilst the producers and growers and cooks who you will read about in this book might more usually be called artisans, they fully deserve to be called artists. Artists of the food world.

People often ask us just what sort of criteria we are looking for when it comes to deciding who it is we finally include in this book. The obvious answer is that we are looking for the very best of everything — the best foods, the best cooking, the best hospitality, the best in whatever environment we encounter it. But it would be truer to say that we are looking for the best people, those artists of the food world, those modest and dedicated people who, in answering a need in themselves, furnish us with so much of the language of pleasure, the language of love.

When we began to write books, we decided to include as many geographical directions as possible, in order to enable people to actually find their way to the cheese house or the sea weed grower or the herb farmer or whatever. Many people, most of whom were, mercifully, decently polite about it, thought we were insane to do this. 'Why should we drive two and a half miles up a mountain after we turn left at the church and keep our eyes peeled for a rusting Morris Minor before taking the third on the left, when we can buy the food in the local shop?', they would ask. Our only answer was that it was fun to put yourself through all those contortions, and great fun, then, to meet the people.

In recent times, fewer and fewer people have doubted our sanity when they read some tortuously involved set of directions, and more and more of them now choose to turn left at the church and head up the hill.

For, in meeting the producer, they get a glimpse of the personality and the passion which is the sole reason for that food being in existence and they come to realise that this is not merely good fun, it is also a vital act of enjoying the food. You may take back with you a cheese or two or an armful of loaves or a clatter of sausages, but you also take back the memories of the person who makes the food, those remarkable people who, for precious little reward, make these foods that sustain us. Ireland is a richer, better place for these artisan artists, these poets and musicians and painters of the food world. We do our best to try to describe and evoke their work, to give some idea of what they do and how you can best enjoy it. But we are resigned to never ever being able to do them justice through words alone, and can only suggest that you discover these people for yourselves, and succumb to the pleasure of the magic you will find in their work.

JOHN MCKENNA
SALLY MCKENNA
Durrus, Co Cork

CONNAUGHT

THE ARAN ISLANDS, COUNTY GALWAY

THE POET SEAMUS HEANEY has described the three islands of Aran as 'stepping stones out of Europe', a precise and poetic sizing of the lonely trio's appearance on a map. There they rest, just a hop, a step and a jump away from Clare, from Galway and Connemara, alone together in the Atlantic, with New York to the west and the sallow gap that is Galway Bay opening away to the east. Inis Mór, Inis Maan and Inis Oirr: Big Island, Middle Island, Eastern Island.

Step out of Europe, onto the stones, and you are greeted with a surround of clean green sea and by limestone, limestone everywhere. Slate grey in colour, threaded here and there by green pastures, and trellised by mile after mile of dry stone walls. The writer Tim Robinson has described this eviscerated landscape: 'This bare, soluble limestone is a uniquely tender and memorious ground... this land has provided its inhabitants — the Neolithic tomb-builders, the celtic cashelor, the monastic architect, the fence-making grazier of all ages — with one material only, stone, which may fall, but still endures.'

One material only, stone, and from that the people of Aran have fashioned, in alliance and in opposition with nature's elements, the intense topography which constitutes their home. In places, out perhaps towards the south-west of Inis Mór, near to the village of Gort na gCapall where the writer Liam O'Flaherty was born, the endless miles of walls, the miles of stones upon stones are so vivid that they can appear, under the haze of a summer sun, to be as articulate as the finest filigree lace work.

Sit amidst them and it seems that each stone amidst the countless legions of stones has been selected for its place in the wall with infinite patience, infinite care. And perhaps they have, for whilst Robinson mentions that the stone may fall, in fact little of it does. Winter storms can be ferocious on the Arans, but the walls survive, the architecture endures. The art of the craftsmen who assembled these monuments to human labour was such that delicacy, here, implies strength.

Within the islands, within the quiet and dedicated air of Inis Oirr, the introverted and cool mellowness of Inis Maan and the frolicsome energy of Inis Mór, there are two further Arans. One is the bustling islands with their summer schools for language students on Inis Oirr, the Synge symposia on Inis Maan, the day trippers in Kilronan.

The other is the quiet Aran, another place found by trawling through the boreens and turloughs, found by defiantly walking on the low road to Kilmurvey Bay, or down from Baile na Caishlean to the lighthouse, in search of gentian violets, bee orchids or other rare flowers, in search of the measure of the place.

Within this quietude, the quixotic immensity of the islands becomes manifest. Here, you learn, is a place where each and every field has a name, an individual title which spells its history, its function. And these fields have been sculpted by human effort: the stones collected and assembled into walls, the surface rock broken and prised apart, before sand and sea weed were laid down to make the light soil which forms the pastures and fields.

Within the islands themselves, there is then further elaboration, for the wall builders in one part will have built their honeycombs of stone in a different style from the islanders who live elsewhere. Perhaps they built differently because they are, in themselves, different, though only a few miles separate them. Folklorists will tell you that people from the western side of Inis Mór, of Bun Gabhla, of Creig An Cheirin, of Eoghanacht, are earthy people, frank about many private things, which is not what one might expect down

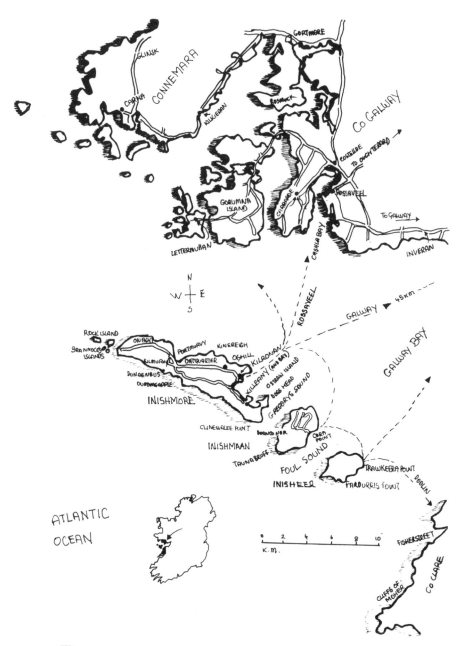

east in Kilronan, or in Cill Éinne.

On Inis Mór one finds more of the blow-ins, the arrivistes who have come to Aran to settle, many of them transfixed by a single visit which decreed that they must return. Unpicking their previous lives, the artful tapestries of lives and lovers which they left behind, is a joyful diversion, as is listening to the way in which the soft lick and lilt of the Irish language has changed the way they speak for ever.

Ask one what the island is like in the dead of winter and she replies; 'Ah, fantastic. You should see the seas, all aubergine coloured'. Poetry, and precision, come as second nature to them after a while. Attracted by the myth of Aran, that endless dream which J. M. Synge's dull little book about the islands fomented and which Robert Flaherty's movie 'Man Of Aran' etched onto celluloid and thence into our consciousness, they soon become a part of it.

One finds this tight knot of history and complexity in many things. The Aran sweaters knitted by Siobhan McGuinness in her little cottage on Inis Mór, near to the Church of the Four Comely Saints, are true Aran sweaters, for Siobhan takes an Aran fleece to begin and, after carding, spinning and washing, she finally knits the gansy. And, even here, the stitches which dictate the pattern of the jumper have a significance beyond mere ornamentation, for they echo the religious beliefs which Siobhan seeks to practice, and there is a story behind each beautiful weave of wool.

Others will tell you that they can identify who knitted a particular sweater just by looking at it, and one remembers that, in the past, drowned islanders would be identified by their sweaters. More happily, the gorgeous sweaters knitted on Inis Maan which find their way to the four corners of the earth can form a happy communion of memories when you see one abroad, far from home.

The slow patience which strolling, clambering and exploring the islands provokes is rewarded not just by an appreciation of the initially mundane. For there are mysteries here also. That turlough, which a few days ago seemed filled with water is, today, a pasture, replete with cud-chewing cattle. You walk down into it and marvel at the profusion of mint which now graces the surface, and find that the only remnant of the glowing lake you saw earlier is a tiny stream of water in which some watercress still survives.

This overwhelming detail — in walls, in wool, in the glottal swoop of soft Irish, in remnants and in faces, in private histories and public monuments — seems all the more remarkable when one stands on the summits and fringes of the islands, high up at Dun Aengus fort, at Synge's Chair up on the highest cliffs of Inis Maan, at the lighthouse on the south side of Inis Oirr.

Then you realise that the land all around can be seen as it tumbles into the sea, for only myth has made the Arans mighty. These stepping stones are tiny, and can seem almost pathetically vulnerable shards of limestone. But the communities of people who have hewn and carved their pasts and their presents into these islands have paid little attention to their violability, and have bequeathed to them a secret, inner life from the fabrics of language and community, and stone.

INIS MOR
KILRONAN

RESTAURANT & ACCOMMODATION
CLIFF HOUSE

The Scrigeen, Kilronan Tel: (099) 61286 Olwin Gill

Olwin Gill's cooking is generous and taste-loaded, able to offer moments of quiet magic as you savour some roasted lamb and a plate of floury spuds, a fresh grilled fillet of sole in a grainy mustard sauce, an absurdly creamy strawberry-layered concoction for dessert. The tastes are true and appropriate, perfect pleasure after a day in the wind-blown wonder of Aran. The bedrooms in the B&B are simple and fine value.

Open for dinner, bookings only, Mon-Sun. Closed Xmas day. Average Price: dinner £££ B&B £££. No Credit Cards. Cliff House overlooks the harbour at Kilronan.

ACCOMMODATION AND RESTAURANT
MAINISTIR HOUSE HOSTEL

Inis Mór Tel: (099) 61169 Joël d'Anjou & Tara Rafferty

Mainistir house has always been a visionary venture, the pursuit of an ideal vision of hospitality and informality, of simplicity and satisfaction, culture and comfort. It is very much the vision of Joël d'Anjou, assisted perfectly by his trusty sidekicks Tara and Mairtin, and it is true to say that no one else could make it succeed.

M d'Anjou makes it work by being a cultured man without a trace of snobbery, by being a private person who loves to share his space with people, by being of such a singular frame of mind that the idea of Mainistir — it is called a hostel but is closer to a pensione in design and orientation — offering accommodation to both backpackers and families, offering sublime food at a knockdown price in the format of a buffet in the evenings, offering at times what seems the essence of Aranness, is an idea made real.

There is nowhere else like it, right from the sound of Gregorian chant on the tape player that begins the day, devolving later on into some Mozart arias, perhaps a little Miles Davis, or Willard White singing spirituals, all of them setting the mood and tone with judicious tempos. The 'Vaguely Vegetarian' buffets which Joël and Tara cook for dinner are happy, intelligent creations: a celery broth, some sweet grains and pulses, maybe even crab quiche, whatever takes their fancy on the day makes its way out to the dining room on top of great big North African plates. In summertime, Mainistir is perfect. For a unique Christmas, it is extraordinary. At any time, you will wish to be nowhere else but here.

Open for dinner 8pm sharp (7.30pm winter). Open for Xmas. Average Price: dinner ££ B&B ££-£££. Visa, Access. No wine licence — wine available in shop. Recommended for Vegetarians. When you arrive on the pier ask for Mairtin.

SNACK AND SANDWICH BAR
PEIG'S

Kilronan

A snack and sandwich bar with tables both inside and out. Good for bumper lunchtime sandwiches as well as muffins and carrot cake.

Open 11am-6pm Tue-Sun

PUB
JOE WATTY'S PUB
Kilronan Tel: (099) 61155
Cold beer, warm chowders, hot sessions.
Open pub hours, selling soup and sandwiches from approximately 12.30pm-7pm

ACCOMMODATION
ST. CIARAN'S
Oughill Tel: (099) 61238 Bernadette Street
Bernadette and Jim Street's house, about a mile up the road from Kilronan, is a house filled with discerning objects, cultured things, items of craft that give pleasure when you

see them first, but give more pleasure when you look at them again. It's a bright, amusing house, with a lovely dining room to enjoy your lovely breakfast, with so-cosy bedrooms, with arse-swaggering ducks outside meandering amidst the squiggly geese and the sleepy pooches.

You will fully need the bolstering charge of hearty porridge and some fresh eggs, perhaps some apple and cinnamon or banana muffins with a belt of strong tea, to persuade you to leave the house in the morning and set about your explorations.

Open for B&B only. Closed 1 Nov-end Apr. Average Price: B&B £££. No Credit Cards. Take one of the mini buses from the pier, or the airport. There will be a small charge but you'll find it's worth it.

ALSO OF INTEREST
AN T-SEAN CHEIBH, Kilronan Tel: (099) 61228 The name means The Old Pier, and this is the first restaurant you stumble across when you arrive off the boat. Simple food, chip shop fare or self-service meals, and a nifty verandah to sit under and watch the arrivistes.
Open 10am-10pm Apr-Nov

DUN AENGUS, Kilronan Tel: (099) 61104 P.J. and Grace Flaherty's restaurant may not boast quite the dramatic fallaway view of the fort after which their restaurant is named, but they don't do too badly as regards scenery. This Dún Aengus overlooks Kileaney Bay and is open from breakfast to dinner. Go for Guinness and seafood, or tea and fruit cake.
Open 10am-10pm 7 days Apr-Nov

M.E. POWELL'S, Kilronan The general shop for the island, so you can buy something to stop birds nesting in your chimney, something to keep off the rain or simply some simple food for your picnic.

INIS MEAIN

CRAFTS
INIS MEAIN KNITTING COMPANY
Tel: (099) 73009 Aine de Blácam
The middle island is tricky to get to — the piers are absurdly short — and can be awkward

to get off, but it would be worth swimming across in order to buy the lovely sweaters of the Inis Meain Knitting Company.

Shop open 8.30am-5pm Mon-Fri, open 7 days in summer

INIS OIRR

ACCOMMODATION WITH MEALS
BRID POIL
Baile an Chaisleáin Tel: (099) 75019 Bríd Poíl
There is no better base from which to seek out the measure of little Inis Oirr than Bríd Poíl's welcoming bungalow in the village of Baile an Chaisleáin. Arrive in the morning and the swaddling smell of just-baked bread might meet you, served with that cup of tea you need to revive the limbs after you have hauled your bags up from the boat or the 'plane.
At dinner time you can expect the comforting odours of sweet lamb, just-right fish, the dry air of floury spuds. Mrs Poíl is a fine cook. An enlivening appreciation and respect for food animates her work, all the way from soft, babbly soups to soporific, creamy cakes. Combined with excellent housekeeping and nonchalant comfort, it adds up to the ideal B&B.

Open for dinner for guests only, from 6.30pm, Closed Dec & Jan. Average Price: dinner ££ B&B £££. No Credit Cards. The house is near the airport, ask directions there or at the pier.

RESTAURANT
FISHERMAN'S COTTAGE
Inis Oírr, Tel: (099) 75073 Enda and Marie Conneely
On a good day you can sit outside, joining well-heeled Scandinavians with good tans and wrinkly Americans with good hats. The food is good, but would benefit from a little more finishing. The seafood lunches are always fun, however: Aran Chowder, goujons of pollock and perhaps an upfront Aussie Chardonnay to help you wonder how the day disappears so fast.

Open noon-4.30pm (5pm high season), 7.30pm-10pm Mon-Sun (limited hours during winter, telephone first). Average Price: lunch ££ dinner £££. Visa, Access. Near the pier.

CONNEMARA

THE LANDSCAPE OF CONNEMARA is as beautiful as heartbreak, as consoling as a kiss. Once you have left the rinky-dink rumble of Oughterard behind you and set out west on the road to Clifden, evening falls with the colours multiplying their shades of shale: rock grey, pool blue and pool black, soft silver, all of them ebbing and flowing underneath a fire orange sky.
As night draws in, the darkness swaddles the mountains in black, just as during the day they will be occluded by waterfalls of cloud. The beauty is frightening, with all its positive energy, its gracious giving. For mile after mile, mile after mile, the mystic ruggedness unwinds, and you reach the pertinacious town of Clifden with your vision totally surfeited.

North of the town, around the lakes with their tickertapes of white ribbon waves, the land almost resembles the Dordogne, in France: craggy and peaceful, sullen and kind, potent.

BALLINAFAD

RESTAURANT/HOTEL
BALLYNAHINCH CASTLE HOTEL
Ballinafad Tel: (095) 31006 John O'Connor
Though it is big beamed like a castle, and grey like an hotel, Ballynahinch has never lost the principle of pleasure-pursuit which led to its being built, originally, as a weekend sporting retreat.
Maharajah Ranjitsinji bought the house in the 1930s in order to entertain his friends during the winter and, today, the Castle Hotel still feels more like a country house than many of the country houses in Ireland. It is the air of unspoken amiability which makes it so charming, and so unusual for an hotel. It is relaxing and unpretentious, and staffed by young people who disport themselves likewise.
Many come here to fish on the skirling river, others to shoot woodcock, others for good-value winter weekends when big fires, agreeable food and the do-nothing ambience of Ballynahinch find the place at its best. The dining room is charming and romantic, the cooking is good without ever perhaps achieving a measure of distinction. Those bedrooms which face the river are well worth the extra money, as these offer the best views and the most space.
Open 7pm-8.30pm Mon-Sun. Closed Feb (open for Xmas). Average Price: pub lunch ££ dinner ££££ B&B £££££. Visa, Access, Amex, Diners. Signposted on the N71 road from Galway to Clifden.

BALLYCONNEELY

HOTEL AND RESTAURANT
ERRISEASK HOUSE HOTEL & RESTAURANT
Ballyconneely, Clifden Tel: (095) 23553 Fax: (095) 23639 Christian & Stefan Matz
The Erriseask is not blessed with the sort of atmosphere that might drag you back to this lonely crag of Connemara irrespective of what the food was like, but in Stefan Matz it has a young cook with skills that are altogether dazzling.
Mr Matz has the sort of surfeit of skill that might be almost dangerous, leading to food that was a marvel to look at but intended more for admiration and contemplation than degustation. But his keenness for flavour never deserts him: a carpaccio of scallops, sliced terrifyingly thin, enjoys a beautiful directness of saline tastes, whilst his homemade noodles in a cream sauce of wild mushrooms trades the scent of the sea for the scent of woodland. A steamed fillet of turbot is served with salmon roe, the pink globules a salty antidote to the mellifluous fish, whilst this fondness for using a salty texture crops up in the Connemara lamb, the loin boned and a perfect gratinate of fine herbs cutting the sweet meat.
His food not only tastes superb, it looks utterly magnificent, right from a little amusée through to richly colourful desserts. This alliance of appearance and appetite makes his

food quite thrilling, and with a good bottle of German wine from an interesting list, you can have a dynamic dinner. If the atmosphere could find a little extra trace of lightheartedness, you would walk on hands and knees to Erriseask, so best maybe to bring some friends in a party and whoop it up amongst yourselves.

Open 6.30pm-9.30pm Mon-Sun. Closed Nov-Easter. Average Price: dinner ££££ B&B £££££. Visa, Access, Amex, Diners. Signposted from Ballyconneely village.

CLEGGAN

SHELLFISH
CLEGGAN LOBSTER FISHERIES
Cleggan Tel: (095) 44664 Danielle & John Foure

Most of the catch from the fishery heads straight off to the continent, but if you are renting someplace in the midst of this gorgeous wilderness, then you can buy shrimps and lobster from the factory.

Open 9am-6pm Apr to Sept. From Clifden take signs for Claddaduff and then Aughrisbeg lake. From Cleggan head south and take the sign for Aughrisbeg.

CLIFDEN

RESTAURANT
THE ARDAGH HOTEL
Ballyconneely Road Tel: (095) 21384 Fax: (095) 21314 Stephane Bauvet

So many times in Ireland you look at what might be described as a 'quiet, family hotel' overlooking a bay and your heart sinks because you know that, despite the beauty of the building and its picturesque surroundings, and with all the good intentions of the owners and staff, that the food will be sloppy and the rooms tawdry. Rarely will you be able to rely on genuinely thoughtful service, well thought-out, welcoming food and a high standard of housekeeping in the rooms upstairs. The Ardagh is one you can rely on.

Food is available in the bar at lunchtime; it will be good soups, open sandwiches which reveal the Dutch background of the owners, and oysters to be drunk with cinnamon-tasting Guinness. The restaurant, which overlooks Ardbear Bay, mixes European influences with the best Irish ingredients: home marinated gravadlax, salad tiede with quail eggs and smoky bacon, black sole with a yellow and red sweet pepper sauce, Barbary duckling with caramelised apples and a Calvados sauce.

Open 7.30pm-9pm Mon-Sun and for bar lunches. Closed Nov-Mar. Average Price: lunch £-££ dinner £££ B&B £££££. Visa, Access, Amex, Diners. The Ardagh is 2km outside Clifden on the road to Ballyconneely.

RESTAURANT
DESTRY RIDES AGAIN ➡
The Square Tel: (095) 21722 Paddy & Julie Foyle

It was Lord Beaverbrook, apparently, who said that the sight of Marlene Dietrich standing on a bar, in black net stockings, belting out 'See What The Boys In The Back Room Will Have', was a greater work of art than the Venus de Milo.

They can't, of course, resurrect Dietrich to stand on the bar in Paddy Foyle's wonderful restaurant, but snatches of 'See What The Boys...' does whoomp out from the music system every so often, allowing you and your friends to hold the ritual Dietrich Debate: could Marlene sing just one note? Or could she sing two?

Who cares. Dietrich was the most brilliant self-invented character of the century, and Paddy Foyle's admiration of the lady has extended not just to borrowing the title from the classic western in which she starred with James Stewart, he has also borrowed some of the lady's capacity for re-invention, and re-made his cooking and his style anew in Destry.

Mr Foyle is best associated with Rosleague Manor, his elegant and impressive country house just up the road in Letterfrack, but a desire to simplify his food, to work in a funkier ambience, has led to this effortlessly enjoyable place. With a talented young chef, and the seamless lack of contrivance he and Julie Foyle gift to any venture, Destry rides along on good humour and an adrenalinated energy.

The menu is simple: five appetisers, a trio of soups, a few fish dishes, a few meat dishes, a clatter of desserts, certain specials of the day, but that Foyle signature — an intuitive grasp for motivating flavour in a dish and finding unusual alliances — is right at the fore. The marinated leg of lamb, for example, is as untypical an Irish dish as you could imagine, the cubes of meat char-grilled to a rich spiciness and offset by a chutney sauce. With a Barbary duck, Mr Foyle extracts the full complement of rich, oilful flavours, with fish he will do clever experiments such as coating white hake in black sesame seeds to produce a dazzling dish.

Clifden has needed a place like Destry for a long time, somewhere that matches the exuberance of the holidaymaker, somewhere that lets tomorrow take care of itself. Sitting in Destry Rides Again, we all become The Boys In The Back Room, little Lord Beaverbrooks in the thrall of the Blue Angel.

Open 6.30pm-10pm Mon-Sun. Closed Xmas (slighly more limited hours off-season, ring to check). Average Price: dinner £££. Visa, Access. Centre of Clifden.

RESTAURANT WITH ROOMS
THE QUAY HOUSE
Clifden Tel: (095) 21369 Paddy Foyle
The latest stage of Paddy Foyle's re-invention is this promising restaurant with rooms in a beautiful location on the waterfront in Clifden, planned to open in spring 1994. The mere association of any venture with Mr Foyle is as close to a guarantee of success as you can get, but readers must consider and examine this for themselves as it has, obviously, been impossible for us to do so.
Telephone for more details.

RESTAURANT
HIGH MOORS RESTAURANT
Dooneen Tel: (095) 21342 Hugh & Eileen Griffin
Clifden at Eastertime. Happy locals, happy holidaymakers smile and say to themselves: High Moors is due to open.

Clifden at the end of September. Unhappy locals, unhappy out-of-season holidaymakers grimace and say to themselves: High Moors closed for the season. Roll on next year.

Unlikely as it may seem, for the Griffins' High Moors restaurant is nothing more than the sitting room of their bungalow revamped into a restaurant for the season, but High Moors is part of the social baggage and the culinary culture of Clifden. The reason why is simple: no one knows his customers better than Hugh Griffin and Eileen Griffin knows just what it is that they like to eat that will bring the hungry up the windy hill to the bungalow. Thirty folk can cram in here comfortably and cram in they do: ten minutes after opening time on a busy night and the place will be buzzing with chat and crack and bottles uncorking. From a seat at the window you can watch the pageant of evening colours which the moors perform nightly, but once the food begins to arrive the scenery is likely to be quickly forgotten.

Eileen Griffin is a good cook, and she has the added security of using vegetables and herbs grown just down the road by Hugh, so there may be fresh crab with a garden herb mayonnaise, spinach, feta and mint in a salad with walnut oil, Carna bay scallops with saffron and chervil, wild salmon with a spinach hollandaise, Connemara lamb with redcurrants and rosemary. Happy, simple cooking.

Open 7pm-9.30pm Wed-Sun. Closed Oct-Apr. Average Price: £££. Access, Visa. Look for the sign 1km from Clifden directing you to a side road off the main Ballyconneely road.

RESTAURANT
O'GRADY'S SEAFOOD RESTAURANT
Market Street Tel: (095) 21450 The O'Grady family
For many visitors to the bric-a-brac town of Clifden, O'Grady's is as automatic a stop as St. Peter's in Rome or Mulligan's bar in Dublin. The food they serve, an unchallenging essay on getting good flavours from simple ingredients, explains why.

Everything is designed to make the diner feel comfortable, and to usher in a relaxed time. The lighting is low, the tables are intimately arranged if you want, socially arranged if you don't, service is charming, and the fillets of fish and cuts of meat are as expected, as you hoped. The business of the O'Grady family has always been to look after people, and they do that by doing their best to help you have a good time.

Open 12.30pm-2.30pm, 7pm-9.30pm Tue-Sat (open Sundays Jun-Sep). Closed Dec-Feb (open for a few weeks around New Year). Average Price: lunch ££ dinner £££. Visa, Access, Amex. In the centre of Clifden.

COFFEE HOUSE
KELLY'S, THE COFFEE HOUSE
Church Hill
Home-made food, Tanzanian coffee, and books and prints to peruse.
Open from 9am-9pm in the summer.

B&B, EVENING MEALS
KILLE HOUSE
Kingstown, Clifden Tel: (095) 21849 Anya Brand Vermoolen
Kille is a house of sumptuous, pristine elegance. You would be happy to be here irrespective of whether the views were dull or breakfasts were any good, but the location of the house near to the Sky road allows for vistas of endless fascination, and Anya not only gives the house great good cheer, she is also a splendid cook: scrambled eggs rich and velvety, softly toothsome meat loaf, splendid salamis, fine cheeses all for breakfast with crumbly warm bread and excellent coffee. The housekeeping is of such an extraordinary

standard that there are few other places in the country to which Kille can be compared, and you fold yourself into a big, snowy-white duvet in a big beautiful bed in a big handsome room and thank the stars you are in Connemara, and here in Kille.

Open 7.30pm for dinner for guests, book by noon. Closed Dec. Average Price: dinner £££ B&B £££. No cards. Ask directions for the Sky Road, and from this you will see the small hand-written sign directing you to the house.

SMOKED SALMON
SALMON & SEAFOOD ➡
Salt Lake Manor Tel: (095) 21278 Jean-Jacques Boulineau

M. Boulineau's little shop and factory is a perennially popular destination not just for French visitors — you can come in here and not hear a word of English, some days — but for anyone who craves the goodness and trueness of correctly smoked wild salmon. His technique achieves both a softer texture and a subtle, less forced, facet of smokiness than most of the fine Irish smoked salmon, making this a very personal and very distinctive food, not to mention a mellifluous accompaniment to crisp white Sauvignon Blanc or un-oaked Chardonnay. M. Boulineau himself has never lost the zeal and energy of a man fascinated by the mysterious salmon, patiently explaining to his customers why the wild fish is so much better than farmed fish, inviting you to compare photographs of the fish to see the difference, showing you around his salted racks of fish, slicing thin tastes of the finished product.

Open salmon season: 9am-7pm Mon-Sat ('till 6pm Sat), out of season 10am-6pm Mon-Sat. Closed Sun. Salt Lake Manor is on the road out of Clifden towards Ballyconneely — after about one mile you will see the house signposted.

CORNOMONA

FISH SMOKER
ATLANTIC SILVER FISH
Cornomona Tel: (092) 48193 Paul Somerville

Paul Somerville smokes wild salmon when he has it, farmed fish when he doesn't. Both can be bought from the shop beside the smokehouse.

Telephone to make sure someone's there if travelling a long distance. Open Mon-Sat. Signposted in Cornomona village.

LETTERFRACK

RESTAURANT AND ACCOMMODATION
ROSLEAGUE MANOR
Letterfrack Tel: (095) 41101 Paddy and Anne Foyle

Rosleague is a therapeutic place. Look out from the bedrooms at the front of the house and the view across Diamond Hill, Letter Hill and Speckled Hill, framed by the inrush of Ballynakill Harbour, is a tonic of pure, devoted wilderness and wildness.

The calm concord of the public rooms and the elegant conservatory pitch the body into baleful relaxation, whether you enjoy a simple lunch at the bar, or repair to them after dinner in order to rest up before resting up.

The cooking remains considerate and impressive, for even though Paddy Foyle has begun to concentrate his energies in Clifden, he has installed a happy team who continue to work under his direction, and the dining room is one of the most beautiful in the country, a commodious space where kids in their pyjamas don't feel discouraged from entering to steal a final goodnight kiss.

Open 12.30pm-2pm (bar lunch), 8pm-9.30pm Mon-Sun. Closed early Nov-Easter. Average Price: lunch ££ dinner ££££ B&B £££££. Visa, Access, Amex. The Manor is well signposted from Letterfrack.

ALSO OF INTEREST

CONNEMARA HANDCRAFTS, Letterfrack Tel: (095) 41058 Irish china, pottery, candles, tablecloths and a coffee shop in which to pause and peruse your purchases. Known as The Possibly Shop ('Possibly the best craft shop in the West'), as distinct from the craft shop near Clifden which came along sometime after and called itself 'Probably the best craft shop in the West'.

Open 9.30am-7pm Mon-Sat, 10.30am-6pm Sun. More limited hours off season. Closed Nov-Feb.

ROUNDSTONE

PUB
O'DOWD'S

Roundstone Tel: (095) 35809

A sepia of nicotine paints the chipped and aged wood of the walls and ceiling in this snugglesome bar, and counterpointing their good pints O'Dowd's also serves some decent food: swordfish and chips, steamed mussels, a good smoked salmon quiche. There is also a simple dining room, but the food lends itself best to the informality of the bar and the proximate presence of a pint.

Open pub hours, food served all day 'till 9.30pm Mon-Sun. Closed mid-Oct-Feb (with limited opening times around Xmas and New Year).

FOOD PRODUCER
JOSIE MONKS

Creeshla Farm, Cushatrower Tel: (095) 35814

Josie Monks sells a fine soft goat's milk cheese, lovely fruity yogurts, cheesecake and milk as well as jams, chutneys and orange and lemon curd. Josie's daughter has joined the business and makes salad dips with home-made mayonnaise and goat's cheese. You can buy from the farm, and sometimes you might see them in the Clifden market on Fri or Sat.

Open 8.30am-8pm Mon-Sun high season (limited hours and limited foods available during the winter). Look for signs about two and a half miles from Roundstone.

ALSO OF INTEREST

ROUNDSTONE PARK, I.D.A., Connemara Along with crafts to decorate the table, you might find yourself buying a hand-crafted Bodhrán, made from goat's skin and decorated with a celtic design — the necessary accompaniment to good music and good crack.

GALWAY

CLARINBRIDGE

PADDY BURKE'S

Clarinbridge Tel: (091) 96107 Ronnie and Rita Counihan

It was Clarinbridge that began the idea of the west coast oyster festival, almost forty years ago now, and Paddy Burke's remains the very exemplar of the great gift of oysters and stout.

Open for bar food 12.30pm-10.30pm, lunch 12.30pm-2.30pm, dinner 6pm-10.30pm Mon-Sun

GALWAY CITY

THE GALWAY SATURDAY MARKET

If you came across Eamonn L. Rynne anywhere else, you might judge him an unusual man. He has the appearance, not to mention the green brocaded jacket and the moustache, of a man brought up, maybe, as a member of minor Austrian aristocracy. You half expect him to sing a few bars from Der Rosenkavalier at any minute. But if he did, the fact that his accent is Canadian, sort of, would be another unusual feature.

Except this is in the Galway market, Saturday morning, as usual, and he is standing in front of a clever arrangement of homemade salamis and you don't think for a second that it is somewhat strange. 'I made them because I wanted to eat them and I couldn't afford to buy them', says Mr Rynne, handing you his card which states that he lives in 'Empress of Russia Lodge'. Well, a salami maker who looks like a refugee from 'The Sound of Music' has to live somewhere.

The surreal gaggle of the Galway Market manages to make everything seem integrated, straight-forward. Joachim Hess could be the lead guitarist in a rock 'n' roll grunge band, if he wasn't a vegetable grower and baker of good breads. The little canopy of the

Brekish Dairy, laden with cheeses and yogurts and breads, has simply decamped from Northern Europe. Willem den Heyer and his amazing sausages sit beside Gert and Vita van den Brink's stall of organic vegetables, and Babs and Cait, the bubbly girls from the Connacht Growers, are camped beside the person selling beautiful driftwood, who is beside the kids with the Rice Krispie cakes and the mammies with the country butter. It is all weird and wonderful, and you wish you were some sort of rural Stephen Sondheim so you could write a musical about them all.

Mr Rynne's salamis, incidentally, are excellent. But, then, so is everything else for sale: Dirk Flake's beautiful vegetables and herbs, Eamon Galligan's fine oysters and mussels, the vociferous flowers, the flouncy-topped carrots, the home-baked cakes. This lovely jamboree, this strange confusion of people, is one of the delights of Irish food.

SOME OF THE PRODUCERS SELLING IN THE MARKET

BREKISH DAIRY, Kylebrack West Tel: (0509) 45246 Hugo Zyderlaan Cheese, yogurts, butter, stout breads.

VITA & GERT VAN DEN BRINK, Lough Ahorick Tel: (0509) 49215. Organic vegetables.

CONNACHT ORGANIC GROUP, Cait Curran & Babs McMullan. Organic vegetables

DIRK FLAKE, Aughinish, Kinvarra. Organic vegetables.

BERNARD GALLIGAN, 2 Pinewood Grove, Renmore. Wild mussels, farmed Pacific oysters.

JOACHIM HESS, Brackloon, Ballyglunin, Tuam. Organic vegetables, bread.

WILLEM & COBIE DEN HEYER, Dromeyre, Kilimore, Ballinasloe Tel: (0905) 76139. Sausages, smoked eel and smoked trout.

EAMONN L. RYNNE, Empress of Russia Lodge, Greenfields, Ower P.O. Tel: (093) 35713 Home-made salamis.

AVALLO APPLE JUICE, Irish Organic Fruit Juices, Gort Tel: (091) 31860. Apple Juice.

PUB
TI NEATAIN
Cross Street Tel: (091) 66172
The pints of Guinness pulled in Neatain's are as soft and flowing as the Galway accent, and their bar food has always been interesting, even creative.

RESTAURANT
ROYAL VILLA
13 Shop Street Tel: (091) 63450 Charlie Chan
Upstairs, away from the crowds, the Royal Villa is a haven of waterfalls, step bridges, vivid Chinese shades and, most importantly, good food. This might be, perhaps, the best crispy duck you'll get to try in Ireland: crispy as it promises on the skin side, light and only slightly oily within. It comes, as tradition dictates, with thin Chinese pancakes and garnishes of slivered cucumber, spring onion flowers, shredded lettuce and hoisin sauce. Other specialities amongst the hot Sichuan dishes will indeed give you what the menu describes as 'that deep throat reaction' while black bean sauces are rich and savoury. With a detective's doggedness, Mr Chan hunts down the sweet, sharp, spicy flavours we love, and brings them to you on a plate.

Open 12.30pm-2.30pm, 6pm-midnight Mon-Sat (Fri & Sat 'till 12.30am), 1pm-midnight Sun. Closed Xmas.

Average Price: lunch ££ dinner £££. Visa, Access, Amex, Diners. The very centre of Galway city.

CAFÉ
HOUSE OF JAMES
Castle Street Tel: (091) 67776
Queue up, grab a tray, point to the open sandwich/bake/salad/cake/cold drink/tea/coffee of your choice, pay at the cash register, help yourself to ice and water and sit down at any of the wooden tables and admire your purchases from the lovely shop downstairs.
Open 9am-5pm Mon-Sat. Closed Xmas. Average Price £-££. No Credit Cards.

GALWAY RESTAURANTS

THE COUNTRY BASKET
Cross Street Tel: (091) 63236
An all-day coffee shop serving stir fries, tofu-based dishes, vegetarian chilli, salads and some meat dishes.
Open 9am-6pm Mon-Sat. Average Price: meals and snacks £. No credit cards

FAT FREDDIE'S
The Halls, Quay Street Tel: (091) 67279
A pizza parlour, with some desserts made by Emer Murray of Goya's.
Open 11am-10.30pm Mon-Sun. Average Price: pizzas £

FOOD FOR THOUGHT
3 Lr Abbeygate Street Tel: (091) 65854
Vegetarian and wholefood restaurant. Lasagne, quiche, pizza, shepherd's pie, nut roast, none of them containing meat.
Open 8am-5.30pm Mon-Sat. Average Price: meal £. No credit cards.

HOOKER JIMMY'S
The Fish Market, Spanish Arch Tel: (091) 68351
This is a lighthearted, bubbly place, run by John Glanville who made The Boiluisce in Spiddal famous for enjoyable seafood and legendary brown bread, and looks set to do the same for Hooker Jimmy's.
Open noon-11pm. Closed Xmas. Average Price: lunch £-££ dinner ££-£££. Visa, Access, Amex.

PASTA MISTA
2 Cross Street Tel: (091) 65550
Pizza and Pasta.
Open 12.30pm-9.30pm Mon-Sat (coffee available from 11am), Average Price: pasta £

THE GRAIN STORE
Lr Abbeygate Street Tel: (091) 66620
Newly refurbished lunchtime restaurant.
Open 10am-6pm Mon-Sat, Average Price: meals £. No credit cards

SEVENTH HEAVEN
Courthouse Lane, Quay Street Tel: (091) 63838

Food from the Pacific Rim.
Open noon-midnight Mon-Sun. Average Price: lunch ££ dinner ££. No credit cards

SUNFLOWER RESTAURANT
Quay Street Tel: (091) 66320
Politically Correct Grub.
Open 9am-midnight Mon-Sun. Average Price: meals £ No credit cards

GALWAY SHOPS

FISHMONGER
FLEMING'S FISH SHOP
29 Lower Dominick Street Tel: (091) 66673 Gay Fleming
A small, choice fish shop, full of good fish and sound advice.
Open 9am-6pm Tue-Sat

BAKERY AND PATISSERIE
GOYA'S ★
19 Quay Street Tel: (091) 67010 Emer Murray
How does Emer Murray manage to do it? How can each detail of each biscuit, each cake and each bread represent such rarefied perfection? Individual Tira Misu redolent with chocolate; fig and walnut cake fine and distinct; individual cheesecakes balancing the high wire between sweetness and nourishment. Each cake, each loaf, from the vivid pink strawberry roulade to the miniature yeasted rolls, each are flawless in their execution.
But even though everything looks straight from the pages of a glossy publication, there is no artifice here, no tricks for the eye. For the ingredients used to construct these towers of taste are good flour, real butter, white wine, whole fruit, fresh cream.
Patisserie must be an indulgence, and be seen to be an indulgence, and from the Whoopii Pies — spiced biscuits flavoured with pumpkin purée and filled with a cream cheese icing — to the rhubarb crumble — icing sugared curves that look like the Burren mountains — Goya's cakes are an indulgence so fine, so much a lot of what you fancy, that they must be good for you.
Open 9.30am-5.30pm Mon-Sat. Incidentally, if you want to taste some of Emer's Tira Misu with a cup of coffee, they serve it just down the road in Mezza Luna.

BUTCHER
SEAN LOUGHNANE ➡
56 Dominick Street Tel: (091) 64437 Sean Loughnane
What Sean Loughnane doesn't know about meat isn't worth knowing. A dedicated and decisive man, his butchering skills are peerless, his meat as fine and enigmatically rich in flavour as you will find in a conventional butcher's shop.
Mr Loughnane will claim that there is no mystery to his fine beef, superb lamb, good pork. The husbandry, the handling, the slaughtering, the hanging: all need to be carefully overseen in order to achieve the correct results, he says, and once you do that you can't go wrong. His dedication has won him not just a devoted local congregation, but also a national reputation as a man who represents the pinnacle of achievement in the

butchering business. You buy each and every single thing in Loughnane's confident that it will be definitive in flavour — beef from a Hereford giving a slowly-arriving flavour amidst the loose texture, that from a Limousin giving a fuller taste with more scents of pepper and slightly stronger tissue — and it is enjoyable to buy it for the staff are as charming as Mr Loughnane himself. Do note that on the other side of town, on Forster Street, Mr Loughnane has another eponymous shop, this time specialising in cooked foods and delicatessen produce.

Open Dominick Street 9am-6pm Mon-Sat. On the Strandhill side of the river in Galway city centre. Forster Street 9am-9pm Mon-Sun

GROCERY AND DELICATESSEN
MCCAMBRIDGE'S ➡

38/39 Shop Street, Tel:(091) 62259 Pat McCambridge

McCambridge's is a delightful shop, its shelves filled with interesting foods, the wine shop with interesting wines and spirits, but above all it is the cheese counter which is of greatest interest. You can find almost all of the Irish farmhouse cheeses, carefully cared for, carefully kept, carefully served, and they also maintain a good selection of cheeses from Europe.

Open 9am-6pm Mon-Fri, Sat 9am-5.30pm.

FISHMONGER AND RESTAURANT
MCDONAGH'S FISH SHOP AND SEAFOOD BAR

22 Quay Street Tel: (091) 65001

The fish shop has a decent array of good fish and the simply cooked fish — baked cod, steamed mussels, fish stew, fish and chips — in the restaurant is reliable.

Open (Shop) 9am-6pm Mon-Sat (Restaurant) noon-10pm Mon-Sun.

FRUIT SHOP & DELICATESSEN
SILKE & DAUGHTERS

Munster Avenue Tel: (091) 61048 Brian Silke & Scott Ishmael

Silke's has transmogrified over the years, with the wholesale side of their fruit and vegetable business slowly taking a back seat to Scott Ishmael's fine food venture, this part of the shop improving steadily and surely. Silke's is now an excellent place in which to find the best Irish artisan foods, cheeses in good condition, good bread and condiments, a good selection of salads.

Open 8.30am-6pm Mon-Sat. On the Strandhill side of the river on the edge of Galway city centre.

KILCOLGAN

PUB/OYSTER BAR
MORAN'S OF THE WEIR

Kilcolgan Tel: (091) 691113 Willie Moran

Few foods give such intense, extraordinary pleasure as the Galway oyster. Its international fame is richly deserved, for no other shellfish manages to so richly evoke and encapsulate the nectar of the sea, to cram the taste senses with such myriad scents and associations.

Once you have discovered the taste for them — and it must be admitted that very many people never do find a sympathy for oysters in themselves — then you will be hooked until your last breath, and indeed as your life passes in front of your eyes it may well be memories of sliding oysters down your throat in Moran's of the Weir that give the greatest culinary pleasure.

The Moran family have their own oyster beds, and the native oyster — Ostrea edulis — which they serve is small and muscular, more full-flavoured than the Portuguese oyster and with a better, more complex texture. You eat it with a glass of stout — Murphy's, because it has less of the edge of toastiness than either Guinness or Beamish, may be best — and small slices of brown bread. A little squeeze of lemon on to the shellfish, a bite of bread, a sip of stout. It is a holy trinity of tastes, altogether something miraculous.

Open for pub food noon-10pm Mon-Sat, noon-2pm Sun. Kilcolgan is a few miles south of Galway city, Moran's is signposted from the N17.

MOYCULLEN

RESTAURANT
DRIMCONG HOUSE ★
Moycullen Tel: (091) 85115 Gerry & Marie Galvin

There is an element of the grandiose in Gerry Galvin's way of thinking about his work in Drimcong House. He will happily declare in his happy book of memoirs and recipes 'The Drimcong Food Affair' that 'Eating is more important than sex — we do it at least three

times a day at all ages and yet it merits little planning and insufficient time both in the preparation and the partaking'.

Yet this fondness for the abstract and the romantic is, nevertheless, bedrocked in the reality of running a professional kitchen, and in trying to figure out just what it is that makes a restaurant work, trying to hit on the secret of just what it is that makes people want to go out to enjoy a meal, just what it is that makes a communion of food and wine and the environment of a restaurant work together to produce the magic of enjoyment.

'We instil in our staff the idea that what we do is enjoyable and not worth doing if it is not', he writes, and what is impressive about his book is not just the pithy epithets, with their ability to finger the truth as sharply as Ambrose Bierce or Brillat-Savarin, it is the fact that they are put into operation every night in Drimcong.

'I have no doubt that the appreciation of food and wine has a civilising influence. There is a direct relationship between care for what we eat and drink and our attitude to land, livestock and environment'. You can hear the sigh of envy of a speechwriter for a Minister of Agriculture when you read that. 'I have yet to meet sustained excellence where profit is the primary motive'. This, surely, the rallying cry of artisan producers, growers and cooks everywhere. 'Children should be nurtured to inventive eating from an early age'. This one to be etched on the blackboard of every kindergarten, as the first step to building a vibrant, appreciative nation of cooks and eaters. 'Menus should be short, seasonable and understandable'. And written in English, surely, with an emphasis on where the food originates, rather than what the chef may do to it in the kitchen. 'I would rather err in excessive experimentation than stagnate in repetition'. This, of course, a necessary apologia for Galvin's own cooking, for he does make mistakes in between the brilliance and the dazzling invention, and you forgive him his sins every time.

Perhaps most crucially, he writes that 'We do strive to instil the desire for excellence in our staff, being fully aware that very often the excellence is in the effort rather than the achievement'.

This remark seems so obvious that you might imagine everyone would subscribe to it. But of course they do not, certainly not the very many chefs in Ireland whose work is characterised not just by laziness and a lack of respect for their own efforts, but also by a lack of imagination. 'Perhaps the rarest asset and the rarest faculty that a chef has is imagination. The number of really imaginative people in cooking is small', says Galvin, an obvious truth that makes his own lively improvisations even more precious.

'My motivation and my guiding light is to experiment and, being Irish, to try to build on what we have', he says. His cooking puts this into action, with clever, sustaining experiments: the famous pudding and oysters with an apple and onion confit or a marvellous black pudding mousse, lovable things such as colcannon soup, tipsy pudding, roast pike, playful games with lovage and bergamot, basil and rosemary. His restaurant, with its splendid staff and their obvious happiness and pride in their work, sets the seal on the secret of just what makes a restaurant work.

Open 7pm-10.30pm Tues-Sat. Closed Xmas-Mar. Average Price: dinner £££-££££. Visa, Access, Amex, Diners. Drive out of Moycullen towards Maam Cross, the restaurant is on your right.

ALSO OF INTEREST

WHITE GABLES RESTAURANT, Moycullen Tel: (091) 85744 Kevin & Ann Dunne 'We were impressed with the value of the table d'hôte, the quality of the service and the general ambience. There is also a delightful à la carte menu' writes a reader from the U.K., and indeed the White Gables is making many friends for its friendly and unassuming personality.

Open 7pm-11pm Mon-Sat, and Sun lunch. Closed Xmas and Jan. Average Price: lunch ££ dinner £££. Visa, Access, Amex. Moycullen village centre.

MOYGLASS

BAKERY
MOYGLASS WHOLEMEAL BAKERY

Moyglass Tel: (0509) 49223 Norbet Illien

The continental loaves you see around Galway town probably come from the Illiens' bakery where they make rye bread, organic yeast bread, sourdough loaves and sugar-free cakes.

Look for the breads and cakes in wholefood shops and delis in all the major towns between Galway and Limerick.

OUGHTERARD

COUNTRY HOUSE
CURRAREVAGH HOUSE

Oughterard Tel: (091) 82312 Fax: 82731 Harry and June Hodgson

Things in Currarevagh have changed little, and it is this lack of change, this refusal to progress, which is what the devotees of Currarevagh like.

They like the gargantuan breakfasts, helping themselves repeatedly to lashings of fried eggs, mounds of June Hodgson's terrific kedgeree, tilting the science-lab coffee percolators repeatedly into their cups. They like the gong before dinner, then the procession into the dining room as if this was Upper Table, then the separate tables, the solid food with its distinct nursery echoes, their bottles of wine originally opened last night, all set to be drained. Later, maybe a walk around the lip of glorious Lough Corrib, or tumble into the deep chairs in the drawing room, before bed.

Currarevagh is a protean vision of gentility, good manners, people all in their place, honey still for tea. If you dislike the modern world and its tiresome confusions, then it will offer solace. Describing themselves, they say, 'For the inner man, Currarevagh has found much favour amongst its followers', but the inner man should want nostalgia, above all, if he wishes to become a follower.

Open for dinner for guests. Closed mid Oct-Mar. Average Price: dinner £££ B&B £££££. No Credit Cards.
Follow the 'Lakeshore' road out of Oughterard.

BUTCHER
EAMONN MCGEOUGH ➥

Lake Road Tel: (091) 82351 Eamonn McGeough

Recipes which promise culinary heaven are often complex and contrived. Here is one which is absurdly simple, involving little more than a spot of jaunting about the West.

First, travel to Oughterard, on the fringe of County Galway. Oughterard is a place where, it seems, Jacques Tati's wonderfully oblique character Monsieur Hulot has organised the traffic arrangements: it is best to simply surrender to the dodgem-style strictures which govern things here.

Turn, carefully, off the main road, taking the one which leads down to Lough Corrib. Stop after a hundred yards, outside Eamonn McGeough's butcher's shop. After buying all the other wonderful enticements which will greet you here — little pastry packets filled with secret goodies, reverberantly dark beef, sprightly pink lamb, maybe a couple of bottles of necessary claret — make sure you ask Mr McGeough — who by this time will have ascertained who you are, where you hail from, where you are going and where you bought your gansy — to slice you some of the corned beef.

Take the corned beef and head back to Galway city. Drive straight to Shop Street. Buy some prepared mustard in McCambridge's shop. Then head down the road to Emer Murray's super patisserie, Goya's. Here, once you have exercised some self-control and told yourself you don't need to buy everything with chocolate on it, do buy some of the sweetly yeasty white bread rolls. Outside, slice or tear the roll apart, squidge some mustard onto the bread, and pack in the corned beef.

This is the sandwich made in heaven.

There is a shorter way to enact this magical alchemy of taste: Mr McGeough's corned beef can be bought in Roches' supermarket in Galway itself, but if you go there you will miss the man's relaxed, wonderful feats of raconteurship. That lazy, sinuous western tone dresses up every expression with imagined mischief, best illustrated perhaps by the story of the woman who came into the shop one morning.

'How are you?', asked the proprietor, perhaps blithely.

'Well, you would know, wouldn't you. You would know!', says the woman.

'Know what?' says Mr McGeough, perhaps innocently.

'You would know I'm pregnant. You'd know'.

This, of course, was the first that anyone, even Mr McGeough, knew about it.

Storytelling aside, the staple of McGeough's is superlatively fine meat. The Connemara mountain lamb which one buys here enjoys the full expression of tenderness and sweetness which this most uniquely Irish meat can offer. Its delicacy means that with even the briefest cooking it loses its pink colour, but the softness and lingeringly herbed flavour persists and persists.

With the return of his son James from Germany, where he had been training in the charcuterie trade, McGeough's has further enjoyed the dynamism of a hungry, gifted young inventor. The parcels of puff pastry are James's idea, and the magnificent corned beef is his work. Perfection, you might say, with the interplay between lubricious jelly and richly flavoured chopped meat, but James is restless, never satisfied. You will sometimes see him in the shop, but often he is out the back, trying something new, refining, refining. 'I saw him this morning when he came to let me go to my breakfast, and I haven't seen him since', says Eamonn, in mid-afternoon. 'He's trying something new with the blades, I don't know what...'

But this happy friction, between experiment and reliability, keeps McGeough's more than up to scratch. You shop here with the certainty that whatever you buy will be at its best, will be the best the family can do. And you shop here eager to catch a story, or some amusingly idle chatter, or at least to find out who is expecting.

Open 8.30am-6.30pm Mon-Sat

COUNTY LEITRIM

T HE VINE MUST SUFFER, to make good wine, they will tell you in Burgundy, in Bordeaux. Something of the same principle — spare the rod, spoil the child — must form the basis of the success of Rod Alston's herb and vegetable growing in Rossinver, for his farm is set fast in inhospitable land, and yet his produce is unsurpassably marvellous, premiére cru quality, as fine as a First Growth.

There would be no chance of growing the vine this far north, of course, though the cliché that surrounds Leitrim — that it is a place of unbridled rainfall with every cloud precipitatory and pregnant — is nonsense. The sense of water comes instead from the lakes, and the lakes are pervasively sensual and thus affecting.

The towns too, with their wide streets, their quiet shops, summon you to try to understand them, but this would take a lifetime. One day, walking through Manorhamilton, a wedding cortège passed with car horns blaring in Friday afternoon revelry. Everyone came out to wave, to smile and the place was filled with a Felliniesque gaiety for a few short seconds — the smiles and waves, the speedy voices, the suddenly surreal colours — before the reversion to normal business returned the town to Bergmanesque garrison grey. Rod Alston, like others in Leitrim, works the land and the land works him. This countryside is demanding, but it rewards effort. Some years ago the North Leitrim Vegetable Growers' Association produced a modest little cookery book, and in an introduction the writer Michael Viney, after a learned discourse explaining why the Irish have historically been indifferent to vegetables, wrote of the curious fact that in 'the quiet drumlin country of North Leitrim (not the first place you would think of as the garden of Ireland) a remarkable co-operative of small growers is selling vegetables in the local market town'. That town is Manorhamilton, and the Co-Op Shop is a treasure house of good food, food rich in the pointed, vibrant, zesty character which the Leitrim climate bestows. Rod Alston's herbs and vegetables best exemplify this character: the vegetables are stubbornly flavoured, as if they have struggled to seize every element and nutrient from the earth, yet the tastes are not clumsy or brash, being instead fresh, typical. The salad leaves are frothy with life and arrogant with energy. The herbs — a huge range is listed in the Eden Plants herb catalogue from Alpine Strawberry and Angelica to Sweet Woodruf and Yarrow — have fluent bouquets and distinct flavours. If, thanks to the harsh terrain, everything must suffer as the vine must suffer, then the results are as pleasing and richly complex as a fine wine. A visit to the farm is nothing less than inspirational, a chance to see a vision made real. A visit to the shop, that 'remarkable co-operative of small growers', is always a treat.

THE CO-OP SHOP
Main Street, Manorhamilton Tel: (071) 66407

EDEN PLANTS ★
Rossinver Tel: (072) 54122 Rod Alston
Eden Plants is 7 miles north of Manorhamilton: take the road to Rossinver and Garrison, in Rossinver go past the post office and shop, turn right immediately after the convent, where there is a sign to the herb farm. Eden Plants is the first turning on the left. Herbs can be bought by mail order: ring or write for their catalogue. Eden vegetables cannot be bought at the house. The herb garden is open every afternoon from 2pm-6pm.

COUNTY MAYO

T HE GREAT JOURNALIST and writer John Healy was a Mayo man, born in Charlestown, and in his classic book 'No One Shouted Stop' he recalls market day in the town: 'Today at the back of your mind you can still smell Wednesday... the new hay, the brown smell of the creaking egg baskets... of fresh meat... fresh herrings and dilisk, salty tanged in this inland town... the camphored black frieze of the widow woman's best coat... the smell of horses and donkeys... of the packing from the tea chests of the travelling man with the delph and the hardware: "everything for the home and the farm" was the chirp of the dealer who may have had a home somewhere but never saw a farm... the day and the town was a symphony of sound and smell'.

The symphony of sound and smell is all too absent these days, and, as Healy further pointed out, the towns of Mayo can appear to be disembodied places, with too few young people about, too little to do. In the north of the county and out to the west coast the roads scutter through wide plains of waving snipe grass and you often find little Marian grottos at roadsides, with white marbled, white robed Virgin Marys, hands joined in imploring prayer and the sculpted gaze always beatific, forgiving.

The contrast between the smooth serene figure and the utter wildness of the terrain is surreal.

ACHILL ISLAND

RESTAURANT
THE BOLEY HOUSE
Keel Tel: (098) 43147 The McNamara family
A Boley House was traditionally a temporary building designed to shelter cattle, but the McNamara family's Boley house endures from season to season. The culinary ambitions of the restaurant are modest, but some of their raw ingredients, in particular the fresh salmon, can be outstanding.
Open 6pm-9pm Mon-Sun. Closed Xmas. Average Price: dinner £££. Visa, Access.

ANNE FUCHS
Dugort, Achill Island Tel: (098) 43233
The milk from Anne's happy goats can be bought from her farm, a couple of miles outside Keel heading for the hills. Sometimes she has home-made cottage cheese for sale as well.

O'MALLEY'S POST OFFICE
Keel Tel: (098) 43125
A reasonable selection of wines is sold here to perk up your picnics.
Open 9am-8pm Mon-Sat, 9am-2pm Sun.

O'GORMAN'S FISH SHOP
Keel
A curiosity: the only fish shop we know of that is actually attached to a private house.
Open 8am-late Mon-Sun

FISHERMAN'S CO-OP
Achill Sound Tel: (098) 45123
Holiday makers and campers can take advantage of the co-op shop to buy the fish straight off the boats.
Open 9am-6pm Mon-Sat

BALLINA

FISHMONGERS
CLARKE & SONS
O'Rahilly Street Tel: (096) 21022 M. J. Clarke
The rod caught salmon that you can buy in Clarke's, in its season, has a deep ruby colour, perfectly distinct to those fish caught in the river Moy.
Open 9am-6pm Mon-Sat

SHOP
BRENDAN DOHERTY
O'Rahilly Street Tel: (096) 21723 Brendan Doherty
Shop here for home-made butter and good communion candles.
Ballina town centre.

JAMS & PRESERVES
ETHEL'S HOMEMADE PRESERVES
Ballyholan House, Downhill Road Tel: (096) 21853 Ethel Walker
Ethel's Preserves, jams, marmalades and technicolour chutneys manage to retain an echo of the kitchen table and the kitchen sink, and are worth hunting down whilst in the west.

SHOP
T. MCGRATH
O'Rahilly Street,(096) 22198 Mr McGrath
A higgledy piggledy packed deli with a good cheese counter, select comestibles and unexpected wines.
Open 9am-8pm Mon-Sat (winter times 'till 7.30pm), 10am-2pm, 5pm-8pm Sun.

CONG

HOTEL AND RESTAURANT
ASHFORD CASTLE
Cong Tel: (092) 46003
Famous, famously expensive.
Restaurant open to non-residents. Open 1pm-2pm, 7pm-9pm Mon-Sun. Closed Jan to 15 Mar. Average Price: lunch ££££ dinner £££££
B&B £££££. Visa, Access, Amex, Diners. Just outside Cong village.

RESTAURANT
ECHOES

Main Street Tel: (092) 46059 Siobhan, Tom & Helen Ryan

It tends to be Siobhan Ryan who garners most of the attention in Echoes. Quite right, of course, for she is the person who devises the dishes and is the instrumental force in getting them from stove to table, but she could not do so without all the other Ryans who man this happy place.

Siobhan's Dad, for example, takes care of all manner of supplies to the restaurant — it can help to have a father who is also the next door butcher, and it helps also to have someone who can dog-sit the customers' four legged friends, while their owners eat upstairs.

Siobhan's brother, young Tom, is not only an award-winning butcher, he also knows fish and fishing inside out and back to front. Fair enough, you might think, except that he is not above hopping into the kitchen to rattle the pots and pans when Siobhan takes a deserved break.

Then there is Siobhan's sister, who brings to the job of waiting on table a feline grace and a skill which turns her work into an art form.

And finally there is Siobhan's mother, who welcomes you, organises the bills and is not above a spot of babysitting should emergency demand. She also cooks breakfast in the restaurant during the summer months.

All of this works to the benefit of the fine food you can expect in Echoes. Ms Ryan has a gentle, instinctive touch and a strong feel for colour and texture. She places a huge helping of their home-smoked wild salmon on top of a springy bed of crisp salad leaves, threads breaded monkfish between slabs of green bacon and onions and peppers, dollops lots of scallops into a mornay sauce then serves them on the shell surrounded by piped potato, or maybe just fries them in the pan with a little garlic. Her lamb is herbaceous and sweet, her ice-creams the stuff you scream for in your dreams.

This deeply comforting food comes in grandly generous portions and the happy family affair of Echoes — as far removed from the self-conscious sense of denial that pervades Mayo as you could imagine — ladles on the hospitality and conviviality.

Open 8am-3pm, 6pm-10pm for breakfast, brunch, lunch and dinner Mon-Sun (shorter hours during winter season). Closed Xmas and Mon nights from Nov 1-Easter. Average Price: breakfast & brunch £ lunch ££ dinner £££. Visa, Access, Diners. Echoes is right in the centre of Cong, next to the butcher's.

BUTCHER'S SHOP
RYAN'S
Main Street Tel: (092) 46059 Thomas Ryan

As well as excellent west coast meat, Ryan's sell fine home-smoked salmon, good farmhouse cheeses and the scones you need to make the cheeses into a picnic.

Open 8.30am-8pm Mon-Sat.

CROSSMOLINA

COUNTRY HOUSE & RESTAURANT
ENNISCOE HOUSE
Castlehill, nr Crossmolina Tel: (096) 31112 Susan Kellett

Enniscoe is a relatively simple place, a modest country house which Susan Kellett is restoring slowly and lovingly, in a part of the country which is modest and under-celebrated. Things are done just right here, just so, and this desire to achieve correctness in simple things makes it a pleasurable house in which to while away some holiday time or an away-from-it-all weekend.

The bedrooms have enjoyed careful renovation. Those at the front of the house, overlooking the grounds, are truly the ones you want to stay in, with their quirky four posters and big lazy canopy beds.

At dinnertime, local ingredients are dotted through the menu: deep-hued salmon from the Moy river, local lamb and beef, soft oozy cheeses and soft, succulent fruit from the garden. It is country house cooking, of course, but whilst in other places it might seem a little obvious, here it feels just right, friendly food within a friendly house.

Best of all, Enniscoe is a place it is easy to relax in, a place to enjoy time alone and apart from the real world, a house that is polite, vivid and perfectly expressive of the strengths of Irish country house hospitality.

Open for dinner if pre-booked. Closed mid Oct-Apr. Average Price: dinner £££ B&B ££££. Visa, Access, Amex. Two miles south of Crossmolina on the road to Castlebar.

DOOHOMA

FISH SMOKER, FISH SHOP & PUB
EAGLE ISLE SEAFOOD
Doohoma Tel: (097) 86829 Eamon Holmes
Out in the wild windy west Eamon Holmes smokes salmon and mackerel, and you can buy both, plus fresh salmon, in his shop between his smokery and his pub.
Open from around 10am 'till when the pub closes. From Bangor take signs to Geesala and Doohoma. Continue until you see the sea, about twelve miles. As you come into Doohoma, Eagle Isle Seafood is the building on the right after the chapel.

NEWPORT

COUNTRY HOUSE AND RESTAURANT
NEWPORT HOUSE
Newport Tel: (098) 41222 Fax: 41613 Kieran & Thelma Thompson
Newport House is a well-turned anachronism in the modern world, a location seemingly occluded from the leavening of time. Ceilings vault. Staircases cascade. Silences ascend. Portraits glower with the power of wealth. In the rooms the women come and go, talking of Michelangelo.

It has the appositely ruddy-cheeked ghillies who wait around in the morning for breakfast to end and fishing to begin. There is the impossibly stooped gardener, the endearingly efficient Miss who counsels a full bowl of soup to counteract intemperate August weather,

the carrot headed waiter with the full-time flushed cheeks, the ageing ladies who wait on the fringes of the dining room and who, should you stay long enough, will elide you under their wings and into their care.

If you belong to that whacky group of people who would walk a country mile in the rain to eat a plate of smoked wild salmon, then Newport House is the place to find not just that smoked salmon but also, usually, a sufficient volume of rain to make your journey seem truly penitential. Newport's smoked salmon is wondrous. Mayo is wet.

They also cure their fish here. Sprinkled then with chopped dill and weighted to form gravadlax, it enters another dimension, allowing cleanness and purity of the taste to come forward. It is truly one of the most distinguished foods Ireland has to offer.

Whilst nothing else may manage to attain the heights of their smoked or cured fish, they work hard at Newport to create interesting and pleasing food. Dinner is a lengthy, multi-coursed affair that is firmly fin de siècle, except the century is the 19th and not the 20th. Creamy soups will follow the gravadlax. A rich fish like turbot will enjoy a rich Champagne sauce, fresh salmon might be char-grilled, the voluble flavours cut by fresh vegetables from the walled garden behind the house. After some salad leaves, a fine cheeseboard, and then a showypiece of desserts: crème caramel under an Ascot hat of spun sugar, home-made ice-cream in a flighty tuille basket.

The wine list is a glorious vinous romp that encourages ardent study and can repay with some decent bargains, though with the celebrated vintages amongst the clarets the price has matured splendidly also. Service is good, though some may find the dining room rather self-consciously formal and quiet, full of well heeled Europeans: bankers from Bologna, lawyers with personal injury practices, Frenchmen who went to the right école, second rate politicians, each and all of them complete with Trophy, or at least Reserve Prize, wives.

In Newport's grand, billowy rooms they babble with each other about the fishing and whatnot, but a decorous distance is always maintained. This is a formal house, and it puts everyone on their best behaviour: at dinner time or breakfast time there will be politesse worthy of Marcel Proust, and a madeleine atmosphere.

Open 7.30pm-9.30pm Mon-Sun Closed mid Oct-mid Mar. Average Price: dinner ££££ B&B £££££. Visa, Access, Amex, Diners. Newport House gates are to be found just at the entrance to the village.

WESTPORT

RESTAURANT
THE CORK
nr The Octagon Tel: (098) 26929 Willie & Jutta Kirkham
Willie and Jutta Kirkham have moved their restaurant from the Westport hills, where it was known as The Ceili House, to this location near the Octagon in town. The menu includes dishes created especially for both vegetarians and vegans, as well as those who like to eat meat and fish. There is also a wine bar with an expanding selection of wines.
Open 6pm-10pm Wed-Sun. Closed Xmas. Average Price: dinner ££-£££. Near the Octagon in the centre of Westport.

FARMHOUSE CHEESE
CARROWHOLLY CHEESE
Kilmeenacoff, Irma van Baalen
Irma van Baalen's lovely Gouda-type cheeses are a valuable and welcome staple of the bubbly Thursday market in the Octagon in Westport and during the summer she can also be found there on Fridays and Saturdays. Both cow's milk and goat's milk cheeses, as well as some fresh cheeses are for sale.

CAFÉ
CONTINENTAL CAFÉ AND HEALTHFOOD SHOP
High Street Tel: (098) 26679 Wendy Stringer
Though the Continental Café has changed hands a couple of times recently, Wendy Stringer has maintained the old favourites — frankfurters, stuffed pitta bread sandwiches — and the shop maintains a healthfood slant whilst specialising in foods for those on special diets.
Open Tues-Sat 10.30am-6pm.

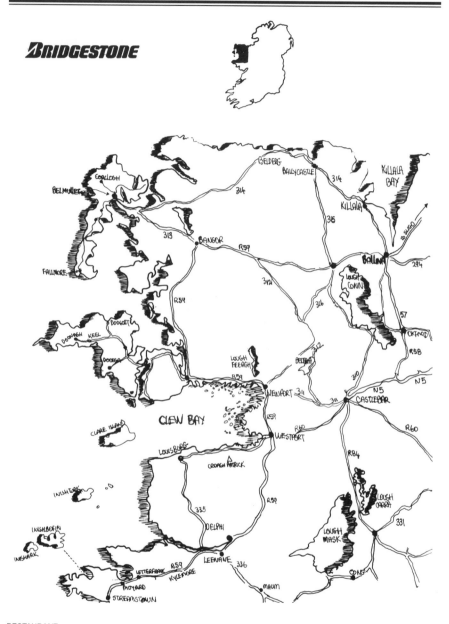

RESTAURANT
CIRCE'S
1 Bridge Street Tel: (098) 27096 Antoinette Turpin and Corry O'Reilly

Corry and Antoinette bake their own bread, serve organic salad leaves and local cheeses,

and their careful sense of choice conspires to give Circe's a fleety holiday spirit and a rumbunctious western character.
Open 10am-10pm Mon-Sat, 7pm-10pm Sun. Closed Xmas and more limited hours during low season.
Average Price: breakfast & lunch £ dinner £££. Visa, Access.

RESTAURANT
QUAY COTTAGE RESTAURANT
The Harbour Tel: (098) 26412 Peter & Kirstin McDonagh
This intimate and enduring restaurant is open all day from noon and from 1pm on Sundays.
Serving simple, agreeable dishes which wisely focus on local seafoods, the Cottage also offers decent vegetarian assemblies. Good quality, given the prices, and a nice atmosphere which seems particularly enjoyable at lunchtime.
Open noon-10pm Mon-Sat, 1pm-10pm Sun. Closed Xmas and Jan. Average Price: lunch & dinner £££. Visa, Access, Amex.

ORGANIC GROWER
WESTERN HERBS AND VEGETABLES
Westport Tel: (098) 26409 Chris & Brid Smith
It is more than likely that the organic vegetables, leaves and herbs which you will find throughout Mayo in shops and supermarkets, and those you will hopefully enjoy in restaurants, will be those grown by Chris and Brid Smith on their few acres near Clogher. They produce almost fifty types of herbs and sell at the Thursday market at the Octagon in Westport as well as in Country Fresh greengrocers in the town.
Visitors to the farm are not merely welcome but encouraged: between May and September for the measly sum of £1.50 with the kids going free you can have a tour between 2pm and 6pm and see how the whole magical process works.
To find the farm take the Castlebar road out of Westport, turn left at the sign for Fahy, travel for one and a half miles when you will see the sign for Clogher and the farm is at the end of the road at the T-junction.

SHOP
WINE & CHEESE
Bridge Street, Anne & Vincent Bourke
Cottage renters and caravan-bound cooks will find much of interest in the Bourkes' unusual shop. Salmon, breads and pâtés are all home made.
Open 10am-6.30pm Mon-Sat.

ON THE QUAY AT WESTPORT
THE ARDMORE RESTAURANT & BAR, The Quay Tel: (098) 25994
Familiar huge menu of pub food with emphasis on fish.
Open 6pm-10pm Mon-Sat (Oct-Apr 7pm-9.30pm). Closed Xmas. Average Price: dinner £££. Visa, Access, Amex, Diners.
THE ASGARD TAVERN & RESTAURANT, The Quay Tel: (098) 25319
Familiar huge menu of pub food.
Open 6.30pm-9.45pm Tue-Sat (open Sun high season). Average Price: dinner £££. Visa, Access, Amex, Diners.

COUNTY SLIGO

R ECALLING LATER THE UNHAPPY PERIOD of his boyhood spent in London, W.B.Yeats wrote 'that I longed for a sod of earth from some field I knew, something of Sligo to hold in my hand. It was some old race instinct like that of a savage, for we had been brought up to laugh at all displays of emotion. Yet it was our mother, who would have thought its display a vulgarity, who kept alive that love. She would spend hours listening to stories or telling stories of the pilots and fishing-people of Rosses Point, or of her own Sligo girlhood, and it was always assumed between her and us that Sligo was more beautiful than other places'.

But this undeniable beauty is grudging, reluctant as a child. The whoops of weather out in western Sligo, which can change the nature of the day from sun to rain and back again in a matter of seconds, is typical of a county that will make little effort to be loved. Sligo demands patience, the patience to wait until the mists of an autumn morning clear and the bare head of Ben Bulben can be seen, patience to wait for the contrary tide so you can grab a bucket of wild mussels or diligently hunt wild oysters in drift pools or set out along Cooleenamore strand with a bag to gather cockles. The impatience of youth might cause you to disregard Sligo. The patience of age will have you agreeing with Yeats: 'There midnight's all a glimmer, and noon a purple glow/And evening full of the linnet's wings'.

BALLINDOON

RESTAURANT AND ACCOMMODATION
CROMLEACH LODGE
Ballindoon, Boyle Tel: (071) 65155 Fax: 65455 Christy and Moira Tighe
Cromleach Lodge is a monument to painstaking application. Neither Christy nor Moira Tighe have a background in the business of running a restaurant with rooms, but their determination to improve, their will to succeed, has meant that Cromleach has steadily acquired an impressive reputation over the last years.

From a distance the house itself is a curious concoction, reflecting the fact that it is the sum of steady accretions over the years, with the original building now difficult to detect amidst the extra rooms and dining rooms which have been added. The rooms upstairs are

super-large and super-comfortable with heartbreak views across fields pinched from a painting by Breughel, out across Lough Arrow and the gorgeous Curlew Mountains.

Moira Tighe's cooking exploits two central commands: firstly, she uses impeccable ingredients from local growers, the bulk of the vegetables and herbs being organically grown, and secondly, despite being self-taught, her cooking strides confidently between modern improvisations — a sausage of chicken and crab, for example — and the classic verities where her work can seem most confidently at home: Lough Gill salmon on a bed of spinach with a lemon and saffron sauce with

white wine, a goat's cheese salad sharply attenuated with vivacious fresh herbs, perfectly subtle and sweet roasted lamb, intricately fine desserts.

Open 6pm-9pm Mon-Sun. Closed Xmas and Jan (open for New Year). Average Price: dinner ££££ B&B £££££. Visa, Access, Amex. Cromleach Lodge is signposted on the A4 just after you leave Boyle and begin to climb the Curlew Mountains; from the junction it is almost 10 miles. It is also signed from Castlebaldwin if you are coming from the Sligo direction, and is 31/2 miles from the main road.

BALLYMOTE

COUNTRY HOUSE, FARM
TEMPLE HOUSE
Ballymote Tel: (071) 83329 Fax: 83808 Sandy and Deb Perceval
The word you most often hear in connection with Temple House is 'perfection'. Nothing more, nothing less. The ability of Sandy and Deb Perceval and this hulkingly handsome house to render people almost speechless with delight is unchallenged in Ireland.
What do people love? The food, says the acclaimed chef. The dinner party atmosphere, say your parents. The whacky and exotic rooms, say your friends, and they list the contents of the Twins' Room: two emerald porcelain washbasins, two wash stands, two bed-end tables, two bedside lamps, two bedside polar bear ornaments, two towels, two flannels, two windows and two fine canopied beds. The friendship, say the people who have already been three times. The sport, say the fishermen and the huntsmen. Temple House is all things to all men and women, and all these things spell happiness.
The house itself is an artful confection, undeniably absurd and splendid, but it is the Perceval's gift to remove any strain of preciousness or pretention from Temple House which makes it work, and makes it appeal to those who love country houses and those who loathe them. Deb Perceval's cooking is an important element of the magic, for she manages always to produce dinners which are exactly appropriate, both for the evening and for the people with whom you share dinner: an onion and blue cheese tart, some of the farm pork in a fillet with a basil sauce, a chocolate meringue gâteau. 'They are able to create a real kind of relaxed caring', says the lady from Germany sitting across from you at dinner. Yes, that's it.

Open for dinner for guests only. Closed Dec-Mar. Average Price: dinner £££ B&B £££££. Visa, Access, Amex, Diners. Temple House is 14 miles from Sligo and is signposted from the N17 if you are travelling from Sligo town or between Collooney and Tubercurry. If travelling from the east on the N4, then turn off the road to Ballymote, travel through the town and you will again see the distinctive blue signs. If lost, ask directions in the Esso garage, or from anyone on the road.

CLIFFONEY

FARMHOUSE CHEESE, GERMAN CHEESECAKE, SOURDOUGH BREAD
HANS AND GABY WALTER-WEILAND
Ballincastle, Cliffoney Tel: (071) 66399 Hans and Gaby Walter-Weiland
Hans and Gaby grind flour, bake breads and cheesecakes, make cheese from cow's and goat's milk, grow vegetables organically and rent out their cottages, and they do

everything with disarming charm and, best of all, with the joyous peal of Gaby's laughter adding a note of frothy irresistibility to their work. The bread, the cheesecake, the cheeses are all filled with joie de vivre, filled with the lovely flavour of zestful love of life.

Cheese is only available in summer months. Telephone for more details of self-catering cottages (open all year, but they book up quickly). Hans' and Gaby's farm is up the narrow road on the right hand side of the road just before the village of Cliffoney, coming from the Sligo direction. Theirs is the fourth house on the left, with the cottage opposite. If you want to order a cheesecake, ring in advance as it takes a couple of days to prepare the quark. Cheese and bread available in Tir na nOg in Sligo town

ALSO OF INTEREST

THE CANAVAUN LOUNGE, Cliffoney Tel: (071) 66123 Mrs Harrison
Superior pub food in a friendly, chatty pub.

COLLOONEY

COUNTRY HOUSE AND RESTAURANT
GLEBE HOUSE

Collooney Tel: (071) 67787 Brid and Marc Torrades
Boredom is a scourge, but maybe also a blessing. Brid Torrades always had a fledgling interest in good food, but it was a stunningly boring period as an au pair in Germany, when she had time to pore over droves of cookery books, which kick-started her nascent interest into decisive action. Back home in Dublin she went daily to catering college, at the same time as running her parents' coffee shop in the village of Malahide, and then reading a newspaper article about Glebe House in Collooney, near Sligo — at the time a splendid ruin, and no more — led to migration to the west coast and to two years solid slog to bring the unruly ruin back to some kind of shape.

By August 1990, Brid and her French husband Marc were open for business, quickly achieving popularity amongst the well-fed citizens of Sligo, a fame which has since spread steadily, by stealthy word of mouth. That quiet fame is well founded, for Ms Torrades allies a tenderly feminine skill as a cook with a rock-solid appreciation of fresh ingredients, most of them grown in the garden at Glebe by Marc.

Ask what her principal influence is and she replies, 'Nature, I suppose. I'm very dependent on what is growing outside in the garden, what Marc is growing, and we try to be as self-sufficient as possible'.

Appropriately, she is happy to accept the description of a customer, who happened to be a French chef, that her style of cooking is 'Cuisine Bourgeois', adding: 'I've always aspired to having fresh herbs and being able to cook using just them, getting the flavour of herbs. It's very simple cooking, I think, where it's simple and simply decorated, and you cook the food avilable at the time. Simplicity is the thing'.

Larousse Gastronomique describes 'bourgeois' as 'The term used for various dishes... that are typical family meals without a set recipe' and this precisely captures the spirit of spontaneity and improvisation which is so happily obvious in Ms Torrades' work. She cooks with great motivation, and has the too-rare gift of being as capable a baker as she is a cook: this means that the vol-au-vent case which cups some wild mushrooms will be melt-in-the-mouth soft, as soft as the puff pastry that enfolds smoked salmon and dill.

The rustic element of cuisine bourgeois finds a good home in her scheme: leg of lamb with Madeira, or sautéed beef with wild mushrooms and garlic, the kind of dishes you want to eat on autumn evenings, when you will pray that the parsnips are in season, for I once ate a purée of parsnips here that made the hairs on the back of my neck stand to attention it was so divine, so right.

These combinations are timeless, as timeless as the tarragon which Ms Torrades teams with chicken or the Pernod she splashes into a seafood selection, but the sparkling quality of the ingredients which Marc Torrades grows and Brid's contented and understated style make them seem brand new. By the time you get around to the dessert trolley, and the bosomy lure of profiteroles with hot butterscotch sauce or a breakheart apple tart, the senses are all a-tingle, and squiffy with pleasure. The rooms in the house are simple, and inexpensive, and allow one to make full use of the good wine list before clambering upstairs to dream such sweet dreams.

Open 6.30pm-10pm (afternoon tea served from 2pm). Open for Xmas. Closed Jan. Average Price: dinner £££ B&B £££. Visa, Access. Signposted from Collooney, just before the bridge.

COUNTRY HOUSE AND RESTAURANT
MARKREE CASTLE AND KNOCKMULDOWNEY RESTAURANT
Collooney Tel: (071) 67800 Fax: 67840 Charles and Mary Cooper
Markree may look like an imposing sort of place as you wind your way up to it along the snaking drive, Gothic and forbidding, but it is a shy sort of castle, a modest pile, an easy-going monument, more Rocky Horror than Hammer Horror. Charles and Mary Cooper's painstaking restoration is beginning to raise Markree from its decades of neglect, when it all but tumbled to the ground, and whilst there remain echoes of boarding school colours here and there, and some of the rooms could enjoy a little more decorative spice, Markree is agreeable and extravagantly simple.

The food in the Knockmuldowney Restaurant is country house modest — mussels in herb butter, baked rabbit, lemon soufflé — but flavours are good, and the wine list is expansive and inexpensive and a real treat for the serious quaffer. Breakfast, in the brightness of the dining room with the babble of foreign tongues all around you and the comfort of solicitous Sligo ladies ushering food to the table, is charming.

Open 7.30pm-9.30pm Mon-Sun and Sun lunch. Closed Xmas and Feb. Average Price: Sun lunch £££ dinner £££ B&B £££££. Visa, Access, Amex, Diners. Markree Castle, near Collooney, just south of Sligo, is clearly signposted from the N4

INNISCRONE

SEA WEED BATH HOUSE
Pier Road Tel: (096) 36238 Edward Kilcullen
We associate the Victorians with prudishness, but they knew something about sensuality. Why else would they have built these bath houses around the coast, and deigned to use sea weed to supply the natural oils in the water, had they not been captivated by the lubricious, evocative sexiness of the experience. Floating in seawater with the unctuous oils lapping your limbs is a bawdy, wanton experience, altogether Rabelaisian.

Open noon-8.30pm Mon-Sun. Closed weekdays in Oct, and Nov-St Patrick's Day weekend.

ORGANIC FARM SHOP
SEA VIEW HOUSE FARM ★

Corballa, Inniscrone Tel: (096) 36255 Anthony & Danny Kilcullen

We holidayed once in Sligo with a friend from England. During the week we bought a fillet of beef from the Kilcullens' farm shop, barbecuing a portion of it first, the rest then quickly chilled and sliced wafer-thin for carpaccio. With a leg of lamb we roasted it with garlic and rosemary, and the remaining pieces went next day into a composed salad with a potato straw cake made with the Kilcullens' floury Claddagh spuds. We also bought their persuasively marvellous hen's eggs and made them into a succulently runny omelette with mushrooms.

Back home in London, our friend invited us for dinner. She bought lamb from a famous and famously expensive French butcher and roasted it expertly. When it was served, she could hardly bring herself to eat it. 'If this is supposed to be lamb', she said, 'then what on earth have they got in Sligo!'.

The answer is that the Kilcullens have some of the best lamb, and beef, and most other things, that you will ever manage to eat. Organically reared, feeding on the lush salty pastures of Inniscrone, the meat approaches sheer perfection. Once eaten, you crave it every time you eat meat from another source, for nothing else, no matter whether you buy it from the finest and most expensive butcher anywhere in the world, will approach this meat for typicity, for tenderness, for pure pleasure.

Anthony Kilcullen's produce is one of the great vindicators of the methods of organic farming and, to convince anyone that organic means better flavour and texture, all you would have to do would be to serve them some of this meat. But beware: you will likely want to eat no other, and likely want to get back to Inniscrone quickly.

Open 6pm-10pm Fri, 2pm-6pm Sat. You can also buy at other times by arrangement. Sea View Farm is almost one mile down the R298, which is clearly signposted on the main Sligo to Ballina road. There is a large sign at the entrance to the farm and the shop.

RATHLEE

DILISK AND CARRAGEEN MOSS
MELVIN'S SEA WEED

Cabra, Rathlee Tel: (096) 49042 Frank and Betty Melvin

'You need to be like a hare to do this', says Frank Melvin, hurdling and jumping from stone to stone on the Long Rock in west County Sligo with the agility of a high-wire specialist. 'You know the fellows that you would come across on the foreshore — and you might surprise them — and they'd be away like mad'.

Frank Melvin springs and leaps amidst the lumpen outcrop of the Long Rock in pursuit of edible sea weeds, in particular the fine sea-salty dilisk (known as dulse in Northern Ireland) and the tangly, khaki-brown restorative which is carrageen moss.

Packed in small plastic bags with the promise 'Harvested in the North West of Ireland' on the label, the weeds are found mainly in health food shops throughout the country. By comparison to other weeds which are produced on a large scale, Mr Melvin's sea weeds are finer and more complete in both texture and taste.

The secret of the high quality of his sea weeds lies not just in the suitability of the Long

Rock and its neighbouring outcrops, but also in his method of drying the weeds: 'The weather will do the bleaching', says Mr Melvin. 'All you need to do is pitch it out, for ten days. But, I believe, to do it right, it must be bleached all around, from the point of view that I can sell that and it won't go soft or go bad at room temperature. If I don't bleach it there will be a tendency that what won't get bleached will go soft'.

Originally a fisherman, Frank Melvin later became the harbour pilot in nearby Ballina before the container ships dried up and died away, forcing him to look for a new method to earn a living. 'I like to work with the sea, the funny thing is if I could make a living I'd work every day at the sea. It's a very healthy place, and there's great peace of mind down there: no one to fight with but the sea urchins!'.

But if the sea shore is a peaceful place, it is also, to the outsider, a place of strange surprise. Summon up the nerve to gambol amidst the rocks with Frank Melvin and a tour of the Long Rock becomes not unlike a tour of Burgundy vineyards.

Over here, just near the water's edge, is a place good for dilisk with fine, long, dark strands — a grand cru site, perhaps. Over there, further out on the water, is where the shorter strands of a type of dilisk known as crannach grows, the fronds of the weed sprouting from tiny shells. 'That's the one the old folk prefer' says Frank, 'They would just walk out and collect it by the handful and eat it'. Its penchant for blooming from the shells, however, means that it is not a good commercial proposition as the strands are too short.

Then, in a premier cru site, one finds the carrageen. 'It's at a different water level, but not far removed', says Frank, 'and it's possible to get it on a day when you won't get dilisk, it's at a higher level. You would only get it in very small proportions when there's a weaker tide, simply because the water is on it'.

With the dilisk, says Mr Melvin, 'Most of the people that I know just chew it, straight from the bag', though a handful of the chopped weed added to a soda bread mixture makes for a cake of bread that is particularly good with cheese.

The carrageen is used for cooking, the inevitable nursery school, blancmange-style pudding, of course, 'though a lot of the people I sell it to use it for colds and flus, for the chest. There are many families even who I supply in the Ballina-Sligo area and they use a huge amount, give it to their kids and bring them up with it, they reckon they never have colds or sickness or anything, they swear by it'.

As a restorative, indeed, carrageen is unbeatable, the weeds soaked and brewed up in water, then strained and mixed with honey and lemon juice. On Aran, notes the writer Tim Robinson, 'Next to whiskey it is the people's most trusted cure for coughs and colds'. A drop of the hard stuff tilted into some brewey carrageen, of course, is surely the perfect recipe for health and happiness.

Available in wholefood stores throughout the country.

SLIGO

WHOLEFOOD SHOP
TIR NA NOG ★
Grattan Street Tel: (071) 62752 Mary, John & Norah McDonnell
Retailers tend, over the years, to mellow, to become timeworn by the pressures of business, the demands of customers. They tend to lose the drive and the focus which

motivated them in the beginning, the desire to sell the foods they love from the producers they respect.

Like any organic environment, a shop and its keepers need to develop and mature, and yet they need to hold fast to their principles, they need to refuse to allow their dedication to become subdued. In Tir na nOg, Mary McDonnell has clung on to her desire to do her best, has held fast to her right to get angry. 'Just look at this! They expect me to sell this!', she shouts, exasperated, and gets on the telephone to let some wholesaler or distributor know that nothing that comes in the door of the shop and goes out the door of the shop is to be anything other than the best and what on earth were they thinking about when they sent.

Mary's fire is balanced by the gentleness of John and Norah, but like her they are devoted to the idea of Tir na nOg as a place of good things, the best foods in their season, chockful of the vigour of the North West climate, the best of the farmhouse cheeses, the choicest dried foods. The shop is a personal reflection of the driven and devoted personalities of the McDonnells', and is an integral and essential part not just of the social culture of Sligo, but of the food culture of this island.

Open 9am-6pm Mon-Sat

RESTAURANT
TRUFFLES ★
11 The Mall Tel: (071) 44226 Bernadette O'Shea

Bernadette O'Shea came to Sligo to open a restaurant which would specialise in pizzas, and everyone thought she was crazy. Now, a few years down the line, in a new premises which has an artfully lovely wine bar above and the coolest staff serving the most exquisite food below, her success has led to the arrival of a host of imitators, folk who think Ms O'Shea simply spotted a trend and went for it, and who believe they can do the same.

They couldn't be more wrong. For Truffles is not simply the new thing, the latest fashion, a new twist on the sort of food people want to eat and a funky new way of serving it. It is, rather, a classic example of the application of the essential skills which every good cook must possess — toughness, determination, skill and dedication, good taste and judgement and a vision of one's work as an artistic enterprise — all of them applied, in the case of Truffles, to the creating and cooking of pizza.

And in Truffles, the creating is every bit as important as the cooking, for Ms O'Shea is an innovator, as restlessly creative as Alice Waters — and we should remember that the creator of Berkeley's Chez Panisse restaurant has a café upstairs over the restaurant which specialises in pizza and pasta — as obsessed with purity as Richard Olney, as devoted to detail as Joël Robuchon.

Each combination on top of the pizza is deliberately thought through to provide confluence and contrast, to offer the most pleasing and sympathetic tastes imaginable even when, in something like the Truffles' Best — roast garlic, roast peppers, ricotta, sautéed onions, parmesan, tomato sauce, olive oil and mozzarella — the list of ingredients becomes potentially overwhelming.

But whilst many of the Truffles' pizzas are culinary Baedekers, tablets of dough informed with all the funky happenings of both classic Italian tastes and New World improvisations — Pizza Mexicano with fresh coriander and sausage meat, Chilli Pizza with hot chilli sauce with sun-dried tomatoes and three cheeses and a salsa of guacamole chutney on the side — Ms O'Shea is always looking to localise her work as much as possible. Thus the pizza with Seven Irish Cheeses or The Californian Classic with sun-dried tomatoes brought back home by the use of Irish goat's cheese. These extraordinary creations are nothing less than music for the mouth.

Open 5pm-10.30pm Tues-Sat, 5pm-10pm Sun. Closed Xmas. Average Price: pizza ££. No credit cards. Recommended for Vegetarians. The Mall is an extension of Stephen's Street, on the main road to Enniskillen going in the direction of the hospital.

PUB
HARGADON'S
O'Connell Street Tel: (071) 42974 Pat Leigh Doyle

Hargadon's has an atmosphere so womb-like wonderful that even the shelves are woozy. Lolling and sagging like Laurel and Hardy on a bender, they are surreally warped, and in Hargadon's they seem perfectly in place, just above the tea and spice boxes, just out front of the assignatory snugs, near to the ancient burner, across from the bar where pints are respectfully pulled, tots of whiskey tilted out of bottles, conversations begun. Hargadon's is a crystaline vision of an Irish pub, frozen in time, preserved perfectly.

DELICATESSEN
COSGROVE'S
32 Market Street Tel: (071) 42809 The Cosgrove Family

If you are no longer young, and prone to nostalgia, Cosgrove's shop may well have you whispering laments for the loss of the local shop, that denizen of carefully selected foods, that warren of excitements, that temple of gossip and information. Cosgrove's is that shop, a splendid, handsome, loving place, with boxes of dried fruits and hanks of cooked meats and soft-smelling tumbles of bread and floorbound bags of salty fresh dilisk. Like Hargadon's pub and the Inniscrone Sea weed Baths, it is resplendently Victorian, an echo from a time now gone.

Open 9.30am-9pm Mon-Sat, 11.30am-1.30pm, 5.30pm-8pm Sun

FARM SHOP
FARMHOUSE VARIETIES
Wine Street Car Park Tel: (071) 70427 Tommy Breheny & Owen Downes

A car park sounds like the last place you expect to find products from the farm, but here in Farmhouse Varieties you can buy good country butter and good country buttermilk, organically reared meat and Irish farmhouse cheeses.

Open 8.30am-6pm Mon-Wed, 8.30am-7pm Thur, 8.30am-8pm Fri, 8.30am-6pm Sat

COOKED FOOD TO GO
THE GOURMET PARLOUR
Bridge Street Tel: (071) 44617 Annette Burke and Catherine Farrell

There isn't anything Catherine and Annette aren't game to have a go at, no taste venture they won't essay, no function too large for them to cope with, no party too small for them

to furnish with food, no demand for Christmas cooking too awkward. This aching willingness to please, and the fineness of their work from bread to ice-cream, from patisserie to pâtés, from chutneys to quiches has made them an essential addition to Sligo's quality-driven food culture.
Open 9.30am-6pm Mon-Sat.

DELICATESSEN
KATE'S KITCHEN
24 Market Street Tel: (071) 43022 Kate Pettit and Frank Hopper
Kate's is the sort of shop that always reminds one of Christmastime. The shelves bulge with those jars of goodies which somehow seem indispensable at a time when you feel you should spoil yourself: aged vinegar, pickled walnuts, cranberry sauce, hand-made chocolates. There is also a catholic selection of wine, and various and plentiful cooked food to-go, for Kate and Frank are truly Irish traiteurs.
Open 9am-6.30pm Mon-Sat

FISHMONGER
KILFEATHER'S
34 Market Street Tel: (071) 43564 Gary Kilfeather
He is a lovely man altogether, Gary Kilfeather, and he runs a lovely shop with fresh fish brought down from Donegal or with rod-caught salmon he buys from local lads during the season that is in it. You couldn't imagine Sligo town without this quiet, splendid shop.
Open 8.30am-6.30pm Mon-Sat

RIVERSTOWN

COUNTRY HOUSE
COOPERSHILL HOUSE
Riverstown, Co Sligo Tel: (071) 65108 Fax: 65466 Brian and Lindy O'Hara
Coopershill can seem a slightly serious sort of house, somewhere likely to have people putting on their best behaviour, their public faces, even with Brian O'Hara's droll and dry sense of humour working hard to put everyone at their ease. Perhaps it is because dinner is taken at separate tables, rather than in communion with your fellow guests, which breaks up the spell of pre-dinner drinks, or maybe it is simply the type of people who are attracted to Coopershill, folk for whom social diplomacies are very important.
Yet, despite this, it is hard to escape the surreal qualities of Coopershill, and impossible not to find amusement and humour in them. These serious other guests, for example, always impress as people with interesting other lives — is this why they put on their public faces? — people with pasts, curious presents. Teasing a little of their mystery out of them over the course of a belter of a brandy after dinner is a joy, though some ill-informed and inaccurate speculation about them as you enjoy Lindy's cooking during dinner will do nicely.
They give a country weekend party feel to Coopershill, an Agatha Christie edge, and everything else about the house, the peacocks, the peacefulness — when the peacocks aren't bleating — the out-of-time atmosphere, colludes with this. Coopershill allows you to

enter a mystery movie by Merchant and Ivory, a Henry James whodunnit. Open for dinner for guests only. Closed Nov-Apr (out of season house parties, incl. Xmas and New Year by arrangement). Average Price: dinner £££ B&B £££££. Visa, Access, Amex. Coopershill is clearly signposted from the Drumfin crossroads on the N4, 11 miles southwest of Sligo.

STRANDHILL

SHELLFISH

The mind's eye is full of farming images, of ladders reaching up to hay lofts, Constable's water mills, field gleaners captured in Impressionist brushstrokes, patient Gainsborough fieldscapes, but there can be no more dignified an image, no vision more worthy of the

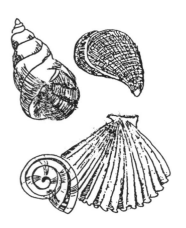

artist's eye, than the stooping silhouette of the shellfish farmer, thigh boots cascading and wading like an aquatic Cyrano de Bergerac, playing tricks on the eye as it swaps focus between the solitary farmer and the mountains that frame him.

The sight of Noel Carter, high-wire walking along the frames of his clam nets down at the shore at Strandhill, brings to mind the famous painting by Jack B. Yeats of fishermen set to launch their boat into the water, their backs turned to us, their unseen concentration rapt. There is sea and sky, the surface of sand, the bodies sharpened in profile by the huge expanse all around. Despite the threat of the sea, these images are ultimately peaceful, natural.

Two such farmers work almost side by side in Strandhill. Noel Carter farms clams, Noelle Woodeson, an actress in her time, farms oysters, and sells them wrapped in seaweed. Mr Carter's clams, raised heroically against the vicissitudes of time and tide and infernal crabs, are small and juicily sweet, Ms Woodeson's oysters saline and pure. Eating them is a pleasure, but simply heading down to the foreshore to buy them — especially the little adventure of crossing the airport runway to get to Mr Carter's place, is glorious.

NOEL CARTER
Strandhill Tel: (071) 68443
NOELLE WOODESON
Coolenamore, Strandhill Tel: (071) 68127

ALSO OF INTEREST
EITHNA'S RESTAURANT, The Harbour Mullaghmore Tel: (071) 66407 Eithna O'Sullivan. Eithna's has a nice location, down near the pier, and judicious choosing should allow for a good lunch or dinner. Open Mon-Sat 12.30pm-10pm, Sun 12.30pm-2.30pm. Closed from end of Sept to Mar..

LEINSTER

COUNTY CARLOW

D
ESPITE ITS LOCATION fifty-two miles south-west of the capital, Carlow looks and feels like a Midlands town. Quiet, cautious, undemonstrative. Ask the locals how things are, how they are doing, and likely as not they'll say 'Ah, not too bad', making you sorry you had asked at all.

It seems all the more surprising then that two of Carlow's restaurants should be places which place great emphasis on their wine lists, and have lists that are distinctive and creative. You might believe everyone in the county to be pint drinkers, pub people: think again.

In The Beams, an old coaching inn comprising a modest link of rooms in the town itself, Peter O'Gorman brings a list of fine wines to food which is understated, French-influenced, and where the fish cookery can enjoy some fine moments. In The Lord Bagenal, just off the main road some miles south of Carlow town as you head for Kilkenny, James Kehoe's inn has been building a reputation for solicitous service and pleasing cooking in the bar and the restaurant, but especially for a wine list which has won more awards recently than any other in the country. A vast, magnificent production that spans the globe in search of the very best bottles, the list is enormous, weighty, chock-a-block with the lithe names of the great wines and the great wine makers, and you read it and remember Robert Louis Stevenson's quote, that 'Wine is bottled poetry'.

THE BEAMS RESTAURANT

59 Dublin Street, Carlow Tel: (0503) 31824 Peter & Betty O'Gorman

Open 7.30pm-9.30pm Tues-Sat. Closed Xmas. Average Price: dinner £££. Visa, Access. Diners.

THE LORD BAGENAL INN

Leighlinbridge Tel: (0503) 21668 James Kehoe

Open noon-11pm. Average Price: ££. Visa, Access, Diners. Leighlinbridge is on the Carlow/Kilkenny road.

DUBLIN

ONSIDERED FROM A COOKING point of view, Dublin barely clutches onto the culinary handstraps when it comes to being regarded as a serious town. It has only one dish which it can call its own and Dublin Coddle, a sluttish stew of bangers, bacon and spuds, is such a resolutely ambiguous concoction that it is difficult to track it down anywhere in the city these days. And, when one finally manages to find it, a single mouthful is likely to convince you that you have found not the holy grail, but some manner of poisoned chalice.

The reason for this disregard of a serious, personal cuisine lies not with a lack of interest in food, however, but more in the fact that the city's heartbeat lies closer to its liver than its belly. The social life of Dublin offers a dichotomy between a restaurant culture which has begun, magnificently, to assert itself over the last decade, and a pub culture which is, unequivocally, the finest in the world. Dubliners have had to learn the style of a restaurant culture, have had to educate themselves to the mores of eating away from home, but each and every citizen and visitor inherits the city's pub culture as a birthright.

The extraordinary temples which offer alcohol, conversation and company are resplendent in their grimery, intoxicating in their ability to coalesce quietude with an adrenalinated hunger. At any time of the day, from floor-washing early morning to raucous late at night, they welcome you with the promise of perfection, a perfection found in the bottom of a glass, and a perfection found all about you: in the stucco mahogany; the fluted ceilings which are likely, late on, to become flootered ceilings; the rotund bellied men behind the bar; the four in the afternoon light which dissects the windows and dances on the tables; the everlasting youthfulness of chucking-out time. 'Time, Ladies and Gentlemen please!' bellow the rotund bellies, but time is just beginning for everyone who finds themselves being cleared out of the boozer at 'round about midnight, dizzy with drink, dizzy with romance, friendship, an implacable beatific kindness to one and all.

Dublin pubs are the greatest in the world because they are populated with and patronised by Dubliners. You can take these people for granted, most likely if you live in the city for a few years. But, move away for even a short while, then return for a couple of days and you see, at about six in the evening when the sun is waning over the Liffey and work is done and fun about to begin, that this city has an energy, a hunger for the good things, and a hunger for the good times, which allows it to be considered as one of the great cities of the world.

Dublin is small, and disparate, mouldy in parts, chock-a-block here and there, but the volatile energy of the Dubs is irreplaceable, intense, heady. Fall in amongst these people, in amongst these pubs, and you feel a part of their quest for a good time, part of their quest to live each moment to the full, part of the immediate here and now. Dubliners do not postpone the need to enjoy themselves, they do not parcel out their pleasures bit by bit, weekend by weekend. The carnival of pleasure, the seizing of the day and the afternoon and the evening, is a daily occurrence, a necessary part of life. In Dublin time, the living always seems to be easy.

This is why Dublin is one of the great cities. It disarms you, almost from the moment you arrive. You settle into its rhythm, settle into its vernacular, find yourself walking at its pace, hear yourself speaking the shorthand of pleasure which is the city's lingua franca: 'Great crack', 'Ah, you're a long time dead', 'Another?', 'Wonderful to see you', 'Let's go try

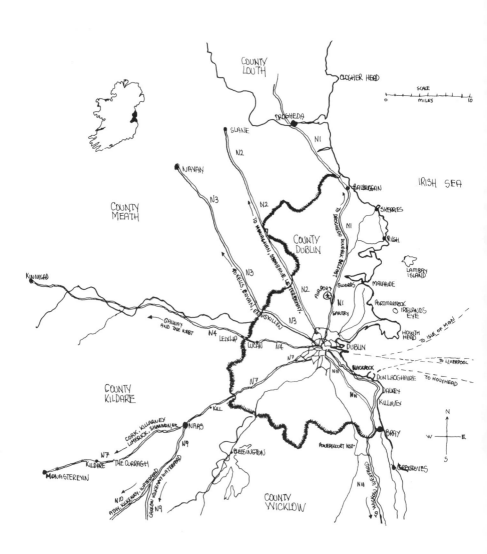

BRIDGESTONE

that place down the street'. The pubs of the city serve alcohol, but you can become intoxicated just by walking down the streets of the city, watching the sunsets, sitting in a park, chatting over breakfast, waiting for your pint of Guinness to transform itself from café au lait brown to thundering black. It is in your veins: pulsing, pulsing.

DUBLIN PUBS

The following are some of the most symptomatic and celebrated pubs of Dublin.

THE BAILEY

2 Duke Street
A super-trendy part of Dublin's social and cultural history which attracts record company hipsters, minor-league musicians, self-conscious actors, very self-conscious actresses, aspiring journalists and pop scribblers. The door to Leopold Bloom's house is the door you walk through.

BAGGOT INN

143 Baggot Street Lwr
The Baggot Inn seems to change its design and orientation as often as some young Dublin women change the colouring of their hair. Rock music gigs are held here, both upstairs and downstairs. Leather jackets are not compulsory, despite appearances to the contrary.

THE BRAZEN HEAD

20 Lwr Bridge Street
The haunt of all those foreign students who come to Dublin to learn English, and almost everyone else who visits the city and must, just must, visit the oldest bar in town.

CAFÉ EN SEINE

Dawson Street
The beauty of Café En Seine can take the breath away: bistro lighting, a long tunnel of the room with high-side seating, and the relentless energy of the super-hip crowd shooting the atmosphere into overdrive. Designed to be like a French café, so there's no need to feel self-conscious if you want coffee rather than alcohol.

DAVY BYRNE'S

21 Duke Street
The pub where Leopold Bloom partook of a gorgonzola sandwich and a glass of burgundy, in Joyce's immortal 'Ulysses'. Nowadays, Davy Byrne's gets a swish crowd, most of whom won't have read Joyce's immortal slice of Dublinese, and lots of tourists who will have read the book and are only too too keen to discuss it.

THE DAWSON LOUNGE

25 Dawson Street
A tiny little downstairs lounge at the bottom of a corkscrew stair case. Cosy in winter, cosy in summer and always, somehow, curiously surreal.

DOHENY & NESBITT'S

5 Lr Baggot Street

At the weekends this glorious old pub is packed to the gills with lawyers, all of them getting more than squiffy and quoting Archbold, Blackstone and the hottest Law Library gossip at each other. Nesbitt's (as it is known) may be best during the week for a contemplative sup in the company of barmen who behave like philosophers: silent as Wittgenstein, stoic as Socrates.

THE DUKE

9 Duke Street

Stalled academics, lesser novelists and Dublin 'characters', all of them wearing tweed jackets and an appropriate disdain for much of life, pile in here. Refurbishment a few years ago did nothing to alter the charm of a place which is both delightful and infuriating.

THE GARAGE

Temple Bar

Attracts a super-hip set who like to park themselves here and lounge around, thanks not only to its post-modern décor but also the fact that rock 'n' roll millionaires U2 are the owners of the bar and The Clarence Hotel which The Garage is a part of.

GROGAN'S

15 South William Street

Creative folk, some who want to be creative but aren't and those who bear the brunt of the hard end of the wedge fill up this neat pub just at the back of the Powerscourt Centre.

HARTIGAN'S

100 Lr Leeson Street

Spartan, serious pub for real drinkers which makes it all the stranger that law students gaggle here at the weekend and try desperately to misbehave.

THE HORSESHOE BAR

The Shelbourne Hotel, St Stephen's Green

If you want to see how the executive, legislative and judicial arms of the Irish Government operate, this is perhaps the best place to start. Forget Leinster House: this is the seat of the Irish Government and a very comfortable seat besides. Affairs of state can get pretty wild late on a weekend evening when the executive, legislative and judicial arms may get a little woozy. An essential and amusing slice of Dublin life.

HUGHES'S BAR

19 Chancery Street
During the day young men contemplating a spell inside may quaff their last drink in freedom here in the company of pitiful relatives and pitiless lawyers. In the evenings some sharp rug-cutting takes over, when excellent sessions and fine set dancing seizes the place.

THE INTERNATIONAL BAR

23 Wicklow Street
If asked to meet for a drink, we would, most likely, suggest meeting in The International, an exuberant wood clad temple which enjoys superb natural lighting. Matt, one of the bar's great retainers, is now pulling pints in some celestial bar, but Simon is still on hand to dispense calm, crafty advice about any subject you care to mention. A good pub for contemplative drinks at 4pm in the afternoon, and a good pub for all sorts of blathery rowdiness at 11pm in the evening.

KEHOE'S

9 South Anne Street
Many drinkers favourite Dublin pub, with grand old snugs but regrettably-difficult-to-get-to loos. The barmen are all existentialists, and have an appropriately jaundiced view of human morality and motivation.

KENNY'S

Lincoln Place
Good sessions can, sometimes, be found in this unassuming emporium at the back of Trinity, a fave rave of students.

THE LONG HALL

51 South Great George's Street
If there is a bar in heaven it will look like this. One of the most exuberant pieces of design you can find in the town, the Long Hall is a veritable Cathedral of Booze. You can sacrifice your brain cells at this shrine without guilt, perhaps chewing the cud about William Morris. Mention him to the staff and they will ask; 'What team does he play for?'. A drole bunch, for sure. Not to be missed by visitors.

MCDAID'S

3 Harry Street
Popularly known as 'The Brendan Behan'. A major Place of Pilgrimage for tourists who want to discover the real literary Dublin and are just dying to ask everyone intelligently daft questions about same. Décor is strictly unreconstructed gothic.

MULLIGAN'S

8 Poolbeg Street
A legendary pint of Guinness — perhaps the most celebrated and discussed in the entire town — is served by blokes who have seen it all and heard it all. Attracts a curious crowd who boast their authentic Dubliner status by talking loudly and pretending to ignore you. Don't miss either the pint or the regulars.

NEARY'S

1 Chatham Street

As a back door to the Gaiety Theatre, Neary's is inevitably a slightly theatrical boozer, but late at night, and especially on rugby weekends, the theatricality tends to affect everyone. Gets mighty crowded late in the evening.

THE NORSEMAN

29 East Essex Street, Temple Bar

This agreeably lackadaisical pub should, of course, be called The Norseperson: per unit of trendiness, one of the coolest and most credible pubs in town. Theatre folk, a rock 'n' roll element, the Temple Bar art community and, heaven help us, some respectable folk as well come here to chat and quaff. Arty and artisan.

O'BRIEN'S

4 Sussex Terrace

Even though one is no more than a couple of hundred yards from the bridge at Leeson Street, O'Brien's, which looks like a handsome, well-worn city pub, nevertheless has a vaguely suburban atmosphere, instead of the sharply tuned frisson of expectation common to the true city centre pubs.

O'DONOGHUE'S

15 Merrion Row

Good impromptu music sessions can be found in this smoky old pub, originally famous as the haunt of musical mini-legends The Dubliners, which draws in Dubliners, visitors and denizens young and old. Its fame as a staple of each and every guide book has not made the staff the slightest bit self-conscious: they just get on with the business of pullin' pints.

O'DWYER'S

7 Lwr Mount Street and 104 Lwr Leeson Street

A pair of busy, rather trendy pubs which concoct an old-fashioned appearance from new materials and clever design. The Mount Street boozer is preferred by the young urban professionals of the town who work round and about it, whilst a younger set, including many students, get their elbow-lifting practice in Leeson Street.

THE OLD STAND

37 Exchequer Street

A very professional and very comfortable pub. Droves of regulars love it, others find it a place that they may visit only rarely.

O'SHEA'S MERCHANT
12 Lwr Bridge Street
Perhaps the sharpest traditional dancing to be found in the city most weeknights, when gaggly civil servants, energetic wives, women in, or just past, their bloom and other keepers of the flame disport themselves with wild abandon.

THE PALACE
21 Fleet Street
For many Dubs, their single favourite boozer and a place they would like to be in when they depart this mortal coil. A lovely old bar which vaults and swirls with wood and glass, and a good pint.

PETER'S PUB
Stephen Street
Peter's Pub is spoken of with touching fondness by many in this town and if you pitch in here at six o'clock on a bright day, this airy, simple place will endear itself to yourself as quickly as any 'First one of the Day'.

RYAN'S
28 Parkgate Street
A beautiful old bar, with a beautiful old bar you will have seen a thousand times in photographs and picture postcards. Wonderful snugs at the back of the pub, and some pretty decent food. A true, well-maintained slice of Victoriana.

SHEEHAN'S
17 Chatham Street
Formerly a comfortable, elbow-patchy, much-loved pub which is now a slightly over-designed and quietly self-conscious watering hole. Irrespective of the changes, Sheehan's continues to attract lawyers, writers and a smattering of the creatively funky classes.

SLATTERY'S
29 Capel Street
Perhaps the best music pub in the city, in the middle of slowly-dying, slowly-decaying, already-desiccated Capel Street.

STAG'S HEAD
1 Dame Court
A very lovely pub which is good for drinking, good for idling away the afternoon hours, good for motoring through the evening hours and, mercifully, good for eating: the food here may be the best in the town. An oaky, smoky bar with relaxed, friendly staff.

THE TEMPLE BAR
Temple Bar
Refurbished a few years back to make it look like an age-old, authentic Dublin boozer, The Temple Bar is permanently stuffed to bursting with raucously trendy types and age-old authentic citizens.

TONER'S

139 Lwr Baggot Street

Authentic Dublin pub which has been tarted up over the years without removing the necessary character which makes it ever-popular: the bar itself is still particularly pleasing. Agreed, by all and sundry, to be a good place.

WHELAN'S

25 Wexford Street

An old pub which looks new, sort of, thanks to careful and clever restoration. Never less than hyper with droves of foreign students and rock and roll heads here for the music.

DUBLIN WINE SHOPS

DEVENEY'S

31 Main Street, Dundrum, D14 Tel: (01) 298 4288

Also at Taney Road, Goatstown (295 1745), 105 Rathgar Road (909366), 16 Upper Rathmines Road (972392), Rosemount Shopping Centre, Rathfarnham (944766), and Sandyford (295 7237)

The Deveney's shops, scattered here and there throughout the city and the suburbs, are good, professionally run shops with a broad range of medium-priced wines from all over the globe, as well as some select and special bottles.

Open 10.30am-10pm Mon-Sat, 12.30pm-2pm, 4pm-10pm Sun

FINDLATER'S

The Harcourt Street Vaults, 10 Upper Hatch Street, D2 Tel: (01) 475 1699 Fax: 475 2530

These vaults below the old Harcourt Street railway station are unquestionably handsome and venerable, but it is possible to feel somewhat ambiguous about their suitability for a wine merchants. The Findlater's premises feel somewhat dispersed, echoey and uncertainly lit, with wines spread around too great a floor space. The air is agreeably cool, of course, a great boon should you wish to splash out on something special or be a subscriber to Findlater's clever Cellar Plan, where you pay a certain amount of money each month and choose wines from the lists which they recommend twice a year. If you don't have anything suitable in which to cellar wines, this is undoubtedly useful. Their range of wines is, of course, excellent.

Open 9am-6pm Mon-Fri, 10.30am-6pm Sat

THE MARKET WINERY

George's Street Arcade, D2 Tel: (01) 677 9522

Tony Ecock's wine shop is sister to the Vintage shops described later.

Open 10.30am-6pm Mon-Fri

MCCABE'S

51-55 Mount Merrion Avenue, Blackrock, Co Dublin Tel: (01) 288 2037 (Also at Vernon Avenue, Clontarf, D3 Tel: (01) 335277)

Jim McCabe's shops are splendid homes to the great wines of the world, pleasing places that entice and lure you into a love affair with the bottle. There are often good-value fine

bargains to be had amidst the batallions of good bottles from all over the world and, if you are on the hunt for a serious vintage, this is one of the most promising places to come. The staff, as you would expect, are excellent.
Open 10.30am-10pm Mon-Sat, 12.30pm-2pm, 4pm-10pm Sun

MITCHELL'S
21 Kildare Street, D2 Tel: (01) 676 0766
The great lure of Mitchell's is not just that it is a splendidly clubbish place in which to buy wines, but also the fact that their recent additions to the range seem to have been chosen with care and an eye for distinctiveness. They maintain a huge range of the professional Mommessin wines from France, amongst a list strong in Burgundies and clarets, but recent times have seen greater divergence away from the Old World, adding interesting Californian and New Zealand wines amongst richly repayable French country wines. One pleasing feature of the shop is the feeling that it is not excessively concerned with fashion, with chasing down the latest bright star to get splashed across the pages of the wine press. They work to their own pace and rhythm, and are to be congratulated for it.
Open 10.30am-5.30pm Mon-Fri ('till 8pm Thur), 10.30am-1pm Sat

MOLLOY'S LIQUOR STORES
Greyhound Inn, Blanchardstown, Co Dublin Tel: (01) 821 012 Also at Crumlin Shopping Centre (531611), Nutgrove Shopping Centre (936077), Block 3, The Village Green, Tallaght (597599), Penthouse, Ballymun (842 8189) and Clondalkin Village (570166)
Though their supermarket 'n' suburb locations may lead you to expect little from the Molloy's shops than clearing houses for beer and plonk, they do have a surprisingly decent range of wines.
Open 10.30am-11.30pm Mon-Sat (11pm winter), 12.30pm-2pm, 4pm-11pm Sun

O'BRIEN'S
30-32 Donnybrook Road, D4. Tel: 269 3033 Also at Blackrock (288 1649), Dun Laoghaire (280 6952), Bray (286 3732), Dalkey (285 8944), Sandymount (668 2096), Greystones (287 4123), Vevay Road (286 8776)
The style of the O'Brien's shops follows a pattern of large windows and glass doors which open out onto simple floor spaces littered with boxes and wooden crates, spanning everything from the very best clarets to a huge range of negociant wines. The shops are usually reliable sources of unusual spirits, and their prices are very keen.
Open 10.30am-9pm Mon-Sat, 12.30pm-2pm, 4pm-9pm Sun

SEARSON'S
The Crescent, Monkstown, Co Dublin Tel: (01) 280 0405 Fax: 280 4771
What a pleasure it is to buy wine in Searson's shop in Monkstown. The simple little room has nothing so formal as a counter, just stone walls, a high ceiling and bottles of good stuff arrayed around the walls and stacked on a fine big sideboard. It is somewhere to contemplate the future, to worry about the legs a modest vintage may have, to smile with delayed delight at the clout and class of a good bottle entering its glory days.
Frank and Charles Searson have a reputation as serious claret men, chaps who only ship stuff that comes in wooden crates, but this image belies the reality. They have a good,

inexpensive house wine in Domaine de Bousquet — nice strawberry fruit in the centre, playful tannins throughout — and have begun in recent years to expand their range to include wines from California and Australia, Spain and Portugal, and to begin to include excellent French country wines alongside their Burgundies and Bordeauxs.

It is possible, therefore, to drop in on the way home from work and to pick up something for dinner that evening, and it is possible to stop by and discuss the staying power of a vintage, should you have come into some Money From America and want to fill your shelves with something fine. Frank Searson is happy to put his trust and his judgement in the best-known claret names — Anthony Barton, Jean-Michel Cazes, Christian Moueix among others — and one buys either the bottle on the way home or the case for the cellar not just with pleasure, but with confidence.

Open 10.30am-7pm Mon-Sat.

SUPERQUINN

Blackrock Shopping Centre, Blackrock, Co Dublin Tel: (01) 283 1511

Irish supermarkets have tended to lag behind the revolution which has energised the wine departments of so many English supermarkets, but Superquinn is a proud exception and the range at Blackrock, their flagship shop, is impressive and keenly priced.

The reason for this is simple. The chaps who are given the run of the wine sections of Superquinn are all enthusiasts, many of them with personal preferences which mean that one shop will have, say, more Portuguese or Spanish or Chilean bottles than another, simply because that is how the local man likes it. Jim Hammond has a keen eye for Portuguese wines and offers a splendid range in the Blackrock shop, but there are also good clarets and Burgundies and fine wines at steep and not-so-steep prices. We once bought a couple of cases of wine in here after noticing that it had been made in the Cave de Sigoules, a village near Bergerac where we once holidayed. Spicy, clean and thirst-quenching, it was cheap as the rain, and gone in a flash. Sadly, when we returned, the shop had no more, so keep an eye out for special offers and don't delay when you come across a good one.

Open 9am-6pm Mon-Sat ('till 9pm Thurs & Fri) Walkinstown and Swords open 'till 7pm

VERLING'S

360 Clontarf Road, D3 Tel: (01) 331653

There is always a great buzz about Verling's, the sort of shop where bottles are always being opened and glasses handed round for the customers to taste some chirpy new arrival, some exciting newcomer that has everyone bright with delight. Jim Verling and Sean Gilley run a splendid wine shop, the kind of place where it is all too easy to loiter and all too easy to spend all too much money.

Never mind. Drinking the results of your splurge will always prove to be delicious, for their wide selection is chosen with care and sound knowledge and the great and the good of the wine world are here, as well as many good bargains: Verling's often proves to be a shop where you can pick up some good quaffing stuff at a keen price. If that happens, of course, you will simply buy more of the booze at a keen price, instead of less of the booze at a costly price. Either way, you win. At least until the monthly bills drop through the letterbox.

Open 10.30am-10pm Mon-Sat, 12.30pm-2pm, 4pm-10pm Sun

THE VINTAGE

Newtownpark Avenue, Blackrock, Co Dublin Tel: (01) 283 1664, 149 Upper Rathmines Road, D6 Tel: (01) 967811

The Ecock brothers' shops have acquired a swisher, more assured completeness in the last few years, and none more so than the shop in Rathmines which always has a busy, commodious atmosphere, doubtless partly helped by the wine appreciation classes which they run from time to time. They import the complete Fetzer range of wines from California, and many other pleasantly surprising wines from Europe.

Open 10.30am-10pm Mon-Sat, 12.30pm-2pm, 4pm-10pm Sun

THE TRIFLES OF PERFECTION

Our broad policy is to try and have the best wine from every appellation, and that's how we operate', says Colm Brangan, a Dublin wine importer who specialises in some of the most applauded and celebrated wines of France. As a merchant, what motivates him most is the desire to chase down new and exciting wines. 'France is going through a revolution which is bringing new and undiscovered wines to the front', he says. But what does he look for when chasing a wine on the wine route?

'One of the things I have always tried to tease out with myself is: why are the great, great wine makers different?', he says, 'and one thing they have, that the mass production, modern technology of new world wines does not have, is this fantastic respect for nature: respecting the vines, the soil, the season. As Lucien Peyraud (of the legendary Domaine Tempier in Provence) always says, in every second or third sentence, "It's the bon Dieu, the good God, who makes it possible".

'And the difference in attitude is that, with a lot of new world wine makers, they are trying to produce a wine to a formula, to a taste, based on the marketing concept: what does the consumer want? Let's produce that. The great wine makers in France are suicidal in their approach to wine at times. They will experiment, and they will produce a wine and risk losing all of it, the complete harvest, and at times they do. But, rather than producing a wine to please the consumer, they are trying to produce an even better wine each year, the best that their particular terroir, soil, grapes can actually produce'.

The difference in attitude, says Brangan, is fundamental. 'Whilst all vine growers are farmers, the really great ones to my mind are artists. You see this when you meet them, talk to them, get to know them. Like Eloi Dürrbach of Domaine de Trevallon in Provence. His mother Jacqueline was a really gifted tapestry maker and, if you go to the Picasso museum down in Monaco, all the tapestries of Picasso's work were produced by her. Eloi's father is the greatest living stained glass artist in France and one of their greatest sculptors.'

'Eloi himself was one of the foremost architects in France, and had a terrific practice in Paris: chucked it all in to go and produce wine in the Valley of Hell, the Valley d'Enfer. He was told "It's impossible, forget it, it's the hottest part of France with temperatures going over forty degrees, the Mistral howls through the place, hard for anything to survive". It seems suicidal, but against the greatest odds, they attempt to do the impossible'.

What the great winemakers enjoy, says Brangan, is 'the challenge. Suicidal or not. They see themselves as artists, producing works of art, and I would agree with them. The great wines of Zind Humbrecht, from Alsace. If it were possible they should be displayed in the Louvre: they are certainly national treasures of France, and when you have the opportunity to appreciate them, by God they are stunning, and you say "Wow!", and it's probably an experience you'll never forget. I shall never forget the first tasting I had with the Humbrechts in Alsace. One wine was more glorious than the next, until I simply ran out of adjectives and just sort of sat there in awe and beamed'.

There is, of course, no mystery to this sublime magic. 'Michelangelo said that perfection was no trifle, and the attention to detail, the trifles that are looked after by these master winemakers, is something else. In Domaine Zind Humbrecht the cork costs two and a half times the bottle, because the cork must last at least twenty five years, because their wines are built to last that long, and longer. The care that the vines get: they use the minimum of sprays because they know that the sprays affect the grapes and the vines, not just in the sense of contamination, but because it will also delay the ripening of the grapes, and may force their ripening into that critical autumn period when the weather is changing'.

When hunting down new wines, Colm Brangan goes right back to basics. 'We try to find out the personality of the person. That, to my mind is the most important thing, and believe it or not, the personality of the wine maker is reflected in their wine. It's astonishing'. But, finding the right personality does not always mean finding the right wine.

'We were searching a few years ago for a wine from a very well-known appellation in France, and I had gone to visit the last twenty or so on our list. I had left the reputed master of the area to last. When I eventually found him I found him in his vineyard and I said "Wow! this is it, this is the guy", because he was working in the vineyard and there was no question it was the perfect location: it was the best site in the whole region and the soil was right, the aspect was right, everything was perfect.

'I spoke to the man, and he brought me back to his cellars and we began to taste the wines and I thought: "Oh, what's wrong here?" The wines were good, but totally not exciting, dull. You are tasting the wines years in advance, and you have to decide if the wines are going to develop. And I thought these wines were going nowhere, they were not going to develop into stupendous wines. I found it very difficult to give him feedback and a winemaker always wants your feedback: it's confirmation to him that you know something about the wines and also he likes to hear them praised, and I found it extremely difficult, I couldn't find it in my heart to praise the wines. We tasted all the wines and I didn't know what to say, I found all of them disappointing.

'So, I was invited back to the house, and we went in and had a meal with his wife and, suddenly, the penny dropped: this man's son and heir had been killed two years previously and the life, the vivacity in their eyes, wasn't there. And you could see this man, who had put his vineyard on the map after a period of dormancy, had brought it to glory, and now there was no future. And the interest was gone. And while he was making reasonable wine he wasn't making the extra effort. And it was so sad I could have cried, it was really, really sad.'

A great wine, says Brangan, 'stands out in any context. Most people think they know very little about wine but in fact I'm convinced that 99.9% of people know a lot about wine, and should have far greater confidence in their tasting. If you give them half a dozen wines, most people will have no problem discerning one from another and picking out the best ones'.

Added to this joyful search is the resolute uncertainty of the whole business: 'This is part of the enthralling interest and enthusiasm which I have and other people have for great wine, and that is: no two wines are the same, and you can never totally predict what is going to happen. And, with the great winemakers, they are trying to push the limits and see what emerges. Very often they don't know'.

Brangan & Company, 7 Deerpark Avenue, Dublin 15 Tel: (01) 821 4052 Colm Brangan's wines are to be found on good restaurant wine lists throughout the country.

DUBLIN RESTAURANTS

AYUMI-YA JAPANESE STEAKHOUSE

132 Lwr Baggot Street, D2 Tel: (01) 622 0233 Fax: 662 0221

Ayumi-Ya literally means 'Ayumi's Place' — named after Mrs Hoashi's daughter Ayumi — and this family operation, that began with a traditional restaurant and shop, now runs a simpler, more modern steakhouse, and a Bento service.

The 'steaks' of the restaurant's title are Teppan steaks, and refer to the manner in which they are cooked — over a hot iron griddle — rather than the cut of beef, chicken, prawn, salmon or even vegetable that you select from the Teppan menu. Also available is a Kushi-age menu: meat, veg or seafood threaded onto skewers, breadcrumbed and deep fried.

But perhaps the best of many good reasons to eat in the Steakhouse is the noodles. These need all the concentration that they are habitually given by the regular clientele of Japanese businessmen who scoop and slurp in the correct fashion at the Soba, or buckwheat noodles, or the Udon, wheat noodles which bask in bowls of soup garnished with batter and deep fried tofu. Ayumi-Ya Ramen are egg noodles with caramel tasting roast pork and slivers of raw root vegetable and there are two Japanese Pasta dishes of pan fried noodles with stir fried vegetable or cod's roe. The basement restaurant itself has been cleverly designed with the cooking area open to the public, so it seems odd to recommend you eat out, but this is the only way to try the Bento. A Bento is a box of cooked food, but there is rather more to it than that. 'The Bento began when people would go to the sumo, the theatre, the kabuki', says Mrs Akiko Hoashi, 'It's portable food'.

The common feature of any Bento is rice — either boiled or fried — but from that point on you can change any of the accompaniments.

So, take the Makunouchi Bento: in a large, rectangular box this may comprise boiled rice with a little pickle on top, then some breaded and fried Prawn Ebifrai, a little macaroni salad in dressing, some chicken Toritasuta-Age, a portion of superb salted and grilled mackerel, a smattering of grilled leeks and peppers and deliciously sweet butterbeans. If you don't wish such a variety of food, then the Yakitori Bento offers skewered, grilled pieces of chicken and onion, full of succulent, baleful tastes, and the cleansing macaroni, sweet butterbeans and toothsome rice.

Open 12.30pm-2.30pm Mon-Fri, 6pm-11.30pm Mon-Thur ('till 12.30am Fri & Sat). Closed Xmas. Average Price: lunch and early evening menu ££ dinner £££. Visa, Access, Amex. Recommended for Vegetarians. Next to the junction between Lr Pembroke Road and Baggot Street.

BATZ

10 Baggot Lane, D4 Tel: (01) 660 0363

A small, attentive lunchtime restaurant tucked just away from the office area of Baggot Street. The simple dishes are best achieved, the atmosphere splendidly unchauvinist.

Open 12.15pm-2.30pm Mon-Fri. Closed Xmas/New Year. Average Price: lunch ££. Visa, Access, Amex. Just past the traffic lights where Lr Baggot Street meets Pembroke Road, turn left and Batz is on the right hand side.

BEWLEY'S

78-79 Grafton Street, D2 Tel: (01) 677 6761 Fax: 677 4021

Part of the folklore and culture of the city, but the old Quaker idiom which once directed Bewley's is now long gone, replaced by a mercantile slickness. Enjoyable still, however, for tea and buns and afternoon idling.

Open 7.30am-10pm Mon-Wed, 7.30am-1am Thu, 7.30am-2am Fri & Sat, 9.30am-10pm Sun. Closed Xmas. Average Price: £. Visa, Access, Amex, Diners. Bewley's is half-way up Grafton Street, which is Dublin's main shopping Street.

BLAZING SALADS II

Powerscourt Townhouse Centre, Clarendon Street, D2 Tel: (01) 671 9552

Blazing Salads serve vegetarian food with just that little bit of extra verve. The best way to enjoy the restaurant is to choose those dishes which offer a little more experimentation and individuality: vegetables packeted in arame sea weed, vegetarian couscous with fiery harissa. The staples of the restaurant are also reliable: the carrot cake, the hearty bakes, the potato salad. There is a small range of organic wine as an alternative to vegetable and fruit juices.

Open 9.30am-6pm Mon-Sat. Closed Xmas. Average price: meal £. No Credit Cards. Recommended for Vegetarians. (also gluten, dairy, yeast and sugar free). At the very top of the Powerscourt Townhouse Centre.

LEO BURDOCK'S

2 Werburgh Street, D8 Tel: (01) 540306
The old coal-fired frier is gone, but the Burdock's edict of fish and chips, fried in fat, with bottles of pop to accompany, endures as if it will last forever. On a summer evening, add your salt and vinegar and take the fish and chips up to the gardens in St. Patrick's cathedral: bliss.
Open 12.30pm-11pm Mon-Fri, 2pm-11pm Sat. Closed Xmas/New Year. Average Price: fish and chips £. No Credit Cards. Not suitable for Vegetarians (chips cooked in dripping). Next to the Lord Edward pub and restaurant, which is opposite Christchurch cathedral.

CANALETTO'S

69 Mespil Road, D4 Tel: (01) 678 5084
Upstairs in Canaletto's there is a neat café-cum-sandwich bar, where fillings like egg mayonnaise are put back on the pedestal on which they belong: fresh eggs, home-made mayonnaise, and the other sandwich fillings include smoked meats, cured fish and strong-flavoured cheeses. Downstairs in Canaletto's piped music, vivid colours and candlelight turn the space into a restaurant with the food still bright and home-made: pastas, composed salads, clever but not smart.
Open 8am-6pm Mon-Fri, 6pm-11pm Mon-Sat. Closed Xmas. Average Price: lunch £ dinner ££. No Credit Cards. Opposite the canal, near Baggot Street Bridge.

LA CAVE

28 Sth Anne Street, D2 Tel: (01) 679 4409
A snatch of what might pass for a quayside bar in Marseille or a little café somewhere in Lyons, La Cave has a knockabout atmosphere — at any time of the day, it seems — and inexpensive food
Open 12.30pm-2.30pm Mon-Sat, 6pm-late Mon-Sun. Closed Xmas. Average price: meal ££. Visa, Access, Amex. La Cave is in a basement, just past the post office on Sth Anne Street: look for the sandwich board outside.

CHILI CLUB

1 Anne's Lane, Sth Anne Street, D2 Tel: (01) 677 3721
Chillis and coconut milk, satays and skewered tofu, kaffir lime and sweet basil, the pungent and verveish tastes of Thailand are best enjoyed in The Chili Club, in a small dining room with a buzzy beat and a gameboy liveliness. This is fun food, gentle yet spicy, very enervating for the senses, very suitable for lots of crisp, cool Chardonnay.
Open 12.30pm-2.30pm Mon-Fri, 7pm-11pm Mon-Sat. Closed Xmas and 2 weeks in Jul. Average Price: lunch ££ dinner £££. Visa, Access, Amex, Diners. Sth Anne Street leads off the middle of Grafton Street, and the Chili Club is on a laneway running south.

THE COMMONS RESTAURANT

Newman House, 85/86 St Stephen's Green, D2 Tel: (01) 475 2597
There is something very self-congratulatory about the Commons. People come here to celebrate those special moments of their lives — successfully achieved anniversaries or birthdays, colleges entered and exams successfully passed, deal clinching power lunches and lavish dinners to sway someone your way. The cooking adds to this back-slapping

carry on: Escoffier style complexity is visited upon prime cuts and designer fillets, but whilst the food strives to be modern it cannot shake off a feeling of being rather old-fashioned, perhaps because it is never allowed to get funky and original, never allowed to shake the decorum. The paintings in the restaurant, by various contemporary artists, are splendid.

Open 12.30pm-2.15pm Mon-Fri, 7pm-10.15pm Mon-Sat. Closed Xmas and bank holidays. Average Price: lunch £££ dinner £££-££££. Visa, Access, Amex, Diners. Beside the Stephen's Green Church on St Stephen's Green South.

COOKE'S CAFÉ
14 Sth William Street, D2 Tel: (01) 679 0536/7/8

One has to applaud the sense of theatre and excitement which John Cooke's Café has brought to the business of eating out in Dublin. Stylish and cool in design, smack up-to-the-minute in cuisine, the café has become the favoured rendezvous of the chattering classes, the contemplative classes and those who just fancy some clever, classy food served in an atmosphere which bristles with brio.

With the benefit of more than a year in business, Cooke's seems to have overcome the problems of off-handed service which made it difficult to enjoy the food at first, and whilst the staff are still not exactly the sort of folk you want to invite to your baby's christening, they are usually polite and proper, and reasonably efficient in getting the job done properly.

This is important, because John Cooke's food, with its sassy, immediate tastes and its vibrant use of colour and contrast, is food that needs efficiency rather than ceremony. You don't linger over this Cal-Ital cooking: you just get right in there and enjoy it.

And enjoying it is easy when the kitchen has such a sharp grasp of how to combine ingredients to show them at their best: an oily avocado crosses with some cool asparagus in a salad; a brilliantly roasted fillet of turbot has a sauce of sweet butter and good oil to set beside the tender tasting fish; fettucine with smoked chicken and field mushrooms has a delicate cream sauce that supports the contiguous tastes of the ingredients and the pasta, especially, is superb.

This is not complicated food, but it is very, very clever in presentation and execution, assailing the eye with a bright sashay of colours, assuaging the appetite with a brace of fine, fresh tastes that run right through to terse-tasting blackcurrant ice-cream, or a fine hazle nut terrine. Mary Gill's breads — the soft foccaccia, the pulpy-red tomato and fennel seed, the earthy soda — were a legend in the town about forty minutes after Cooke's Café opened, and they deserve their reputation. The wine list is thoughtful, though it could benefit from offering more information, and the only problem remains the proximity of the tables one to the other.

Open 9am-noon brunch, noon-6pm lunch, 6pm-11.30pm dinner. Closed Xmas. Average Price: lunch & pre-theatre menu £££ dinner £££. Visa, Access, Amex, Diners. At the back of the Powerscourt Townhouse Centre, on the corner at the zebra crossing.

LE COQ HARDI

35 Pembroke Road, D4 Tel: (01) 668 4130/668 9070

One's estimation of John Howard's restaurant throughout its long history has always been of an archetypal bourgeois eating palace, somewhere that slings history right back to the days of César Ritz and Auguste Escoffier, an uninterrupted blow-out of classical cuisine and claret. Yet, whilst this image can be true, and the restaurant likes to present itself as someplace for racehorse owners to land their helicopters at after a successful day at the Curragh, there is actually as much of the soft and ageless nature of French peasant cuisine — long-cooked oxtail braises, plump terrines, root vegetables — to be found here, as much that is as ruddy as it is ritzy, as there is cooking that is grandiose and verbose. If you do have a successful day at the Curragh, then the Coq has one of the great wine lists, just waiting to soak up some of your winnings.

Open 12.30pm-3pm Mon-Fri, 7pm-11pm Mon-Sat. Closed Xmas and 2 weeks in early Aug. Average Price: lunch £££ dinner £££££. Visa, Access, Amex, Diners. On the right hand side when driving from Baggot Street towards Ballsbridge.

CORA'S

1 St Mary's Road, D4 (just off Lwr Baggot Street) Tel: (01) 660 0585

A little Italian café, and a sweet, wholesome place. Bring the babies and let the female staff members scoop them from your arms and hand them around whilst you eat a little lasagne, some meatballs, sip some wine.

Open 8.30am-6pm Mon-Fri, 9.30am-3pm Sun (closed Sat). Closed Xmas week and 3 weeks in Aug. Average price: set lunch: ££. No Credit Cards. Take the first on the left after Baggot Street Bridge, heading south towards Ballsbridge. Cora's is a hundred yards ahead on the right.

CORNUCOPIA

19 Wicklow Street, D2 Tel: (01) 677 7583

Cornucopia has settled into the groove of Dublin life, its vegetarian pies, curries, bakes and salads appealing to both veggies and non-veggies, fulfilling a valuable role in the everyday goings on of the capital.

Open 8am-11pm Mon-Sat. Closed Xmas. Average Price: main courses £. No Service Charge. Visa, Access. Recommended for Vegetarians. Half way up the Grafton Street end of Wicklow Street.

L'ECRIVAIN

112 Lr Baggot Street, D2 Tel: (01) 661 1919

Derry Clarke's cooking arrives at success not just by virtue of clever sourcing of good foods, or astute and confident skills in the kitchen. Not, indeed, even by virtue of a team of waiters and waitresses who are so assured and professional as to make you blink with delight. No, Clarke's food works because of the astute application of oodles of common sense, a strain of common sense which ushers food out to the customer in a pristine, lively state, full of taste, full of tense, alert flavours. He will dress oysters up in a bechamel with a little concasse of tomato then show them the grill, and they will be hopping with flavour and vigour. He will wait for an order, then pile a pillow of puff pastry with fresh vegetables and sharpen the taste with fresh herbs to make a vegetarian delight. With some mignons of beef, tarragon will coax on the flavour of beef which is so tender it melts in the mouth like a meat chocolate. This common sense is so well understood that it lets no obscene complication get in the way. Clarke works in a tradition which, for many cooks, has come to represent something of a cul-de-sac: Cuisine Française is often misrepresented in this country because cooks overcomplicate the processes needed to prepare the food. Where Clarke wins out is in waiting for an order, then springing into action to both begin and finish a dish in the shortest possible time.

Having a small number of seats in this intimate, clubbable restaurant allows him the luxury of individual service, and Clarke's staff could give Masterclasses in the art of waiting on table. Clarke himself could give Masterclasses in the art of culinary common sense. The family also now run Parker's Restaurant in the Lansdowne Hotel on Pembroke Road, where the menu retains some classical influences but also offers pasta and vegetarian dishes and draws on the funky flavours of the Mediterranean.

Open 12.30pm-2pm Mon-Fri, 6.30pm-11pm Mon-Sat. Closed Xmas. Average Price: lunch £££ dinner ££££. Visa, Access, Amex, Diners. In a basement on the corner of Baggot Street and Fitzwilliam Street.

ELEPHANT & CASTLE

18 Temple Bar, D2 Tel: (01) 679 3121

At any time of day or night, the Elephant & Castle serves the food you want and becomes the place you want it to be. From 8 in-the-morning omelette breakfasts, perhaps after you've just got off the boat, are going into work or have just wrapped up the night shift, to a mid-morning gouter, to a pasta lunch with a girlfriend, maybe a late afternoon pick-me-up tuna and guacamole sandwich or pre-theatre chicken wings that have you licking your fingers right through the performance, onwards to a late night romantic rendezvous with a loved-one, even post-pub burger and fried potatoes, perhaps a family table for Sunday brunch. All of the foods for all of these occasions can be found here. You can even, indeed, eat in the E&C more than once a day, and find it is different, find the style of food will have changed to suit the time of day.

The food is democratically priced, but never cheap: with these ingredients it could never be. The basic menu has evolved little, if any, since it opened, with innovation and experimentation coming from the daily specials, which are always worth trying: lamb korma with relishes; fettucini with chicken, shiitake mushrooms and asparagus, grilled fillet steak and rouille served with herb mashed potato; Sichuan chicken with spicy stir-fried noodles.

Open 8am-11.30pm Mon-Thur, 8am-midnight Fri, 10.30am-midnight Sat, noon-11.30pm Sun. Closed Xmas. Average Price: ££. Visa, Access, Amex, Diners. In Dublin's Temple Bar, just on the south side of the River Liffey.

FITZERS CAFÉ

24 Upper Baggot Street, D4. Tel: (01) 660 0644

The culling of influences in Fitzers is decidedly Pacific Rim in style, slowly working its way back home via Indian flavourings and then deeply into the soul of the Mediterranean. No restaurant can ever achieve authenticity with such a broad range of food styles, so it is best to take Fitzers as somewhere that achieves a suggestion of a style rather than the real McCoy, and to enjoy the buzz and some good Rioja, and the company of friends. Value for money is very keen.

Open 8am-11.30pm Mon-Sat. Closed Xmas. Average Price: lunch ££ dinner £££. Visa, Access. Between Searson's pub and the Baggot Street hospital.

LES FRERES JACQUES

74 Dame Street, D2 Tel: (01) 679 4555

There are plenty of judicious people who will select Les Freres Jacques as their favourite Dublin restaurant, and it is easy to see why. Walk down the little lane and through the door and the restaurant invites you in with that dim-lit light that suggests Parisian oyster bars or London clubs, suggests privacy and cosseting and pleasure.

For solo diners, Freres Jacques is just perfect: one day, a quiet spinster who peered through the window at the passers-by, and a dog-collared priest who slugged cognacs were some other soloists enjoying the effective, tasteful food and the uncondescending way in which it is served. And the food is effective: a mussel and fennel soup rendered perfectly and perfectly compatible with bread flavoured with curry powder, some lobster ravioli with a fillet of turbot then a vanilla bavarois. Sprigs of chervil decorate with simplicity and the fact that a bill can quickly add up as soon as you wander away from the set menus hardly matters.

For special occasions, the restaurant has that assured rhythm which derives from experience and confidence, but they don't let it slip into swagger, and their French correctness has, over the years, been tempered with an Irish affability. It is a very French restaurant, but it is very definitely in Dublin.

Open 12.30pm-2.30pm Mon-Fri, 7pm-10.30pm Mon-Thur ('till 11pm Fri & Sat). Closed Xmas/New Year and bank holidays. Average Price: lunch ££ dinner £££. Visa, Access, Amex. A few doors down from the Olympia Theatre on Dame Street.

FURAMA CHINESE RESTAURANT

88 Donnybrook Road, D4 Tel: (01) 283 0522

The most pleasing aspect of Furama is not just that their Chinese food is better than almost everywhere else in Dublin, but that their efforts to maintain authenticity and to cook true Chinese food are met by such an appreciative audience. At weekends the Furama is full of Dublin 4 types enjoying the lush, sensual scents and flavours which this food gives: excellent Yuk San to be parcelled up into lettuce leaves, roasted duck with its oily, smoky allure intact, steamed black sole with ginger and scallions, this last one a delight because they slip into silver service mode and fillet the fish at the table. Indeed, The Furama exploits more varied techniques than most Chinese restaurants, so there is much greater variety to be enjoyed, and they also maintain a splendid vegetarian's menu.

Open 12.30pm-2pm, 6pm-11.30pm Mon-Sat (Fri & Sat to midnight), 1.30pm-11pm Sun, 6pm-11pm bank holidays. Last orders half-an-hour before closing time. Closed Xmas. Average Price: lunch ££ dinner £££. Visa, Access, Amex. Recommended for Vegetarians. Opposite the rugby ground.

GOOD WORLD RESTAURANT

18 Sth Gt George's Street, D2 Tel: (01) 677 5373/677 5404

Dublin's Chinese community fill the Good World on a Sunday afternoon. They come for the dim sum and all the favourites are here: some crisp, deep-fried won ton, char siu cheung fun, a lovely glutinous pancake filled with shards of pork, rice dumplings, prawn har gau. Mix them to run the gamut of tastes and textures: sharp, spicy, sticky, slurpy and slithersome, and, with a pot of jasmine tea, this makes a fine, affordable treat.

Open 12.30pm-midnight Mon-Sun. Average Price: dim sum around £2-£3 lunch ££ dinner £££. Visa, Access, Amex, Diners. Near the corner of Sth Gt George's Street and Exchequer Street.

RESTAURANT PATRICK GUILBAUD

46 James Place, Baggot Street Lwr, D2 Tel: (01) 676 4192 Fax: 660 1546

Patrick Guilbaud's eponymous restaurant is claustral in its pursuit of a classic idea of French food, pernickity as Martin Luther when it comes to the edicts of cooking. 'We are very classical', M. Guilbaud will tell you. 'All our sauces are the way they should be done. If we say we do a beurre blanc we do a beurre blanc, if we do a bearnaise we do a bearnaise, but the real way. We do everything the way it should be done'.

And this is true, and can make for fine eating, for you find you can recall years later the procession of tastes in a simple lunch, for example: duck liver mousse, brill with a buttery veloute sauce and some smoky asparagus, pistachio and dark chocolate gateau. The precision of tastes which chef Guillaume Lebrun can disclose from ingredients is never less than impressive and he can arrive at some magnificent alliances, though seasoning is always slightly on the aggressive side. And yet Guilbaud's has remained a restaurant that is easy to admire yet impossible to love. You admire the hard-headed determination which created this purpose-built place, the well-drilled staff with their cloche synchronicity honed to the nth degree, the keenness of the prices for set menus. But admiring is one thing, and affection another, and Guilbaud's has never lost an air of cool distance, of hautiness. This makes it perfect for entertaining, for they get on with their work while you get on with yours and they never but never get in the way. But if you cherish humour, spontaneity, improvisation, cooking that comes from the heart rather than the head, you must look elsewhere.

Open 12.30pm-2pm, 7.30pm-10.15pm Tues-Sat. Closed Xmas. Average Price: lunch £££ dinner ££££. Visa, Access, Amex, Diners. Behind the Bank of Ireland on Baggot Street.

IMPERIAL CHINESE RESTAURANT

12a Wicklow Street, D2 Tel: (01) 677 2580 Fax: 677 2719

The cooking in The Imperial is tilted a little heavily in favour of Western tastes and Western styles of eating, though if you pay a little more for the select dishes on the menu the food is very expertly realised, but the real treat of this restaurant is Dim Sum, served every day during the day but best enjoyed on Sunday at lunchtime. Then, the room fills with local Chinese families munching on glutinous rice dumpling, sesame croquettes with lotus paste, Char Siu, prawns in rice paper, with the heads of the kids peering up each time a new bamboo steamer of food arrives at the table, anxious to see what is inside, hungry to get at it. Terrific fun, terrific value.

Open 12.30pm-midnight (dim sum served 12.30pm-5.30pm) Mon-Sun. Closed Xmas. Average Price: lunch ££ dinner ££ dim sum £2-£3 per dish. Visa, Access, Amex. Half-way down Wicklow Street, off the lower end of Grafton Street.

THE IRISH FILM CENTRE

6 Eustace Street, Temple Bar, D2 Tel: (01 677 8788 Fax: 677 8755

The idea and the ideal of good food in a public space has been one of the guiding lights of The Irish Film Centre on Eustace Street. You can have a glass of beer and a sandwich downstairs, a muffin and a coffee, or you can pitch up the stairs to the lean space of the restaurant, with its funky modernist seats and cat-walk arrangement of tables.

The food in the IFC is not just efficiently rendered, it also tastes very true, very real. Partly this is due to the clever simplicity of chef Eddie Bates, a cook who never shows off and who manages to bring home the true taste of a dish whether it hails from Morocco or Mullingar. He is as good with Baba Ghanoush as with deep fried scampi, as comfortable with Chinese Chicken and Bean Sprout pie — a provocative series of soy-rich flavours bundled up in melting pastry — as with Vegetable Strudel, the parcel of filo packed to bursting with pine nuts and set on a light tomato sauce, with a tumble of couscous beside. The rusticity of the food is an ironic counterpoint to the architectural modernism of the IFC, but the mixture works perfectly. Prices are very keen, especially in the evening when the menu opens out — Chicken Jambalay, Fusilli with Courgettes and Mussels, dry baked Salmon with Roasted Pepper and a Balsamic Vinaigrette — but at lunchtime, when light pours in through the roof windows, through the sun-comprehending glass, this is a lovely space.

Open 12.30pm-8.30pm Sun-Tue, 12.30pm-11pm Wed-Sat (last orders) Bar snacks available from 10am. Closed Xmas. Average Price: bar snacks £ lunch ££ dinner £££. Visa, Access. Recommended for Vegetarians. The IFC is next to Quaker House, just off Dame St.

KAPRIOL RESTAURANT

45 Camden Street Lower, D2 Tel: (01) 475 1235 (298 5496 home)
Egidia Peruzzi's food can sometimes hit on a taste which is nothing other than the pure, distilled essence of food: a Lasagna Venata with the yielding lure of mushrooms is so distinguished you lick the plate clean with your fingers, veal dishes of melting tenderness, toothsome risotto with the rice carrying the unalloyed sweetness and sea saltiness of prawns and squid, a charming zabaglione. When this concatenation of tastes happens, you can enjoy some blisteringly fine food in The Kapriol, and the charming little room — imported, it seems, straight from the Alps — seems the perfect place in which to enjoy it. For some, however, the charms of Egidia and Giuseppe Peruzzi's restaurant remain mysteriously elusive, for others the sheer individuality and personality of the place gives it a homeliness and distinctiveness which is all too rare in Dublin.

Open Mon-Sat 7.30pm-midnight (last orders). Closed Xmas, bank holidays and last 3 weeks in Aug. Average Price: dinner ££££. Visa, Access, Amex, Diners. At the southern end of Camden Street, on the corner where the road divides.

LOBSTER POT RESTAURANT

9 Ballsbridge Terrace, D4 Tel: (01) 668 0025/660 9170
You can't really describe the Lobster Pot as old fashioned, for what they do in here has nothing to do with fashion. As ageless as a gentlemen's club, and just as cosy, they brew up bisques, pair the day's catch of fish with proper sauces, proffer generous helpings of vegetables and give great advice about wines. It's delightful, but it is expensive.

Open 12.30pm-3pm Mon-Fri, 6pm-10.30pm Mon-Sat. Closed Xmas/New Year and bank holidays. Average price: lunch and dinner ££££. Visa, Access, Amex, Diners, Airplus. Just to the north side of the bridge at Ballsbridge. On the first floor, over the group of shops.

LOCKS

1 Windsor Terrace, Portobello, D8 Tel: (01) 543391
Clare Douglas works closely with the organic grower Marc Michel, who maintains one enormous tunnel on his farm in Wicklow with fruits and vegetables grown just for the restaurant. This professional and careful approach to her supplies runs right through Ms

Douglas' approach to the restaurant itself, one of the most meticulous and professional operations in the city, and one of those places where you slide and sink into the ambience, reluctantly emerging a few hours later and disappointedly slinking back into the real world. The audience of professional folk who are the principal habitués of Locks, and devotees of its solid and classical French-style food, behave like little puppies getting their tummies tickled. But then, it is nice to get one's tummy tickled, on occasion.

Open 12.30pm-2pm Mon-Fri, 7.15pm-11pm Mon-Sat. Closed Xmas. Average Price: lunch ££ dinner £££.

Visa, Access, Amex, Diners. Between Portobello Bridge and Harold's Cross Bridge, facing the Grand Canal.

THE NATIONAL MUSEUM CAFÉ

Kildare Street, D2 Tel: (01) 662 1269

The enchantingly lovely room which the Museum Café occupies is a happy, handsome space in which to enjoy cooking which one Dublin journalist, appositely and accurately, described as 'simple, unpretentious food... cooked with care and attention'.

Those factors of care and simplicity have always been the hallmark of Joe Kerrigan's cooking. He is unique amongst Dublin cooks in actually being at the Fish Market early each morning, in personal pursuit of the best fish he can buy and when he brings it back, Kerrigan likes to do as little as possible to it: lightly fried, maybe with some mashed potatoes, some creamy carrots or bright, steamed broccoli. He makes a demon Dublin Coddle, the ancient dish augmented with a little cream to modernise it, and throughout his work you see the mark of someone who respects the mantra that one must respect the intrinsic flavour of a dish and work only to bring it to its best. This he does with the super baked ham which is always for sale, the full-tasting salads, the dreamy cakes. This is, indeed, simple and unpretentious food, for Kerrigan has no arrogant ego, and wants only to make food that will satisfy and give pleasure. There are many treasures in the National Museum, and the Café is the latest one.

Open 10am-5pm Mon-Sat, 2pm-5pm Sun. Closed Xmas. Average Price: lunch £-££. Visa, Access.

NICO'S

53 Dame Street, D2 Tel: (01) 677 3062

Ageless tratt food, which suits buckets of wine, flaming sambucas and suits the lovers of all sexes who love Nico's for its grand guignol and its piano player. The waiters are a theatre of chauvinism and panicked cool.

Open noon-2.30pm Mon-Fri, 6pm-12.30am Mon-Sat. Closed Xmas. Average Price: lunch ££ dinner £££. Visa, Access, Amex, Diners. Just down from the Central Bank on Dame Street (travelling away from Trinity).

101 TALBOT

100-102 Talbot Street, D1 Tel: (01) 874 5011

101 Talbot has grown into one of the essential restaurant spaces in the city, and for a very simple reason: the cooking speaks of personal care and personal preferences, the big room oozes quiet charm, and the calm personalities of Margaret Duffy and Pascal Bradley make it feel like a restaurant where the owners are more than overly concerned that you should have a good time, enjoy the food, want to come back.

Margaret Duffy is one of those cooks who bring a meticulous feel for goodness and taste to their cooking, so the culinary grab-bag of foods which 101 offers — Italian pastas, Provençal bakes, up-to-the-minute sandwiches, Yankee desserts, stir-fried vegetables, Irish roasts and game — can be approached with assurance, for the kitchen is determined to get them right, to get them such that you will enjoy them and regret, when they are gone, that they are gone. At any time of the day, this food is a delight, and the space is perfect for solo diners of both sexes, babies, paramours, theatre-goers, cineastes, even your mother, maybe.

Open 10.30am-10.30pm (Mon 'till 4pm) pasta served all day, Lunch menu noon-3pm, dinner menu 6.30pm-11pm. Closed Xmas. Average Price: lunch £-££ dinner £££. Access, Visa. Recommended for Vegetarians. Between the Abbey Theatre and the Pro Cathedral.

PIGALLE

14 Temple Bar, Merchant's Arch, D2 Tel: (01) 671 9262

Pigalle is aptly named, a loose-limbed restaurant that adds a dash of North Africa to a kitchen that is rooted in Paris. A place that hides rigorous culinary disciplines behind unmatching plates, informal service and an atmosphere that is more retrograde right bank than self-conscious left bank. Rather more Montmartre than Montparnasse.

The table d'hôte menu is good value, smoothy soups, rare lamb on well constructed sauces, gravity-defying pastries on colourful fruit purées and vanilla custards.

Like a true French restaurant Pigalle doesn't evolve or innovate, it simply does what it does and does it with unmatched charm.

Open 12.30pm-2.30pm, 6.30pm-11pm Mon-Sat. Closed Xmas. Average Price: lunch ££ dinner ££. Visa Access. Pigalle is in the heart of the Temple Bar, on the first floor over Merchant's Arch.

PIZZERIA ITALIA

23 Temple Bar, D2 Tel: (01) 677 8528

No-nonsense Italian tratt grub: Spag Bol, Pizza Margherita, all the old standbys to be drunk with rough red wine that is happily priced as rough red wine. Its Italian colours flag the beginning of the Temple Bar cobblestones and the counter seating is suited for looking out and looking in. If the toasty smell of rising pizzas doesn't drag you into the restaurant, you can buy yourself a wedge-to-go from its side street kitchen window.

Open noon-11pm Tue-Sat. Closed Xmas/New Year, last 2 weeks in Jun. Average Price: lunch ££ dinner ££. No Credit Cards. In Temple Bar, on the corner where it becomes Fleet Street.

THE RAJDOOT TANDOORI

26-28 Clarendon Street, Westbury Centre, D2 Tel: (01) 679 4274

Not just the best Indian cooking in the city, but one of the most consistent restaurants in the country. The Rajdoot is part of a small chain of Indian restaurants based in the U.K., but there is no feeling of factory-line production here.

The food is reverberantly lush in the northern Indian Moghul style, with their tandoori dishes torchily and aromatically spicy with the waft of charcoal blessing chicken shashlik or beef tikka, their curries a serene meld of butter and tomatoes, yogurt and cashew nuts and not the jumble of junk so many Indian restaurants are content to serve, the biryanis fluffy and precise, each element distinct.

Breads are marvellous, vegetarians are almost spoilt for choice, service perfect, and prices keen.

Open noon-2.30pm, 6.30pm-11.30pm Mon-Sat. Closed Xmas/New Year. Average Price: lunch ££ dinner £££. Visa, Access, Amex, Diners. Recommended for Vegetarians. At the back of the Westbury Hotel.

ROLY'S BISTRO

7 Ballsbridge Terrace, D4 Tel: (01) 668 2611

Roly Saul's eponymous venture has proven to be the biggest hit in Dublin's restaurant culture in recent times, and the clever calculation behind it all reveals the shift in eating styles which is driving through the restaurant trade.

For a start, though called a bistro this is really a brasserie — the upstairs dining room is handsome and endearing — but the prices belong almost to a café with lunch, in particular, a whacking great bargain. Secondly, the food betrays no tension between care and necessary speed of service. The cooking, however, is well crafted: poached cod, coq au vin, loin of pork, venison pie, bistro fare that is suitable for lunch, perfect for dinner. Finally, it is a fun place. No matter whether you are eight or eighty, the secret of Roly's success is that you can extract from it what you want: a quick lunch or a lingering dinner, a family party, maybe impressing the kids at the weekend when you have access and they don't want to go to the zoo again. Other restaurants in the city cottoned on to this idea a while back and they have proven to be successes also. Roly's is the latest addition to a pantheon where the demands of the punter are paramount.

Open noon-4pm, 6pm-11pm Mon-Sun. Closed Xmas. Average Price: lunch ££ dinner under £££. Visa, Access, Amex. On the corner between Ballsbridge and Herbert Park, just down from the American Embassy.

LA STAMPA

35 Dawson Street, D2 Tel: (01) 677 8611/677 3336
Perhaps the most beautiful dining room in the city, and the food can be good, though a succession of changes in the kitchen have made for some uncertainty over the last few years.
Louis Murray's policy seems to be to hire very high profile chefs — Paul Flynn, right hand man to Nico Ladenis for the last decade has just followed Michael Martin — so there can be dazzling food to match the dazzling room.
Open noon-2.30pm Mon-Sat, 6pm-11.30pm Mon-Sat ('till midnight Fri & Sat). Closed Xmas. Average Price: lunch £££ dinner £££-££££. Visa, Access, Amex, Diners. Opposite the Mansion House.

TOSCA

20 Suffolk Street, D2 Tel: (01) 679 6744
One of those restaurants that features endlessly in gossip columns, on account of its attraction to visiting starlets and rock stars, which means the food garners precious little attention. A pity, because whilst the modern Italian influences are obvious, there can be interesting tastes, and the staff are excellent. The same owners run Dillon's Dublin Deli next door, serving what they call cuisine nua.
Open 10.30am-midnight Mon-Sun ('till 1am Thur-Sat). Closed Xmas. Average Price: lunch £ dinner ££. Visa, Access, Amex, Diners. Half-way up Suffolk Street. Dillon's Dublin Deli Tel: (01) 6774804

TROCADERO

3 St Andrew's Street, D2 Tel: 775545/679 2385
An integral and unmissable part of Dublin culture. The food is just what you will expect it to be, but the crack will be a whole lot better. Go very late and join the thespians, rock'n'rollers, paparazzi and assorted night owls. Don't worry about your hangover.
Open 6pm-12.30am Mon-Sat, 6pm-11.30pm Sun. Closed Xmas. Average Price: dinner £££. Visa, Access, Amex, Diners. St Andrew's Street runs between Wicklow Street and Suffolk Street.

UNICORN RESTAURANT

12b Merrion Court, off Merrion Row, D2 Tel: (01) 676 2182
The Unicorn should actually be called Pitcher's, for this is where you go to be seen pitching an idea for a television series, a new autumn range, a change in fiscal policy, a book-and-big-screen tie-in, or to have the said ideas pitched at you. It is customary to eat a little food whilst you are either pitching or being pitched at.
Open noon-3pm, 6pm-10pm Mon-Sat. Closed bank holidays. Average Price: lunch £ dinner ££. Access, Mastercard, Visa. In a courtyard just off Merrion Row, just a few steps from St Stephen's Green and the Shelbourne Hotel.

THE WELL FED CAFÉ

Dublin Resource Centre, Crow Street, D2 Tel: (01) 677 1974
Politically correct ambience and vegetarian food, but enjoyable even if your politics are decidedly dodgy.
Open 10.30am-8.30pm Mon-Sat. Closed Xmas/New Year and bank holidays. Average Price: £. No Credit Cards. Recommended for Vegetarians. In the Temple Bar area, parallel to Fownes Street, beside the Central Bank.

THE WINDING STAIR BOOKSHOP AND CAFÉ

40 Lwr Ormond Quay, D1 Tel: (01) 873 3292

Kevin Connolly's Winding Stair has always sold coffee and cakes to enable you to while away hour after hour in this beautiful second-hand bookstore, listening to music, perusing the shelves, peering out the window at the River Liffey. Recently, since Kevin's sister Eileen began to cook soups and to make bumper sandwiches at lunchtime, the shop has begun to attract hordes of the hungry and these, too, have succumbed to the innocent seductiveness and chippy hilarity of the Winding Stair. The atmosphere is so unpretentious and crystalline calm, the girls and guys cooking and serving the food so full of sappy sang froid, that the Winding Stair is irresistible.

Open 10.30am-6pm Mon-Sat, Soup served from noon; coffee, cake and rolls and sandwiches available all day. Closed 25th Dec-1st Jan and bank holidays. Average Price: £. No Credit Cards. Note: all soups are Vegetarian. The Winding Stair looks down from the North side of the River Liffey onto the Ha'penny Bridge.

ZEN CHINESE RESTAURANT

89 Upper Rathmines Road, D6 Tel: (01) 979428

The Zen looks like a Chinese restaurant which has been designed by a returned Christian Missionary who wants to praise the Lord and simultaneously practice with his chopsticks. High-beamed, the tables set wide apart, plain of ornamentation, it hits that spot were church hall meets college common room. It is, in fact, an old meeting hall, and the feeling of spaciousness and light are a delightful antidote to the over-heated design of all the other Chinese restaurants in town.

But, you can't eat furnishings, so it is a happy thing that the food is so good, leaning mainly in the direction of Sichuan specialities: beef with preserved vegetables on a bed of beansprouts is busy with the sharp taste of peppercorns and black beans, whilst tofu adds a nicely soulish taste. Dan Dan noodles are excellent, arriving in a deep, dark soup with shoots of spring onion here and there. It is reassuring to see, also, a modest sized menu rather than a huge array of dishes built around a series of basic ingredients. The Zen is a surprise, a nice surprise.

Open 12.30pm-2.30pm, 6pm-midnight Mon-Fri, 6pm-midnight Sat-Sun. Average Price: lunch ££ dinner £££. Visa, Access. Take-away service available.

SOUTH COUNTY DUBLIN

BLACKROCK

AYUMI-YA JAPANESE RESTAURANT

Newpark Centre, Newtownpark Avenue, Blackrock Tel: (01) 283 1767

The parent of the Ayumi-Ya Steakhouse in Dublin city, and one of the longest established restaurants in the county, the Ayumi-Ya continues to move through the years with grace and the promise of good food. Mrs Hoashi's food is as ornamented and as fine as one expects of Japanese cooking, whether you choose the Teppan-Yaki tables and have the food cooked immediately in front of you, or decide to go native and sit on the floor and enjoy the calming service by the waitresses. The set menus are excellent value, but sometimes it is fun to allow the restaurant to compose a menu for you — they even suggest that first-timers choose the Omakase-Menu, where the chefs select the food — and to indulge in a succession of sublime and sinuous and sympathetic dishes: tempura with its clamouring batter, tofu with its mellow indifference sharpened by deep-frying or mixed with sesame oil, shabu-shabu of thinly sliced beef washed in broth with grated radish.

Open 7pm-11pm Mon-Sat, 6pm-10pm Sun. Closed Xmas. Average Price: dinner £££. Visa, Access, Amex, Diners. Recommended for Vegetarians. At the Blackrock end of Newtownpark Avenue, amongst the small group of shops set back from the road by a small car park.

CHINA-SICHUAN RESTAURANT

4 Lower Kilmacud Road, Stillorgan Tel: (01) 288 4817

Forget those beloved sizzling dishes which you scoff on tipsy Saturday nights in your local Chinese eating house, those fake concoctions of MSG and culinary myopia. In the China-Sichuan you will find the real thing: the musky, coffee-odoured thrill of Hot & Sour Soup,

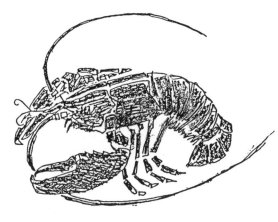

dumplings either pan fried with a fathom-black dipping sauce or in a hot sauce with spicy chilli. Then, some chicken in a garlic sauce, the dish offering endless nodes of viscous flavours, some monkfish with cashews perhaps, the fish jumping with freshness and the tentacular cuts putting you in mind of the roof of the Sydney Opera House. With these, some voluptuously slinky Dan-Dan Mein noodles, or maybe some clean boiled rice. Expect to cough, occasionally, as the toxic charge of chillies hits the back of the throat: apply Australian Chardonnay immediately. For dessert, some gloriously cool almond bean curd, the taste like an incredibly exotic marzipan, comes as a delicious surprise, the perfect ending to a series of surprisingly accessible and delightful tastes.

Open 12.30pm-2.30pm, 6pm-11pm Mon-Fri, 6pm-11pm Sat, 1pm-2.30pm, 6pm-11pm Sun. Closed Xmas. Average Price: lunch ££ dinner £££. Visa, Access, Amex. Recommended for Vegetarians. On the Kilmacud Road, just up from the Stillorgan Shopping Centre.

CLARET'S

63 Main Street, Blackrock Tel: (01) 288 2008

Alan O'Reilly's food has always been correctly achieved and presented, the influences of both classical and modern French cooking assimilated into menus and dishes that are understated, interesting and good value.

Open 12.30pm-2.30pm, 7pm-10pm Tue-Sat. Closed Xmas and bank holidays. Average Price: lunch ££-£££ dinner ££££. Visa, Access, Amex. Situated on a one-way street (driving back in the direction of Blackrock) — opposite the Library.

LA TAVOLA

114 Rock Road, Booterstown Tel: (01) 283 5101
Excellent service, great atmosphere, nice spicy arrabbiata for penne, crisp and well-balanced pizzas, fresh, lively salads, super ice-cream. Good value.
Open noon-11.30pm Mon-Sat. Closed Xmas. Average Price: Pizzas £-££, Pastas & main courses ££. Access, Visa. The Rock Road is part of the main thoroughfare between Dublin and Dun Laoghaire, opposite Booterstown DART station.

DALKEY

IL RISTORANTE

108 Coliemore Road, Dalkey Tel: (01) 284 0800
Roberto Pons brings a modern sensibility to traditional Italian food in this small, upstairs room, beginning with the clean lines of modern design rather than traditionally overblown décor, and continuing with a kitchen which adds a slant of revision to classic Italian fare.
True, there is liver and onions, risotto, veal with Parma ham and sage, minestrone and tiramisu, but portions are modernistically arranged on big white plates and Il Ristorante energetically tries to resuscitate these classics.
Open 7.30pm-9.45pm Tue-Sat. Closed Xmas, and 2 weeks from end Jan-beginning Feb. Average Price: dinner ££££. Visa, Access, Amex. At the fork in the road in the centre of Dalkey, turn left and the restaurant is just on the right, over The Club.

TORULA'S

21 Railway Road, Dalkey Tel: (01) 284 0756
You can get simple snacks in the bar during the day, and more considered, luxurious, food upstairs during the evening.
Open 6pm-10.30pm (wine bar open from 12.30pm). Closed Mon during Jan and Feb. Average Price: early menu ££ dinner £££. Access, Visa. Railway Road is on the right at the end of the main street in Dalkey.

DUN LAOGHAIRE

KRISHNA INDIAN RESTAURANT

First Floor, 47 George's Street Lwr, Dun Laoghaire Tel: (01) 280 1855
The lighting is almost dusky dark, but the food is bright with careful flavours and personal care.
Open noon-2.30pm Mon-Sat, 6pm-midnight Mon-Sun ('till 1am Fri and Sat). Closed Xmas. Average Price: dinner £££. Visa, Access, Amex, Diners. Recommended for Vegetarians. A few doors up from Dunphy's pub on the same side of the street. Upstairs over the butcher's shop.

ODELL'S

49 Sandycove Road, Dun Laoghaire Tel: (01) 284 2188 Fax: 284 0613
The cooking here is smooth-edged, friendly, almost suburban, but this suits the modest ambitions of Odell's and they are able to achieve good flavours and create a nice ambience

to help one to enjoy an evening.

Open 6pm-10.30pm Tue-Sun. Closed Xmas. Average Price: dinner £££. Visa, Access, Amex, Diners. Upstairs, opposite Fitzgerald's pub in Sandycove.

GLENCULLEN

FOX'S FAMOUS SEAFOOD KITCHEN

Glencullen Tel: (01) 295 5647

They claim that Fox's is the highest pub in Ireland — for some reason many other pubs make this claim, perhaps to make you feel lightheaded even before you have a drink — and maybe it is the altitude, here in the Dublin/Wicklow hills, which makes this place so giddy. During the summer, and on a Sunday especially, the place is positively riotous, with music and dancing and golfing and what-not. The what-not, however, is one of the best reasons to go, for their seafood is excellent: they get the crab meat and claws from Ted Browne in Kerry and they need to do little or nothing to them to extract the sweet, pure flavour.

Food served noon-10.15pm Mon-Fri, noon-8.45pm Sat, 4pm-10pm Sun.

NORTH COUNTY DUBLIN

HOWTH

ADRIAN'S

8 Abbey Street, Howth Tel & Fax: (01) 391696

'I'm into the flavours, the purity of flavours', says Catriona Holden, 'and getting them at source and trying to encapsulate it in the end product. I try to get the perfect flavour of a thing, without changing it'. Ms Holden manages to achieve her ambition, largely through an astute alliance of taste and tactility: superb fresh fettucine with crab toes; queen scallops, prawns and squid in a dreamy creamy sauce that clings to the excellent noodles; or perhaps the same fettucine with a sauce as simple as chilli oil and black pepper, this trumped with sharp, fiery scallions scattered on top. She will skin and fillet plaice and serve it with little melon balls of roast potatoes, green cabbage with sour cream and caraway seeds and fantastic crispy, peppery carrots and each detail will be precise, proper, and full of life. Tactile. Tasty.

Catriona and her father do everything in Adrian's, a simple pair of rooms just off the waterfront in Howth, though they have to pull in a waitress and a dishwasher at the weekends when things get busy.

If good tastes are the leading feature of her work, then excellent value is also something that drags you back: the food is very keenly priced, and the simplicity and youthful heart of the restaurant make it especially enjoyable.

Open noon-late afternoon, 7pm-9.30pm Mon-Thur, noon-3pm, 7pm-9.30pm Fri-Sat, noon-5pm Sun (during summer dinner starts from 6.30pm and lunches stretch on longer). Closed Xmas. Average Price: lunch ££, dinner £££. Visa, Access. Recommended for Vegetarians. Abbey Street runs up the hill from the seafront in Howth.

KING SITRIC

East Pier, Howth Tel: (01) 325235 Fax: 392442

Now over 21 years old and with the key to the door in hand, Aidan MacManus's restaurant sails ever on, its cuisine bourgeois orientation slightly trimmed for modern sensibilities, but the essential concept of luxurious eating intact. Great wine list.

Open 6.30pm-11pm Mon-Sat, Oyster Bar May-Sept, 12.30pm-3.30pm. Closed Xmas and Easter week and bank holidays. Average Price: dinner ££££. Visa, Access, Amex, Diners. Vegetarians dishes available with advance notice. The King Sitric is the big green building at the end of the pier facing the yacht club in Howth.

MALAHIDE

BON APPETIT

9 St. James Terrace, Malahide Tel: (01) 845 0314/845 2206

There are clever and ingenious specialities in Patsy McGuirk's cooking, and the restaurant pulses with the attentive concern of the chef-proprietor.

Open 12.30pm-2.30pm Mon-Fri, 7pm-11pm Mon-Sat Closed Xmas and bank holidays. Average Price: lunch £££ dinner ££££. Visa, Access, Amex, Diners. At the crossroads take the coastal road back to Dublin. Bon Appetit is one of the houses on the long Georgian terrace on the left.

OLD STREET WINE BAR

Old Street, Malahide Tel: (01) 845 1882

Gail Sinclair's menu suits the style of her little place, whether you find yourself there on a quiet Monday lunchtime or late on a bumptious Friday night when the buzz is good. There are placid vegetable soups— good mushroom, a curried parsnip — quiches that enjoy good pastry, and hearty peasant stock such as Irish Stew, a vegetable and ginger stir fry, shrimp and tomatoes together with pasta. There is, naturally, a chocolate biscuit cake, apple pie from Mum, and even apple and strawberries together in a tart. It is a thoughtful menu — there are always at least four or five vegetarian options — and it doesn't require more than a second's thought to decide that you want to go back to Old Street and enjoy it again.

Open noon-3pm, 6pm-11pm Mon-Sun. Closed Xmas. Average Price: lunch £ dinner ££-£££. Visa, Access. Turn left before the traffic lights, just after the Church. The wine bar is on the left.

ROCHE'S BISTRO

12 New Street, Malahide Tel: (01) 845 2777

Orla Roche's culinary ambition is mighty, and her quiet flair manifests itself in dishes which combine tension and release in much the same way that a good thriller will manipulate your emotions. Beneath filo pastry lies a supreme of chicken, and inside the chicken is Cashel Blue cheese. An escalope of salmon promises to be smoochy, before its companion lemon vinaigrette blows in your ear to wake you up. Duck is given the boozy consolation of Armagnac, but is then sobered up by green peppercorns. This is clever food, in that the processes required to achieve it are relatively simple, and these are dishes which the little kitchen can handle coolly and confidently. Nice atmosphere, good prices.

Open noon-2.30pm Mon-Sat, 7pm-10.30pm Thu-Sat. Closed Xmas/New Year. Average Price: lunch £££ dinner £££. Visa, Access, Amex, Diners. At the traffic lights, head down towards the sea and Roche's Bistro is on your left a few doors down.

SKERRIES

RED BANK RESTAURANT

7 Church Street, Skerries Tel: (01) 849 1005 Fax: (01) 849 1598

The way Terry McCoy does it, cooking and running a restaurant seems easy. Source your foods from local growers, suppliers, fishmongers and fish smokers, oyster farmers and flour grinders, so that the foods of the region will have the tastes of the region and be cooked in the region.

Then, bring to them some quiet but well-tuned skills, and treat the foods with, as McCoy himself will say, 'sympathy and respect': no crazy culinary miscegenation here just for the sake of it, no amateur forays to the Pacific Rim, no dalliance with this year's new thing. Just the occasional innovation that has come from a trip abroad where you learnt of some alliance, some suitable technique, and which you find can be made to work in you own kitchen.

Cook, then, with grace and good humour, and get things right: smoked salmon with tarragon, steamed cockles and oysters, hake with the energetic kick of horseradish, perhaps a smoked loin of pork or roasted Barbary duck. The meat dishes, like everything else, will be correct and flavourful, but it is with fish and shellfish that McCoy shines, and you find yourself going 'ooh' and 'aah' with pleasure at the succulence and promise of each mouthful. Fish cookery is all about sources and sauces, and Terry McCoy understands this better than almost anyone.

Open 7pm-9.45pm (last orders) Tue-Sat. Closed Xmas, 2 weeks in Jan. Average Price: dinner ££££. Visa, Access, Amex, Diners. Skerries is 29km north of Dublin and signposted from the N1 Dublin/Belfast road. The restaurant is in the centre of town.

SWORDS

LE CHATEAU RESTAURANT

River Mall, Main Street, Swords Tel: (01) 840 6353/840 6533
John Dowd, Le Château's chef and patron, is a confident, bustling sort of bloke with a confidence in his skill which might seem out of place in a quiet town like Swords, until one remembers that Swords is no longer some satellite nowhere on the road between Dublin and Belfast. Its energetic and fiercely proud folk are building a strong sense of community out of their town and Le Château is an important part of that self-confidence. You might normally expect to see someone like Dowd in the city centre, but maybe pitching up here was just the right thing to do.

His skill is best discovered in his lively, free-flowing visitations on great classic dishes, dishes he still manages to invest with energy and commitment: rack of lamb with berry chutney, sea trout with two sauces, an excellent seafood with marie rose sauce, all of them good bistro dishes which need good ingredients and energetic cooking skills to show them at their best. They find both things here.

Open 12.30pm-2.30pm Tue-Fri, 7pm-11pm Tue-Sat, 12.30pm-3pm Sun. Closed Xmas and bank holidays. Average Price: lunch ££ dinner £££. Visa, Access, Amex, Diners. Down a side lane in the centre of Swords village. One-and-a-half minutes from the N1, five minutes from the airport.

OLD SCHOOLHOUSE

Coolbanagher, Swords Tel: (01) 840 2846 Fax: 840 5060
The ambitions of The Old Schoolhouse explain the reasons for its enduring success. In here, the intention is to provide food which is enjoyable without presenting any unfamiliar challenges. People like The Old Schoolhouse: its unpretentiousness, its feminine efficiency and feminine charm, its simple food, which can be effective and tasty: smoked pheasant with gooseberry sauce, poached hake with hot pepper sauce.

Open 12.30pm-2.30pm Mon-Fri, 7pm-10.30pm Mon-Sat. Closed Xmas and bank holidays. Average price: lunch £££ dinner £££. Visa, Access, Amex, Diners. The Old Schoolhouse is just off the main street in Swords, down the hill, five minutes from the Airport.

DUBLIN SHOPPING GUIDE

DUBLIN CITY CENTRE

ASIAN FOOD STORE
THE ASIA MARKET
30 Drury Street, D2 Tel: (01) 677 9764
The Asia Market is one of the smallest shops in the central city, but within this bedroom-sized space there lies a paradise of ingredients. One of Dublin's greatest shopping adventures is to seek out and find some queer foodstuff that, until you read Yan Kit So's recipe for Almond Bean Curd or Eileen Yin Fei Lo's Chiu Chow Lo Soi Duck, you'd never heard of and certainly never cooked with before. Despite its size, you could be cooking every day of the year and still find some new exotica on the groaning shelves of the Asia Market with which to experiment.
Open 10am-7pm Mon-Fri, 11am-6pm Sat and Sun

CHOCOLATES
BUTLER'S IRISH
51a Grafton Street, D2
One of the very first Irish made chocolate companies, Butler's Irish are distributed throughout the country from their small factory at Unit 5 Enterprise Centre, Pearse Street, D2 Tel: (01) 671 0599. Recently they acquired their own shop at the top of Grafton Street, from where you can buy their entire range.
Open 9am-7pm Mon-Sat (Thur 'till 8pm)

CHINESE FOOD STORE
CHINACO LTD
67 Bride Street, D8 Tel: (01) 478 4699
Chinaco is reminiscent of the Chinese supermarkets in London's Soho, a bit of a barn of a shop spilling over with giant woks and spatulas set beside colourful tins, cabinets of frozen oysters and taffeta-green flourishes of bok choy. Part warehouse, part retail outlet, from the outside you might not imagine that the shop is even open to the public. The service within is cool — it's sensible to have an exact idea of what you want before you get here, because advice is seldom given.
Open 10am-6.30pm Mon-Fri, 11am-6.30pm Sat & Sun

BAKERY
COOKE'S BAKERY
31 Francis Street, D8 Tel: (01) 549201; 32 Dawson Street, D2 Tel: (01) 6772270 Fax: (01) 6790546
Walking into Cooke's bakeries is, in bread terms, the equivalent of stepping out of monochrome into the charged fission of technicolour. Forget the sober, simple stuff on which you were reared, the no-nonsense sliced pans and dour soda breads, for the breads in here are day-glo dizzy, acid-crazed hallucinations that seem to have sprung more from a Salvador Dali dreamscape than from the fusion of flour and water.
There are torridly coloured breads with tomato and fennel seeds. Shiny, egg-washed

sourdoughs. Sternly brown rye breads. Flour-flecked sodas. Great big whirls of foccaccia dotted with tomato. Threaded lengthy plaits of white bread, the whole kit and caboodle of them as bright with vivid colour as some pop art poster. You might almost be happy to just look and not eat, but one bite — of the subdued but certain sourness of the sourdough, of the succour of the plaits or the sweet joy of the foccaccia — and you will be booking a return visit.

The breads are complemented by excellent cakes: two custard cake, almond amaretto cake, apple and calvados, chocolate pecan and a kaleidoscope of others, and at lunchtime the sandwiches are only splendid for slaughtering your hunger.

Open 10am-5pm Mon-Sat, 10am-2pm Sun

GROWERS' MARKET
THE DUBLIN FOOD CO-OP
St. Andrew's Centre, Pearse Street, D2 For membership Tel: (01) 872 1191 Fax: 873 5737

We polarise neatly into two distinct and diametric camps, those of us who line up each second Saturday morning for the Dublin Food Co-Op.

There are, firstly, the hard-working volunteers whose zealatrous energy keeps this ingenious show on the road. These selfless souls shovel oat flakes into bags, weigh out shoals of aduki beans on the little scales, diligently arrange the rice crackers in their boxes beside the Ecover bleaches and the wholewheat spaghetti. They line up the alternative magazines, pin up notices for shiatsu and house-sharing, before scooting around the Saint Andrew's Hall with their power purchasing leaflets, hoovering up the necessary Tanzanian coffee, sesame oil, miso and brown rice.

They are a diverse crew: beards, Doc Marten's and Traidcraft dresses. All around the hall their day-glo kids are alternatively meek and mischievous as they cavort together. They are the backbone of the Co-Op: dedicated to an idea of alternative purchasing which has created an aspect of community around the whole venture.

And, then, there are the hedonists.

We are here to buy some of Silke Cropp's wanly wonderful goat's milk cheeses, driven down from Cavan by the cheesemaker herself. We are here for Nicky Kyle's mum's eggs, those hearty, muck-speckled orbs of delight which glare at you from the Sunday morning frying pan with their defiant freshness. And, today, Nicky's mum also has pâté and hummus, pickles and chutneys, and box-bursting duck eggs.

We line up to see just what organic herbs and plants Laura Turner has for sale, then splurge politely on fragrant mint and lissom tarragon, spruce thyme and — we have been waiting for this — some aristocratic basil. Next door Deirdre O'Sullivan has freshly dug spuds with some Kildare soil still on them, or deep-green cabbages or lovely Swiss chard which will go into that favourite Raymond Blanc tart recipe with some Gruyère cheese.

Deirdre Keogh's organic vegetables always seem to echo their mistress's blooming good health, whether vibrant scallions, or plump heads of various varieties of lettuce which you want to rush home for lunch. Next door to her will be Penny Lange's table of biodynamic produce, in season veritably groaning with unimpeachably wonderful vegetables which, a few hours ago, were snugly embedded in Wicklow soil. Here one finds the curious rarities such as salsify and scorzonera, purple baby cauliflowers, yellow finger-size courgettes. Our greedy eyes feast, our swiftly evacuating wallets and purses disgorge once more, our bags are filled up and up.

All around us the hard work of the Co-Op carries on, but we hedonists are locked into oblivion, thinking of nothing further than lunch, then dinner, then Sunday lunch and Sunday dinner. Some of the basil will go towards a fresh pesto sauce for pasta, the goat's cheese will be barbecued gently, the spuds and baby turnips and celeriac milled into a white purée, the new garlic baked in a brick with chicken until it is oozingly soft. If, at the stall where the Inisglass community sell their flours and breads, we can find some of their yogurt mixed with fresh fruits, then dessert is a cinch.

The workers fortify themselves for more work with aduki bean pasties from the little stall manned by Sage foods. We hedonists, famished by our expedition, do the same, and promise ourselves that, one day, we will come along and volunteer and do some work and help out and keep the whole thing going. But that, well, that will have to be next time. For now, it is lunch, and dinner, and lunch, and dinner, and that is as much as matters.

The Dublin Food Co-Op is open from 10.30am-5pm every second Sat. St Andrew's Hall is in the middle of Pearse Street.

PATISSERIE
THE GALLIC KITCHEN ★
Christchurch Market, 40-48 Back Lane, D8 Tel: (01) 544912
From about ten yards away, the scent suddenly jumps up into your nostrils. The scents of butter, of baking, of pastry quickly crisping to splendid perfection, of glazes caught just as they thicken, of fruit liquescing into docile deliciousness. It is Sarah Webb's Gallic Kitchen you are approaching, it is Gallic Kitchen smells which are causing you to spontaneously salivate, and it could be nowhere else in this town.

Ms Webb is a superb baker. Not a trace of ego or arrogance gets in the way of her search for flavour, for savour. Where other patissiers like to show off with façile complication, Sarah Webb sticks to the basic tenet of pleasurable deliciousness as the goal of her work.

So, pain au chocolat is crumbly and fulsome; sausage rolls with their pair of bangers in between buttery, break-heart pastry urge you towards gluttony; the baby quiches with their flecks of spinach and dice of ham are the perfect picnic lunch.

The white breads with their mantle of browned egg wash are serene and sweet, the potato bread so confoundedly delicious that you curse yourself for the fact that you cannot emulate them, but console yourself with the fact that Ms Webb turns them out, perfectly, every time.

A dogged, professional consistency explains why Ms Webb's business gets bigger every year. Year in, year out, winter, spring, summer or fall, all you have to do is call here and, after the initial delightful assault on the nostrils, you can bet your bottom dollar that the pear tart this time will be as good as last time, the salmon roulade as enjoyable, the crunchy pizzas just as terrific as everything else.

Market Stall Open 10am-5pm Fri-Sun

WHOLEFOODS
THE GENERAL HEALTHFOOD STORE
93 Marlborough Street, D1 Tel: (01) 874 3290
A small, friendly little wholefood shop with an interesting range of breads and good snacktime cooked foods — spring rolls, vegetarian pasties, lentil burgers.

Open 9.30am-6pm Mon-Sat

GREENGROCER
HERE TODAY
25 South Anne Street, D2 Tel: (01) 671 1454 and the Corporation Markets, D7
The laid-back, slap-dash service aside, Here Today is an essential place for every manner of fruit and vegetable, especially for a good selection of organically grown produce.
Open 6.30am-6.30pm Mon-Sat (Market shop open 5am-2.30pm Mon-Sat)

KITCHEN SHOP
KITCHEN COMPLEMENTS
Chatham House, Chatham Street, D2 Tel: (01) 677 0734
Ann McNamee's shop spills over with the sensual, superb stylings and designs of the finest makers of kitchenware, the producers of the most alluring and must-have pots, pans and paraphernalia. On two floors intersected by a steeply winding staircase, you will find, and will be charmingly helped to find, any and every necessity to transform you from a kitchen Cinderella into the new Alice Waters. Calphalon pans, Sabatier knives, crushingly complicated texts for cake decorating, every little fidgety item and finickety necessity you need to unleash the huge culinary potential that lurks within you is to be found here.
Open 10am-6pm Mon-Sat ('till 7pm Thurs)

CHOCOLATES
LIR CHOCOLATES ➥
IDA Enterprise Centre, East Wall Road, D3 Tel: (01) 878 7800
Lir chocolates are veritable orgies of confected intensity, narcotic in their sweet splendour, profound in their ability to reduce the eater to the state of gluttonous chocaholic in seconds. Finely balanced between sweetness and fruit intensity, they are aristocrats of the sweetie world: ordinary chocs are to Lir as Mantovani is to Mozart.

DELICATESSEN
MAGILL'S
14 Clarendon Street, D2 Tel: (01) 671 3830
An excellent cheese counter with French and other European cheeses alongside the best Irish farmhouse cheeses; Stone Oven bread brought in every Thursday morning; a good sausage and cooked meats counter — though some of the wonderful charcuterie from Continental Sausages in Kerry would surely add extra spice and sophistication to this section — and every manner of oil, preserve, salad and condiment make up the splendid selection of Magill's long-established deli. Prices are generally on the steep side, but with such a satisfying array of foods on offer who minds the extra few shillings.
Open 9.30am-5.45pm Mon-Sat. Opposite Powerscourt Townhouse Centre.

FISHMONGER
MCCONNELL'S
38 Grafton Street, D2 Tel: (01) 677 4344
A fine fishmonger who sells only what came from the market that morning and then shuts up shop. This almost-eccentric commercial behaviour is your guarantee of fresh fish, but whilst browsing amongst the wet fish, don't overlook their smoked salmon also.
Open 9am-5.30pm Tue-Fri, 9am-1pm Mon & Sat if fish is still for sale.

FISHMONGER
THOMAS MULLOY

12 Baggot Street Lower, D2 Tel: (01) 676 6133

Mulloy's always have a good selection of fish and shellfish in their unusually-designed shop, including wild salmon in season. All of their smoked salmon is wild.

Open 8.45am-6pm Mon-Fri, 8.45am-4pm Sat

GREENGROCER
OW VALLEY FARM SHOP

Powerscourt Townhouse Centre, D2 Tel: (01) 679 4079

Invaluable little place for finding unusual doo-dahs: girolles, good olives, fruits and nuts, tomatoes on the vine in season.

Open 8.30am-6pm Mon-Sat ('till 7pm Thur)

KNIFE SHOP
THOMAS READ & CO

4 Parliament Street, D2 Tel: (01) 677 1487

Read's is the oldest shop in Dublin, and one of the nicest, with beautiful glass counters exhibiting every manner of cutting instrument, from cut-throat razor to cutlass, from boning knife to nail clipper, that you could desire. Vitally, they have an excellent knife sharpening service so rather than entrusting your precious tools to the blunt attentions of a domestic instrument if you want to sharpen up your act, it is both more profitable, and more fun, to bring them in here.

Open 9am-5pm Mon-Fri

GREENGROCER
THE RUNNER BEAN

4 Nassau Street, D2 Tel: (01) 679 4833

The trestle tables of this busy shop spill out into Nassau Street under a couple of great big canopies, and it is always busy with both the mundane and the magnificent of the fruit and vegetable world.

Open 8am-6pm Mon-Sat ('till 7pm Thurs)

CHEESE STALL
RYEFIELD FOODS

Mother Redcap's Market, Back Lane D8

Ann Brodie's happy stall of cheeses benefits not only from the younger-than-springtime nature of the lady herself but also from the expert eye of a cheesemaker, for Mrs Brodie is responsible for the fine Ryefield cheeses, made back home on the farm in County Cavan and, you guessed it, available here. But, then, so is almost every other Irish farmhouse cheese you can think of, all in expert condition and sold in conjunction with breads and cakes, pickles and jams, hand-made sweets and a host of other delicacies. Mrs Brodie manages to cull the best foods from her neighbours, meaning that everything here is charmed with natural, instinctive, organic flavours.

At Christmastime, especially, the Ryefield Foods' stall is invaluable for real Christmas cakes and puddings, crumbly sweetmeat pies, all the fare of the festive season. There is a second Ryefield Foods' stall run by other members of the Brodie family at the weekend market in Blackrock, County Dublin, enjoying the same fine range of foods.

Open Mother Redcap's 10am-5.30pm Fri-Sun, Blackrock 11am-6pm Sat-Sun

KITCHEN SHOP
SWEENEY O'ROURKE

34 Pearse Street, D2 Tel: (01) 677 7212

Whilst it is mainly professional cooks, on the hunt for a brace of ladles or a giant-sized sieve, who habituate Mr Sweeney and Mr O'Rourke's lovely kitchen shop, the domestic cook has much to gain from a visit here, not least the keen prices and the fact that the shop aims to cater for every culinary need. So, if the design of the shop is higgledy-piggledy, this only adds to the fun of hunting through mountains of stainless steel in search of the right sized mixing bowl, or pulling through boxes to find the right pestle and mortar.

Open 8.15am-5.15pm Mon-Fri (closed for lunch)

FRESH YEAST
THE YEAST SHOP

College Green, D2

Little tablets of fresh yeast are for sale here on Mondays, and — if there's any left — Tuesday mornings. The shop itself has not advanced since the days when De Valera was Taoiseach, and long may it refuse to do so.

NORTH CITY

BUTCHER
HANLON'S
20 Moore Street, D1 Tel: (01) 873 3011
One place in Dublin where, amongst all the other Moore Street multifariousness, you are likely to find rabbit, usually from Wicklow and usually at a very good price.
Open 9am-5.30pm Tues-Sat ('till 5pm Mon & Fri)

ITALIAN FOOD SHOP
LITTLE ITALY
68 North King Street, D7 Tel: (01) 872 5208
An essential place for anyone with a copy of Ada Boni, Giuliano Bugialli or Marcella Hazan. Good dried pastas from De Cecco, good dried porcini, good Lavazza coffee, a belting range of Italian wines and liqueurs, and essential cheeses and cooked meats. Many restaurateurs use the shop to stock up on the necessities of take-away and trattoria food, but in amongst the tomato purée and the cooking oil there are lots of good foods to be found.
Open 9am-5pm Mon-Fri, 10am-1pm Sat

GROCERY SHOP
NOLAN'S
29A Stoneybatter, D7 Tel: (01) 677 0656
They don't make neighbourhood shops like Nolan's anymore, and more is the pity. Staffed by gentle gentlemen of all ages who know exactly what you want better than you know yourself, they sell lovely baked ham and good soda breads with which to encase it in a sandwich, and a complete range of comestibles. But the atmosphere of the place, with a word always about the weather and the ways of the country, is what makes it special.
Open 8am-6pm Mon-Sat (closed for lunch 1pm-2pm Mon-Fri)

SOUTH CITY

JAPANESE FOODS
AYUMI-YA
Newpark Centre, Newtownpark Avenue, Blackrock, Co Dublin Tel: (01) 283 1767
If you have eaten the — cooked — ingredients in Mrs Hoashi's restaurant underneath the Ayumi-Ya shop, you may be tempted to try your hand at this ethereal and intricate cuisine. This is where to begin assembling the soya, beancurd, seaweed, marinated plums and other staples which will, assuredly, see you on the road to success.
Open 5pm-7pm Mon-Sun (Sat 1pm-5pm)

BAKERY
BRETZEL KOSHER BAKERY
1A Lennox Street, D8 Tel: (01) 475 2724
The more moderne bakeries which have opened in Dublin in the last few years have not

knocked the venerable Bretzel out of its stride. Just take a peek in the window and you see that all the old favourites survive, today as ever: great big hanks of gloopy pizza, milky coffee-coloured onion rolls, bug-eye gingerbread men, foldaround croissants, sugar-smack cakes, rustic rye breads. The confectionery here has a happy, kiddyish concept of sweet foods, with more piled on top of more in the pursuit of surfeit and a happy disregard for patissier's finesse.

Open 9am-5.30pm Mon-Sat

TRAITEUR
DOUGLAS FOOD CO.

53 Donnybrook Road, D4 Tel: (01) 269 4066

An eye of intricate discrimination rules over Richard Douglas's lean, minimal shop in Donnybrook.

The Spanish olive oil they sell from the barrel is soft and fat tasting, neither too spicy nor florid. The cheeses, artisan French abetted with farmhouse Irish, will be in pristine condition: a pungent Brie, an unguent Gaperon, an urgent Roquefort, a Gubbeen in immaculate prime. The bread, from Cooke's Bakery, cannot be bettered. The chocolate, the coffee, the vinegars, the olives and the essential what-nots are all chosen for their finesse.

This finesse crosses over into the cooked food sold here, for the Douglas Food Co. is, effectively, an Irish trâiteur, a cooked food shop. The window offers hearty crubeens set solidly in their fat, a curried herring salad, finely rendered quiches, terrines and pâtés with sharp colours and supple contours, tartlets, roulades and marquises of shattering beauty.

The sense of discrimination is unerring, so you shop with confidence, allowing the Co. to take the slog out of a dinner party or allowing yourself the benefit of a night off, with nothing to do but warm the food through when you get it home. There are good wines — at caution-causing cost, admittedly — to complete the menu. The Douglas Co. may be nascent, but one is already looking forward to its adolescence.

Open 10am-7.30pm Mon-Fri, 9am-6pm Sat

GREENGROCER, DELICATESSEN AND WHOLEFOODS
FITZPATRICK'S

40A Lower Camden Street, D2 Tel: (01) 475 3996

Fitzpatrick's was one of the first good food shops in the city, and it retains its essential status by virtue of diligent and dedicated hard work, patiently expanding its range whilst maintaining precise standards with everything it stocks. Along with an ever-present range of vegetables and fruits from Organic Foods, there is a choice array of wholefoods, a good cheese counter and fine breads for sale. So much good stuff, in fact, that Fitzer's is almost a one-stop shop.

Open 8am-6.30pm Mon-Sat

DELICATESSEN
FOTHERGILL'S

141 Upr Rathmines Road, D6 Tel: (01) 962511

Terry and Breda Lilburn's shop has such a sweetie-pie air of innocence about it that it seems like a cake kindergarten, inviting you to Please Look After This Chocolate Sponge

Cake. The innocence, however, ends with the Lilburns and their splendid staff: many indeed have been the customers who have come in here with the intention of giving a decent home to a chocolate torte or a chocolate bombe or a selection of drooling eclairs or what-have-you, only to then pass it off to their coffee morning cronies or dinner party dilettantes as their own work. Would that they were half such talented bakers as this quiet and hard-working couple, who augment their sweet thing skills with excellent savoury foods — you can make up a very fine picnic or sandwich here at lunchtime — and choice deli foods and wines.

Open 9.30am-6pm Mon, 9am-6.30pm Tue-Fri, 9am-6pm Sat

GREENGROCER AND DELICATESSEN
ROY FOX

49a Main Street, Donnybrook D4 Tel: (01) 269 2892 Roy Fox

Tumbling out onto the pavement there is an imaginative display of fruits and vegetables — priced in groups, like a market: '6 limes for a pound' — inside there's a fruitful display of deli goods: Silke Cropp's fresh cheeses from Cavan, breads from Cooke's Bakery, plus nuts, spices, rices and other such niceties.

Open 9am-7pm Mon-Sun

DELICATESSEN
THE GOURMET SHOP

Rathgar, D6 Tel: (01) 970365

A strange shop that happily appears to be almost time-warped, and which quietly offers some fine, locally baked foods, salads and meats and some excellent, unusual wines.

Open 9am-7pm Mon-Sat

SUPERMARKET
C MORTON & SON

15 Dunville Avenue, D6 Tel: (01) 971254

There is something distinctly bright and breezy about Morton's lovely supermarket.

It's not just the design, a slice of 1960s' modernism, which creates the effect, though this and the vogueish sliding glass door do their bit to build an air of grace and lightness.

It's not even the outdated but timeless layout of the shop, with its modest scale and low level shelving, its quietude and modesty, though all this does make for a supermarket which is a distinctive and enjoyable place to loiter around.

No, the bright and breezy nature of the place comes from what is on the shelves, and the careful selectivity which puts it there: Cooke's Bakery bread in all its splendiferous glare, Drumiller yogurt, Rudd's sausages and bacon; Marc Michel's organic produce from County Wicklow; a host of berries, cherries and currants in season; crème fraîche and buffalo mozzarella and the other essentials of a cool cabinet; a selection of wines which runs from cheap Argentinians and Bulgarians to decent Medocs and other interesting clarets; and then, naturally, those necessary little bits and bobs for the house and the garden.

You get the impression in Morton's that they want to sell these foods because they are proud of them, just as they are proud of their own cooked foods and their meat and fish counters. Their pride makes not only themselves optimistic, but also their customers: a

·hand-written sign in the window offers for sale a car and describes it as '59,000 miles: As New'. One would need to be an optimist to buy that.
Open 9am-6.30pm Mon-Sat

ITALIAN SHOP
NATURALLY NICE
Dunville Avenue, D6 Tel: (01) 973411
From the outside, with its trays of fruit and veg nestling under a canopy, Naturally Nice looks like a conventional shop: nothing more, nothing less. But, in fact, its speciality is Italian foods, and most anything from mozzarella to Montepulciano d'Abruzzo is for sale. Beside serried rows of familiar foods, they prepare a selection of their own dressings.
Open 9am-7.30pm Mon-Sat, 9am-2.30pm Sun

BUTCHER
DANNY O'TOOLE
138 Terenure Road North, D6W Tel: (01) 905457
Oh for the simple certainties of the professional butcher, and the peaceable charm of the professional butcher's shop. Danny O'Toole is a model butcher and runs a model butcher's shop: simply styled and unostentatiously furnished, with a small array of meats set out on display and some necessities — onions, spuds, a few tins of this and that — also available. But his quiet confidence touches everything informing his dealings with meat, and you shop here quietly confident that everything you buy will be the best, and will have those typical taste characteristics that announce meat which has been properly slaughtered and properly hung. Mr O'Toole also specialises in meat from organic farms, and will alert you whenever an order arrives and is ready for collection, but even if you want no more than a pound of sausages or a single pork chop for supper, shopping in O'Toole's always gives one a taste of skill and charm at work.
Open 9am-6pm Mon-Sat (lunch on Wed 1pm-2.30pm)

PUFF PASTRY
QUINLAN'S
87 Morehampton Road, Donnybrook Tel: (01) 668 9529
Quinlan's is always full to the brim with lurid coloured cakes, light sweet biscuits and spongy old-fashioned pastries. The spoon-faced, white-haired lady behind the counter will try to charm you into buying some of these, but do not let yourself be waylaid from asking for their uncooked puff pastry which is sold in half pound slabs, folded in greaseproof paper. Splodges of butter within the paste let you know that this is handmade. It always puffs perfectly, and who but the truly dedicated would go through the rigours of turning and folding and rolling, when you are unlikely to improve on Quinlan's recipe?
Open 7am-6.30pm Mon-Sat, 11am-2pm Sun

ASIAN AND AFRICAN STORE
UNIVERSAL FOODS
11 Upr Camden Street, D2 Tel: (01) 478 4617
Shiny shards of ginger, chillies that throb with lurid red and green vibrancy, shaggy coconuts, Brazilian coffee, rice of all manner of origin and specie sold from big buckets:

there is always a torrent of quizzically arousing foods in the Universal, the best place in town to find the more unusual African and Asian foods. The shop itself has all of the splendidly disorganised air of someplace in Karachi or Bangalore.

Open 10am-7pm Mon-Sat, 2pm-6pm Sun

NATURAL GOURMET SHOP
WHAT ON EARTH ➡
255 Harold's Cross Road, D6 Tel: (01) 965111

Jim Dempsey just can't help himself. Every time he discovers something new which he thinks will complement his shop, then he has to have it, whether it be some new kiddies' food produced to Demeter symbol standard, an appellation controlée rice from someplace in Spain he read about in a magazine, or just some onion bhajis cooked by Sage Foods, or lovely, slow-burning De Rit wax candles. Maybe just some baked beans which are the best he has ever tasted.

The urge for self-improvement, the enthusiasm to get better and to get better things, powers him on: 'This is not really a wholefood shop', he says. 'What I'm aiming to achieve is what you might call The Natural Gourmet, good pure foods with pure flavours'.

And so he sources the excellent Salkeld flour, Organic standard Corleggy Cheeses from County Cavan, some splendid Organic standard wines from France and Italy, vegetables from Penny Lange in County Wicklow. What On Earth is one of few wholefood shops which have decisively and definitely shaken off the tired old mantle of quack pills and dried pulses, replacing it instead with a distinct, personal ideology that searches out good foods both locally and internationally. The Natural Gourmet, indeed.

Open 10am-6.30pm Mon-Fri, 10am-6pm Sat

SOUTH COUNTY DUBLIN

SAUSAGES AND BREADS
BOSWELLS
11 Sydney Terrace, Blackrock, Co Dublin Tel: (01) 288 2237

Part of the sausage-making chain that originated in Co Wicklow (see Wicklow town for more detail).

Open 9am-7pm Mon-Sat

DELICATESSEN
CAVISTON'S DELICATESSEN
59 Glasthule Road, Sandycove, Co Dublin Tel: (01) 280 9120

Venture into an argument about which is the best shop in Dublin and the County and the chances are that, after many names and places have been canvassed, most considerate souls will agree that Caviston's is hard to beat.

And it's not just because it has everything you desperately need and desperately want, though it has all of those things, from a super fish counter with everything that swims, lies and crawls in the ocean for sale, great vegetables, super cheeses, excellent salads and breads and choice dried goods. But, vitally, Caviston's also has the breezy, busy-bee atmosphere of the best shops, that helpful, running-here-and-there air of young folk working hard, preparing, assisting, serving. This is the factor that makes it special, the very deliberate hands-on policy of the Cavistons themselves, their intimate knowledge of each and everything they sell, their desire that you should be happy with each thing you buy and that you should always get what you want. This is a very old idea of service, done with a smile, and it makes it great fun to shop here.

Open 9am-7pm Mon-Sat

TRAITEUR
THE GOOD FOOD SHOP

Glenageary Shopping Centre, Glenageary, Co Dublin Tel: (01) 285 6683

Sue Farrell's shop is as bright and fresh-faced as the proprietor herself, a carefully considered traiteur filled with cooked food, and with the added bonus of a boulangerie, for Ms Farrell bakes excellent breads on the premises.

Every day there are terrines and soups available, perhaps a slice of some handsome rare-roasted beef, maybe some sliced ham or salami to pile into a sandwich. The bakes and cakes are sleekly executed and sumptuous and the necessary peripherals — wine, teas and coffees, condiments, mustards, pulses and what-not — are all chosen with care. It is a friendly shop, eager to please, keen to know just what they can do to help you to enjoy their cooking to the utmost, happy to assume all the responsibility for getting your party — or just your dinner — as right and proper as they possibly can.

Open 9.30am-6pm Mon-Sat

BUTCHER
HICK'S BUTCHERS ★

Woodpark, Sallynoggin, Co Dublin Tel: (01) 285 4430

Ed Hick is the best pork butcher in Ireland, a young man with an unquenchable hunger for experiment and a joy in good food. Where the great skills and tradition of pork butchering have, for the most part, been lost in Ireland, and the days when a talented butcher would creatively make use of every part of the pig — for you can use 'everything except the squeal', as legend has it — are gone, Mr Hick, with the assurance and confidence of years spent training in Germany behind him, is an echo of the noble theme of the expert charcutier.

Mr Hick's skill is so great that if you buy something relatively straightforward from him — say a few ribs of Kassler, the smoked loin of pork — it will be so good that, when devising dinner, you should allow it as much centre-space as possible. Rustle up a white purée of potatoes, celeriac, white turnips and garlic with plenty of warm milk and butter, serve alongside the kassler, and you need do no more in order to have your friends and guests drooling. They will admire your purée, of course, but it will be merely the foil to a piece of pork the like of which they will have never eaten.

As a butcher, Ed Hick is especially valuable in the modern, factory-farming age, for his work is hedged with concern and care for the animals he works with, and the humaneness and awareness he practices are, ultimately, not just to the benefit of the customer's taste buds, but also of benefit to the customer's conscience.

Almost every time you go into the shop there is some delicious surprise awaiting you, some new twist on the art of the pork-possible. Sausage with orange and fennel seed. Flavour-filled pancetta and speck. A brilliant smoked white pudding. A marinated dish ready for the barbecue — and do note that Mr Hick will barbecue an entire pig for you for a special outdoor party. There often seems no limit to the things he does to amuse himself, to keep his skills up to the mark, to keep the shop moving forward, ever motivated. Assisted by the darling service of Miss Flannery, it is a thrill and a delight to take yourself up to Sallynoggin.

Open 8.30am-5.30pm Tue-Fri, (closed for lunch 1pm-2pm Mon-Wed). Open 'till 5pm Sat

BAKERY
MCCAMBRIDGE'S FINE FOODS
Arkle Road, Sandyford Industrial Estate, D18 Tel: (01) 295 8868
McCambridge's were making decent ice-cream in the innocent old days when a poke and a slider meant a cone and a wafer. Their crumbly and elegant brown bread is also widely available around Dublin.

WHOLEFOODS AND SPICES
MONKSTOWN FINE FOOD CO
16a Monkstown Crescent, Monkstown, Co Dublin Tel: (01) 284 4855
Anne Kendrick's shop is a friendly little place with an eclectic mixture of wholefoods and spices, but it is of especial interest because of the broad range of dried spices she sells. You want three different types of paprika? This is where you will find them, available to buy in modest amounts so they won't go stale on you. There are dozens and more to choose from, so even the most recalcitrant recipe specification is likely to be satisfied here.

Open 10.30am-6.30pm Mon-Sat

DELICATESSEN
THOMAS'S DELICATESSEN
1 Cornelscourt Village, Foxrock, D18 Tel: (01) 289 6579
This long narrow warren of a shop is a pleasing place in which to find judiciously chosen foods, both in their raw state and cooked. There are good breads and excellent cakes and assorted bakes, a fine cheese counter selling many of the Irish Farmhouse cheeses alongside their Continental colleagues, and there are plenty of quaffable wines at decent prices. Thomas's always feels like a keen, eager place, somewhere to find the good things.

Open 8.30am-7pm Mon-Sat, 10am-2.30pm Sun. Right at the end of a strip of shops in Foxrock village

NORTH COUNTY DUBLIN

SAUSAGES AND BREADS
BOSWELLS
The Diamond, Malahide, Co Dublin
Part of the sausage-making chain that originated in Co Wicklow (see Wicklow town for more detail).
Open 9am-7pm

FISHMONGER
NICKY'S PLAICE ★
Howth Harbour, Howth, Co Dublin Tel: (01) 323557
'My people were all fisherfolk from the word go, right down the generations of McLoughlins', says Nicky McLoughlin, whose little lean-to shop at the end of Howth Pier is a Mecca for fish lovers. 'My mother wanted something different for me, but the call of the sea is always there. I got a secondary education, and I worked until I was nineteen, but then I went to sea. You just couldn't keep me away'.
Thanks heavens for the call of the ocean, for Mr McLoughlin's knowledge and appreciation of good fish is second to none. 'I wouldn't take fish unless it was good quality', he says. 'You know by feeling the fish, if it's firm, and you look under the gills, but you wouldn't actually have to look under the gills once you feel it is firm: then you know it is good quality'.
He has seen the Irish way of eating fish evolve from the days when it was mere penance food, the staple of the mortifying classes. 'When I came in fish was only appreciated on a Friday, it was a Friday meal and that was it. But when the Friday thing went, everything changed. Now, if you were down here any day, no matter what time of day, there are people who want fish'.
Ironically, the old days were days of plenty: 'When I was fishing you would come in with maybe 100 boxes a day, and now they wouldn't see 100 boxes for a month. When you had the boats that were fishing here years ago, what we called the day boats, they would go out in the morning at six and come in in the evening at six, and we got the fish straight off them. And the fish you were getting in was beautiful: it was firm, you filleted it that day, people had it that evening. It was from the boat to the shop to the customer'. But this ideal is becoming increasingly difficult to realise: 'Most of the guys on the boats do look after the quality of the fish, I will say that about our Irish fishermen. They try to keep it as well as they can, but they're restricted nowadays because they have to go such a distance to get the fish and to bring it back. Okay, you can have it as good a quality as they give it to you, but it's not like the fish you'd be getting years ago.What the boats have to do now is to maybe stay out for four or five days, and go further away for their fish, so the fish is not like fish off a day boat'.
The fishermen travel further, and stay at sea longer, simply to net sufficient fish to make it worth their while. This is the caustic irony which has paralleled the transformation of fish from penitential fare to boutique fashionability. 'The thing about it is, years ago they only ate fish on a Friday and there was so much fish there it was unbelieveable. Now, they'll eat fish every day, and we can't get the fish'.
The reason for this, says Mr McLoughlin, is that the Irish Sea is overfished. 'It's due to

modern technology and the modernisation of fishing gear, it's due to the fact that the Irish Sea is an easy access for everyone, they can get to England and they can get to Holland and they have all kinds of boats in the Irish Sea, and it's been completely overfished'.

Mr McLoughlin still hunts out the best fish he can, but is rueful for the old days of plenty: 'At the time we were fishing out there, you would catch so much fish you would have to dump it, and I remember years ago some of the old people saying; "You're going to live to regret that"'.

Open 6am-8.30pm Mon, 8am-9pm Wed-Thur, 8am-6.30pm Fri

SUPERMARKET CHAINS

ROCHE'S STORES

54 Henry Street, D1 Tel: (01) 873 0044; Frascati Shopping Centre, Blackrock, Co Dublin Tel: (01) 288 5391; The Square Tallaght, Tallaght Town Centre, D24 Tel: (01) 599566

The quiet dignity of Roche's Stores supermarkets attracts a loyalty from their customers that is usually the preserve of the corner shop. Shunning the bully-boy tactics of some of the other supermarket chains, Roche's carries on doing what it does well and doing it quietly, always offering a selection of organic foods beside other supermarket paraphernalia. The Henry Street branch, in particular, has an easy charm that comes as a surprise given its bustling inner-city location.

Open Henry St 9am-5.30pm ('till 8pm Thurs); Blackrock 9am-6pm ('till 9pm Thurs & Fri); Tallaght 9am-6pm ('till 9pm Wed-Fri)

SUPERQUINN

Head Office, Sutton Cross, D13 Tel: (01) 325700

Other branches: Ballinteer Avenue, D16 Tel: (01) 298 9332; Blackrock Shopping Centre, Co Dublin Tel: (01) 283 1511; Blanchardstown Shopping Centre, D15 Tel: (01) 821 0611; Castle Street, Bray, Co Wicklow Tel: (01) 286 7779; McKee Avenue, Finglas, D11 Tel: (01) 341182; Knocklyon Road, Templeogue, D16 Tel: (01) 942421; 9 Nth Main Street, Naas, Co Kildare Tel: (045) 76706; Northside Shopping Centre, Coolock, D5 Tel: (01) 847 7111; 116 Sundrive Road, Kimmage, D6W Tel: (01) 921336; Sutton Cross, Sutton, D13 Tel: (01) 322744; Superquinn Shopping Centre, Dublin Road, Swords, Co Dublin Tel: (01) 840 6222; Walkinstown, D12 Tel: (01) 505951, Newcastle Road, Lucan, Co Dublin Tel: (01) 624 0277

The Feargal Quinn diktat of supermarket management is entitled 'Crowning The Customer' and its core philosophy is that the customer, having shopped once, must return to the store time and again. In order that this might happen the various stores are equipped with much more than simply a wide selection of good food: there are crêches, wide aisles, no sweets at checkouts and a large number of attentive staff whose motivation and helpfulness is delightful and which is consistent from store to store. Ultimately, Superquinn aim to live up to an idea that shopping should be enjoyable, and not a scream-sundered trudge with a wheeley-basket that has you quivering with fatigue at the end of it. The stores are commodious, accessible, the friendly atmosphere a direct counterpoint to the frightened-rabbit blankness of staff in other Irish supermarkets. As a flagship, the store in Blackrock in County Dublin is peerless, a splendid space which nevertheless doesn't suffer from any sense of self-congratulation. You can scan the shelves in other supermarkets and find that they have everything you need, and nothing you want.

Superquinn actually have the things you want.

All stores open from 9am. (Walkinstown, Lucan, Naas, Knocklyon and Blanchardstown open 'till 7pm Mon-Wed, other stores open 'till 6pm.) All close 9pm Thur & Fri, 6pm Sat.

COOKERY SCHOOLS

ALIX GARDNER'S

Kensington Hall, Grove Park, Lower Rathmines Road, D6 Tel: (01) 960045

This is the longest-established cookery school in Ireland and Alix Gardner — who was trained in both London's Cordon Bleu and Leith's cookery schools — teaches the principles and techniques of Escoffier, progressing, only when these are truly learned, to look at modern trends and recipes from around the world. Classes in the 12-week certificate course are divided according to use of ingredients and the techniques which bring each to its best are then discussed and practised. Guest lecturers are cleverly chosen and have included Sarah Webb of the Gallic Kitchen and both Paul and Jeanne Rankin from Roscoff.

THE COOKERY CENTRE OF IRELAND

2a St Patrick's Ave, Dalkey, Co Dublin Tel: (01) 285 8728

Bee Mannix-Walsh is Cordon Bleu trained, studying in the schools of both London and Paris, and her education includes time spent in the Culinary Institute of California. 'The pursuit of excellence' is the rallying call to all the students who enrole here and Mrs Mannix-Walsh has built a steady reputation for her 'Fun' courses where young children are encouraged to enjoy time in the kitchen.

SANDY O'BYRNE'S SCHOOL OF FOOD AND WINE

Garden Level, 89 Ailesbury Road, Donnybrook, D4 Tel: (01) 283 7539

'The combination of food and wine and their essential partnership is fundamental to the philosophy of the school' writes Ms O'Byrne, and, in the 12-week certificate course, the school specialises in providing a comprehensive wine course based on the educational modules established by the Wine and Spirit Educational Trust. Part-time courses include a masterclass in Italian cooking given by Roberto Pons of Il Ristorante in Dalkey.

DISTRIBUTORS

GLENEELY FOODS

Merchants Yard, East Wall Road, D1 Tel: (01) 743275

Percy Covitz's operation is the organisational animus which distributes much of the fine Irish artisan foods found in Dublin's best shops.

ORGANIC FOODS

Unit 26, Hills Industrial Estate, Lucan, Co Dublin Tel: (01) 628 1375

This splendid organisation collects and distributes into Dublin shops, with startling speed and efficiency, the produce from a large number of Organic growers. Contact Clare Mooney for further information regarding the thirty or more stores they supply.

TRADITIONAL CHEESE AND PINNACLE FOOD SERVICES

Limekiln Lane, Walkinstown, D12 Tel: (01) 509494 Eugene Carr

Eugene Carr's twin organisations distribute the Irish farmhouse cheeses countrywide. Traditional Cheese distributes the cheeses, enlivening the cheeseboards of restaurants and the cheese cabinets of shops as it does so. Pinnacle Food Services concentrates on popular delicatessen items.

WHOLEFOODS WHOLESALE LTD

Unit 2D, Kylemore Industrial Estate, D10 Tel: (01) 626 2315

Gladys and all the others of the Wholefoods Wholesale team are super-fast and super-efficient in the business of dispensing and distributing to wholefood shops both in Dublin and throughout the country.

PROFESSIONAL BODIES

THE IRISH ASSOCIATION OF HEALTH STORES

c/o 47 Highfield Park, Dundrum, D14 Tel: (01) 298 1574 Fax: 298 1574

The representative body for the country's health food shops, the IAHS lays down guidelines for members and strictly controls their vegetarian credentials.

IRISH COUNTRY MARKETS ASSOCIATION

Swanbrook House, Morehampton Road, D4 Tel: (01) 668 4784

Governing body for the splendid Country Markets found in the nooks and crannies of most Irish towns.

COUNTY KILDARE

G AMBLING, n. A pastime in which the pleasure consists partly in the consciousness of advantages gained for oneself, but mainly in the contemplation of another's loss. It is not known where Ambrose Bierce, author of The Devil's Dictionary from which this sagacious definition of gambling is taken, ended his life — he set off in 1913 for the revolution in Mexico and was never seen again — but the sharpness of his definition suggests he may well have ended his time in Kildare, wasting his money on the gee-gees.

Kildare is racing country, a land of stud farms, race courses and gentle rolling acres grazed by valuable bloodstock, someplace where your fortune is likely to be depleted and your heart is likely to be broken. If only, says you, I had wasted the time and the money on something with two legs, rather than four.

ATHY

RESTAURANT
TONLEGEE HOUSE
Athy Tel: (0507) 31473 Mark and Marjorie Molloy

'I should like particularly to congratulate the Molloys. Nothing was ever too much trouble, and the food was exceptional'. This remark in a letter from an English traveller who could declare that during their holiday in Ireland — with a couple of exceptions — 'everyone, everything and everywhere was magnificent', is the kind of talk-talk you hear about Mark and Marjorie Molloy's Tonlegee House.

Partly, this affection is built on the basis of Mark Molloy's cooking, an ambitious, charged cuisine which wraps itself up in culinary complexities — boudin of chicken with pistachio nuts and a Pommery mustard sauce, escalope of salmon with mussels and a fresh basil sauce, guinea fowl with roast garlic and a thyme flavoured jus, chocolate and almond flavoured marjolaine (this a dish in tribute to his wife, perhaps?) — but which is always capable of making flavours hit home, creating dishes that are often truly memorable.

But it is the atmosphere created by a young couple working hard in their own place and slowly improving it, slowly knocking it to rights, adding on a quintet of comfy rooms to truly turn it into a restaurant with rooms, it is this motivation which creates the energy and the thrill of Tonlegee, makes it a place where nothing is too much trouble.

Open 7pm-9.30pm Mon-Sat ('till 10.30pm Fri & Sat). Closed Xmas. Average Price: dinner £££-££££ B&B ££££. Visa, Access. In Athy, cross two bridges and take the Kilkenny road out of town. Very soon you will see their sign telling you to go left.

BUTCHER
MACSTAY'S BUTCHERS
Duke Street, Athy Tel: (0507) 31868 David MacStay

'All I ever knew about was steak, chops and roasts' said one of Mr MacStay's new and now ever-loyal customers, when introduced to his enormous variety of meat recipes: herb lamb burgers and lamb sausages spiced with natural spices imported from Germany; Mexican steaks ('as thin as a newspaper') ready to be quick-fried; lamb 'Swiss Roll' ('I mince it, mix it with herbs and bring it home to Bernadette who rolls it in puff pastry, and we sell it by the slice'); free-range turkey, boned and stuffed and 'a terrible lot of other home-made things' besides.

'I work six days a week, and never enter for any awards' says Mr MacStay, who still manages to find the time to be a member of the Athy Amateur Dramatic group. His awards come in the form of praise from his devoted customers: 'If ever you could say this is a place built with love' said one 'this is it'.

Open 9am-6pm Mon-Sat. Facing the Shore's Car Park in the centre of Athy.

KILCOCK

FARMHOUSE CHEESE
MARY MORRIN
Kilcock Tel: (01) 628 7244 Mary Morrin
Mary Morrin adheres to the disciplines of both organic and bio-dynamic farming, and, using the milk of her Hereford cow, makes a cream cheese, sometimes flavoured with

fresh herbs, sometimes flavoured with dried herbs and cumin seeds. She also makes country butter, and chicken and ham pies using a home-made shortcrust pastry and free range animals where possible.

You can buy the produce of Mary's farm at the Naas Country Market, Fri mornings, 10.45am-12.15pm.

MOYVALLEY

ROADSIDE DINER
MOTHER HUBBARD'S
Moyvalley Tel: (0405) 51020 John Healy
Mother Hubbard's is the trucker's equivalent of restaurant Paul Bocuse. Just as, if you eat in M. Bocuse's famous restaurant near Lyons, you are confronted with images of the great man on every wall, on the wine bottles, on the plates, in bronze sculptures, photorealist paintings, everywhere — someone once described it as like eating with Stalin — so John Healy's Mother Hubbard's shouts loud and clear the message and the moniker.

The t-shirts which the staff wear advertise their place of employment, and you can buy them for yourself, to further broadcast its fame. The name is on the napkins. It is on the biros which they leave for you to fill in the little questionnaire enquiring if you are happy with their efforts. There are pictures of the diner on the table-mats. Outside there are a couple of signs beaconing the name in neon. M. Bocuse simply cannot compete with Mother Hubbard's.

Who needs culinary rosettes when you have this much confidence?

They are unlikely to collect any culinary rosettes in Mother Hubbard's, but if your image of a roadside diner is someplace where someone shoves something like food in your direction whilst straining to keep their cigarette ash out of the pot, think again. This is one of the most thoughtful, pristine, efficient places you will find in Ireland. True, it's someplace which truckers swear by and largely dominate, but the food is properly done, the service is solicitous, there are splendid facilities for changing baby, they broadmindedly provide condom machines in both the loos, and there are showers and telephones and newspapers, and some refuge from the road.

Open from 6.30am-11pm Mon-Sat, Sun 8am-11pm. On the N4 to Sligo and Galway, a few miles before the road divides at Kinnegad.

STRAFFAN

HOTEL AND RESTAURANT
THE KILDARE HOTEL AND COUNTRY CLUB
Straffan Tel: (01) 627 3333 Ray Carroll
Less of an hotel and country club than a temple, this one firmly devoted to Mammon, whom Ambrose Bierce defined as 'The god of the world's leading religion'. Lavishness is unrestrainedly embraced in every detail, though Michel Flamme's cooking can unearth modest grace notes amongst the classic French disciplines.

Open 12.30pm-2pm, 7pm-10pm Mon-Sun. Open for Xmas. Average Price: lunch ££££ dinner ££££-£££££ B&B £££££. Visa, Access, Amex, Diners. Signposted off the Dublin/Cork road.

COUNTY KILKENNY

W^E SHALL RECOGNISE again that within a few square miles we should have everything which we can possibly need. Here in Kilkenny the earth is fruitful and the neighbours are intelligent, imaginative and kind; their minds are well adapted to poetry and jokes and the propounding and solving of problems'.

Intelligent, imaginative and kind, adapted to poetry and jokes, to propounding and solving problems. Yes, you think, well that was surely a Kilkenny man who could and would  describe the locals so fondly. And, true, this quote comes from the Kilkenny essayist Hubert Butler, from a book called 'Escape from the Anthill'. But Butler did no more, here, than to describe the local character, and to give some idea of the richness of culture which Kilkenny exudes, the span of influences, the comfort of history. The city is, perhaps, the most beautiful in Ireland, with an aristocratic mien, and the land is fruitful — there are excellent organic and bio-dynamic growers — and rich in mystery, rich in craftspeople producing pottery, leather, glass, precious metals.

BENNETTSBRIDGE

FLOUR MILL
KELL'S WHOLEMEAL FLOUR
Bennettsbridge Tel: (056) 28310 Billy Mosse
The River Barrow powers the wheel which grinds Billy Mosse's flour, giving it sagacious, deep tastes which many professional chefs appreciate. You need to buy it in10 kilo bags, or otherwise content yourself with the widely available brown bread mix which can be found in shops and supermarkets.

CAFÉ AND CRAFT GALLERY
THE MILLSTONE
Bennettsbridge Tel: (056) 27644 Eavan Kenny & Gail Johnson
A new venture, organised by the Mosse family but run by Eavan and Gail, who both have Ballymaloe backgrounds. The menu is reassuringly short — kibbled wheat scones, watercress soup, pasta with tomato and basil, lemon roulade, chocolate fudge pudding.
Open noon-6pm Wed-Sun, 6pm-9.30pm Thur-Sat

POTTERY
NICHOLAS MOSSE POTTERY
Bennettsbridge Tel: (056) 27126 (shop) 27105 (factory) Nicky Mosse
Nicky Mosse's work fuses a gentle Edwardianism in his palette of colours — baking bowl brown, soft blues and greens — with a delicate, plainness of design that is ruddily functional. His work is quietly distinctive, made from Irish clay, fired by water power, a very homey and consoling series of earthenware.
Open Jul & Aug 10am-6pm Mon-Sat, 2pm-6pm Sun

POTTERY
STONEWARE JACKSON POTTERY
Bennettsbridge Tel: (056) 27175 Michael Jackson
Handsome tableware, also porcelain and stoneware.
Open 9am-5.30pm Mon-Fri, 9am-6pm Sat. Closed lunch 1pm-2pm

INISTIOGE

RESTAURANT
THE MOTTE
Inistioge Tel: (056) 58655 Alan Walton & Tom Reade-Duncan
In its artfully confected contrivance, The Motte is a charmingly regressive space, just what you want a restaurant dining room to be when you are out for that special night, just how you want a restaurant dining room to appear when you walk in out of the evening.

Drapes tumble and flow to the ground and shudder up to the ceiling, the art on the wall is striking, full of presence, the music is stagy and whacky, gleaming glasses gleam, linen is crisp and tactile. It is a genuinely intimate little room: five tables, low lights, service which works at a properly pedestrian pace, instantly slowing you down and quickly setting you up for the evening.

Alan and Tom like to tinker and toy with tastes, like to twist conventional cooking a little awry, so calf's liver comes sweet and sour, smoked salmon has an orange couscous, a mango purée completes the Pacific Rim whirl which a coconut crêpe contributes to a warm breast of chicken.

Pork cooked in milk is nothing new, but pork fillet with coconut milk is, while roasted pheasant has not only a deep chocolate sauce but also a scattering of Chinese straw mushrooms to add an unexpected savoury note to a cloying and rich dish.

It is all good fun, this playfulness with contrasts and confections, though desserts opt simply for drop-dead deliciousness: sticky profiteroles or a white chocolate cheesecake.

Alan and Tom orchestrate the controlled waywardness of The Motte perfectly, with clever gags, digressions into local history, friendly chit-chat. A charming evening, a charming restaurant, a charming village. The name, incidentally, is not pronounced in the way a Dublin youth might use the sound to describe his girlfriend — 'mott' — but takes on a refined, Kilkenny character to become 'moat'.

Open 7pm-10pm Mon-Sun ('till 9pm Sun). Closed Xmas.
Average Price: dinner £££. Access. Visa. Up the hill in Inistioge town centre.

KILKENNY

GREENGROCER
THE AUBERGINE
74 High Street Tel: (056) 63274 Mr Farrell
Locally grown organic vegetables can often be found in Mr Farrell's shop, with a full complement of conventionally produced produce. The L&N supermarket across the road also sells organic produce.
Open 9am-6pm Mon-Sat ('till 7pm Fri)

ORGANIC GROWERS
MAEVE BRENNAN, CLARA BRICKEN
Clifden Tel: (056) 65588
You can buy Maeve's produce from the side of the road, where you will often see a little trestle table set up, and a sign with it which signals that there is someone at home to sell produce from the field and the tunnel. Look out for the apples, and maybe even pluck them from the tree yourself.
About two miles out of Kilkenny on the N10 going east,

CRAFT SHOP AND CAFÉ
KILKENNY DESIGN CENTRE
Castle Yard Tel: (056) 22118 Kathleen Moran
The shop sells the most gorgeous Irish crafts from all over the country, the restaurant sells clever, simple food for those who are almost dropping from the shopping.
Open 9am-5pm Mon-Sat (10am-5pm Sun). Closed Xmas and on Sun between Jan and Mar. Average Price: £- ££. Visa, Access, Amex.

RESTAURANT & ACCOMMODATION
LACKEN HOUSE ➡
Dublin Road Tel: (056) 61085 Eugene & Breda McSweeney
You could select any dish from the menus which Eugene McSweeney prepares and cooks in Lacken House, the homely, peaceful restaurant with rooms which he and his wife Breda run just on the outskirts of Kilkenny, and no matter what the choice — steamed breast of chicken with a nettle mousse, let's say, or goose with a purse of apple and walnut stuffing, poached silver bream with tomato and fresh herb sauce — and no matter what the individual tastes and the distinct techniques which would be involved, you will find yourself always confronted by two simple truths.
The first is that with everything he cooks, Mr McSweeney exploits the long-learnt skill of the professional cook — the chicken will be perfect, the goose hearty yet refined, the poached silver bream was described by a writer for America's Bon Appetit as 'one of the best fish dishes I've ever eaten'. Skill, here, is used to extract flavour, to reveal the character and essence of a food. Mr McSweeney never shows off, never lets things get complicated just for the hell of it.
But you will also find that the cooking shows someone who has never lost touch with the scents, attractions and satisfactions of the garden and the ground: he likes to spirit the green, wild tastes of herbs and leaves such as nettles and parsley into dishes to offer a

counterpoint to the luxury of prime cuts and complex tastes. Involved food needs simple, earthy tastes to make it both enjoyable and digestible and Mr McSweeney knows, as surely as Hubert Butler knew, 'that within a few square miles we should have everything which we can possibly need'. He keeps his chain of suppliers as short as possible, though he will wander down as far south as Clonakilty to secure Edward Twomey's black pudding in order to make his livelysome twice-baked black pudding soufflé, but otherwise everything is local. Local, also, is the character of Lacken House, for the rooms are simple but appropriate, the staff are warmly welcoming, and you find the true tastes of Irish food, and Irish hospitality, here.

Open 7pm-10.30pm Tue-Sat. Closed Xmas. Average Price: dinner ££££ B&B ££££. Visa, Access, Amex. On the Dublin Road just as you go into Kilkenny.

MUSHROOM HUNTING

THE WORLD OF MUSHROOM HUNTING is crepuscular. Scramble off the beaten track or away from the open field into the woods, and it will take about thirty seconds before the eyes acclimatise to the tree twilight. Then, magically, one begins immediately to see the smooth caps, the flirtatious fling of the hoods, the sinewy stalks that were previously invisible. To go mushroom hunting you must, first, immerse yourself in the habitat of the fungi.

This can make for mysteriously lovely experiences. Who has not been in a wood sometime in the late afternoon when a spear of sunlight comes through the clouds and falls down amongst the leaves and trunks. Then, quickly, one is in that almost surreal world filmed in Alfred Hitchcock's thriller 'Vertigo', when Kim Novak leads James Stewart on a dizzy, druggy trail through the woods. The light is spectral, focused, as if a huge arc light from a movie set has been lit up just at the edge of the trees.

Fungiphiles watch this great movie, watch the play of shimmery light weaving through the trees, and they want to be there. Not, of course, to go courting with Kim Novak or to be led astray like Jimmy Stewart. No, fungiphiles just want to see if there are any chanterelles to be found underfoot, perhaps, if it is to be a good day, some hedgehog fungi, maybe even a boletus to send you home triumphant. For moviemakers, woods spell mystery. For some of us, woods spell mushrooms.

And there are many factors, aside from the reward of collecting dinner, which compound the pleasure of the mushroom hunt. Firstly, there are the evocative juxtapositions in which one finds the fungi. The sticky, bright white Porcelain fungus which sits obediently high up on a branch reminds one of a smugly grinning Cheshire cat, plucked from a storybook. The Jew's Ear fungi dangling from a rotted branch of elder are like an array of Burgundian Wine Chevalier's soft hats. A pair of puffballs stuck up an elm are fungal Jack and

DELICATESSEN
SHORTIS WONG
74 John Street Tel: (056) 61305 Mary Shortis & Chris Wong
The name sounds like a fusion of Irish and eastern, and thus Chris and
Mary's shop has the perfect title for somewhere that bakes great soda
bread — Chris Wong has an assured, light touch in his baking — or
perhaps lamb murtabaks — Chris Wong has a demon touch when it
comes to street food — and which otherwise offers all the good things of
the area with every manner of spice, seasoning and soul food from
around the globe also for sale.
Open 9am-7pm Mon-Sat, 10.30am-2.30pm Sun

Jills, gone up the hill. Best of all, a mighty Dryad Saddle sidles out of a rotting
trunk like one half of an outlaw's pack, something to be picked up and tossed
over your shoulder as you mosey down Main Street.

There is, then, the infernal intelligence of the fungi. We are happy to tug out
some white parasols, found in the middle of a field, because we know they are
delicious to eat, but it is the hunt in the woods which really drags us back, the
competition of pitched wits. There is no evidence, it seems, to suggest that fungi
adapt themselves in order to hide in their environment, but then why do those
false chanterelles hide away with such chameleon cunning? Why are the
desperately desirable mushrooms always the hardest to find, demanding endless
patience, patience?

The hunt, usually disappointing, can also be a funny experience. Take a look at a
gaggle of fungiphiles from a distance and they are a ridiculous sight. Backs
huddled like penitents making the circuits on Lough Derg, they finecomb the
woods with the fixed eyes of forensic detectives, obsessively on the hunt for the
diaspora of the spores, looking for clues.

And there is the nice joke implicit in the appearance of the mushrooms: the
sticky, strawberry jam colours of the truly nasty ones like the poisonous Fly
Agaric, the bride-white lure of the False Deathcap. The names are good for a
laugh also: Plums and Custard, warns Roger Philips, is 'Considered Edible by
some but not recommended'. The Deceiver is, appropriately, 'very variable in
appearance and therefore often difficult to recognise at first sight'.

Ultimately, perhaps, we hunt fungi because we know, at the end of the day, that
we shall brush them off, slice them up and, just by simply frying them, secure
that elusive edge of desiccation which makes certain foods so desireable.

There is a subtle crescendo of disintegration to be found in foods such as blue
cheese, game, offal, and particularly in the Pinot Noir grape. A rooty decay,
strangely, makes some foods and wines alluring. Fungi, with their love of rotting
habitats, absorb the air of disintegration and desuetude in which they prosper.
They reek of natural mulch, they sprout hungrily from compost, they are the last
foods of rotting earth and, in seizing them, we pick life and food from just before
the fall.

WINE SHOP
THE WINE CENTRE
15 John Street Tel: (056) 22034 Maureen & Eamonn O'Keeffe
An excellent range of wines and a shop with the sort of cloistered atmosphere that makes it a pleasure to browse amongst the bottles.
Open 9am-6pm Mon-Sat (closed 1pm-2pm lunch)

LAVISTOWN

FARMHOUSE CHEESE/SAUSAGES/MUSHROOM HUNTS
LAVISTOWN FOODS ➡
Lavistown Tel: (056) 65145 Olivia & Roger Goodwillie
Olivia Goodwillie's Lavistown cheese is a subtle thing, refined where other cheeses are blowsy, cerebral where other cheeses are ruddy. It is made in a style which approximates to an English Caerphilly, so the texture is pale white and slightly crumbly, and the cheese seems to be made up, when it is young, like a series of curd pieces joined together like the chains of an atom.

A little ageing alters this curdiness, and the cheese then dries slightly and takes on softer, more lengthy flavours. It is perfect, then, to match with red wine, but is also very good for cooking, for it melts obligingly and its sweetness forms a perfect cloak for gratins and bakes.

Mrs Goodwillie also makes splendid sausages from the happy pigs reared on the farm, bangers which are a million miles removed from the conventional sausage, for these enjoy pork and garlic and a little seasoning and that is all. They are perfect, then, for complicated, agrestic stews and casseroles, the sweet meat conjoining with your tomatoey, herby beans and cuts of game, perfect for that Irish cassoulet you are thinking of inventing one of these days.

Lavistown also doubles up as a study centre, when Roger Goodwillie runs courses on organic gardening and related green and environmental matters. They also organise mushroom hunts when the season is on, and these are mighty fun indeed.

Laviston cheese is distributed throughout Ireland, the sausages are available from Shortis Wong, and both these and the cheese is available from the farm.

PILTOWN

HONEY
MILEEVEN
Owning Hill Tel: (051) 43368 Eilis Gough
Joe and Eilis add various spirits to their honey, but truth be told the Mileeven honeys have little need of any spicing up, for the subtle scents of clover which they exhibit are narcotic enough in their own right. Do look out for the wonderful honey and cider vinegar which they make, a sweet, rich, altogether joyful splash of vigour to contribute to any salad, particularly one where the leaves have a bitter edge which needs to be slightly alleviated.

The honeys and the cider vinegar are widely available in good shops.

STONEYFORD

JERPOINT GLASS STUDIO
Stoneyford Tel: (056) 24350 Keith & Kathleen Leadbetter
The Leadbetters' glassware is intended for the table, so those seeking distinctive hand-made glasses for quaffing and swallyin' should take themselves down to Stoneyford, near to Mount Juliet.
Open 9am-6pm Mon-Fri, 11am-6pm Sat.

COUNTY LAOIS

IS THERE A BENEFIT to being somewhere small, easily set to the back of the mind, as modest and unsung a place as County Laois is? Perhaps. What may be grandiose elsewhere, it seems, is unforced here, unassuming. A pub like Morrissey's in Abbeyleix, were one to transport it to Dublin or Galway, would quick become a pickled tourist trap, somewhere famous for being famous. In Abbeyleix, this extraordinary pub simply gets on with the business of serving drink, as it has done for decades, refusing to allow time to change it, still with a counter of foods, still with the old biscuit tins, still with the respect for a fine pint of stout which they have always pulled. Anywhere else, Morrissey's might be a self-conscious sort of place. But not here. It is likewise with Pat and Joan Highland's soft Abbey Blue Brie, an effective, tasty, surprising cheese which, allowed a little ageing, develops salty and compex flavours, but is always an unassuming, modest thing.

This modesty extends to the pair of country houses which you find in Laois, a pair of country houses which are amongst the most affectionately regarded in the entire country. No man, woman or beast can resist the maternal grace which Allison Dowling casts over Glebe House. 'Allison Dowling is a gem... we felt like good friends by the end of our short stay', wrote some English travellers, and they spoke for all who find themselves in this crook of the woods. No one knows more about the county than Mrs Dowling, so a stay at Glebe allows for the opportunity to discover the county following Allison's advice: expect to be charmingly surprised by what you find.

Similarly, in Frank and Rosemary Kennan's Roundwood House, an air of pleasure-filled idyll pervades, and you could almost believe it was the product of the air that sweeps down Slieve Bloom, such is the ease with which this house operates. Roundwood is so story-book super, with its commingling ducks and its horses, its wide rooms with tall windows, you might imagine yourself transported to some never-never land.

They have changed the name of Laois before — it was Queen's County, once upon a time — so maybe they will change it again, this time to Never-Never County.

MORRISSEY'S
Abbeyleix Tel: (0502) 31233 P.J. Mulhall
Sandwiches served all day.

ABBEY BLUE BRIE
Ballacolla Tel: (0502) 38599 Pat & Joan Highland

GLEBE HOUSE
Ballinakill Tel: (0502) 33368 Allison & Michael Dowling
Open for dinner for guests, and for non-residents if pre-booked. Closed Xmas, New Year. Average Price: dinner £££ B&B ££££. Visa, Access, Amex, Diners. Signposted from the Dublin-Cork Road.

ROUNDWOOD HOUSE
Mountrath Tel: (0502) 32120 Frank & Rosemary Kennan
Open for dinner and Sun lunch for guests, and for non-residents if pre-booked. Closed Xmas. Average Price: dinner £££ Sun lunch ££ B&B £££££. Visa, Access, Amex, Diners. Roundwood House is signposted from Mountrath. If in doubt follow signs for Slieve Bloom.

COUNTY LOUTH

L OUTH CAN SEEM THE LEAST ADORNED of the counties of Ireland, a place devoted to work, with little or no time for play. The towns still feel industrial, though today they can only seep with a nostalgia for the times when they were busy, bustling. The villages, for the most part, exude a hard-headed, no-nonsense stertorousness that speaks of hard working farm folk who cull their living from the land. The Louth accent itself, that babble of flat vowels and subdued expressiveness, indicates a mindset that prefers to look on life in a straightforward, matter of fact way.

This plainness of mind and of manner dictates the social eating of the county. Food must always deliver the satisfaction of a full belly at dinner's end, and prices amongst the restaurants are fiercely keen for there is little money here to waste on eating, even though there is money about. But Louth, with its Amish contrariness and certainty, is not someplace where you might exhibit wealth.

ARDEE

RESTAURANT
THE GABLES HOUSE AND RESTAURANT

Dundalk Road, Ardee Tel: (041) 53789 Michael and Glynis Caine

It is a measure of the seriousness of The Gables House that their menu is written in French, but don't imagine that the ethos of the cooking is anything other than richly ruddy food for hungry people. Those County Louth culinary signatures which the locals demand — hearty helpings, lavish sauces laced with booze, an unapologetically domestic ambience —are in full swing here. Michael and Glynis Caine's food begins from a French sensibility but their classicism quickly subsides in favour of surf 'n' turf favourites — quails stuffed with prawns, chicken filled with crab meat — the calming certainty of steak with stilton or pork with Calvados, and the consoling familiarity of deep fried cheese with blackcurrant sauce, prawns with a thermidor, lamb with rosemary.

Open 7pm-10pm Tues-Sat. Closed 2 weeks in early Jun, 2 weeks in Nov. Average Price: dinner £££, B&B £££. Visa, Access, Amex. Off the N2, about 50 metres from the Carrickmacross Junction.

CARLINGFORD

PUB & BISTRO
JORDAN'S PUB & BISTRO

Newry Street, Carlingford Tel & Fax: (042) 73223 Harry and Marian Jordan

Harry and Marian Jordan describe their cooking as 'parochial', but don't imagine that this amounts to nothing more than parish pump food. Parochial, here, means the best the parish can offer: tamed oysters from Carlingford Lough and wild samphire from its salt marshes, puddings laced with the local, succumbingly delicious Tyrconnell whiskey, local mushrooms. In genuine bistro fashion they sometimes offer crubeens and fish'n'chips, both fancified somewhat: the trotters boned and stuffed, the fish an elegantly poached monk tail with deep fried julienne of turnip. With County Louth typicity everything is

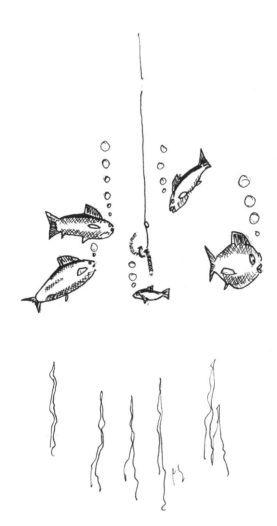

served with a generous spirit, clever but never too serious and the happy style of the food colludes charmingly with this disarmingly seductive village.

Open 6.30pm-7.30pm early bird menu summer months, 7pm-10pm Tue-Sun. Closed two weeks in Nov.
Average Price dinner: ££. Visa, Access, Amex.

COLLON

RESTAURANT
FORGE GALLERY RESTAURANT

Collon Tel: (041) 26272 Des Carroll & Conor Phelan

The Forge indulges its customers with Falstaffian generosity, ladling vast portions of simply prepared food in your direction and, just when you think you have surely surfeited, along will come another dish of, perhaps, courgettes in a tomato sauce, to accompany the potatoes boulangere and the boiled potatoes, the carrots and the broccoli and the what have you, which are already accompanying your chicken in filo or fillet steak. It may be wise to pass a busy day on the farm snagging turnips or to arrive here hungry from a game of football to best make your way through this County Louth belt-busting. The paintings and some of the antiques exhibited are for sale.

Open 7pm-10pm Tues-Sat. Closed Xmas. Average Price: dinner £££. Visa, Access, Amex. Recommended for Vegetarians. In the centre of Collon village.

DROGHEDA

RESTAURANT
THE BUTTERGATE
Millmount Centre, Drogheda Tel: (041) 34759 Fidelma McAllister
Its location, just a slight turn off the road on the outskirts of town, makes The Buttergate a useful lunch stop, though the sheer size of the portions on offer are conducive more to somnolence than speedy work. The food is diverse, but choosing carefully can allow for a decent meal.
Open 12.30pm-2.30pm Tues-Sun, 7.30pm-10.30pm Thurs-Sat. Closed Xmas. Average Price: Look for the signposts to the Millmount Centre on the N1.

GROCER
KIERANS' BROTHERS
15 West Street Tel: (041) 38728 Mark Kierans
This fine shop can appear, initially, to be indistinguishable from the slough of supermarkets and other retailers which cluster around West Street, but there are good breads and hams and other carefully selected foods to be found amidst the standard plastic-clad produce from dairy and farm. The smoked meats they prepare themselves are especially rewarding
Open 9am-6pm Mon-Wed, 9am-8pm Thur, 9am-9pm Fri, 9am-6pm Sat

DUNDALK

CONTINENTAL BUTCHER
THE CONTINENTAL MEAT CENTRE
20 Clanbrassil Street Tel: (042) 32829 Ann & Alo Putz
Ann and Alo are such quiet, hard-working people, and so modest about their skills that you wonder if they know just how good they are at the business of charcuterie.
For they are very good indeed, with a wealth of experience underlying everything: every slice of pastrami, with its dark, peppered exterior and invitingly pink interior, every slice of orangey-ochre pepperoni that falls on top of the pizza bases in many of the best pizzerias in the country, every piece of bratwurst or mettwurst, sechi or speck. Alo's expertise is not confined to the prepared meats, however, for the raw meats are splendid — dark hued beef, carefully prepared lamb — and you can also buy breads and pâtés to construct a quick picnic.
Open 9am-6pm Mon-Sat ('till 1pm Thurs)

DUNLEER

FLOUR MILL
WHITE RIVER MILL
Dunleer Tel: (041) 51141 Gerard O'Connor
A slow, ponderously powerful stone wheel grinds Gerard O'Connor's flour and bran in the

White River Mill, and anyone who seeks the solace of an elemental pace should call here to buy some flour and to watch this beautiful process at work. Nationally, the wholemeal flour is sold under the Lifeforce label, but locally you can find both it and the bran sold under the White River Mill label.

The Mill is on the left hand side of the road as you head south, just driving up the hill going out of Dunleer: look out for the track. If in doubt, the folk in the supermarket will be able to point the way.

KNOCKBRIDGE

FARMHOUSE CHEESE/COUNTRY BUTTER
TARA CHEESE
Dunbin, Knockbridge Tel: (042) 35654 Caroline Meegan
Ever since she began to sell her wanly yellow country butter in Superquinn, Caroline Meegan has been barely able to keep up with demand. Even though the milk she uses is pasteurised, the flavour of the butter is soft and lactic, perfect as a sauce just melted in its own right over some asparagus. Caroline's cheese, Tara, is likewise mellow in taste, a gentle Louth gouda, and as it is very low in fat is perfect for the weight conscious.
The butter is for sale in the Ryefield Stall in Mother Redcap's market in Dublin and in Superquinn stores. Tara cheese is widely available.

RIVERTOWN

WHISKEY DISTILLERS
COOLEY DISTILLERY
Rivertown, Dundalk Tel: (042) 76102 David Hynes
Cooley Distillery's single malt takes its name from the famous single malt made originally in Derry by the company of A.A. Watt, a firm which, late in the last century, ran the largest distillery in Ireland. The Watt family also had a racehorse named The Tyrconnell and, in 1876, it won The Queen Victoria Plate at the lotteryish odds of 100 to 1, leading to a label being created for the whiskey to honour the success.
This is the label that is on bottles of The Tyrconnell Single Malt today, for the company of A.A. Watt has been revived since 1986 by the Cooley Distillery and one hopes that the company will be able to replicate the unlikely success of its four-legged predecessor, for this is a fine whiskey.
The first sip impresses with the distinguished, almost amazing softness of the spirit, before muted floral aspects enter into the taste frame. The whiskey gives no burn in the mouth and is well-balanced and pleasing.
If you see a bottle of The Tyrconnell, snap it up, for Irish Distillers has bought the Cooley Distillery and will be running it down.

TERMONFECKIN

RESTAURANT
TRIPLE HOUSE RESTAURANT
Termonfeckin Tel (041) 22616 Pat Fox
Pat Fox's keen interest in wine spills over happily into his cooking: wild mushrooms with shallots and Madeira; smoked pork with a Loire wine sauce; lamb with a Malmsey sauce; hake with beurre blanc Noilly Prat. Mr Fox is a quiet, characterful man, and his food is thoughtful and unshowy.
Open 1pm-2pm, 7pm-9.30pm Tues-Sat (early bird menu 'till 7.30pm). Closed Xmas. Average Price: lunch ££ dinner £££. Visa, Access, Amex. 5 miles north east of Drogheda on the Boyne River road.

COUNTY MEATH

WHILST THE EASTERN PART of County Meath has been increasingly colonised by families who commute daily to Dublin, the county has not lost a strong sense of individual identity. You feel, once you are in the middle of it, with the big broad blue sky arcing away to a seemingly infinite horizon, that you are decisively in the midlands, far away from the powerful grip of the capital.

Even when, in the evening, from the south east of the county you can see the eerie glow of

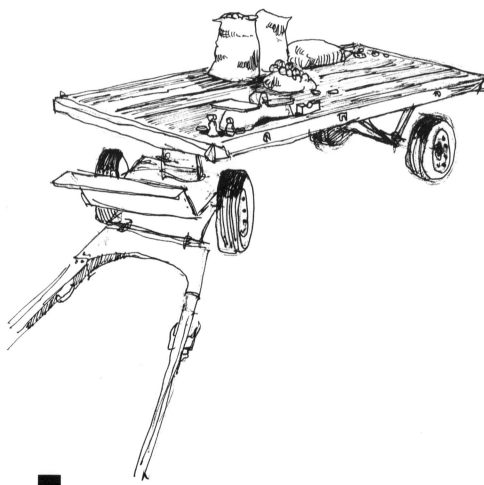

the big city, Meath nevertheless is rural, pastureland, fervidly fertile.

In the midst of this agricultural cradle, Paul Groves cooks a very personal interpretation of hâute cuisine in the Dunderry Lodge Restaurant.

His orientation is decidedly modern, with leanings towards the fresh tastes of the Mediterranean and accents from both the Middle and Far East. Carpaccio, borrowed from Italian cooking, may begin dinner, rack of lamb with a very Middle Eastern aubergine purée may follow, or fillet of beef on Chinese leaves with a five spice sauce, while an îles flottantes may close proceedings on a delighted Francophile note. What all the dishes will enjoy will be Mr Groves' ability to reveal basic, integral tastes and to find harmonious accord between them.

Near by, in the town of Navan, Richard & Trish Hudson's bistro serves a funky, informal menu: spicy chicken wings, hummus, pasta pesto, chicken stir-fry, homemade burgers and lamb kebabs char-grilled. Over on the coast, in Maureen Hassett's Coastguard Restaurant, it is specialities such as her own smoked salmon and a worthy chowder which cull attention.

Close to Bettystown, the Sonairte ecology centre at Laytown has an interesting garden and an obscure selection of apples come the season, with other vegetables for sale during the rest of the year. Another Meath speciality to look out for is James Tallon's super-coarse Martry Mills flour.

DUNDERRY LODGE RESTAURANT
Dunderry, Robinstown, Navan Tel: (046) 31671 Paul and Fiona Groves
Open 7pm-9.30pm Tues-Sat, 1pm-2pm Sun (Sat and lunches by arrangement in May-Aug). Closed Xmas. Average Price: lunch £££ dinner ££££. Visa, Access, Amex, (but no Amex at lunch). Recommended for Vegetarians. From Navan take the Athboy road. Drive for four-and-a-half miles and you will see signs for Dunderry village and then Dunderry Lodge.

HUDSON'S
Railway Street, Navan Tel: (046) 29231 Richard & Trish Hudson
Open 6.30pm-10.45pm Tue-Sun. Closed Xmas. Average Price: dinner £££. Visa, Access.

COASTGUARD RESTAURANT
Bettystown Tel: (041) 28251 Maureen Hassett
Open 7pm-late Mon-Sat. Closed Xmas. Average Price: dinner £££. Visa, Access, Amex, Diners.

MARTRY MILLS
Martry, Kells Tel: (046) 28800 James Tallon

SONAIRTE

THE NINCH FARM
Laytown Tel: (041) 27572 Mary Perry
At Julianstown on the main N1 road take the sign for Laytown. The centre is about a mile down the road on the right hand side, behind a long wall. Ring for details of opening times and availability of produce.

COUNTY OFFALY

I T CAN BE A PITY TO FIND YOURSELF always driving through County Offaly, dissecting the county as you head in the direction of any of the six counties which fringe it north, south, east and west.

For there is a strong element of discrimination here, reasons to make the effort to stop, look, examine. You find this in a town like Birr, with locally grown fruits and vegetables, countrywide farmhouse cheeses and good breads and cakes to be found if you look carefully.

The focus of your trip should be Birr Castle, where you can enjoy home cooking in the Cottage Coffee Shop at its gates. The coffee shop sells cakes and light meals during the day, and runs a bring your own wine restaurant some evenings. Game is occasionally on the very reasonably-priced menu, and they describe their cooking as 'a little bit of Italian, a little bit of French and some Irish — very exciting!'

Also at the gates you can buy the produce of the castle gardens: asparagus in spring, tomatoes in summer and old varieties of apple come autumn.

In the dower house of the castle estate just a mile outside the town, you find Susie and George Gossip's Tullanisk. This country house has acquired droves of admirers for its comfortable rooms, the crack of the communal dinners, and the calming fact that here in the middle of the country you feel happily in the middle of nowhere.

Way down south, just before the county fades away into Tipperary, David and Prue Rudd make perhaps the county's best known foods, their excellent bacon and bangers and black puddings. The bacon is gently cured by rubbing on — rather than the usual injecting — salts and sugars and allowing the meat to cure in its own juices. Consequently Rudd's pork products compare to other meats as cheese does to chalk.

BIRR CASTLE GARDEN PRODUCE

(0509) 20799 Mrs Doolin

Open 9am-1pm, 2pm-5pm, and open for telephone orders Mon-Sun (longer hours and no lunch hour in the high high season).

COTTAGE COFFEE SHOP

Tel: (0509) 20985

Open 11am-5.30pm Mon-Sat, 7.30pm-9.30pm Wed-Sat (with much more limited hours off season).

TULLANISK

Tel: (0509) 20572 Susie & George Gossip

Open for dinner for guests. Closed Xmas and Feb. Average Price: dinner £££ B&B £££££. Visa, Access. Signposted from the Banaher Road

PRUE & DAVID RUDD

Busherstown House, Moneygall Tel: (0505) 45206

The Rudds' pork products are to be found in all Superquinn shops as well as a number of local shops in Offaly.

COUNTY WESTMEATH

NOEL AND JULIE KENNY'S Crookedwood House occupies a vital role in this quixotic part of the country, where the flatlands of Dublin and Meath quickly expire in the face of a rush of lake water and the topographical ruggedness which signals that you are, suddenly, making your way into the west of the country.

One anticipates dinner in Crookedwood secure in the knowledge that Mr Kenny's skills are capably diverse and that the sensuous combinations he can create will make the hack to Crookedwood worth the bother of all those windy Westmeath roads. He likes to mix shellfish with pasta — mussels with fettucine, maybe prawns laced with Pernod to accompany the starchy staple — and is a great utiliser of the local venison, served maybe in a gulyas with spatzle, or paired with wild duck in a red wine sauce. Even with the sort of surf 'n' turf specials which ruddy Westmeath appetites savour, Kenny works out the equation by combining a honey-roasted pork steak with salmon in filo and serving it with two sauces. This is clever cooking, but the intelligence is used to achieve pure, comforting tastes.

Whilst the other Westmeath restaurants may dance to the beat of a different, simpler, drum, they are all unified by a sense of hard work, whether you are in Steven and Martina Linehan's Le Chateau Restaurant in Athlone town, have followed Ray Byrne and Jane

English from their old popular stomping ground at the Castle Pantry in Tyrellspass to their latest venture at The Wineport Restaurant in Glasson, or join the locals at The Glasson Village Inn, in the same village of Glasson.

Otherwise, the speciality of the county is the fine venison reared on the Clonhugh farm at Multyfarnham by Anke and Gunther von Bunau, and the quite brilliant charcuterie of Volker Gonserowski, which can be bought at Streamstown House. Mr Gonserowski is a member of that highly distinguished group of butchers who hail from Germany but now live and work in Ireland, and his produce — frankfurters, pâtés, smoked and cured hams, sausages and brawns — is superb.

CROOKEDWOOD HOUSE

Mullingar Tel: (044) 72165 Noel & Julie Kenny
Open 7pm-10pm Tue-Sat, 12.30pm-2pm Sun. Closed Xmas and 2 weeks Oct/Nov. Average Price: dinner £££ Sun lunch £££. Visa, Access, Amex, Diners. Coming from Mullingar, turn right at the hospital on the road to Castlepollard, then drive to Crookedwood village. Turn right at the Wood pub, then one and a half miles further along you will see the house.

RESTAURANT LE CHATEAU

Abbey Lane, Athlone Tel: (0902) 94517 Steven and Martina Linehan
Open 6pm-10.15pm Mon-Sat (Sun in high season). Closed Xmas. Average Price: dinner £££ Visa, Access, Amex.

WINEPORT RESTAURANT

Glasson, Athlone Tel: (0902) 85466 Ray Byrne & Jane English
Open noon-10pm Mon-Sun. Closed Xmas and winter hours 6pm-10pm Mon-Sat, noon-10pm Sun. Average Price: lunch ££ dinner £££. Visa, Access, Amex.

THE GLASSON VILLAGE INN

Glasson, Athlone Tel: (0902) 85001
Open 7pm-10.15pm Tue-Sat, 12.30pm-2.30pm Sun. Closed Xmas. Average Price: dinner £££ lunch ££. Visa, Access, Diners

GOKI'S MEATS

Streamstown House, Streamstown Tel: (044) 26340 Volker Gonserowski
Goki's meats can be bought from Streamstown House 9am-6pm Mon-Tues, 2pm-6pm Wed, or otherwise by appointment. Streamstown is centrally situated between the N4 to Sligo and the N6 to Galway and is easily accessible from either major road. From the N6 turn north at Horseleap, then take the first left and the first right. You will see the large stone house on the left, and the shop is at the back of the house. From Mullingar take the R390 to Athlone, then branch off at the R391 and follow the signs to Streamstown. Turn left at the pub and the white gates and long drive of the house will follow on your right.

CLONHUGH DEER FARM

Clonhugh House, Multyfarnham Tel: (044) 71117 Anke & Gunther von Bunau
The gates of the farm lead from the main N4 road between Longford and Sligo. Go past the Foxe's Covert pub on the right-hand side and three quarters of a mile further on you will see the house.

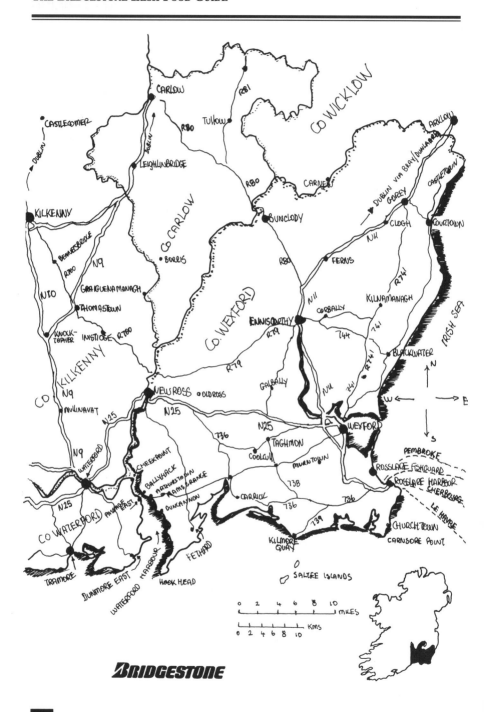

BRIDGESTONE

COUNTY WEXFORD

IN HIS FINE BOOK of 'States-side peregrinations 'Hunting Mister Heartbreak', the writer Jonathan Raban, freshly out of Liverpool on board a massive cargo vessel but perturbed by the imminent arrival of a modest hurricane called Helene, notes 'the quick dit-dit flash of Tuskar Rock ahead of us. Rosslare, a few miles short of it, was a good deepwater port, and County Wexford is a genial and beautiful place to find oneself stormbound'.

Unfortunately for Raban, Helene did not oblige the crew and passengers, consigning them to a few days stormbound shore leave, a brief spell in which to enjoy the geniality and beauty of County Wexford. But whether you glide by the coast of the county in a boat or pitch your way in a car or on a bike through the rollicking hills which dump and crest all the roads down here, Wexford is a place where you want to find yourself becalmed, confined to shore, unable to do little more than admire the slow stroke of light in the sunsets, the pleasantly inviting scale of the fields and the roads, the low hills, the what's-around-the-corner surprise which this modest county offers in its towns and in its countryside.

It is this sense of modesty which makes Wexford so genial. Nothing is ever overstated here, either in the way people speak or the way they behave: they take their good weather for granted and pass little remark upon it, they organise their festivals with expertise and endeavour, but they do it for themselves rather more than for the interest or approbation of the rest of the country, or the rest of the world, for that matter.

Arrive here, at the fine port of Rosslare, and as you scoot along the roads Wexford will seem beautifully integrated, comfortable, a place which keeps its own counsel. Within fifteen minutes, it will have absorbed you into its confidence, its geniality, its beauty.

BALLYEDMOND

RESTAURANT, PUB FOOD AND TAKE-AWAY
EUGENE'S RESTAURANT ➡

Ballyedmond Tel: (054) 89288 Eugene & Elizabeth Callaghan

Ballyedmond village is just a clatter of thatched cottages, some new bungalows, a couple of shops. It unwinds along peaceably, just kids on bikes and gangly dogs. Eugene's Restaurant sits beside a pub, with a take-away sandwiched in the middle. Hardly auspicious. The dining room of the restaurant is a simple, four-square space, the colours are pastel-quiet, the loos are immediately at the end of the room which has enough tables to seat thirty or so.

If this all seems a bit glum, then the menus, written in an agreeable hand-scribble, will cause you to look up at your family, slightly in disbelief, to check that they, too, have a menu which offers the same things as yours. Are they promised Sauté Sea Scallops with lightly Spiced Lentils? Warm Mediterranean Salad with Balsamic Vinegar? Braised Shank of Lamb with Root Vegetables? Pork Fillet with Ginger and Soya? You are in a room that looks like a diner, beside a chipper beside a pub, and the menu is promising food straight from the cutting edge.

Strange to relate and even stranger to believe, in Ballyedmond, not too far from Wexford town, Eugene's Restaurant, beside the chipper beside the pub, is run by Eugene Callaghan, winner a couple of years back of the Roux Brothers' Young Chef of the Year title, until recently right-hand man to Paul Rankin in Belfast's Roscoff, and one of the hottest culinary talents to be found anywhere in Ireland.

Mr Callaghan could pull a job anywhere in these islands and name his price but he has come to Ballyedmond, with his wife Elizabeth and their twin babies Emma and Sarah, and it is in this trio of establishments that he cooks not just for the restaurant but for the bar — scrambled eggs with smoked salmon and chives, fillet of plaice with lemon and parsley butter, panfried steak with mustard cream — and for the chipper where he batters the cod and fries the chips.

The strength of Eugene's cooking can be seen in the dish of Braised Shank of Lamb with Root Vegetables. This is something we would associate as a quintessentially French dish: the lamb cooked to melting tenderness, the vegetables soft and caramelly, the arrangement simple, still-life pleasing. Eugene Callaghan cooks this dish to utter perfection. The call of ruddy country tastes is here, the sublime melt of gentle turnip, the lacy, floury flirtatiousness of a good potato, the intelligent, up-front pleasure of the lamb. But whilst the arrangement of the dish is classically French, with the lamb sprouting a sprig of thyme and the turned vegetables festooned around the edges of the plate, Mr Callaghan reclaims this dish as being triumphantly Irish.

No other country could offer basic ingredients with these flavours, and one marvels at the ability of this cook to genuflect to the French for direction and inspiration, but to return so confidently to the unique tastes of the Sunny South-East. Cooking, the famous dictum goes, is when things taste of themselves. Mr Callaghan can top this: he gets things to taste not just of themselves, but also of their place of origin.

Open 12.30pm-2.30pm Mon-Sun, 7pm-9.30pm Mon-Sun (closed Tues evenings). Bar lunch and evening meals, takeaway open 'till 12.30am. Closed Xmas. Average Price: Bar lunch ££, lunch ££ dinner £££. Visa, Access, Diners. Ballyedmond is on the R741 between Gorey and Wexford.

BANNOW BAY

SHELLFISH
BANNOW BAY FISHERIES
Clifton, Spawell Road Tel: (053) 42182 Ross Lee
In the curl behind Hook Head, Ross Lee farms Pacific Oysters as well as clams and mussels.

BLACKWATER

FARMHOUSE CHEESE
CROGHAN CHEESE ★
Ballynadrishogue, Blackwater Tel: (053) 29331 Luc & Ann van Kampen
'Goats are natural foragers, not grazers' says Luc van Kampen. Just walk behind his happy herd as they return to their fields after milking and you soon see what he means, for the greedy curiosity of the goats quickly transforms them from behaving like an unruly

dragoon of squaddies, lazily sauntering out after a lazy lunch, into a busy raggle of foragers, bounding up ditches and hedgerows like so many basketball players pitching for a basket. By the time they are back in their pasture, the young bucks will already be locking heads to joust and fight, whilst the more sane and sagacious will be breezily chewing the cud. Mr van Kampen, meanwhile, will be likely back at work, beginning to create the curd from which Croghan will eventually emerge. 'It's a process, it's alive, it's a creative thing really', he says and the sense of excitement and pride which this gentle, almost Doonesburyish man takes in his work is palpably evident in his cheese. Croghan is a masterly food: handsome to look at in its ice-curl shape with a mottled, bluey-pink rind caused by being rubbed with Bacterium Linens for a few days, inside it is pure white and tender, with a tense lactic thoroughness that delivers a powerful aftertaste. As Luc points out, 'there are no indigenous Irish recipes for cheese and though most are based on a Continental model, they take on their own character after a while'. None more so than Croghan (pronounced, alternatively, as 'Crockan' or 'Crowan': the name refers to a mountain in north Wexford). The cheese resembles a Reblochon, but no French cheesemaker could arrive at tastes like these, their subtle, supple intensity a perfect parallel for a fine, aristocratic claret. Croghan reaches its best at about six weeks old and it is the autumn cheeses, made in September and October, which are perhaps the most characteristic, though the out-of-slumber freshness of the cheeses made in April and May is delicious.

Cheese can be bought from the farm, but telephone first to check that there is some available. From Wexford, take signs to Curracloe, Blackwater and then Ballyvaldon. Half-a-mile out of the village there is a difficult-to-see turn to the right. Follow this to the end, keeping to the right.

CROSSABEG

ORGANIC FLOUR, VEGETABLES, BREAD & YOGURT
INISGLASS TRUST
The Deeps, Crossabeg Tel: (053) 28226 Anthony Kaye
Much of the produce of the Inisglass Trust makes its way up to Dublin for the fortnightly Dublin Food Co-Op, whilst the Inisglass flour is widely available in good wholefood shops throughout the country. One good reason to make the trip to Wexford, however, is the fact that they have an excellent nursery of fruit trees for sale, so those with the patience to begin planting for the next generation should head for Crossabeg.

The Dublin Food Co-Op holds its market every second Saturday. See Dublin chapter for more details.

ENNISCORTHY

FARMHOUSE CHEESE
CARRIGBYRNE FARMHOUSE CHEESE
Adamstown, Enniscorthy Tel: (054) 40560 Paddy Berridge
Paddy Berridge's cheese is the biggest selling, and probably the most widely available, of the farmhouse cheeses, recognisable instantly by the multi-sided little wallets in which the Saint Killian brie is sold. If you have the patience to allow the cheese to age a little, for,

typically, wholesalers and retailers always sell the cheese when it is still sprightly young, it can mature into something rich and creamy in flavour. So, make a deliberate policy to buy a Saint Killian when it is right at its Sell By Date, then leave it alone in a cool room for a while, then open a bottle of red wine.

CHARCOAL
PHOENIX TIMBER PRODUCTS
Ballinabarna, Enniscorthy Tel: (054) 34005
Natural charcoal without additives from the by-products of sawmills. It not only smells

attractive, it looks genuine, and is a vital ingredient of a successful barbecue.
Available in shops and garden centres

FOULKSMILLS

RESTAURANT & FARMHOUSE ACCOMMODATION

CELLAR RESTAURANT, HORETOWN HOUSE

Foulksmills Tel: (051) 63706 Fax: 63633 Ivor Young

Horetown is a plain old pile of a country house, catholic in its capaciousness, calvinistic in its plainness, and it comes as little surprise to discover that its history interlinks with Cromwell — who granted the townland of Horetown to William Goffe, a puritan — and later on with the Quakers.

The house, then, exudes the power of wealth, but in no way betrays a passion for money, so one's final impression is of somewhere defiantly Victorian, proud of power but ambiguous about riches.

This curious architectural ambience is met, inside, by a sort of Arsenic and Old Lace plainness: Horetown feels like the sort of house a maiden aunt might own, and has just the sort of time-dated accoutrements of unsophisticated plumbing and heating which your aunt might have installed in the 1950s. Downstairs, the Cellar Restaurant has a kick-off-your-shoes, devil-may-care character, which explains why so many people enjoy coming here time and again, and Ivor Young's straightforward, easy-going food is old-fashioned and welcoming.

Open for dinner for non-residents. Closed Jan-Mar and Xmas. Average Price: dinner £££. No credit cards.
From Wexford direction, turn left in Taghmon village (opp. Furlong's), drive for exactly 3.5 miles on the L160 to Horetown House sign.

GOREY

RESTAURANT AND COUNTRY HOUSE

MARLFIELD HOUSE

Gorey Tel: (055) 21124 Mary Bowe

A super-plush country house.

Open 1pm-2pm, 7.30pm-9.30pm Mon-Sun. Closed Dec & Jan. Average Price: lunch £££ dinner ££££. Visa, Access, Amex. 2km from Gorey on the Courtown Road.

RESTAURANT

GOREY CHINESE RESTAURANT

50 Main Street Tel: (055) 22104

The décor leaves a lot to be desired, but the cooking here is greatly more authentic than

most Chinese restaurants.
Open 12.30pm-midnight Mon-Sun. Closed Xmas. Average Price: lunch £££ dinner £££. Recommended for Vegetarians. On the main street in Gorey.

SHOP
THE HONEY POT
4 Main Street, Gorey Tel: (055) 20111
Bread from Arklow, good coffee and crafts.
Open 9am-6pm Mon-Sun

TACUMSHANE

B&B WITH FULL BOARD
FURZIESTOWN HOUSE
Tacumshane Tel: (053) 31376 Yvonne Pim
It is the inherent thoughtfulness she brings to everything that makes Yvonne Pim's house so special. Furziestown is little more than a nice farmhouse way down here in the heel of the country, but Mrs Pim's care and concern for her guests has elevated the house into one of the most highly regarded places to stay in the country. You feel welcome. Mrs Pim spoils you. You love it.

And you will love the food: one dinner began with Scandinavian fish mousse, then organic roast lamb with garden herbs, served with steamed scarlet runner beans, broad beans in a

light bechamel sauce and roast potatoes, with rosemary and crab apple jelly and fresh mint sauce to garnish, before a bombe of summer berries. Mrs Pim also does menus for vegetarians — mushroom croustades on a bed of mixed greens, chick peas in spiced lentil and coconut sauce with mixed rice, then a carrageen moss mousse — and for vegans — carrot and apple salad, then sesame tofu with stir-fried vegetables and mixed rice with courgettes and cashews. One friend described Furziestown to us as 'perfect', and that may just be right.

Open for dinner for residents only. Closed end Nov-Feb. Average Price: dinner £££ B&B £££. No Credit Cards. Recommended for Vegetarians. Signposted from Tacumshane (telephone for detailed directions).

WEXFORD TOWN

RESTAURANT
THE GRANARY
Westgate Tel: (053) 23935 Paddy and Mary Hatton
The Granary is an enthusiastic place, darkly lit, and with the tables divided up into quiet, private spaces. The cooking is familiar and hits many good points, but could benefit from being a little more relaxed.

Open 6pm-10pm Mon-Sat (open on Sun during the Opera Festival). Closed Xmas. Average Price: dinner £££. Visa, Access, Amex, Diners.

SHOPS

DELICATESSEN AND CAFÉ
LA CUISINE DELICATESSEN
80 North Main Street Tel: (053) 24986 Philip & Brigid Doyle
The shop is the thing here, for alongside some decent bottles of wine there are farmhouse cheeses and cooked meats. The café at the back relies as much on the microwave as many other Wexford eateries, so seeking something simple makes for the best eating.

Open 9am-5.45pm Mon-Wed & Sat, 9am-6pm Thur & Fri (coffee shop closes at 5.30pm)

WHOLEFOOD SHOP AND BUTCHER
GREENACRES
56 North Main Street Tel: (053) 22975 James G. O'Connor
A copious array of vegetables and a small counter selling meat from the Pure Meat Company of Wexford.

Open 9am-6pm Mon-Sat

WHOLEFOOD SHOP
HUMBLE NATURAL FOODS
Walker's Mall, North Main Street Tel: (053) 24624 Heike Weiehagen
Heike's shop has all the potions and lotions and pulses of wholefoodery, but you can also find organic vegetables, real breads and, occasionally, very good honeys.

Open 9.15am-6pm Mon-Sat

FISHMONGER
JAMES MEYLER
The Bull Ring Tel: (053) 22339/41990 James Meyler
A nifty fish counter, and the staff are hospitable and informed.
Open 9am-6pm Mon-Fri, 9am-5pm Sat

FISH
ATLANTIS
Redmond Road Tel: (053) 23309 Mr Doyle
Redmond Road is near the Wexford quays, and from this caravan, the Doyles sell the fish that they catch themselves in their three trawlers. This, and the fact that theirs is the fish used by many of the better local chefs, is something of a guarantee of freshness.
Open 9.30am-5.30pm Mon-Wed, 9.30am-5pm Thur-Sat

HOTEL
FERRYCARRIG HOTEL
Ferrycarrig, Wexford Tel: (053) 22999
During the Opera Festival, the Ferrycarrig is the place to go when you're in your fab evening gear. At other times of the year the bar enjoys good views and a sunny location.
Bar open 10am-11pm Mon-Sat, noon-11pm Sun

COUNTRY HOUSE
NEWBAY HOUSE
Wexford Tel: (053) 42779 Fax: 46318 Paul & Mientje Drumm
What kind of place is Newbay? It is the kind of place where, after a splendid breakfast, you might decide that the best thing to do to get the day rolling would be to, well, just go right back to bed. And so you do, with a clear conscience and, with the lightsome light of Wexford filtering through the curtains when you wake up a couple of hours later, you might decide that this was one of your most inspired decisions. That's the kind of place Newbay is, one of the most relaxing and convivial of the country houses. Partly this comes from Min Drumm's social skills and the expert ease with which she sets everyone into the pace of the house as they sip sherries as a prelude to dinner. Partly, its the unpretentious design of the house, the light sense of space thanks to the stripped pine furniture — a speciality of Paul Drumm's. But it is also the excellent cooking: well judged, both interesting and satisfying, a cross between professional assurance and an amateurish charm. On a good night,

with the big table ringed by happy diners gaustering away one to the other and the food and wine flowing seamlessly, it is perfectly charming.

Open for dinner for guests (book by 12.30pm). Closed Nov-Apr. Average Price: dinner £££, B&B £££££. Visa, Access. Newbay House is signposted from the N25 which curls around Wexford town.

ALSO OF INTEREST

TALBOT HOTEL, Trinity Street Tel: (053) 22566 Famous locally for the tripe and onions, served as part of their popular bar lunch.

Bar menu available 12.30pm-3pm, 6.30pm-8.45pm Mon-Sat

LOBSTER POT BAR Ballyfane, Carne Tel: (053) 31110 Seafood lunches are served in the bar, including crab claws in either garlic or cheese sauce, and various seafood salads.

Bar menu served all day and into the evening from noon to about 10pm (no food between 5pm-6pm).

ROSSLARE

KELLY'S STRAND HOTEL

Rosslare Tel: (053) 32114 Fax: 32222 The Kelly family

The mere idea, the very thought, of criticising Kelly's is something which the many apostles of this ageless place would consider on a par with suggesting that Mother Theresa is in cahoots with the Mob.

For its devotees, this venerable hotel is above and beyond criticism, a place so deeply sunk in their affections that they cannot do anything other than advocate its corn-fed cosiness, its disarming lack of pretension, its happy family conviviality.

And it is easy to see why they like it. Kelly's has a Seaside Spa air, whether you are there in

the middle of balmy August or blustery March. Its multifarious methods to help you relax — everything from Crazy Golf to Sing-Alongs, from Beauty Bouquets to Swedish Back Massage — attract the city-weary, folk who want to trip-out into private time, who want to let the cares of the world slide off them in the course of an Aromatherapy session or a meaningful encounter with a third gin and tonic before dinner. Snug in the midst of the busy and beautiful dining room at 8.30 in the evening, they will want this procession of pleasure to go on forever and ever, or at least for another couple of days.

But the enjoyment which Kelly's offers could be improved upon. While the price of dinner is very keen, and they do serve expensive foods such as foie gras and lobster on the set menu and serve them to huge numbers of diners, the foie gras is after-dinner-mint thin and, though the lobster is splendid, its splendour reveals that some of the other ingredients could benefit from greater quality control. The rooms, meanwhile, are anonymous and one suspects that the residents in Kelly's don't spend a lot of time in them, such are the demands on their time from the countless diversions.

But where Kelly's should make a conscious policy change relates to the fact that if one is spending a night here before catching the Rosslare ferry, the dining room does not open for breakfast until 8.30 am. You, by this time, will probably already be aboard the boat, probably dissatisfied with a 'Continental' breakfast that could not muster a good cup of coffee. It would be so easy to change this — a single cook starting at 7.30 am would do the job — and it would bring this deficit into line with the other fine points of the hotel: the brilliant staff, the holiday atmosphere, the superb, beautifully constructed wine list which features many wines imported from France by the hotel itself and which is, delightfully, one of the most interesting and clamorously quaffable in the entire country.

Restaurant Open 7.30pm-9pm Mon-Sun. Closed early Dec-end Feb. Average Price: lunch ££ dinner £££. Visa, Access, Amex. Signposted from the Wexford/Rosslare road.

COUNTY WICKLOW

Wicklow IS A DANDYISH KIND OF PLACE. Inland, in the autumn, the hedges throw out berries that are Restoration red in colour, sharp as lipstick, done up for a Congreve comedy.

In summer, up among the hills, the cool yellows and acrid purples of the flowers are foppish and playful, easy to admire but difficult to take seriously. The hills tumble down to the lakes as if arranged ready for inexpert landscape painters to come and capture some aspect of Arcadia.

You might walk amidst an early morning mist and see lazy grouse take into the air with fat indecisive flaps of their wings, or you might stroll along the seafront of a spectacularly silly resort such as Bray with its arcades and ices and toasting flesh and wonder why everything here seems so contentedly clichéd.

The leafy roads, the middle-class markets, the out-of-town ambience, the manicured gardens, the kiss-me-quick frivolity, all of these are found in Wicklow and it contributes to a feeling that the County is less elemental than anywhere else in Ireland, that Wicklow sets out to be an idealised place, somewhere where nature is tempered, tamed.

This is partly true, and partly not true. Great estates landscaped Wicklow here and there, but up in the hills nothing can shake the resolution of wayward heather and sulphurous bog. Even the towns and villages themselves seem slightly disassembled, loose at the edges, fringed with a nervous energy. Wicklow is not polite and genteel, as it can seem at many moments. It is as typically voracious as anywhere else in Ireland, with just a few smooth surfaces offered here and there as a diversion.

ARKLOW

BAKERY
THE STONE OVEN BAKERY
65 Lower Main Street Tel: (0402) 39418 Egon Friedrich

'The secret of good bread is heat, and steam', says Egon Friedrich, hunched down, peering deep into the innards of the eight-ton baker's oven he personally disassembled, transported from Hanover, and then re-assembled in The Stone Oven in Arklow.

If only it were that simple. The secret of the fine breads which Mr Friedrich produces, in the introverted little town of Arklow, lies not just in the correct, quick application of thunderous heat to make the bread rise, followed by the play of steam in order to achieve a correct crust. It lies also in the happy co-mingling of those traditional skills — flour-milling, hand-kneading, natural proving, wild yeast sourdough starters — which announce a style of bread diametrically opposed to the spongy, supermarket gunge made by the Chorleywood process.

The Stone Oven Bakery is a veritable balm. The grey bread loaves — which are not grey, of course — sit in little Moses baskets, quietly proving. There are the joyful party rings, large spirals of white bread dotted with seeds that contribute a warm oiliness to the palate as you crunch through. In the window of the shop, cheerfully hanging by coloured ribbons, are crunchy pretzels, and buying some bread here means that one can enjoy the pain of feeling famished, as the odour of sausage rolls or apple strudel has your nose puckering the air like a Bisto kid.

But if Mr Friedrich works according to the traditional rules of bread making, he is not above some cheeky improvisations. Immediately after he has milled wheat, grown by Desmond Thorpe in County Wexford, Mr Friedrich will 'pour warm flour into the mix, against all the rules. But with the warmth of the milling process in the mixture, you use that heat, and it works. A lot of bakers say you have to leave the flour or you disturb the gluten. But it's done a lot of times now on the continent, where bakeries run their mills to produce this nutty, crunchy taste'.

A modest, amusing man, his business philosophy is simple: 'You make sure nothing goes on the counter which isn't fit for sale. We all make mistakes, but so long as you're not trying to sell them, and trying to take someone else's money for it, you're okay', and as straightforward as his modesty: 'I think the oven is the secret', he says. 'It forgave me all my mistakes, it always baked the stuff good and it's encouraging to bake with something like that. You put something in and it works. At my farewell party in Germany I baked for my friends in my gas oven and they said, "Ah, you're off to Ireland to be a baker, great", and then this thing came out, all flat, kaput! They said, "You'll be back in a month". With this thing, it works'. Mr Friedrich has not gone back.

Open 9.30am-6pm Mon-Sat, closed half day Wed

SMOKED TROUT
I.D.A.S. SMOKED TROUT
Woodenbridge, Arklow, Tel: (0402) 35233
I.D.A.S. Smoked Trout comes filleted and vac packed. The flavour is subtle and the fish have good texture. Good for salads.
Available from all branches of Superquinn.

AVOCA

CRAFT SHOP & TEA ROOM
AVOCA HANDWEAVERS
Avoca Tel: (0402) 35105 (Also at Kilmacanogue)
A useful and enjoyable stop, not just to peruse the desirable crafts, but also for revitalising cups of tea and cake. There is another branch in Wicklow, just off the road at Kilmacanogue Tel: (01) 286 7466
Open: Avoca 9.30am-5.30pm Mon-Sun; Kilmacanogue 9am-5pm Mon-Fri, 9.30am-5pm Sat & Sun

BRAY

GREEK CYPRIOT RESTAURANT
THE TREE OF IDLENESS
Sea Front Tel: (01) 286 3498 Susan Courtellas
Few other chef/patrons in Ireland were so intimately associated with their restaurants as was Akis Courtellas with his much-beloved Tree Of Idleness. His too-early death robbed the country of a major cooking talent, for Courtellas had begun in recent years to refine

BIO-DYNAMIC FARMING

PENNY AND UDO LANGE farm thirty-six acres in County Wicklow according to the principles of Bio-Dynamic farming, a code of practise first suggested in a short series of lectures in 1924 by the educationalist Rudolf Steiner. Some of the steps they take in their farming practices can seem arcane, even obscure-for-the-sake-of-it, but there is a delightful, delicious conclusion to the hard work they so assiduously undertake. Their produce, quite simply, is stunning: full of flavour, full of heart, full of real scents and mineral elements, full of simple goodness, a term so easily forgotten — so deliberately sidelined — in today's boisterous food world. We have seen people look at Penny Lange's produce with nothing less than amazed stupefaction as she sets up her stall in the fortnightly Dublin Food Co-Op. Strong-veined fennel with long, wavy fronds that reek of caramelly scents. Glistening, rubied broccoli and tightly nuggeted cauliflower. Celery that actually has an odour, a clean, vibrant smell. Everything — from salad leaves to cut herbs to root vegetables — has such vigour, such ruddy health. And this is before you talk about the carrots, chunky, crunchy dangles of pure health, which have achieved an almost legendary reputation.

Udo Lange describes the principles of bio-dyn as designed to promote the idea of each farm as an 'individuality': 'We look at farming as an organism and what we strive for is towards a healthy, complete organism', he says. 'We have animals producing the manure so we don't buy manure. We look at the cow as a very important animal, the cow gives something back through her digestion. She helps to fertilise the ground and this is very important to the fertility of the farm. Our aim is to produce all the feed on our farm, and in growing we try to produce the seeds. We call each farm an individuality'. And, he adds, 'I think a plant which is raised in a particular place is more able to give what it is supposed to give when it is raised, planted and then harvested all in the same place'.

The Langes lived abroad for some years and on returning to Ireland they were struck by the fact that the country 'still felt untouched' and thus a perfect environment in which to farm bio-dynamically. 'Steiner tried to make people aware of the cosmic forces working on the soil', says Mrs Lange. 'He tried to make us look at the soil in a new way, to bring about a creative way of looking at what is around us, to assess it from a less materialistic point of view and from more of a living point of view'. Mr Lange adds: 'The impulse from Steiner is a way to bring us back to the natural processes, the life processes, which at this stage we have totally lost'. Their foods, grown in harmony and rhythm with the land, seem imbued with these simple processes, seem suffused with the very life force.

PENNY & UDO LANGE ★
Ballinroan House, Kiltegan, Co Wicklow Tel: (0506) 73278
The Langes' vegetables are sold in the fortnightly Dublin Food Co-Op on Pearse St, in What On Earth in Harold's Cross and in certain branches of Superquinn and Quinnsworth.

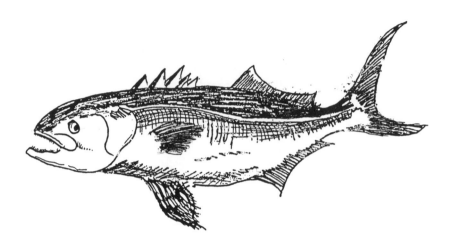

and re-define the nature of Greek-Cypriot cooking, a cuisine held in low regard for the most part but which, Courtellas showed, could be raised to heights of sublime and resonant achievement when in his hands.

Susan Courtellas has continued to run the 'Tree and, assisted by the devoted staff who ran the show when Akis was alive, she has made the transition smoothly.

The menu is still composed of dishes which Akis Courtellas either' created or upon which he stamped his interpretation — spinach ravioli filled with chicken mousse and wild mushrooms with a carrot sauce, grilled ewe's milk cheese with a tahini sauce, three fillets of beef, lamb and veal in a mustard sauce, smoked lamb with a blackcurrant and wine sauce, whilst the great standards of the Eastern Mediterranean — Imam Bayildi, moussaka, saddle of lamb with feta cheese and olives — are given an ever-new interpretation. The great dessert trolley, an Archimboldesque explosion of exotic fruits with accompanying ices and desserts, is unique, the wine list deeply serious and rewarding.

Open 7.30pm-11pm Tues-Sun ('till 10pm Sun). Closed Xmas and 2 weeks in Aug/Sept. Average Price: dinner ££££. Visa, Access. The Tree Of Idleness overlooks the seafront in Bray

SHOP
THE NUT KEG

The Boulevard, Quinnsboro Road Tel: (01) 286 1793

Wholefood shop which also has lots of good organic vegetables during the summer season.

Open 9am-6pm Mon-Sat ('till 7pm Fri)

DUNLAVIN

COUNTRY HOUSE
RATHSALLAGH HOUSE
Dunlavin Tel: (045) 53112 Fax: 53343 Joe and Kay O'Flynn

'Dear Mr & Mrs McKenna, My husband and I spent five glorious days last week at the Rathsallagh House and we look forward to returning every year, if possible'. So began a letter from the 'States which, after this enthusiastic encomium, went on to roundly denounce us for failing to express ourselves in the language of devotional delight which the adherents of Rathsallagh use to describe their favourite place. And my goodness but they are effusive and devoted to this lovely house, and to the fine dinners and breakfasts which Joe and Kay O'Flynn prepare. Mention to them that you feel prices in Rathsallagh are steep and they will look at you with incredulity, as if to say: What price perfection?

The secret of Rathsallagh is, surely, that it feels like an enclave, a cosy enclave of civilisation, set apart from the barbarous world. It is this feeling that so captivates people, the impression that everything elsewhere has ceased to exist, and this bubble of wooded grounds, misty mornings, fireside breakfasts, the coven of the courtyard rooms and the roisterous dinners is a magical mysteryland, all on its own. A masterly illusion, when you consider that Dublin City is scarcely up the road, but a narcotic one.

Restaurant Open 7.30pm-8.30pm Mon-Sun. Closed Xmas. Average Price: dinner ££££ B&B £££££. Visa, Access, Amex. Signposted from Dunlavin Village.

ENNISKERRY

RESTAURANT
CURTLESTOWN HOUSE
Enniskerry Tel: (01) 282 5083 Colin & Theresa Pielow

Curtlestown feels old-fashioned, in the nicest possible way. Deep colour walls and warm fires add up to a slightly convoluted sense of grandeur and together conspire to make you feel good, make you feel welcome, as the ceremony of dinner gets under way.

And ceremony is the word. Soups come in tureens for tables to help themselves. Every dish is attractive as well as generous, and even the napkins have little bow-tie holders. Elsewhere this might well be killingly twee. In Curtlestown it is just another aspect of a very innocent, very true motivation.

This motivation works right through the ceremony of dinner, for smoked salmon and terrines are flavourful, lamb is fine and sweet, game is achingly rich, and vegetables are veritably jam-packed with flavour. Playful nursery puddings, and the baleful state of relaxation you have achieved as dessert beckons may encourage you to dip into a bottle of something luscious, golden and sweet, and the wine list has enough good choices to satisfy ardent quaffers. The food, overall, is restrained and a little shy, but in the context of an evening in Curtlestown, which is most definitely not restrained and shy and can warm up to house party temperatures pretty quickly, it winds up being exactly what you felt like. Good house party food, indeed.

Open 8pm-10pm Tue-Sun, 12.30pm-2.30pm Sun. Closed Xmas. Average Price: dinner £££. Visa, Access. Leave Enniskerry on the Glencree Road, and the restaurant is on the left.

GREYSTONES

RESTAURANT
THE HUNGRY MONK

Greystones Tel: (01) 287 5759 Pat & Sylvia McKeown

Long-established restaurant which places a special emphasis on Sunday lunch. Renowned wine list.

Open 7pm-11pm Tues-Sat, 12.30pm-3pm Sun. Major cards. ££

WICKLOW AND SOUTH DUBLIN COUNTRY MARKETS

NONE OF the other Country Markets held throughout Ireland seem to buzz with the same sense of possessive pride as those of Wicklow and south County Dublin. On Saturday mornings, in modest church halls and simple community centres, gangs of ladies, and the occasional gentleman, assemble, tense with expectation, wicker baskets readied, granny elbows sharpened, to fight their way through yet another bruising encounter with their neighbours and friends. Their quarry is the spanking fresh salad leaves and soil-laden spuds, still-warm breads and cakes, jars of jam, conserves and chutneys, armfuls of flowers and occasional niceties like free-range chickens or farm-made buttermilk, which these splendid organisations assemble for the committed and the curious. In Roundwood, the atmosphere is that of a polite jamboree, in Kilcoole it is cooler, a little more sedate, in Kilternan it is little other than warfare, a thunderous, adrenalinated struggle to grab as much as you can in the shortest possible time.

They are exhilarating adventures into the soul of a community, surprising glimpses of the just-under-the-surface social tensions which make life worth living. Forget the gentility with which this part of the eastern seaboard is traditionally associated: the Country Markets are for those who relish the shout and the shove and the fight of real life, the physical and spiritual charge of real shopping.

Camaraderie between neighbours is set aside, family is enlisted in the dedicated, concentrated pursuit of fresh, hand-made foods, and may the devil take the hindmost.

NORTH WICKLOW COUNTRY MARKET
St Patrick's Hall , Kilcoole
(10.30am-11.30am Sat).

ROUNDWOOD SUNDAY MARKET
Parish Hall
(Mar to Dec, 3pm-5pm Sun).

KILTERNAN COUNTRY MARKET
Golden Ball, Kilternan, Co Dublin
(10.30am-noon Sat)

WHOLEFOOD SHOP
NATURE'S GOLD
Killincarrig Road Tel: (01) 2876301 Brod Kearon
Locally grown organic vegetables and a thoughtfully serene atmosphere make Brod
Kearon's shop always a pleasure to visit.

KILMACANOGUE

GOAT'S AND COW'S MILK YOGURT
COPSEWOOD YOGURT
Kilmacanogue Tel: (01) 286 2081 Edward Drew
Copsewood is perhaps the longest-established yogurt in the country, and one of the best.
Both cow's and goat's milk varieties are made, and they are widely available in both
Wicklow and Dublin.

KILPEDDER

ORGANIC FARMER
ORGANIC LIFE ➡
Tinna Park House Tel: (01) 2819726 Marc Michel
Marc Michel compares to the standard organic farmer as Yves Montand compares to
Bing Crosby. His pony mane of blond hair could get him a gig with any garage band in
San Francisco. His cowboy boots could get him a bit part in 'Hud' and, whilst his torn
jeans signify age and hard work, they have the sorts of holes and patches which suggest
the slashes of the fashion pages. He is a modern vision of the Organic Grower as Rock 'n'
Roller, the Rolling Stone of the compost crowd.
If Michel's appearance is a surprise, and a surprise given the hours of hard work he puts
in on his forty acres — five-forty-five is the summoning hour for a man who says he has
been growing vegetables 'all my life' — then his astuteness and assurance when it comes
to marketing and selling his produce is no less of a surprise. The Organic movement is
dotted here and there with folks who reckon that making a living is slightly distasteful and
who think that improving the availability and appearance of organic foods is tantamount
to selling out.
Michel, on the other hand, markets his superb produce with a marketing-man's wizardry,
zaps it out under the banner 'Organic Life' in bright big boxes, in smart packs with his
signature clearly visible. Not only is the produce superb, packed tight with the elegant and
understated flavours which the Wicklow air and the Wicklow climate gift to his graft, but
they look cool, hip. You want these chunky little tomatoes with their soft red skins, those
flouncy lollo rossos, the rainbow-bright peppers in red and yellow, the noble Home
Guards with their dusting of soil, and you want them not just because they are full of
goodness and will do you good, but also because they are hip, fashionable. The spud as
fashion accessory. Organic vegetables as part of your World of Interiors.
The backbone of Michel's operation, just off the main road as it scoots past the drowsy
village of Kilpedder, is a sextet of fifty-metre tunnels, packed with tomato plants slowly

succouring to perfection, full of broad beans hanging droopily, low-lying aubergines, hidden sweet peppers. 'It's the tomatoes which require the most care' he says, for each plant must be trained to climb as it grows, continually wrapped around hanging cord like a tightrope walker clambering up to the high wire. Side shoots must be continually

cleaned away and each plant shaken from time to time to assist pollination.

The result of this care is tomatoes which are stuffed with that play of sweet flesh and sharp pips which can make them so delicious. Pluck an Ailsa Craig from the vine and munch it and it has that nettle greenness and unpredictable volubility which modern strains of tomatoes have abandoned. 'The Ailsa Craig has the best flavour, and is one of very few old strains still grown', says Mr Michel, who supplements them with gardeners' delights,

beef tomatoes and a modern hybrid imported from Holland.

One tunnel is reserved for produce grown especially for Lock's Restaurant in Dublin, and indeed it is the hope of restaurateur Clare Douglas that soon her restaurant will use nothing but produce from Michel's tunnel. This conjures up a particularly lovely relationship between restaurateur and grower, the sort of thing which Alice Waters of Chez Panise in San Francisco has made such a feature of over the last twenty years. Other Dublin restaurant foragers should begin their search for fine foods here.

Organic Life produce is widely available in Supermarkets and Healthfood Shops in Dublin and Wicklow.

LARAGH

RESTAURANT & B&B
MITCHELL'S SCHOOLHOUSE
Laragh Tel: (0404) 45302 Margaret and Jerry Mitchell
The food they cook and serve in the cosy little dining room of Mitchell's is dinner party tasty and Irish generous: a ramekin of chicken liver pâté, a gratin of crab and salmon, then maybe silverside of spiced beef, or pork with redcurrants, with plenty of good vegetables. The food is good value, and the comfortable rooms make for inexpensive and

easy-going lodging at the end of a day exploring, or at the end of a meal socialising. Do note that, unusually for Ireland, children are not permitted in the restaurant.

Open 12.30pm-2pm, 7.30pm-9.30pm Mon-Sat, 1pm-2.30pm Sun. Closed Xmas. Average Price: lunch ££ dinner £££ B&B £££. Visa, Access, Amex. Driving into Laragh from Roundwood, bear right and the restaurant is on the right.

RATHNEW

HOTEL
HUNTER'S HOTEL

Rathnew Tel: (0404) 40106 Fax: (0404) 40338 Gelletlie Family
On a sunny summer Sunday afternoon tea taken in the primly concocted gardens of Hunter's Hotel is a nostalgic treat.

Open all year. Tea served between 4pm-5.45pm Average Price: tea £

RESTAURANT & COUNTRY HOUSE
TINAKILLY HOUSE HOTEL

Rathnew Tel: (0404) 69274 Fax: 67806 William & Bee Power
They are great sports, William and Bee Power. You might think that the slog — the hard slog — of running a well-run country house throughout the year might allow them, come Christmas time, to pile their feet up and pour themselves, rather than someone else, a drink.

Not a bit of it. Christmas at Tinakilly is bright with the same sort of merriment the Powers bring to their year-round task and, perhaps appropriately in this big old Victorian pile of a house, the theme they adopt is Dickensian: pots of punch, a plenitude of goose and turkey and plum pud, ponies and traps and smoochy mistletoe and, doubtless, someone offering Tiny Tim's salutation: 'God bless us everyone!'.

For the rest of the year, the Powers-that-be allow this thoughtfulness to infiltrate the house wholesale: good menus and a kitchen which is happy to prepare dishes plainly, a good wine list with plenty of half-bottles and lots of clarets, plenty of peace and quiet and comfort if you want it in both the house and the acres of gardens. 'Ambience and service are first class', a gentleman wrote to us once, just one voice in a consistent chorus.

Open all year, 12.30pm-2pm, 7.30pm-9.30pm Mon-Sun. Open for Xmas. Average Price: lunch ££-£££ dinner ££££ B&B £££££. Visa, Access, Amex. Signposted from the Dublin/Wicklow Road.

ROUNDWOOD

RESTAURANT
THE ROUNDWOOD INN

Roundwood Tel: (01) 281 8107 Jurgen & Aine Schwalm
If you feel like heading out of the city to aimlessly drive around County Wicklow on a Saturday morning, do time things in order to allow yourself to arrive in Roundwood at lunchtime, for the food in The Roundwood Inn is solid, sustaining and just right for weekend lunchtimes. They make gulyas in the Irish fashion, can concoct a good squid

salad, and the atmosphere is easygoing, enjoyable.

Open 1pm-2.30pm, 7.30pm-9.30pm Tue-Sat, 1pm-2.30pm Sun. Bar food served all day. Closed Xmas.
Average Price: lunch ££ dinner £££. Visa, Access. Right in the middle of the village of Roundwood.

WICKLOW

SAUSAGE MAKERS
BOSWELL'S SAUSAGES
The Mall, Main Street Tel: (0404) 69462 Leonard Boswell & Sean Kelly
When Sean Kelly and Leonard Boswell talk about sausages they use words like 'marketing plan', 'competitive pricing', 'growth potential' and 'export range'. When you buy their sausages you are served by young people in natty uniforms, sporting baseball caps. The Boswell sausages were launched with the help of Introductory Press Releases and brochures, fliers and copylines ('Positive Eating, Positive Living'). The story of Boswell's is one of those Big Ideas that you read about in colour supplements.

Neither Sean Kelly nor Leonard Boswell have ever served their time behind a butcher's block. Sean was a hotel executive and Leonard a restaurateur and, thanks to their Big Idea, they now run what they hope will become a chain of shops selling sausages.

There are many flavours, some classic, some zany. The meats for the sausages — pork, lamb, beef, venison — are all carefully sourced and each banger comes with the guarantee of no artificial or synthetic ingredients, no soya substitutes and no mechanically recovered meat.

The sausages are meaty, and while being a little short on finesse they deliver a good chunky punch and are good for barbecuing and grilling.

You can also buy their home made breads, made in the day-glo flavours of California: tomato and onion, celery and Edam, fennel and tarragon, as well as olive oils and home-made relishes and chutneys.

Open 9am-6.30pm Mon-Sat. Branches also open in Blackrock, at 11 Sydney Terrace Tel: (01) 288 2237
(Open 9am-7pm Mon-Sat) and Malahide, County Dublin.

RESTAURANT & COUNTRY HOUSE
THE OLD RECTORY
Wicklow Tel: (0404) 67048 Fax: 69181 Paul & Linda Saunders
If Linda Saunders did not exist, then the citizens of the County of Wicklow would have had to invent her.

A vital and essential asset to the town and the county, her character seems to sum up this delightful place — quietly complex, slightly reserved, but pretty bloody determined behind it all — and her effusive and intricate cooking is a perfect reflection of the strengths and delights of Wicklow.

She uses fine organic ingredients, grown locally, and this explains firstly why her food always has a vibrancy and freshness about it: it seems to reflect and express the sunshiney, youthful nature of the Wicklow hills.

To this, she brings a degree of invention and expressiveness — and an intuitive feeling for the architecture of taste — which few other country house cooks can match. Indeed, this sense of complex but compatible flavouring in her food is reminiscent of the structure of a perfume, with alluring scents and mellifluous taste structures to be enjoyed both in main dishes and in their compatriot sauces: a warm terrine of salmon and sea trout will swim along with a green herb sauce, parsnips will pair off with red beans for a soup, whilst the elegant ruddiness of a carrot and cucumber tart will have the warm spice of marjoram underpinning it.

But there is more to Linda Saunders' skill than just the ability to conjure intricate tastes with skill. She also, bravely, can construct entire dinner menus to arrive at compatibility and complexity and, to celebrate the Wicklow Flower Festival, cooks a dauntingly daring ten course Floral Dinner: kale flower purses in filo; gazpacho ropjo with iced borrage blossoms; roast quail stuffed with apple, pine nut and sage flowers, the joyful jamboree of tastes is delightfully endless.

The extension of the dining room has gifted the Old Rectory with greater light, perfect for a cuisine of such delicacy, and the wine list is terrifically thoughtful, with an unusual accent of good Spanish wines. Rooms in the house are cosy comfy, and whilst the Rectory is a good base for exploring Wicklow, you will likely find that you will want to eat nowhere else but here.

Open 8pm Sun-Thurs, 7.30pm-9pm Fri-Sat. Closed Nov-Mar. Average Price: dinner ££££ B&B £££££. Visa, Access, Amex. Recommended for vegetarians. On the left hand side of the road as you drive into Wicklow town heading south.

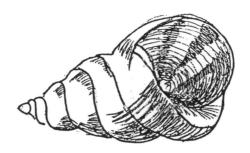

MUNSTER

COUNTY CLARE

THE BURREN

N O MATTER FROM WHICH DIRECTION you approach it, a first glimpse of the Burren always provokes the same words of description: Barren. Lunar. A Place Apart. Travelling south, turning away from Galway and east into Clare, and the shaley, sullen hills that nestle Corcomroe Abbey look like massive, dormant armadillos, ancient hibernating monsters who might, at any second, awaken.

Travelling north, away from the silly seaside towns of Lisdoonvarna and Doolin and, looking over towards the frothy reaches of the hill of Mullaghmore, one appears to see nothing but naked rock. Crushed, impacted, scattered limestone is everywhere but here, on this lovely lonely hill, the rock is so artfully confected that it might have been cornetted from a celestial ice-cream machine. Look east then, from the Aran Islands over towards the coast of Clare, and the stern fall of the Cliffs of Moher is congratulated in the hinterland by the tumble of unending rock just north of the Cliffs. Burren, you remember, is a word derived from the Irish term boireann: a rocky place.

But there is another reality to this most forbidding of places. Corcomroe, a Cistercian abbey which dates from the 13th century, is dedicated to Sancta Maria de Petra Fertilis: Our Lady of the Fertile Rocks. The columns of the Abbey, some of them, have tender carvings of flowers to decorate their capitals, little plaits set in stone, the earliest botanical carvings in western Europe. Outside, on the hills, one finds the natural echo of this man-made gesture. For here, amidst the rock, and all around the rock, can be found a uniquely vibrant world of flora and fauna, all of it thriving within the hospitality of the fertile rock.

Endless geological seizures and shifts throughout the millenia have given us the surface of the Burren, a surface geologists refer to as karst. In certain lights the karst will appear darkly lilac in colour, in other lights it will revert to gun metal grey. Crouch down close to the surface in order to look across it and it can appear as a huge vellum manuscript, wrinkled, rolled, speaking of its age and the hands that fashioned it. Even when you are scrambling over the top of it and the grave-tomb clank of the stones rings out below your boots, it seems unambiguous. Not just deathless, but deathly.

But peer down into the gullies over which you have to step so carefully and, there, you see a greedily tentacled hart's tongue fern, its leaves hungrily clinging and clawing to the sides of the rock. Beside it, some bracken will have peered above the stone and left its fronds resting on the rock, gold against grey. Here is the fertile rock to which Corcomroe Abbey is dedicated and this rock is truly fertile.

To walk a country mile through the Burren takes a long time. The richnesses encountered simply by walking the roads and searching the hedgerows helps one to realise, quite quickly, that each road here is not just a line going from A to B — a means to take the traveller from one place to another — but is a place in and of itself.

Each track, littered with flora, becomes a modest expedition of hunting and gathering. Amble around the ring of roads at the base of Mullaghmore, perhaps in the early autumn, and the hazel scrub will be shielding its slowly-budding nuts. There are sloes to be searched for, and juniper to hunt down. The berries on blackberry branches are thick and fat, ripe for jelly-making, a dark counterpoint to the dangly lanterns of fuschia.

Botanically, the true glories of the Burren are the elusive and elitist orchids — the fly and bee orchids, the early purple orchid, any of the two dozen or so varieties which can be found here — and, of course, the gentle Spring gentian. Between April and June, the perfect blue blueness of the gentian is profuse; it is plentiful on the limestone, and found right down at sea level. In 1880 the botanist T.H. Corry evoked the fragile intensity of the flower perfectly when he wrote:

> Blue—blue— as if the sky let fall
> a flower from its own caerulean wall.

This Spring gentian, nowadays both symbol and shorthand for the entire Burren area, typifies the atypicality of the Burren. 'Plants normally found in regions as far apart as the Arctic and the Mediterranean occur together in the Burren', writes the naturalist Gordon D'Arcy. 'Some which have a distinctly Atlantic distribution grow beside others which are normally associated with Alpine meadows. To complicate matters further, plants which would normally be thought of as upland or montane species occur almost at sea level and alongside coastal plants. Moreover, plants which are normally found in woodlands grow in the open or in the limestone where there is no sign of tree cover'.

This series of inexplicable occurrences might lead one, fancifully, to speculate that the Burren encourages such eclectic profusion because it offers its own form of shelter to the plants. Once, visiting the cheesemaker Anneliese Bartelink, who lives in a straight-out-of-a-storybook thatched house in the south of the Burren, we had to clamber down and up hills to get to her house and cheeseroom but, inside, the house felt terrifically snug. It seemed imbedded, implanted, in the limestone against which it was built, secure against any ravages.

The towns of the Burren offer this feeling of enclosure also. Ballyvaughan, with its lovely tea rooms and pubs and quiet resort-style atmosphere, is modest and amiable, a place one looks forward to returning to. Sitting in the flustered dimness of a Lisdoonvarna pub, one can easily forgive the town its commercialised gaudiness, and begin to see traces of the once respectable spa town.

This feeling of enclosure can strike you at surprising occasions. Climb up the steep path between the Gleninagh Mountain and Cappanawalla, a few miles west of Ballyvaughan and, as you crest the hill, a glorious silent valley opens out before you. In a mild rain, on a fine day, with just the warm brown hues of the moor and the light skirting of green hazel, you forget that you are almost a thousand feet high, and are aware only of the easeful peace in this forgotten place.

This seizing and shifting of the ages has given us not just the appearance of the Burren, but also the secrets of the Burren. It looks naked, but is profuse with life. It looks invincible but, in fact, it is being eroded and eaten all the time, every second.

'Boireann may be a rocky place, but water, not rock, is the essence of The Burren', writes E. Charles Nelson in his book on the wildflowers of the area. 'Water brought the rock into existence; aeons later frozen and running waters fashioned the karst landscape. Water, moreover, will be The Burren's ultimate destroyer'.

Here is another sign of the hidden Burren, for underneath the stone is an underworld of caves. The play between limestone and water which produces the karst means that the water of the Burren runs underground. There are many turloughs, places where the water,

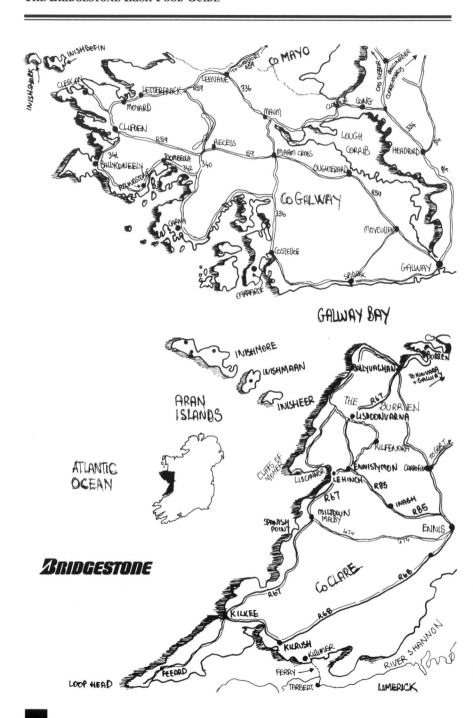

mysteriously, will be one day present and the next day disappeared. Take a tour through the honeycombed tunnels of the Ailwee caves and one sees in the decisive, tireless destruction carved out by the subterranean water, in the powerful falls of the streams as they pummel the soft stone, how all of this magnificent natural intricacy will, one day, be worn to oblivion. Underneath the karst, that grey, schismed pavement with its secret wealth of flora, the stone is being steadily, ceaselessly disembowelled. And this is the ultimate secret of the Burren. It exists as it is because it is balanced, at the end of the land and the edge of the sea, made of rock that was once eroded from above and is now being eroded from below. It is barren in appearance, but uniquely fertile, thanks to its pollution-free location, though the pollutions of the modern age are unlikely to be kept away for ever. From a distance it looks forbidding, a rocky place, a place apart. Up close, it invites the visitor to be tender and cautious and inquisitive towards it. It invites our respect, and it needs our respect.

BALLYVAUGHAN

RESTAURANT
CLAIRE'S RESTAURANT
Ballyvaughan Tel: (065) 77029 Claire Walsh
In Claire's Restaurant, on a good night, you will see more people completely and graciously at their ease than at anytime you can likely remember. This is the sort of place that summons relaxed, boozy laughter whether you are feeling in that vibrant holiday mood or not, whether the place is packed with duos and quartets, or troops of bikers and hikers, or flora and fauna explorers, whether it is Saturday night in August or Wednesday in May. All you have to do is to eat the local foods — mussels feuillete, baked Burren cheese, good, fresh lobster cooked to toothy perfection, sweet Burren lamb which melts in the mouth — allow the glam young women who deal with everything so sveltly to look after you, and get on with raising the roof. Leaving, you will find yourself promising to return soonest, for when in Clare, you want to be in Claire's.
Open 7pm-10pm Mon-Sat (more limited hours off-season). Closed Oct-Xmas, New Year-Easter. Average Price: dinner £££. Visa, Access. In the centre of Ballyvaughan

CAFÉ
AN FEAR GORTA
Pier Road Tel: (065) 77023 Fax: 77127 Catherine O'Donoghue
An Fear Gorta is a splendid and beautiful tea rooms-cum-restaurant with a gorgeous conservatory at the back which is one of the nicest dining places you will find. Sitting here at lunchtime in the summertime, surrounded by members of the judiciary, assorted Cosmo bike-girls with their Amy Tan novels, earth mothers and others of the odds and sods found in Ballyvaughan during the season, all munching on their pristine salads, scoffing their all-too-super cakes and bakes, is a total joy. Catherine O'Donoghue's food is full of taste, full of fun, and the staff are great, especially the elderly Miss Tiggywinkle who waits on table with such beatific kindness that you want to insist she sits down while you get her a cup of tea.
Open 11am-5.30pm Mon-Sun. Closed Sept-May. Average Price: lunch £

SNACK BAR/SHOP
AILWEE CAVE COMPANY
Ballyvaughan Tel: (065) 77036 The Johnson family
A tour of the Ailwee cave complex is thrilling, maybe even slightly chilling as you delve deeper and deeper into this extraordinary series of excavated caves. After you emerge into daylight, the visitors' centre offers not just splendid crafts and books but also an excellent tearooms/café, with hunger-slaughtering food that is carefully made and enjoyable and, a few hundred yards down the hill, Ben Johnson makes Burren Gold, a tender, buttery, Gouda-style cheese, which is for sale alongside other desirable comestibles.
Open 10am-5.30pm Mon-Sun. Average Price: meals and snacks £. Access, Visa, Amex.

FARMHOUSE CHEESE
BARTELINK
Poulcoin, Kilnaboy, Annaliese Bartelink
Annaliese Bartelink has been making cheese in Ireland for about fourteen years, and her cheese has a depth and complexity of flavour that comes from deep experience as a cheesemaker. These gouda-style cheeses can be richly, vibrantly fulsome and loaded with fine, mineral notes. One look at the rocky surroundings all about her Hansel-and-Gretel farmhouse and you can see how the rich flora of the Burren gifts the milk with these floral, erudite tastes, but the surprise is just how creamy the cheese can be, for this is rocky land, and you assume pastures are scarce and poor.
Like all the creamy, buttery Irish gouda-style cheeses, Annaliese's cheeses are at their very best with a good deal of ageing: when over twelve months old — admittedly and unfortunately it is difficult to find it this old — it is truly memorable. But, even if bought young in the locality, it's a cheese that reflects the smells and scents of the Burren, and this is its singularity. Try both the cow's and goat's cheeses with different flavourings, but the expertise of the Bartelinks often leads you back to the original, unflavoured, cheese where the good Burren flavours come through unchallenged.

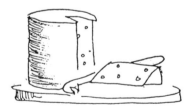

BUNRATTY

RESTAURANT
MACCLOSKEY'S

Bunratty House Mews Tel: (061) 364082 Gerry & Marie MacCloskey

The MacCloskey banquets given every night in this restored basement, are similar to those given in nearby Bunratty Castle in that they are sumptuous and generous. They differ, however, in more than one respect. Instead of using your fingers — medieval style — as they do in the castle, this restaurant offers more tableware and cutlery than we have ever come across before, or since. Secondly, and more importantly, Gerry MacCloskey's cooking is true and genuine and not some theatre of the absurd which you might find just down the road. His food is calm, uncomplicated and very polished, and his work with the great staples of the area such as Burren lamb, west coast mussels, and other local ingredients locate true flavours with unerring accuracy.

Open 7pm-10pm Tues-Sat. Closed Xmas and Jan. Average Price: dinner £££. Visa, Access, Amex, Diners. The restaurant is signposted in Bunratty

B&B WITH RESTAURANT
CAHERBOLANE FARMHOUSE

Corofin Tel: (065) 37638 Brid Cahill

By itself, Caherbolane is a very ordinary farmhouse, just a quartet of unadorned rooms upstairs for guests and a dining room below. But the energy and good cheer of the Cahills is addictive and the cooking by Patricia Cahill in the front room they convert to a restaurant is excellent: spicy chicken wings with a blue cheese dip, a slice of sirloin cooked to pinky perfection, a trio of delicious lamb cutlets, perfect chocolate and Grand Marnier mousse, making for a perfect base from which to scoot around the county.

Open 7.30pm-9.30pm Mon-Sun. Open all year. Average Price: £££. No Credit Cards. Three miles outside Corofin on the road to Gort.

ENNIS

DELICATESSEN & COOKED FOOD SHOP
ABBEY MEATS — THE FOOD EMPORIUM

Abbey Street Tel: (065) 20554 T.J. McGuinness and Brenda Dearing

The Emporium is a truly surprising place, a shop that fuses the elements of a French charcuterie, a trâiteur and a patisserie: good raw meats, good cooked meats, excellent baking and a fine display of deli foods and good vegetables. Very useful for making up a picnic lunch.

Open 9am-6pm Mon-Sat

RESTAURANT AND PUB FOOD
THE CLOISTER

Abbey Street Tel: (065) 29521 Jim Brindley

The Club Sandwich has, somehow, echoes of the jet set age, something which makes this food-all-day bar a particularly appropriate spot if you've just arrived from a transatlantic-hopping plane and are heading north to 'Do' the west coast. The Cloister sells these totems of the modern age, as well as Croque Monsieurs, toasted goat's cheese, local mussels and revitalising cakes, all splendid, rev-up food.

The bar menu, served around the bar itself as well as in the patio with its surround of a high walled garden, runs all afternoon, servicing locals as much as it does blow-ins, plane hoppers, travelling salesmen, those who are simply hungry. In the evening the food formalises, and The Cloister switches itself into a seafood restaurant.

Open noon-9.45pm (pub food), 7pm-10pm (restaurant) Mon-Sun. Closed Xmas. Average Price: restaurant £££ bar ££. Visa, Access.

OFF LICENCE
ALEXANDER KNOX & CO
18 Abbey Street Tel: (065) 29264 Michael O'Grady
A good shop for those essential bottles of hard stuff and softer wines.
Open 9am-7pm Mon-Sat

WHOLEFOOD SHOP
OPEN SESAME
29 Parnell Street Tel: (091) 31315(home) Sally Smyth
Sally Smyth sells the organic vegetables of local grower Helga Friedmacher and the local Kilshanny cheeses in her cute little shop.
Open 10am-1.30pm, 2.30pm-6pm Mon-Fri, 10am-6pm Sat

ENNISTYMON

BAKERY
UNGLERT'S BAKERY
Tel: (065) 71217 Mr Unglert
Continental breads, such as those flavoured with rye flour are the speciality of this German bakery in the pub-filled town of Ennistymon. You can also eat in here, in a little café which is attached to the bakery and have coffee to go with your cake. If you're planning a picnic, the wholefood shop Country Lane, which sadly closed in 1993, has been re-incorporated into the leatherwork shop, just round the corner, and promises to continue the tradition of selling good cheeses and sausages and salamis from the Killaloe Delicatessen company.
Open 9am-7pm Tue-Sun

INAGH

FARMHOUSE CHEESE
INAGH FARMHOUSE CHEESES ★
Inagh Tel: (065) 26633 Meg and Derrick Gordon
If Meg and Derrick Gordon moved to Kowloon, or maybe Madagascar, and brought their herd of beautiful goats with them, the cheese they would make in their new location, be it

Des Moines or Dubai, would be just like the cheese they make in Inagh. Other cheesemakers utilise the strengths of the environment in which they work, and to this add a soupçon of personality. With The Gordons, their goat's milk cheese seems to be the product more of themselves than of their environment, though that must, of course, play a role.

But, for the most part, this is a cheese which you feel you could almost have a conversation with, if you have met the cheesemakers and can hear their chirpy voices ringing in your head as you take a bite. The Inagh cheeses are alive with a wiry, sparky zestfulness, a sharp and laconic attitude, an ironic and well-versed fluency.

All the cheeses, whether the Lough Caum semi-hard cheese with its marbled paleness, or the St. Tola log, white like the sun behind the clouds, or the little crottins of soft cheese pressed in paprika or crushed peppercorns or fresh herbs, offer a concentrated and evocative lushness, a tingling satisfaction that becomes a tremor. You can use the St. Tola for cooking, and it is fresh and rich with pasta, superb grilled on a barbecue or with some dressed salad leaves as a starter, even a raspberry vinaigrette. The Lough Caum suits a wintry evening and a good cheese knife with which to peel off slices as you demolish a bottle of claret. And all the time you hear the voices of its makers in your head, that babble of life right through the ballet of tastes.

Inagh cheeses are available throughout the country, and are sold from the farm. Ask directions in the village of Inagh. You can also have the cheese sent through the post, which is surprisingly efficient. Telephone for details.

LAHINCH

RESTAURANT
BARRTRA SEAFOOD RESTAURANT
Lahinch Tel: (065) 81280 Paul & Theresa O'Brien
Paul O'Brien counts in the little red returning fishing boats from his window overlooking Liscannor Bay and, if he sees them going out and then sees them coming in, he knows that the speciality of the restaurant — lobster — will be on the menu tonight. Oysters, home-smoked salmon, smudgy home-made rolls and Kilshanny cheeses make up the rest of this simple, just-right menu.

Open 1pm-3pm, 6pm-9pm Mon-Sat, 1pm-3pm Sun. Closed late Oct-late Mar (Xmas and New Year parties by arrangement). Average Price: lunch £-££ dinner £££ Signposted from the Lahinch-Milltown Malbay Road.

FARMHOUSE CHEESE
KILSHANNY FARMHOUSE CHEESE
Derry House, Lahinch Tel: (065) 71228 Peter and Aaron Nibbering
There are a quintet of different flavours used by father-and-son Peter and Aaron to make the much-respected Kilshanny. The plain cheese has a lush and up-front milkiness, especially when young. The pepper version gives a spicy, but not too spicy, kick to the milkiness, whilst it is the cheese flavoured with garden herbs which is perhaps the most appealing, for the greenness of the flavouring seems very suitable for such a pasture-rich cheese. The cumin cheese has a pronounced savoury note which suits red wine, and the garlic cheese is pungent but still controlled. You will find the Kilshanny cheeses much in

evidence in County Clare, where they are well supported, and they are for sale on Saturday mornings at a small stall in the Limerick market. If you are on the hunt for cheeses which are more mature, then it is perhaps best to follow the signs for the farm and to buy them there.

The Nibberings are delighted to sell from the house, which is well signposted ('Derry House') from Kilshanny village. Coming from Lahinch, go north. Cross over the bridge and take a right turn before you come to Liscannor. Otherwise the cheese is available from most of the surrounding supermarkets and many restaurants in the area.

KILRUSH

FARMHOUSE CHEESE
ST MARTIN CHEESE

Carnanes, Kilrush Tel: (065) 51320 Eileen O'Brien
Eileen's cheese is a simple and soulful product, not much seen except in the locality —
look out for it in the Supervalu in Kilrush — and maybe as far away as Ennis in Knox's,
but it is rich and buttery in flavour, great for picnics.
Cheese can be bought from the farm which is just outside Kilrush. Telephone for details and directions.

LISDOONVARNA

RESTAURANT AND HOTEL
SHEEDY'S SPA VIEW HOTEL

Lisdoonvarna Tel: (065) 74026 Fax: 74555 Frank & Patsy Sheedy
Little about either the exterior or the interior of Sheedy's Spa View Hotel, in the drowsy
resort of Lisdoonvarna appears to set it apart from that multitude of mousy hotels found
the length and breadth of Ireland.
Walk inside and you can see those fabulous old ladies you expected to find in someplace
like Lisdoonvarna, sitting just where you expected to find them. 'That's lovely that, isn't it?
What is it?', one old darling asks of her lady companion.
But Sheedy's is different. Frankie Sheedy cooks proper food, real food, not the sort of food
you expect to find in an hotel in a remaindered spa town like Lisdoon: local black pudding
with stewed apple and sweet onions; gravadlax served with nasturtiums, borage flowers,
salad leaves, baby tomatoes and cashew nuts; breast of chicken amidst a pool of toothy,
creamy yellow lentils; Irish blue shark on a bed of crisp kale underlaid with ribbons of
carrot. The staff are just as sweet as the desserts, and with keenly priced wines and the
holiday town atmosphere to help, it is easy to enjoy yourself.
Open breakfast, bar food and snacks 8.30am-9.45pm, restaurant open 6.30pm-9pm Mon-Sun. Closed end
Sept-mid Mar. Average Price: dinner £££. Visa, Access, Diners, Amex.

SALMON SMOKER AND PUB
THE LISDOONVARNA SMOKEHOUSE AND ROADSIDE TAVERN

Lisdoonvarna Tel: (065) 74084 Peter & Brigitte Curtin
One of the most surprisingly delicious toasted sandwiches we were offered in recent years
came in the Roadside Tavern. It was made with white bread, and filled with Lisdoonvarna
Smokehouse home-smoked salmon, a few slices of tomato and a minimum of finely sliced
onion. Then, the alliance of fish and whatnot was toasted, so that the salmon 'cooked'
slightly within the bread. It was a surprise, and a delicious one.
Peter Curtin's Roadside Tavern expanded to include a smokery thanks, or perhaps no
thanks, to the general economics of the area, which is to say the hard times that makes
everyone have to look to maximise every opportunity they can. So let us be thankful for
the benefit of hard times, for it has meant that Peter Curtin's smoked salmon, eel and
mackerel — all most competitively priced, all distinctively true in flavour — are now
distributed far and wide around Clare and its neighbourhood counties. But, perhaps, it is

in the Roadside Tavern itself, in this quixotically timeworn pub, that they are enjoyed best of all.
Smokehouse open 9am-6pm. Bar food served 12.30pm-8.50pm

NEW QUAY

PUB FOOD
LINNANE'S BAR
Tel: (065) 78120
When she won the 1993 Ladies Oyster Opening Championship in nearby Clarinbridge, prising a dozen of the little fellows out of their shells in a mere eighty-eight seconds, Anne Hardiman of Linnane's Bar punched the air and exhorted all and sundry to 'Party on, Dudes!'. This is good advice to follow, if you should be in this charming pub, looking out over the quay. Lobster and oysters suit the excellent brown bread, and Peter Curtin's smoked trout is excellent. Most everything suits another pint of stout, so party on, dudes.
Pub food served noon-9pm

FOOD PRODUCER
THE POT-POURRI
Bridgetown Tel: (061) 377443
County Clare's own herb grower, with a splendid list that encompasses regular kitchen herbs such as chives, fennel, parsley and marjoram and extends and extends to such luxuries as French tarragon, camomile, bergamot and Corsican mint.
Sold locally as well as in the Galway Saturday Market.

ALSO OF INTEREST
BRUCH NA HAILLE, Broadford, Doolin Tel: (065) 74120. Perfectly placed for sourcing the seafood in which the restaurant specialises.
Open 6pm-9.30pm Mon-Sun. Check opening times out of season.
THE DOOLIN CAFÉ, Doolin Tel: (065) 74429. For a cup of tea and a relaxing browse through assorted papers and books, the Doolin Café is hip and friendly, with good breads and good coffee.
Open 9.30am-2pm, 6pm-9pm May-Sept.
CAFÉ ON THE QUAY, Kinvara. They get the simple stuff right in here, and it is a sweet room in which to eat lunch: a BLT, some chunky chowder, a good brown stew or maybe shepherd's pie, then some ice cream or some ginger cake, and a bottle of sharp white wine. Nothing flashy, but the standards are high.
THE LAZY LOBSTER Doolin Tel: (065) 74390. Anne Hughes & Conor McGrath. Well established seafood restaurant.
Open 6pm-9.30pm Mon-Sun. Closed Oct-Mar. Average Price: dinner £££. Visa, Access. Turn towards Roadford rather than taking the road to Doolin Pier.
MR EAMON'S, Lahinch Tel: (065) 81050 Eamon & Rita Vaughan. Popular with holidaymakers.
Open 7pm-9.30pm. Closed Xmas. Average Price: dinner £££. Visa, Access, Amex.

COUNTY CORK

ITS GENEROUS SIZE and rich amplitude of climate and cultures allows County Cork to offer greater diversity in its foods than anywhere else in Ireland. There are several different worlds here, sprawling throughout the county from west to east and south to north, quietly and unfussily commingling one with the other.

Up in the north, temperaments are settled, inward, and the politics of the place are deeply conservative, the most conservative politics, indeed, of the entire country.

To the east, from the border with Waterford right to the city itself, the lay of the land is serene, untroubled, peaceful; a sense of composure is your constant companion as you waddle around exploring the coastline or the ululating inland hills.

And, then, the city itself adds an energy to this serenity. This is someplace which is still, in essence, rather naïve, still populated with hopeless but wonderful shops, places where spinsterly young girls smile at you as they dust uninteresting volumes in second-hand bookstores, or fat men in second-hand record shops peer at their dismally enticing racks of remaindered discs, or wide-boyish old fellas strike up chat with you in their sing-sing voices before you decide, apologetically, that you aren't interested in what they are selling, after all.

In the Covered Market, or the English Market as it is also called, this play of musical accents selling alluring schlock with great commercial vigour reaches a happy apogee. What is different here, however, is that a diligent hunt will unearth some good, fine foods from amidst the dross: fish bristling with freshness, cheeses that drool with lactic pungency, tripe and drisheen that threaten with their odorous energy. This is where one gets a glimpse of the splendid and singular food which Cork can offer, and the creative commonsense which the better growers, farmers, cheesemakers, bakers, butchers and fishwives have at their fingertips.

Many of these artisans work way out west of the county, in the kiddy-coloured villages with their promising names — Timoleague, Courtmacsherry, Skibbereen, Ballydehob, Rosscarbery — an appealingly playful series which ends with the ominous brevity of the village of Schull, a place which, even in the soft-soft accent of West Cork, can be nothing more than a bony sound: Skull.

But if Schull sounds threatening, its beauty and boisterousness make it one of the most captivating places to be found anywhere in Ireland. To the south, fishermen and yachtsmen will tell you, it is bounded by the Fastnet Rock, a Mecca of arrival for the seafaring. To the north, a geologist may say, it is bounded by Mount Gabriel, with its noded observation posts.

But the crucial points of entry to Schull are really the cheesemakers who sit at opposite ends of the village, to east and west. And the vital points in between are the restaurants, shops, bakers, pubs, butchers and craftspeople who are pinioned along each side of the climbing Main Street.

The riches of an artisan food culture and its capacity to support and encourage a lively and creative culinary society are seen here in perfect focus: Schull is both teacher and preacher, though its sermon of good food and the good life is, as always, issued in those break-heart syllables and vowels, in accents so soft you can never imagine them being raised in anger. Way out west, the voices may be impenetrable, but they are always beautiful, beautiful to behold.

The chapter on County Cork is arranged in the following order: North Cork, East Cork, Cork City, South and West Cork, The Far West Peninsulas, The Islands of West Cork.

NORTH CORK

BALLINGEARY

FARMHOUSE CHEESE
CARRAIG GOAT'S CHEESE
Ballingeary Tel: (026) 47126 Aart and Lieke Versloot
Come rain or come shine you will find Mr Versloot with his little stall of goat's milk cheeses at the Bantry Friday market. A mountainy man, his clothes and beard perfumed with turf, he makes an instinctive, expert cheese that is fresh with the goodness of the Ballingeary hills, the aftertaste furnishing a mellow cleanness that comes with experienced cheesemaking technique and pristine milk. Carraig cheese is sold when it has aged a matter of weeks, usually somewhere around about seven weeks, but it will happily last much much longer, developing smoothly and richly into something special.

BALLINEEN AND ENNISKEANE

ORGANIC MEAT, EGGS, CHEESE AND VEGETABLES
MANCH ESTATE
Manch, Ballineen, Tel: (023) 47507 Fax: 47276 Iris & Janet
In a country that supposedly loves the potato, it is sad to reflect on how rare it is in Ireland to be able to buy a sack of spuds and know that every one will have a tight fitting skin and no softness or blemishes within. The waxy organic Desiree potatoes that you can buy on the farm in Manch are each and every one immaculate. Seamus O'Connell in The

Ivory Tower Restaurant in Cork uses them to make a crispy, ruby-tinged potato cake, and they're made for both mashing into a smooth, milky purée and for baking into a slumberously dry mouthful.

But it's not only the potatoes that are expertly produced. The hairy pork chops have a toothy density and a good layer of fat that begins with happy well-cared for pigs who wander around outside in the orchard, and the sausages and cured pork are perfect items of charcuterie. The cheese, made from sheep's milk is creamy white, clean tasting and can sink perfectly into an olive oil, garlic and herb coating.

It is very joyful to be at the farm in Manch and to watch a tractor thundering into the yard and then to realise, suddenly, that instead of some macho farmer behind the wheel, it is either Janet or Iris, getting on with the work, doing each and everything, doing it right.

Manch is a few miles east of Dunmanway, with a sign at the entrance to the farm saying 'Free Range Eggs'. Janet and Iris also sell their produce at the Tuesday market in Macroom.

FARMHOUSE CHEESE
ROUND TOWER CHEESE
Bride View House Tel: (023) 47105 Nan O'Donovan

Thanks to Nan O'Donovan's unceasing energy, wedges of Round Tower Cheese can be found for sale all over the county. Round Tower could be described as a classic Irish Gouda, the taste always gentle and milky, a bundle of sweet and communing tastes which remain very fresh. If you can ever get the chance to try it, do look out for, or do inquire about, the small cheeses which Nan matures for up to nine months, for one then sees an entirely different Round Tower: forceful where the young cheese is mild, concentrated where the milkiness of the young cheese is diffuse, altogether something special and marvellous.

COOLEA

FARMHOUSE CHEESE
COOLEA CHEESE ★
Coolea Tel: (026) 45204 Dick and Helene Willems

Such an extraordinary concatenation of tastes are contained within a properly kept, happily aged Coolea that it can seem almost impossible to enumerate them. One finds the smell of sweetly old Parmesan, the buttery redoubt of Cheddar, the wise satisfaction of an Appenzeller, the cleanness and perfect construction of a good Gouda, the intensity of flavour of a Tomme or a Reblochon. But these names, and the styles of cheesemaking they signify, are no more than allusive signposts to the specific and special nature of Dick and Helene Willems' cheese, its essential uniqueness

Sometimes you think it is like a concentration of toffee — this perhaps if you buy one that is eighteen months old — other times the cheese will be cake-sweet, a sugary confection of milk, a baby-pleasing piece of utter delight, kaleidoscoping with lush, sexy flavours. More than perhaps any other Irish farmhouse cheese — though Coolea's near-neighbour Ardrahan does manage to achieve something similar — Coolea is a deep, deep concentration of tastes and flavours, so tongue-ready and upfront that they may leave you tongue-tied. Dick and Helene have adapted and refined a classic Dutch Gouda technique

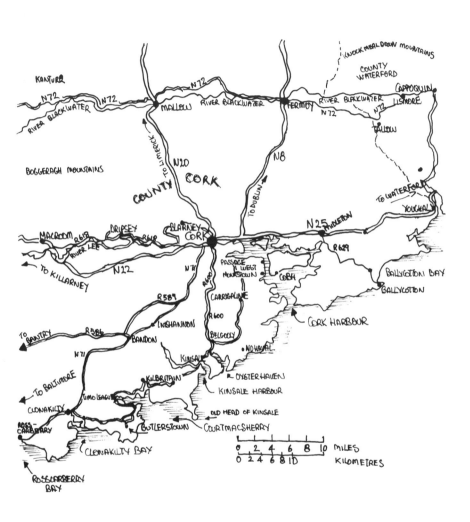

to suit the full flavour of the Coolea milk, making not just one of the most consistent cheeses sold in Ireland, but in the process creating one of the most perfervid tastes found in any Irish food.

KANTURK

FARMHOUSE CHEESE
ARDRAHAN CHEESE

Ardrahan House Tel: (029) 78099 Mary & Eugene Burns

'I never met anyone in the cheese business who wasn't nice', says Eugene Burns. This comes as no surprise, for when you meet Mr Burns you can't be anything other than nice, for so charming and hospitable are both he and Mary that the devil himself would have to respond warmly to them.

Like all of the farmhouse cheesemakers, the cheese they make is constructed from their personalities as much as their skills, and Ardrahan is a mirror to Eugene and Mary: the true essence of the country, intense, splendid, something instinctive and organic and devoid of artifice. The milk from this part of North Cork has long been celebrated for its richness and its complex flavours, and these powerful tastes make their way into Ardrahan, allying with Mary's skill as a cheesemaker to create a semi-soft cheese that can exhaust the senses with delight.

COUNTRY HOUSE & RESTAURANT
ASSOLAS COUNTRY HOUSE ➥

Kanturk Tel: (029) 50015 Fax: (029) 50795 Joe and Hazel Bourke

Assolas is gifted with being one of those houses that makes you feel very glad you are there. It is dashingly romantic, whether at night when the house is dappled with lights and you wander alongside the river and tiny bats career around splashing onto the surface of the water like bellyfloppers, or on a warm morning amidst the sprucely manicured hedges and shrubs as you maybe swing on the tree swing and think of your salad days.

It is welcoming, thanks to Joe and Hazel Bourke and their assiduous and assured youthful energy, their easy wit and style. Mrs Bourke cooks, and she does so with a great feeling for both acuity of flavour and texture in a dish. With a twice-baked soufflé made with Mary Burns' Ardrahan cheese, the effulgent, energetic flavours will be tempered with a subtle cream sauce ringed around the soufflé. Rosscarbery oysters, wisely, are just left alone, served on the half-shell. A baked fillet of brill will have a counterpointing dice of bacon as vivid contrast to the svelte fillets of fish and the pointed comfort of a herby cream sauce. Cream cheese and courgette will be used to stuff a breast of chicken which is then wrapped in filo and the dish will meld with comforting flavours.

But where Hazel Bourke's cooking demonstrates her confidence best of all is with her use of the fresh herbs, many of them grown out back in Assolas' vegetable garden. The torchy spice of rosemary will scent the jus with a loin of lamb, garlic ramsons and the unfurled umbrella of a chive flower will sit amidst a ring of salad leaves, elderflower will add a muscatty bite to a soft gooseberry fool, a dish of batoned carrots will be singing with the tastes of ginger and orange.

Such wonderful food, enjoyed in the quiet comfort of the red-walled dining room, makes you doubly glad to be at Assolas and, days after, images from the visit come back into the mind: the whites-clad cook walking back across the lawn after collecting herbs; the sea-green colour of a bowl of asparagus soup; the bursting orange and red colours of a breakfast compote; the lush comfort of the rooms. Precious memories.

Open 7pm-8.30pm (non-residents booking essential). Closed Nov-mid Mar. Average Price: dinner ££££ B&B £££££. Visa, Access. On the Mallow to Killarney road, follow signs to Kanturk. Four-and-a-half miles before Kanturk you will see signs for Assolas House.

ALSO OF INTEREST

NORTH CORK CO-OPERATIVE SOCIETY LTD, Kanturk Tel: (029) 50003 Sean McAulis. The milk collected from farmers within a ten mile radius of Kanturk is pasteurised by the Kanturk Dairy in exactly the same way as any other milk in any other dairy. So, how then is one to explain why the Kanturk Dairy milk is richer, creamier, more satisfying than other commercial milks? Heaven only knows, but better it is, with a fulsomeness and sweetness beside which other milks seem positively emaciated. You can find Kanturk Dairy milk and their cream — sold as North Cork Co-Op Society — in Millstreet, Macroom, Kanturk and the small villages creeping into west County Limerick.

MACROOM

MACROOM OATMEAL ★

Walton's Mills, Manor Villa Tel: (026) 41800 Donal Creedon

You just can't hurry Donal Creedon's delicious oatmeal. Like many of the best breakfast foods — still-warm soda bread, slowly coagulated scrambled eggs, gently cooked rashers — it needs the indulgence of time. So be wise, then, and indulge it, take the time to prepare this artful, artisan food, for nothing else in Ireland so repays the expenditure of effort, so rewards the indulgence in minutes.

To get it at its best, soak a few spoonfuls in water overnight. In the morning, pour off any excess water, then mix the appropriate quantity of fresh water — you can use a portion of milk to make it creamy — and add some salt. Slowly, slowly bring it to the boil, then slowly, slowly simmer it, with the little puckering popfuls of hot air breaking the surface. Stir every so often. Wait for it to achieve a creamy, gentle emulsion, which may take fifteen, maybe twenty minutes. Then spoon it into a bowl, and scatter rich brown sugar on top. Pour on sinfully thick cream, and do not spare it, for this is no penitential Calvinistic

MACROOM TUESDAY MARKET

EACH AND EVERY TUESDAY there is an all-day street market in Macroom town. On one side of the street you find the conventional growers, selling brilliant orange carrots and snowy white parsnips gathered together by their feathery green leaves, sacks of potatoes and whatever else might be in season. On the other side of the street you find the artisans led by the marvellous Manch Estate growers who sell sheep's cheese and lamb salamis, fabulous potatoes, and some pork products.

food, but a serene, indulgent, sweet thing of joy. Eat it slowly, and savour the sustenance of deep flavour, with the fresh warmth of oats to warm every part of the soul. There is nothing else like it.

MALLOW

RESTAURANT & COUNTRY HOUSE
LONGUEVILLE HOUSE AND PRESIDENT'S RESTAURANT ★
Mallow Tel: (022) 47156 Fax: 47459 William, and Jane Aisling O'Callaghan

It was a happy year spent working in England with Raymond Blanc that energised the ambitions and skills of William O'Callaghan. 'He opened my eyes', says William. 'He gets into it, he gets into the food, he doesn't keep himself apart from anything. A lot of chefs just do it and get it out, but he gets involved in it. So that involvement is what I want'.

That involvement is what you get in Longueville House. Mr O'Callaghan is an outrageously talented cook, and his culinary fluencies seem to know no boundary. He manages with each dish to use his technique to evoke the inherent flavours and strengths of the food, and in the case of Longueville this has particular resonance, for the house is almost self-sufficient and in eating here one eats the food of the area in the area.

This unity — the son of the house cooking where his father taught him and exploiting the produce of the farm — is of great importance to William O'Callaghan, for he is obsessive about ingredients. 'The cucumbers coming in now, the taste of those is just incredible', he says. 'You can't compare the spinach we have here and the stuff that comes in plastic bags'. And there are the trips a little further south to gather chanterelles, and the farmer nearby who breeds suckling pigs specially for the house, and the plans for the future: 'I'm going to get into the pigs maybe next year, because I'm getting a little boniff and I want to train it to try and get some truffles. We have a lot of beech and oak around the property, no reason why they shouldn't be there'.

One hopes so, for whilst most chefs dream of working with truffles, most of them in reality wouldn't be able to exploit the elusive and haunting flavour to the full. William O'Callaghan has such ability that you hope he can get his hands on the finest things, and you will happily abnegate any responsibility in his presence: if he wants to cook it, then you want to eat it. To this end, perhaps the best way to enjoy Longueville House is to opt for the Surprise Menu, the Chef's recommendations of the day. A charlotte of Longueville lamb fillets and baby courgettes set in a tomato concassé begins, the marbling of the meat and the vegetables perfectly rendered, the sweet flavours offset by a herb vinaigrette. Then a ravioli of prawns with the juices scented with basil, and on to pan fried fillets of black sole with a gâteau of garden vegetables. Pause for lemon sorbet, then breast of farmyard duck with a ginger and coriander sauce, this accompanied by a potato straw cake, and desserts begin with a stunning hot lemon mousse, and conclude with a blackcurrant sorbet wrapped in a pancake and gratinated with a sabayon.

This sublime indulgence demonstrates many facets about Mr O'Callaghan. Firstly, his food is balanced, and the courses follow seamlessly, with nothing discordant or gross ever allowed to interrupt the procession. Secondly, the use of herbs is liberal, but they play much more than a supporting role, strongly influencing the final flavour of the dishes. Thirdly, he can cook anything: the ravioli is as expert as the fish is expertly simple: the lemon mousse is as torchily exciting as the charlotte. And that is the key to his magic: he is excited by food, excited by cooking, he gets into it, and the result is deliriously delicious.

Open to non residents for lunch and dinner, if pre-booked by phone Closed mid Dec-mid Mar. Average Price: lunch £££ dinner ££££. Visa, Access, Amex, Diners. Recommended for Vegetarians. 3 miles west of Mallow on the N72 to Killarney.

ASPARAGUS GROWER
JUNE WILLIAMS
Doneraile Tel: (022) 24316

Perhaps it is the painfully short season which makes the pert shoots of asparagus seem so precious when they do duck out from under the soil late in April and early in May. Maybe it's their not-too-sweet cleanness of taste, or the promise of dishes to come as you bring them home: steamed then served with scrambled eggs; in a sharp green soup; with just a hollandaise sauce; maybe nothing more than a knob of butter on top oozing over the stalks and the dark tips. Like corn, they are best eaten as soon out of the ground as possible, so heading to North Cork to buy some stalks freshly cut by the Williamses is great fun.

'You can almost see them growing', Mr Williams says proudly of the plant's vigour. 'You can cut in the morning and by the evening there's more'. The more, of course, doesn't last long, and, as the classic seasonal food, asparagus should be savoured then forgotten until next year.

Telephone to inquire about availability and to get directions.

MITCHELSTOWN

FOOD DISTRIBUTOR
HORGAN'S DELICATESSEN SUPPLIES
Mitchelstown Tel: (025) 249892 Michael Horgan

Michael Horgan's company is one of the principal handlers and distributors of the Irish farmhouse cheeses and other speciality artisan foods, as well as handling a vast range of imported specialist cheeses and deli foods.

EAST CORK

CARRIGTWOHILL

OYSTER FARMER
ATLANTIC SHELLFISH
Tel: (021) 883248 Fax: 883702 Con Guerin

'See that house over there', says Con Guerin, looking far across the quiet bay where he farms the fabulous Rossmore oysters. 'That was a childless couple in there, and so they started eating oysters. Next thing you know, the wife has twins! Then they had to stop eating them! It's the zinc that does it, you know.'

It may indeed be the high zinc content that creates the aphrodisiacal quality of oysters, but the saline thrill delivered by eating Mr Guerin's native oysters is such that you could be forgiven if all you thought about at the end of eating half a dozen was eating another half dozen, and then six more for good measure. Narcotically powerful in taste and succulent and full in texture, few other foods found anywhere else in the world suggest such purity of taste, such perfection of the pleasure principle.

The farm is incredibly awkward to find and very easy to get lost when trying to do so, so telephone for details of the Rossmore delivery service.

FERMOY

COUNTRY HOUSE
BALLYVOLANE HOUSE
Castlelyons Tel: (025) 36349 Fax: 36781 Merrie and Jeremy Green

Ballyvolane sits comfortably and happily on the hillside at Castlelyons, quietly luxurious amongst quietly luxurious grounds, amidst the infernally swollen charm of north east County Cork. This entire area is suffused with a meandering obliqueness, a relaxed and relaxing air of procrastination, nicely lazy sort of country.

Inside, the house is full of the right sort of burnished mahogany, and while portraits of long-gone ancestors glare down at you from the walls, anything ominous in their gaze is dissipated by the air of giddy, giggly fun which swaddles everyone staying here. The dinner party cooking, the bright fires, the gin and tonics: it's so appropriate it deserves to be satirised.

Open for dinner for guests. Closed Xmas. Average Price: dinner £££ B&B £££££. Visa, Access. The house is very well signposted in the area and from the main Dublin-Cork road.

RESTAURANT & CREPERIE
LA BIGOUDENNE
28 McCurtain Street, Fermoy Tel: (025) 32832 Rodolphe and Noelle Semeria

La Bigoudenne restaurant is as prototypically French as the queer-shaped pointed hat which gives the restaurant its name. During the day it is a simple café, serving filled baguettes, chunky pâtés, home-made soups, while at night the menu becomes rather more formal: a glass of kir to begin, then veal with ceps, fresh river trout, fresh lobster with butter, the techniques and styling brought straight from the French provinces and allowing for good direct tastes and a confident, calm atmosphere. The speciality of the restaurant, however, and one that makes it worth travelling any distance to try, are the northern French crêpes, sweet ones — filled with stewed apple, chocolate, pear and ice cream — and savoury ones — ham and egg, egg and cheese, chicken and mushroom with cream, salad and blue cheese. They are splendid on-the-road food, giving the energy a lift, brightening the soul.

Open 12.30pm-10.30pm (the restaurant menu gets going around 7pm, but they are helpful and flexible).

Open for Xmas, closed 2 weeks end Sept. Average Price: lunch £-££ dinner ££-£££. Visa, Access.

FOTA

RESTAURANT
NIBLICK'S

Fota Island Golf Club Tel: (021) 883667 Michael and Catherine Ryan

Michael Ryan, of Arbutus Lodge and Isaacs Brasserie, is the force behind this restaurant within the Fota Golf Club.

It's a big airy upstairs room with high, open beamed ceilings and despite its size the room retains a cosiness that comes from the warmth of stone walls and dark wood. Square pedestal tables with matt black wood finish, and bentwood chairs fill the space; chunky clean stainless steel cutlery is pre-laid in an 'instruments for the use of' mode (a lá dentist) on double ply white napkins. The air is filled with the sound of rock music, the type that is usually interrupted by the D.J. saying 'traffic down town is moving slowly... ' which seems out of place in the sedate surroundings of a golf club.

The laminated menu culls specialities from north and south of the Mediterranean: Penne Arrabiatta, Tapas, Salad Tiede, Tagine of Lamb. The food is colourful, glossy, but sometimes needs a little oomph to get the other senses working full tilt. The staff are friendly and natural, but work to their own pace.

Niblicks follows a formula that has worked well in other parts of the country, as well as in the tremendously successful Isaacs in Cork city. It will be interesting to see how the formula develops in the unusual surroundings of a golf club.

Open 12.30pm-2.30pm, 6pm-9.30pm Mon-Sun (no dinner Sun). Average Price: lunch ££ dinner £££. Visa, Access. Take the turning for Cobh just past the Carpet Factory on the Cork/Youghal road, then look for signs to the Fota Golf Club.

KILLEAGH

FARMHOUSE
BALLYMAKEIGH HOUSE

Killeagh Tel: (024) 95184 Mrs Margaret Browne

'My girlfriend and I travelled to Ireland for Valentine's Weekend and we had a whopping great time at this gem of a place', writes a Mr McKenna from London — no relation, we hasten to add — before hitting overdrive in order to describe Margaret Browne's

Ballymakeigh House. 'The house was so welcoming and warm with every comfort one would need, big fires, fresh flowers, crisp linen, rich and warm décor. The warm welcome even extended right through to the tea leaves'.

All of this is completely true, utterly unarguable. But there is more. 'The food deserves a special mention. It all tasted so fresh, wonderful and light. I just happened to mention one morning that I love hot oysters and roast duck and that night that was exactly what Mrs Browne served to us for dinner — all at a very reasonable cost'. Unsurprisingly, Mr McKenna concludes: 'I shall definitely return there again'. Perhaps we should hold a convocation of McKennas at Ballymakeigh, Mr McKenna?

Open dinner for guests only, book by 4.30pm. Closed Xmas. Average Price: dinner £££ B&B £££. No Credit Cards. Killeagh is between Midleton and Youghal on the N25: watch for the sign to the house on the road.

MIDLETON

FISHMONGER
BALLYCOTTON FISH SHOP
Main Street Tel: (021) 613122 Anthony Coffey-Walshe
An excellent fish shop, with the aquatic congregation on sale brought from as near as Ballycotton Bay.
Open 9am-6pm Mon-Sat

SHOP & RESTAURANT
THE FARM GATE
Coolbawn Tel: (021) 632771 Kay Harte & Morag O'Brien
Flowers everywhere, food books and magazines scattered around and about, some unknown string quartet sawing away happily on the stereo, a great big table of desserts laid out to make you salivate the second you walk in, a giddy assortment of sculptures and paintings for decoration. It is a happy space, the Farm Gate, very feminine, very understated, and how very nice it is to be here. They do nice things to simple food, like cooking a shepherd's pie upside down so the spuds are on the bottom, make a proper event out of something like a crab sandwich, and their pancakes and pastas are flavoursome, friendly, food to spend time over.

Out front, meanwhile, the Farm Gate shop is packed with choice cheeses, cakes, bakes and bread, good vegetables and comestibles.

Open 9.30am-6pm Mon-Wed, 9.30am-5pm, 7.30pm-9.30pm Thurs-Sat. Closed Xmas. Average Price: lunch £-££ dinner £££. Visa, Access.

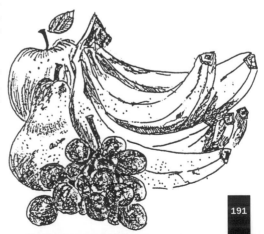

DISTILLERY
JAMESON HERITAGE CENTRE
Midleton Tel: (021) 613594
The home of the tortuously expensive Midleton Single Malt, and nowadays the site of conducted tours which explain the magical process of distilling.
Open 10am-4pm Mon-Sun. Closed Nov-Mar except for bookings.

SHANAGARRY

COUNTRY HOUSE & RESTAURANT
BALLYMALOE HOUSE ★
Shanagarry Tel: (021) 652531 Fax: 652021 Ivan and Myrtle Allen
Food and philosophy have proven to be uncomfortable bedfellows in the past. Ludwig Wittgenstein never minded what he ate, so long as it was exactly the same thing each and every day. Pythagoras was amongst the earliest vegetarians, refusing to eat meat due to his belief in the transmigration of souls. Too often, too much deep thought has tended to result in reasons not to eat certain foods, rather than digging up excuses to actually enjoy, and encourage enjoyment in, the eating of food.
Myrtle Allen has a philosophy of food and, like her own philosophical musings, it is durable, homespun, essentially simple. Encourage a circle of producers around and about you to produce the very best foods they can manage and, vitally, support them as best you can. This helps to keep everything local and, by virtue of this small-is-beautiful creed, you have the benefit of foods which express themselves in terms of the micro-climate in which they are produced and reared: local industry and agriculture, local foods, local flavours. In addition to this, you should attempt to be as self-sufficient as you can: grow your own spuds, make your own chutneys, produce as much of the food you need through your own endeavours as is possible. Then, when it comes to the cooking of this food, do it from scratch and do it with ingredients which are as pristinely fresh as possible. Don't allow any egotism to blunt the edge of the cooking: strive to find a method of preparing each dish which allows the food to speak of itself.
Then, when it comes to serving the food, do it simply, but courteously and as graciously as you can. No theatre, no theatricals, no spurious, self-congratulatory or fashionable convolutions. Deep-coloured dining rooms, good paintings to lift the soul, good wines to salve the spirit. All of this must be done with an air of concern and with the maximum dialogue between customer and cook, a culinary conversation.
This is a simple modus, and its simplicity means that many, if not most, cooks overlook it. Myrtle Allen has never lost sight of this creed of simplicity, this respect for plainness in thinking and cooking, for more than twenty five years. During that time, the philosophy of Ballymaloe has remained consistent: respect for the fruits of the land, air and sea. Respect for the long-held culinary codes which best transform these fruits. Respect for the person who will enjoy the fruits of the cook's labours and, just as important, respect demanded for the efforts of the cook and respect for the culinary arts.
Many people find it difficult to see this simplicity at work. Where they want crescendo, Ballymaloe offers diminuendo. They want swagger, and are disappointed by subtlety. They want overstatement, they get understatement. But there are many, still, who see in the

Ballymaloe philosophy a logical, conscientious, concerned and kind way of working with the world and for them it is this deep thread, just as much as the delicious presentations on a plate or the baleful comfort of the house, which makes Ballymaloe special.

Is this any consolation to abstemious philosophers? Wittgenstein, surely, had a Ballymaloe dinner menu in mind when he decided that he didn't want anything other than the same thing, and perhaps he feasted each day on something like a typical May menu: chicken and garlic soup, then a salad tiede with lamb fillets and kidneys and a walnut oil dressing, followed by chicken baked with cucumber and chardonnay served with buttered turnips and grilled scallions with a dessert of, perhaps, some orange mousse with a soupçon of chocolate ice-cream. Then, back to work on the Tractatus. Pythagoras, likewise, would have been well pleased, for Ballymaloe is one of the few restaurants to offer a complete vegetarian menu every evening.

Open buffet lunch 1pm, dinner 7pm-9pm Mon-Sun (buffet dinner Sun). Closed Xmas. Average Price: lunch £££ dinner ££££. Visa, Access, Amex, Diners. Recommended for Vegetarians. Ballymaloe House is signposted from the N25.

COOKERY SCHOOL
THE BALLYMALOE COOKERY SCHOOL
Kinoith House, Shanagarry Tel: (021) 646785 Darina & Tim Allen
'Real food with true flavours' is the simple ethos from which the Ballymaloe School has built a world-wide reputation. It is an imprimatur which Darina Allen has been handed from her mother-in-law, Myrtle Allen, and which she is in the process of handing on to scores of eager students on the lengthy three month courses; to B&B matrons taking a weekend out to learn how to make better bread and simpler food; to those from pubs who want to be able to do obvious things but do them well; to vegetarians who wish to add some cooking kudos to their best efforts. Occasionally during the summer there will be guest cooks taking part in short courses for a couple of days, and these can prove to be terrific fun, not to mention a terrific challenge.

KITCHENSHOP
BALLYMALOE KITCHEN SHOP
Ballymaloe House, Shanagarry Tel: (021) 652032 Wendy Whelan
Behind the excellent craftshop at Ballymaloe there is an excellent kitchen shop. It's one of those shops that, no matter how many times you return, you always find some new discovery, some exciting new implement. But nothing is chosen for its gimmick value, from a simple nutmeg grater, to a pizza stone, to the complete range of le pentole saucepans, everything here will work when you take it back to your own kitchen, everything is bought because it's built to last. The shop echoes the philosophy of Ballymaloe itself, simplicity, excellence, and great fun.

Open 9am-6.30pm Mon-Sun

PRESERVES
BALLYMALOE RELISH
Caherlog, Glanmire Tel: (021) 353358 Yasmin Hyde
'Would you like relish on your hot dog?'
'No, not for me thank you, just plain.'

'It's Ballymaloe relish...'

'Oh yes! I love that, yes please'.

So goes the conversation with the non-gourmet.

'What is the basis behind that wonderful sauce for your char-grilled lamb?'

'Oh, don't tell anyone, but it's Ballymaloe relish actually'.

So goes the conversation with the gourmet.

All around the country, and no doubt around various parts of the globe, people are discovering just how good Ballymaloe Relish is. Perfect in a cheese sandwich, perfect with a barbecue, perfect for cooking. And it makes an ideal present — because you know the recipient will love it.

The principal ingredient of the relish is tomato, red-ripe tomato. The texture is of soft chutney punctuated by the odd well-cooked sultana and the occasional spice seed.

The recipe for the chutney was an original Myrtle Allen concoction, and, says her daughter Yasmin 'It was always an essential part of the table, even before the restaurant opened. I liked it, partly because it was so versatile' she adds, 'and partly because it keeps very well without having to add armfuls of additives'.

Ballymaloe Relish is distributed in shops and supermarkets throughout the country.

BUTCHER

J. CUDDIGAN

Church Street, Cloyne, Shanagarry Tel: (021) 652521 Mr Cuddigan

On the right side of the splendidly hewn and gnarled butcher's block which serves as the counter in Mr Cuddigan's fuss-free shop there is a trio of old, brown paper wrapping spools, the sort of thing that was once a staple of every shop in the country and is now effective by its absence. It is still here, and so is the plainness of style, the commonsense of mind and the excellence of product which signals a true artisan. Mr Cuddigan's meat is delicious: beef as herby as you have ever tasted, lamb as sweet as dolly mixtures, offal as clean tasting as you can imagine. You rush it home, wrapped in brown paper, maybe singing to yourself about brown paper packages tied up with string with, inside, some of your favourite things.

Open 9.15am-5.45pm. Closed lunch 1pm-2pm and half day Wed

POTTERY
STEPHEN PEARCE POTTERY
Shanagarry Tel: (021) 646807
Stephen Pearce's traditional design of pottery has been much imitated, but never improved on. The calming russet-tinged colour of the local clay, dug near the river Blackwater, needs nothing other than the occasional swirl of pale white to bring it to life. Best of all, just as the clay colour evokes the essential earthiness and ruddiness of the potter's art, Mr Pearce's work also has a deeply pleasing grainy tactility and weight in the feel of the plates and jugs and cups, an honest feeling.
Open 8am-5pm Mon-Fri, 10am-5pm Sat, 2pm-5pm Sun

MUSTARDS & PRESERVES
BRECON LODGE PRESERVES
East Ferry, Midleton Tel: (021) 652352 Robert Nunn
A broad and popular range of mustards — they actually grow the seeds for the mustards themselves — chutneys and savoury jellies, widely available in supermarkets and choice delis.

YOUGHAL

RESTAURANT/PUB FOOD/ACCOMMODATION
AHERNE'S SEAFOOD BAR
163 North Main Street Tel: (024) 92424 Fax: 93633 The Fitzgibbon family
Each and every year new followers are added to the fold of those for whom Aherne's personifies bliss itself. Charmed by the intimacy of the dining room, succoured by the comfort of the food, lulled by the promise of the wine list, they speak afterwards in enraptured tones, these presidents, actresses, food journalists, visitors from abroad. No-one, it seems, is immune to the charms of the pinky art-decked dining room, or the cosy bar where you are left alone to drink in the atmosphere.
It is unusual for a fish restaurant to endear itself into the hearts and minds of so many. There are scores of restaurants where carnivores will insist that you'll find the best steak in Ireland, there are numerous vegetarian, wholefood and other faith — rather than food — led restaurants.
But Aherne's manages to beatify itself with a fillet of cod or a fried john dory, done just right, just perfect, on occasion achieving a certain transcendence of taste.
Open 12.30pm-2pm, 6.30pm-9.30pm Mon-Sat, 6.30pm-9.30pm Sun (pub food available 10.30am-closing time). Closed Xmas. Average Price: lunch ££-£££ dinner £££. Visa, Access, Amex, Diners. On the Main Street in Youghal at the Waterford end of town.

GOAT'S MILK AND CHEESE
ARDSALLAGH
Ardsallagh House, Youghal Tel: (021) 92545 Kornelius Korner
Farmhouse goat's milk cheeses, some soft, some hard and also goat's feta. Some of them flavoured, some spiced in oil, goat's yogurt, and goat's milk and goat's butter. Found in the locality, and occasionally in Cork city.

CORK CITY

RESTAURANTS

ARBUTUS LODGE

Montenotte Tel: (021) 501237 Fax: 502893 Michael & Declan Ryan

Recent years have seen a greater informality make its way into the serving of food in Arbutus and nowadays one of the biggest attractions of the hotel is the very modern and delicious dishes served in the bar at lunchtime. Whilst relatively simple food, it is always executed with professionalism and is just as suitable as the more formal cooking of the dining room when it comes to matching a good bottle of wine from the extraordinary wine list to accompany it. The list continues to attract plaudits and awards every year, and it deserves each and every one of them.

Open restaurant: 1pm-2pm, 7pm-9.30pm Mon-Sat, bar lunch 12.15pm-2.30pm Mon-Sat. Closed Xmas.

Average Price: bar lunch ££ restaurant lunch £££ dinner ££££ B&B £££££. Visa, Access, Amex, Diners. Cork city centre, signposted from the Cork-Dublin road.

CLIFFORD'S ★

18 Dyke Parade Tel: (021) 275333 Michael Clifford

Michael Clifford impresses as a man who works incredibly hard, and impresses as a cook who has an intense seriousness of purpose. Yet, what is most enjoyable about his food is the fact that it is not at all po-faced or intense, but impish and amusing, full of little tricks and sleights of hand which bring a smile to your lips before the tastes bring another smile to your lips.

Like many other chefs in Ireland, Clifford has his own Clonakilty Black Pudding recipe. He serves it with a purée of local mushrooms and blinis, the tender little blini resting on top of the dish, angled like a foppish hat. A little coriander will be sidled into a butter sauce which is served with fillets of john dory that tumble over each other like scrunched velvet.

A velouté of chicken will have the resuscitatory addition of pearl barley to make a rich soup. Never mind the hotch-potch concocted by Alexis Soyer to feed the hungry during the famine, this is a dish which would sustain any nation, and bring joy to the world at the same time.

All of Clifford's food shows great respect for the basic melodies of classical cuisine, but the impishness shows with the way he twists your expectations of a dish just slightly off key, the way he will vary the tempo and give his own interpretation of a standard. This is perhaps best demonstrated with his radical re-working of a basic Irish Stew, where the dish is totally disassembled and yet still respects the basic simplicity of this peasant classic. Underlying this playfulness, always, is a rock solid technique and a determination that everything should be as perfect as possible: no more, no less.

In this ambition, Clifford is assisted by a team who are superbly in control of their duties: service is assured and always appropriate, enthusiastic — ask for a glass of water and they say 'Certainly. Indeed. Yes' before hurrying off for it — with the depth of information and good grace the waiting staff have at their fingertips second to none. The wine list has improved in recent times, and there are now lots of good bottles to pair with this heady, articulate cooking.

Open 12.30pm-2.30pm Tue-Fri, 7pm-10pm Tue-Sat. Closed Xmas week, 2 weeks in Aug and bank hols. Average Price: lunch ££ dinner ££££. Visa, Access, Amex, Diners. Clifford's is a minute's walk from Jury's hotel; turn left, then right at the first set of traffic lights and you will see the restaurant on the corner.

ISAAC'S BRASSERIE AND HOSTEL

MacCurtain Street Tel: (021) 503805 Canice Sharkey

It's an awkward thing, deciding just what time of day it is that you most prefer to go to Isaac's.

For lunch, with the big tall room light and bright, it is a splendid place, the food full of suggestions which inspire the appetite: a shellfish soup with a soft pink rouille served alongside; some colourful fresh pasta ribboned on the plate and swathed with fresh asparagus and parmesan; a swaggering chicken pie under a crown of pastry; a charcoal-grilled steak sandwich served with big fat chips. The food suits either a simple, speedy bite or a luridly long excursion with plenty of white wine that tails off somewhere late in the afternoon.

At dinnertime, however, the catholicity of Canice Sharkey's cooking always seems apt, always seems able to offer just what you feel like, whether that be true tasting crab cakes in the American style, a stew of beans with Clonakilty black pudding, a subtle lamb curry or some of his splendiferous pasta. Such an international array of dishes on one menu may suggest that the food will be no more than ersatz, but Mr Sharkey is a self-controlled cook and the flavours in his food are as buzzy and happy as the atmosphere in the dining room.

If you wish to make the most of that atmosphere, then the rooms in the Isaac's hostel are simple, spotless, reminiscent of a European pensione, and a valuable remembered taste of your salad days. It's the kind of place where the sound of some trumpeter playing some cool jazz may come quietly drifting across the quad as you lie on your bed on a warm afternoon and you ask yourself, just who was he, that young man that you once were.

Open 10am for coffee, 12.30pm-2.30pm, afternoon tea, 6.30pm-10.30pm Mon-Sat, 6.30pm-9.30pm Sun. Closed Xmas. Average Price: lunch ££ dinner ££ B&B £££. Visa, Access. Cork city centre, north of the river.

THE IVORY TOWER RESTAURANT

The Exchange Buildings, 35 Princes Street Tel: (021) 274665 Seamus O'Connell

'I would like to open people's minds about food. I find there is no one who is really surprising people with cooking, challenging people with new ideas'.

Other chefs say similar things to this all the time, but there is a difference when someone like Seamus O'Connell says it, for he is an almost preternaturally gifted cook. In the, simple, almost minimalist room that is The Ivory Tower, Mr O'Connell hopes for a restaurant that will evolve into somewhere that 'the diners would have such confidence in that they would come regardless of what is on the menu.

'I could say, "Look, I'm just doing one menu a night with maybe three choices at a set price". Then I would have free rein to follow the seasons, and to organise what I want to'.

This is a good stratagem to follow with Mr O'Connell, for his food is devilishly exciting, right from the thrill when you first see a menu he has prepared: Sun-dried Tomato Hummus and Crudities. Chicken Chimichanga Guacamole and Salsa. Sautéed Squid and

Fresh Pasta with a Tomato and Basil Sauce. Organic Strawberries in Millefeuille Caramel. But not only can he write them, he can cook them. A brilliant Mussel, Saffron and Orange soup; an extraordinary Duck and Aubergine Pizza with Brie, made with a croissant pastry — this one influenced by the Californian restaurateur Wolfgang Puck; a georgeous Pigeon Terrine with the best potato Straw Cake; a grain-perfect Couscous to accompany some hot, spicy Lamb Sausages; a gloriously, richly caramelised Tarte Tatin. With his devilish ability to synthesise masses of foreign influences, his hunger to create and his lavish kitchen skills, Mr O'Connell is as individual and as exciting a cook as you will find anywhere in Ireland. Time will allow the restaurant to acquire more adroit service and more of the heady buzz which will add further lustre to this dynamic food.

Open noon-4pm Mon-Sat, 6.30pm-11pm Wed-Sun. Closed Xmas and 2 weeks Jan. Average Price: lunch ££-£££ dinner £££. Visa, Access. Recommended for Vegetarians. Princes Street leads off St Patrick's Street.

LOVETT'S

Churchyard Lane, Well Road, Douglas Tel: (021) 294909 Fax: 508568 Dermot & Margaret Lovett

You can pick and choose the type of Lovett's you wish to enjoy. At lunchtime the food in the bar is informal but carefully attended to, keenly priced, charmingly served. If you wish for something more formal, then the food in the restaurant is perfect for a light lunch, maybe a fillet of salmon or sole and some floury spuds to mop up a buttery sauce. This time of day tends to be the province of local businessmen, who tend to watch their waistlines but pay somewhat less attention to their blood-alcohol level, thank heavens.

In the evening, the menu is more formal, and this is the time to make the most of Lovett's massive and select wine list. Dermot Lovett is a passionate student of the wines of the Wine Geese, those hearty souls who fled Ireland during the seventeenth and eighteenth centuries and slowly worked themselves into positions of enormous importance in the wine industry of Bordeaux. Mr Lovett's concern makes this a good location to splash out on something aristocratically bibulous, secure in the knowledge that the wines will have been cosseted with care.

Open 12.30pm-2pm, 7pm-9.45pm Mon-Fri, 7pm-10pm Sat. Closed Xmas and 2 weeks in Aug. Average Price: lunch £££ dinner ££££. Visa, Access, Master, Amex, Diners. From Cork take Route 609 to Douglas. Turn onto the Well Road, and the restaurant is on your left.

CAFÉ
THE CRAWFORD GALLERY CAFÉ

Emmet Place Tel: (021) 274415 Fern Allen

The Gallery is a lovely space, femininely alert and appealing, with food to match. Fern Allen is a scion of the great Ballymaloe clan and much of the food in here comes from there, not just physically but temperamentally and creatively as well. This is comfort cooking: crumbly brown breads and cakes to accompany coffee, soulful soups that seduce you into deep contentment, chicken baked with butter, or maybe cooked with cream and gentle spices and served with rice, some sparky fish from Ballycotton. At lunchtime it is a delightful place in which to consider and recharge, at dinnertime it becomes appropriately fey and romantic and perfect for relaxing.

Open 10.30am-5pm (lunch served 12.30pm-2.30pm) Mon-Sat, 6.30pm-9.30pm Wed-Fri. Closed Xmas and bank hols. Average Price: lunch £-££ dinner £££. Visa, Access. The city centre restaurant is on the ground floor of the gallery.

BAKERY AND CAFE
THE GINGERBREAD HOUSE

Frenchchurch Street Tel: (021) 276411 Barnaby Blacker

Barnaby Blacker came to Ireland with a background working in the St Quentin Bakery in London. He first worked for a spell as pastry chef in Ballymaloe House, absorbing Myrtle Allen's instinct for fresh, simple flavours as he did so. The Gingerbread House opened in 1991 and is a slightly excitable space, full of good baking, good preserves and excellent filled sandwiches which pack Armin Weise's salamis with the wonderful Ballymaloe Relish for an unbeatable lunch. Croissants, sausage rolls and pain au chocolat can all be taken away or eaten in, in the slightly cramped, slightly charged premises.

Open 9am-6.30pm Mon-Sat

VEGETARIAN RESTAURANT AND WHOLEFOOD SHOP
QUAY CO-OP

24 Sullivan's Quay Tel: (021) 317660 Arthur Leahy, Maura O'Keefe

The Co-Op has for many years been a reliable destination for wholesome wholefood, always managing to furnish its punters with good food even through a series of changes in direction and orientation. During the day it operates as a self-service restaurant, offering tried and tested vegetarian staples. At night the menu explores some of the newer ideas to influence vegetarian cuisine, offering table service and a moody, dusky ambience that invites you to open up a bottle or two. The shop downstairs is an excellent source of good foods, organic vegetables and occasional exotica.

Open shop 9.30am-6.30pm, restaurant 9.30am-6.30pm self-service, 6.30pm-10.30pm table service Mon-Sun. Closed Xmas. Average Price: lunch £ dinner ££-£££. Visa, Access. Recommended for Vegetarians. Just south of the river in the city centre.

PUB
THE LONG VALLEY
Winthrop Street Tel: (021) 272144

Strange and incredulous as it is to tell, but we witnessed, once, on a Wednesday lunchtime, The Man Who Ate Two Rounds of Sandwiches in The Long Valley.

He sat down with the two paper plates, each with a Long Valley sandwich, balanced one on top of the other. After solemnly eating his way through one baked ham, egg mayonnaise, lettuce, tomato and onion wedged between spongy soft brown batch bread, he removed the top plate and without pausing settled into eating his second cheese, onion, ham and tomato lodged between toasted white tablets of thick pan loaf.

Satisfied, The Man Who Ate Two Rounds of Sandwiches in The Long Valley drank down his Lucozade, wrapped his large coat around his somewhat larger stomach and returned to work, perchance to snooze.

Around and about him the gay eccentricities of this weirdly wonderful bar carried on unabashed. But, we who had seen him, we knew that we had seen something.

Pub food served all day.

WINE SHOP/OFF LICENCE
GALVIN'S OFF LICENCES
37 Bandon Road Tel: (021) 275598; Watercourse Road Tel: (021) 500818; 22 Washington Street Tel: (021) 276314 Barry Galvin

The range of both wines and spirits in Barry Galvin's shops is splendid, a keen balance struck between easy-going quaffers at decent prices and the more serious wines which need age and a more profound financial supplement on the part of the customer.

Open 10.30am-11pm Mon-Sat, noon-2pm, 4pm-10pm Sun

WHOLEFOOD SHOP
NATURAL FOODS
26 Paul Street Tel: (021) 277244 Wendy O'Byrne

Wendy O'Byrne's little nook and cranny of a shop may well be the best wholefood bakery in the country. If this summons images of well intentioned but crushingly dull baking, think again. The breads and cakes here — sourdoughs, wholemeals, pittas, famous cherry buns, sweet slices of apricot bake — are executed with an alert and well-tempered hand, and at lunchtime they are formed into truly fine sandwiches. The shop is a busy warren of good things, with organic vegetables for sale, bags of Macroom Oatmeal, many of the good foods of the county.

Open 9.30am-5.30pm Mon-Sat

BUTCHERS
O'FLYNN'S BUTCHERS
36 Marlborough Street Tel: (021) 275685/272195 John O'Flynn
The Messrs O'Flynn are dogged, dapper men. Every time you walk into their capacious shop just off Patrick Street there seems to be some clever new experiment — lamb sausages with a little more spice, venison sausages, maybe, a helping of rare duck livers or osso bucco — alongside their great staples: the kassler which has made them so famous, the well-marbled beef, the soft and tender lamb, all the necessities of a good butcher's shop. And there will be good advice also, and some chat about the ways of the world, and the infernal nature of politics, and the comings and goings of your mutual friends.
Open 9am-5.45pm Mon-Thurs, 8am-6pm Fri & Sat

MARKET
CORK COVERED MARKET
The Cork Market, confusingly known also in local parlance as the Old English Market, can seem at first glance like little more than a cross between abattoir and emporium. Meat dominates most counters, and much of it is grimly unappetising, but a little patience unearths the jewels in this crown: the Maucnaclea cheeses, Isabelle Sheridan's stall of cooked meats and pâtés, the buttered eggs, the tripe and drisheen for those who can abide this most effulgent of foods, the lovely fish stalls towards the rear of the Market, Mister Bell's stall of Asian foods. It is an eternally lively place, reverberant with noise and activity, the don't-touch scolding looks of some stallholders, the pell-mell come-and-go of lively shopping and gossiping.

MR BELL'S
Mr Bell
Spices and all the sorts of stuff you need for cooking and eating Eastern: couscous, Shaosing wine, pulses, the lot.

LA CHARCUTERIE
Tel: (021) 270232 Isabelle Sheridan
Madame Sheridan might well have simply taken her cart of mousses and pâtés, saucissons and terrines, hams and meats straight over from some little local market in France. Happily one finds the hoped-for decisiveness and subtleties of taste of good charcuterie in all her work. Do look out for the pigeon and chocolate.
The stall is open 10am-5.30pm Wed-Sat

MAUCNACLEA FARM CHEESES ★
Tel: (021) 270232 Martin Guillemot & Anne-Marie Jamand
Within the world of Irish farmhouse cheesemakers, the work of Martin and Anne-Marie is unique. Rather than concentrating obsessively on a single style of cheese and concentrating then on replicating it each and every day, they experiment according to the amount of milk they have, strolling effortlessly between creations that use cow's milk and those that use goat's milk, ageing some cheeses while others are sold with the bloom of freshness. Some are soft, some are semi-soft, some are allowed to develop to a harder texture. Some will be allowed to develop a blueness, and occasionally they

themselves will slice open a cheese, unsure of just what they will find inside. They produce fabulous butter and the most divine double cream imaginable.

Is there anything that unifies their work? The answer is that the Maucnaclea cheeses are unified by Martin and Anne-Marie's staggering skilfulness, their ability to create and mature cheeses to immaculate fullness of taste, precise exposition of flavour and break-heart beauty. One day you buy a piece of goat's milk camembert and also a slice of camembert made with cow's milk: the former is flinty and oozing, the taste balanced between careful acidity and a fresh completeness, the latter will be rich and evocative, the saltiness summoning the concentrated flavours of the milk out of the cheese.

But then, you also buy some cottage cheese, and a tub of cream and butter and what-have-you, for these cheeses, perhaps more than any others in Ireland, can genuinely be classified as irresistible, sublime, plangent.

The stall is open 10am-5.30pm Wed-Sat.

IAGO
Tel: (021) 277047 Fax: 277750 Sean Calder-Potts
Imagine being able to fax in your orders to the Old English Market. Sean Calder-Potts allows you to do this. On sale are pasta and ice cream from Isaacs, unusual breads and an expanding selection of Irish farmhouse cheeses, including Silke Cropp's Corleggy cheese from Cavan.

MOYNIHAN'S BUTTERED EGGS
Tel: (021) 272614
Buttering the eggs helps to keep them fresher for longer, but it also seems to impart a buttery character to the eggs.
Open Mon-Sat.

KAY O'CONNELL'S FISH STALL
Most of the fish stalls in the market have a splendid selection of wet fish and crustacea, but Mrs O'Connell's stall manages to almost always have what you want and to have it in pristine condition.
Open Mon-Sat

O'REILLY'S TRIPE AND DRISHEEN STALL
Tel: (021) 966397 Stephen and Maurice O'Reilly
Drisheen is a blood sausage made with sheep's blood and is unerringly pungent. Some love it, most don't, but what sort of person would you be if you never tried it? So do give it a go.

FARMHOUSE CHEESE
CHETWYND IRISH BLUE
Castlewhite, Waterfall Tel: (021) 53502 Jerry Beechinor
Jerry Beechinor's mild blue cheese is made with pasteurised milk and has a quiet, tongue-teasing contrast between the spicy saltiness of the roquefort blueness and the alloyed canvas of the milk on which the blue rests. Widely available, it is vastly superior to any

imported blue cheese, swapping the blandness of the foreign cheeses for a considerate and gentle texture and taste.

ALSO OF INTEREST

RESTAURANTS

FLEMING'S, Silver Grange House, Tivoli Tel: (021) 821621 Michael Fleming
French-influenced food. Open 12.30pm-3pm, 6.30pm-9.30pm Mon-Fri. Closed Xmas. Average Price: lunch ££ dinner £££. Visa, Access, Amex, Diners.

JACQUE'S, 9 Phoenix Street Tel: (021) 277387 Jacqueline & Eithne Barry
Somewhat dated but impeccably maintained, Jacque's is always a fresh and lively restaurant, keenly motivated. Self-service during the day, cosily comfortable at night. Open 9am-3pm Mon, 9am-10.30pm Tue-Sat. Closed Xmas. Average Price: lunch £-££ dinner £££. Visa, Access, Amex, Diners.

O'KEEFFE'S, 23 Washington Street Tel: (021) 275645 Tony & Marie O'Keeffe 'Positive flavours' is the phrase Tony and Marie use to describe their cooking in this intimate bistro. Open 6.30pm-10pm Mon-Sat. Closed Xmas. Average Price: dinner £££. Visa, Access, Amex, Diners.

CAFÉ PARADISO, 16 Lancaster Quay, Western Road Denis Cotter and Bridget Healy. A new vegetarian café with a most interesting menu: potato and lovage tortilla, foccaccio sandwich with roasted vegetables and melted mozzarella, butterbean and hazel nut croquettes, leek and mixed peppercorn tart. Open 10am-10.30pm Mon-Sat. Average Price: lunch £ dinner ££-£££. Bring-your-own wine.

SOUTH & WEST CORK

BALLINHASSIG

RESTAURANT
BILLY MACKESY'S BAWNLEIGH HOUSE

Ballinhassig Tel: (021) 771333 Billy Mackesy

There is a lot of the personality of Billy Mackesy in his food. He is a thoughtful man who can sometimes seem quietly quiet, though you find yourself always on the alert for an explosion of personality. His cooking is as generous in flavour as it is in portion, as welcoming as it is challenging, and the surprises of sharp personality that peek through its subtleties are refreshing. Mackesy likes to use robust cuts of meat, fish and game: pink pigeon breasts, breaded sweetbreads topped with citrus fruit, salmon that has been smoked and in an inspired move is served simply with potato, brill teamed with the loudest of all herbs, basil, in a cream sauce, a venison steak that has been first marinated and then char-grilled. But there is never a loss of delicacy in the cooking, volume does not compensate for flavour.

The service is memorable in its humour, enthusiasm and knowledge, and you feel the

restaurant is run as a team, by a team. The interior design, however, could never be described as chic, arriving somewhere close to a typical Irish front room without the religious portraits or the television sets. But, because everything is done right and done so spiritedly, you find yourself pleased by this lack of artifice, and it makes Mackesy's a place where you can relax and let your hair down.

Open 7pm-10.30pm Tue-Sat. Closed 2 weeks in Oct and Xmas. Average Price: dinner ££££. Access, Visa, Amex. On the Cork-Bandon road (N71) you will find the Half Way village about 7 miles from Cork. Proceed through the village over the bridge and take the first left (sign Kinsale). The restaurant is on the right after about 3 miles.

BANDON

POTTERY
THE BANDON POTTERY
82-83 North Main Street Tel: (023) 41360 Robin & Jane Forrester
The intense blueness of Jane Forrester's work is as much of a signature as the unmistakable cuspy orange hued apples which are found on all the Bandon Pottery products. The many pieces made by the Forresters are pleasing and tactile, but should not be regarded purely as ornaments: these are plates and dishes intended to be used. You can deliberate decisively about what to snap up in the shop whilst you enjoy their coffees and home baking and peruse the other crafts, Jerpoint glass, Con Doyle Woodcraft, handwoven scarves, silk, wool, leather and candles which they sell.
Open 9am-6pm Mon-Sat. The shop is just on the way out of Bandon, heading west after the traffic lights.

THE BANDON FRIDAY MARKET
The Ladies in the print dresses and the sensible cardies run the Bandon market with a firm hand, the array of cakes and sweet things, the table of fresh eggs, the fine organic vegetables and the lovely Jersey butter — this and many of the vegetables produced by Kim Lois and Ian Paul in Ballineen — are all lined up lovely and inviting, on best behaviour.
Friday 2pm-4pm The Hall has a sign at the top end of the main street, just around the corner.

BUTLERSTOWN

RESTAURANT
DUNWORLEY COTTAGE RESTAURANT ➡
Dunworley, Butlerstown Tel: (023) 40314 Katherine Norén
You will find tastes in Dunworley Cottage that are not to be found anywhere else in Ireland, and find a style of cooking which no one else in Ireland could even consider replicating. In this eclectic mix of Scandinavian commitment — Katherine Norén, who runs Dunworley, is from Sweden — and the very finest Irish ingredients, the result is a powerfully flavoursome cuisine of unerring individuality.
Indeed the food presents such a thunderous panorama of tastes that one is glad that the restaurant itself offers little distraction: it is a plain and simple place, cosy but near-

monastic, and this simplicity actually makes the verve and fortitude of the food seem even more pronounced.

So what to eat? You must try the celebrated nettle soup, of course, a green, green brew of wild garden tastes, and naturally the marinated herring, served with a variety of sauces. This, with an eye-boggling glass of aquavit to partner the fish, is one of the finest things you can eat in Ireland, a dish which is so sexy and sinuous as to beggar belief.

But, then, you will also want the salmon soup, fresh little cubes of fish plying against the caramelised taste of the broth, and likely as not you also cherish the gravadlax, and the eggs with a trio of mayonnaises, and the warm globe artichokes with vinaigrette, and on no account must you miss the blanquette of veal, for Mrs Norén gets fine, milk-fed beef and the blanquette is so fudgy and chocolatly, almost syrupy in its sweetness, that you will vow to eat no other veal until you come back here.

Dunworley succeeds because it offers foods which are totally honest in taste, so pure and unadulterated that they seem as fine as the wild air that rushes off the sea at this wildest of spots.

Open high season from 6.30pm Wed-Sun (with lunch at 12.30pm-3pm during Jun-Aug). Weekends only Nov and Dec. Always telephone to check first. Open for Xmas. Closed early Jan-St Patrick's Day (again, always check). Average Price: lunch £££ dinner £££. Visa, Access, Amex, Diners. Recommended for Vegetarians. The restaurant is well signposted as you drive from Timoleague.

COUNTRY HOUSE
SEA COURT
Butlerstown Tel: (023) 40151 (Caretaker Tel: 023 40218) David Elder

The light around this area of Cork shades everything it touches in pastel colours. Only the sea itself can break the peace that it generates. And in this environment the Sea Court sits colourfully oblique, a place which has the mute confidence of a long history.

David Elder himself seems to fit perfectly in these surroundings, a quiet-spoken, cultured American, he oversees all aspects of the house from the careful cooking to the authoritative renovation of its five colourful bedrooms.

Furnishings in all the rooms are happily sparse — no nonsensical clutter — and the total effect is nothing less than uplifting. Absorb deep lungfuls of the clean, clean air and you are unlikely to need any other sort of nightcap.

Breakfasts and dinners are simple and correct, fine value, completing the profile of articulate restraint which drives you back to the soft sensibility of Sea Court.

Open for dinner for guests (book by noon). Open for short season only mid Jun-end Aug. Average Price: dinner £££ B&B £££. No Credit Cards. Signposted from Butlerstown.

CARRIGALINE

COUNTRY MARKET
CARRIGALINE COUNTRY MARKET
The GAA Hall, Crosshaven Road Tel: (021) 831340

'Please no shopping until 9.30, except for flowers', pleads the felt-tip sign on the table as you walk into the Carrigaline community hall and wait for the Friday morning market to kick off.

It's a necessary commandment, for retaining self-control when faced by the disarming riches of the biggest and best Country Market in the country presents enormous difficulties. You want to hoover up yardarms of lolloping flowers, grab reams of vegetables all spruce and happy in their fresh glory. Caution, and calorie counting, can go hang whilst you deliberate over whether to get one chocolate topped sponge or two, or just one and a battenburg, or a battenburg with a gooey Swiss roll.

And then there are the obligatory additions: some of Pat O'Farrell's Carrigaline cheeses, made just up the road outside the town. Some candle-white beeswax. A jar or two of orchard-brown apple chutney. A second bag of those deliciously dark chicken livers. A second mortgage so you can buy everything in the place.

The market is a riot of good food, food which is not just good to taste but is good in every sense. Local food, made by local folk, sold at its best in the locality from which it has drawn its character. Transported to France and plonked in a market square, coachloads of camera-laden tourists would come to pay homage and mutter to themselves about 'culture'. Here, in the softlands of the county, the locals know how valuable this institution is, but pass no great comment on it.

Like the other markets scattered throughout the country, Carrigaline is a splendidly pleasurable place in which to shop. The atmosphere is punctuated with kind advice — 'It's not a bit fussy, put it in a border, it's dead easy', says a woman to an elderly man making up his mind whether or not he will buy a potting plant — and the comfort of close friends, fresh gossip, the goings and comings of the community, the expectation of fresh new foods as they come into season.

Whether or not you actually buy anything, a stroll around the Carrigaline Community Hall on a Friday morning is delightful. 'Everyone in the market is a producer' says Catherine Desmond, the Chairperson of the Committee which manages the whole splendid adventure. 'It's housewives, it's an interest, it's a co-op'. It's more than that, of course. It's an idealised, and ideal, aspect of a local community looking after its own needs, valuing its own resources, actually giving meaning to the term 'community'.

Friday mornings 9.30am-10.30am For details Tel Catherine Desmond: (021) 831340

FARMHOUSE CHEESE
CARRIGALINE FARMHOUSE CHEESE
Marello, Leacht Cross Tel: (021) 372856 Pat O'Farrell
This cheese represents the epitome of a farmhouse operation. Pat O'Farrell milks the cows, makes the cheese with his wife, and then can be relied upon to promote the cheese at great lengths at food fairs around the country. One wonders when anyone gets a chance to sleep in this household. The cheese itself is mild in taste, as gently flavoured as Pat's accent is whisper-soft, and comes under an enveloping wax coating. Some of the cheeses are flavoured with garlic and herbs.

PRESERVES
OWNABWEE PRESERVES
Ballynametagh House Tel: (021) 372323 Phil Thompson
Phil Thompson's Ownabwee Preserves can be relied on to give the professionalism of a cottage industry allied to the taste of jams and jellies that could have been made on the kitchen stove.

RESTAURANT
SEAN NA MBADS

Ringabella Tel: (021) 887397 Fiona McDonald

No signposts signal this out-of-the-way restaurant and pub near Carrigaline, but it's worth hunting down. An old stone two storey house, it's divided into a couple of bars, a billiards room and a dining room lined from wall to low ceiling with books. But whilst this might sound like an amateurish big house dinner-party sort of a place, one look at the menu reveals that a professional touch is behind what was once a simple country pub. Saddle of Rabbit is confidently roasted, a maigret of duck given a port wine sauce and accompanied by a purée of leek and mushrooms. Brill is made into a mousse, poached and served with mussels with a sauce studded with tomatoes and chives. The wine list is short, just eight bottles, with a Muscadet that compares to a Toyota Corolla: comfortable, effortless, but hardly stylish. You can book a table but they don't, in fact, reserve them.

Open 7pm-9.30pm Thurs-Sun (bar open 7 nights from around 5pm). Closed Xmas. Average Price: dinner £££. Visa, Access. Telephone for directions.

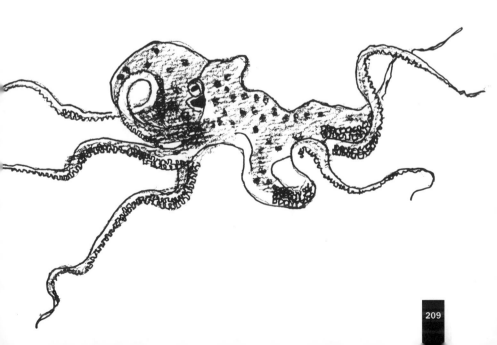

CLONAKILTY

RESTAURANT
FIONNUALA'S

30 Ashe Street Tel: (023) 34355 Fionnuala

Fionnuala cleverly describes her raggle-taggle collection of tables, chairs, and candle-wax encrusted Chianti and Amarone bottles as a 'Little Italian Restaurant', clever because this spells her culinary strengths. Pizzas and pastas are generous with the spicy flavours of pepperoni and sweet peppers, food that is comforting at lunchtime, and fun for the evening. The dining room, with its appropriately well-worn feel, looks like the stage set of some amateur dramatic production, but there is nothing stagy about the friendliness and the good heart of the cooking.

Open 12.30pm-2.15pm, 6pm-9.30pm Tue-Sun. Limited hours in winter. Average Price: lunch £-££ dinner £££. Visa, Access.

HOTEL BAR AND RESTAURANT
O'DONOVAN'S HOTEL

44 Pearse Street Tel: (023) 33250/33883 Tom O'Donovan

The industrious O'Donovans run this hotel with vigour and enthusiasm. The bar, with its Guinness surfer roof mural, its old bottles and glasses, is a maze of family paraphernalia. There's a marvellous old polython in the café, and the corridors are lorded over by the five generations who have run the hotel since it opened, one of whom was Auntie Cat, the first woman in Clonakilty to smoke in public and wear trousers.

Open pub hours, with restaurant open all day and throughout the evening. Average Price: meal £-£££ B&B £££. Visa, Access. Clonakilty town centre.

BUTCHER/PUDDING MAKER
TWOMEY'S BUTCHERS ➡

16 Pearse Street Tel: (023) 33365 Edward Twomey

Black pudding is not a foodstuff which the Irish take seriously. It is something to be sliced and fried for Sunday breakfast, and then pay no more moment to it. So, how can one explain the extraordinary success of Edward Twomey's near-legendary Clonakilty pudding, a rusky, mealy mouthful of delight which has captured the imagination of Irish chefs throughout the country.

One chef will pair a few slices of pudding with oysters and a mustard dressing. Another, this the famous invention of Gerry Galvin of Drimcong House, will team it with the oysters and an apple and onion confit. Eugene MacSweeney in Kilkenny will use the pud for a twice-baked soufflé. Canice Sharkey in Cork will top a Mediterranean bean stew, rich with tomatoes and peppers and an assortment of beans, with a couple of slices of the pudding on top. Why this sudden fever pitch, this rush of pig's blood to the heads of all these distinguished men?

One might suggest that the answer lies with the pudding, and certainly it does. Mealy and mellow in taste, the Clonakilty pud has the ability to ally itself with many diverse foods, thus making it ideal company for the feverishly creative mind of a cook.

But, just as importantly, the secret lies with Mr Twomey. Slowly, surely, he promoted and made public the Clonakilty pudding. He insisted that it be taken seriously, demanded that it find a function away from the Sunday fry-up. And his dedication, and his sweetly charming character, worked. Harrington's Original Recipe Clonakilty Black Pudding is now as famous an Irish food as Galway Oysters or Guinness, and it is all thanks to Mr Twomey, whom we might describe as the Henry Ford or Harry Ferguson of Black Pudding, an Irish Bocuse of the boudin. His achievement is remarkable. As remarkable as his pudding.

Open 9am-6pm Mon-Sat

PUB
AN SUGAN

41 Strand Road Tel: (023) 33498 Kevin and Brenda O'Crowley

This is a friendly little pub, and they work hard to keep the bar food up to scratch, so there are pleasures on the plate as well as in a glass.

Open noon-10pm Mon-Sun (Sun closed between 2.30pm-4.30pm)

COURTMACSHERRY

B&B WITH RESTAURANT
TRAVARA LODGE

Courtmacsherry Tel: (023) 46493 Mandy Guy

Travara Lodge sits looking out on the sea in the beautiful, pastel-painted village of Courtmacsherry, and Mandy Guy works hard to make a success of both the little restaurant downstairs and the rooms upstairs. The food is simple, fillets of fish, fillets of steak, cordon bleu chicken, and it's always fine value. The rooms have pummeling showers and comfortable beds and, with those at the front of the house, super views.

'With advance notice we do our best to accommodate any requests, i.e. ground floor room, cots, baby sitters, sea view, dogs, vegetarian meals, packed lunch, early breakfast etc', they say, and they do mean it.

Open 7pm-9.30pm Mon-Sat ('till 9pm low season). Closed Nov-Apr. Average Price: dinner £££ B&B £££. Visa, Access. Just on the waterfront in Courtmacsherry.

GLANDORE

THE RECTORY

Glandore Tel: (028) 33072 Sean O'Boyle
A handsome venture in one of the handsome villages of south west Cork, Kieran Scully's cooking quickly won admirers when The Rectory opened.

Open 7pm-10pm Mon-Sun (Tue-Sat in winter with possible closing period in spring). Average Price: dinner £££. Visa, Access, Amex. On the harbour at Glandore.

KINSALE

B&B
THE OLD PRESBYTERY

Cork Street Tel: (021) 772027 Ken & Cathleen Buggy
Everything you encounter in Ken and Cathleen Buggy's Old Presbytery has a purpose. Everything works to add meaning and character to the house, everything conspires to build an aesthetic, to add an extra patina of personality, to contribute something witty, something humorous.

The beautiful hand operated printing press which cradles a selection of books. That great big whicker linen basket. The smooth round of the butter churn. Mr Buggy's paintings and streetscapes which decorate the walls, the clever cartoons he has drawn that have you chuckling away to yourself with mirth, years after you first saw them, when the memory of one of them rushes back into the mind. The fascinatingly useless pulp novels. The fabulously baleful big brass beds with their come-hither softness and crisp sheets of snowy-white.

It may sound eclectic and uncritical but, assembled all in one place, these artefacts construct a house which is marvellously articulate, which reveals an eye devoted to correctness, to putting the right thing in the right place, to finding the right thing for the right place. The Chinese believe that the organisation of a room greatly affects personality and good fortune. The Old Presbytery will greatly influence your character and good fortune: you will be over the moon to find yourself here, and hardly able to believe your luck.

Ken and Cathleen complete this spatial paragon, with Mr Buggy's breakfasts never anything less than perfect — the soda bread crumbly, the porridge a smooth fougasse of oats and cream, the eggs fresh, the bacon smoky — and Mrs Buggy as calm, collected and charming as you wish you were yourself.

Open for dinner by special arrangement. Closed Xmas. Average Price: dinner £££ B&B £££. No Credit Cards. Just at the corner of Cork Street, opposite the church.

BROWN SODA BREAD

BREAD IS SIMILAR TO WINE in that it is often understood to evoke something larger than itself, the regional soil, the character of the place and people who make and eat it' writes Paul Bertolli in 'Chez Panisse Cooking', and this is true of the brown soda bread made in Ireland.

Ireland's regional soils and their characters give us a flour that is trenchant and unsophisticated. The lack of a burning sun means that the proteins in the wheat never fully develop; fluffy baguettes and puffy pastries need a flour that is nimble and fast working, and that could never be said of Irish flour.

The people who have shaped Irish soda bread are a people who have experienced famine, and their character has given us a plain loaf that puts nourishment on a higher level than indulgence.

That said, in its proper context and eaten with the best Irish foods: salmon, fried bacon, lamb stew, oysters, there can be no better accompaniment to breakfast, to lunch, to dinner.

The secret of soda bread-making is simplicity. There are few rules and few ingredients: flour, milk, soda and salt. But, like anything that is simple, the margin for error is enormous. Common mistakes and problems make a bread that is too crumbly, too hard, too yellow in colour and, at its worst, bread that tastes of an indigestion tablet.

Stirring, rather than kneading, gives the loaf good body. The dough should be damp with a texture like a roux.

The flour should be coarse. The milk must contain acid, it could be buttermilk or sour milk. Some recipes contain cream, others add an egg. Breadmakers in Ireland use 'Bread Soda' rather than bicarbonate of soda or baking powder. Pure bicarbonate will work, but use less of it, otherwise you'll get a bad taste and a yellowy colour. Baking powder is not used as it contains an acid that is already present in the buttermilk.

After that, it is every man to himself. Anybody who makes soda bread has their own technique. Some put the bread in a low oven and then give it a firey blast at

TOWNHOUSE
THE OLD BANK HOUSE
Kinsale Tel: (021) 772968/774075 Michael & Marie Reise

A handsome, town-centre B&B in a building that was, once, the Munster and Leinster Bank, The Old Bank House is an oasis of cool sanity, somewhere that seems especially valuable during holiday times when Kinsale appears on the brink of overheating on an hourly basis. The trappings of the modern age are all here: direct dial telephones, multi-channel TV, big, elegant bathrooms, but Michael and Marie Reise never allow the house to sink into formulaic blandness.

Open all year except Xmas. Average Price: B&B ££££-£££££. Ask about evening meals. Visa, Access, Amex.

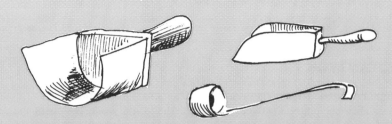

the end, others put it high and leave it for an hour, half an hour, turn it down, turn it round.

Siobhan McGuinness, who makes her living from knitting, makes a wonderful loaf on the Aran Islands: 1lb brown flour, 1pint buttermilk, 2 teasps bread soda, 1 teasp salt. 'Put all dry ingredients into a bowl' she writes 'and mix together with your hand allowing air through. Add buttermilk and mix bit by bit until mixture is very soggy but not on the side of being over liquified. Pour into a bread tin (floured on the bottom) and place in oven. Light oven to high gas then, and leave for about 15 mins. When there is a slight crust formed lower to about half flame or slightly less for remainder of 1 hour or until bread is completely cooked. Sorry I can't give gas marks', she continues 'for my oven has given up the ghost on that line and I just judge the height of the flame'.

Ken Buggy of the Old Presbytery in Kinsale in Co Cork is probably the best teacher if you want to learn the art of soda bread making. First he gives you a list: 'teaspoon, knife, flour, wooden spoon, bread soda, mixing bowl, buttermilk, oven on high, floured baking tray'.

Gather together the above. Put one overfilled kitchen cup of white flour into the bowl, and add 2 heaped cups of brown flour. Sieve in 1 rounded teaspoon of bread soda (the soda is the only thing you sieve). Add three-quarters pint buttermilk. Whizz round with the wooden spoon as if constructing a roux. Lightly bring together the dough, finally using a little more white flour to seal it. Shape into a ball and place on loaf tin. Cut deeply — nearly all the way through as it will heal together — in the shape of a cross. Bake for half an hour.

RESTAURANTS

THE BLUE HAVEN

Pearse Street Tel: (021) 772209 Brian and Anne Cronin

The latest string to the bow of this professionally run hotel is a fine wine shop and off licence with an excellent range of good plonks and zestful spirits to lift the spirits. Amidst much that is familiar and friendly there are some stellar wines: the legendary Cloudy Bay Sauvignon from New Zealand, the legendary Domaine de Trevallon from Provence, the splendid and surprising Hamilton Russell Chardonnays and Pinot Noirs from South Africa, unlikely and impressive Rieslings from Spain and the excellent new whiskey,

Tyrconnell, from Rivertown, just north of Dundalk. The hotel is also a good spot for bar lunches.

Open 10am-11.30pm Mon-Sat, 12.30pm-11pm Sun (winter hours they stop serving at 11pm). Food served in the bar 12.30pm-3pm, snacks 3pm-5.30pm, evening meals 5.30pm-9.30pm.

CHEZ JEAN MARC

Lower O'Connell Street Tel: (021) 774625 Jean-Marc & Fiona Tsai

This grand, handsome temple of a restaurant has an admirable confidence about itself and a zesty air which quite suits the Kinsale spirit. The food is generous — portions are trencherman massive — and whilst there can be successes, precision and sympathy of flavour in the food can sometimes seem elusive.

Open 7pm-10pm Mon-Sun. Closed Xmas. Average Price: dinner ££££. Visa, Access, Diners. Behind Acton's Hotel, just a little up the hill, in the centre of town.

MAN FRIDAY

Scilly, Kinsale Tel: (021) 772260 Philip Horgan

Man Friday's popularity may be explained by the generosity of its portions, and its decision to bank on old favourites like prawns and steaks. The restaurant always has a great buzz and is always busy: the food comes out fast and efficiently, often with two sittings a night.

Open 7pm-10pm. Closed Xmas. Average Price: dinner ££££. Visa, Access. On the hillside of Scilly, looking down at the town.

PIAZZETTA

1 Newman's Mall Tel: (021) 774311 Dagmar and Dieter Reckers

Piazzetta may not be much to look at, its menu may not seem to promise the sun, moon, earth and stars, but it is possible to enjoy a super lunch or dinner here which features real

flavours and real pleasures: stone oven-baked pizzas, pasta with appropriate sauces, monkfish marinated in olive oil and herbs, a simply divine Alsatian onion tart, gnocchi with parmesan and hot butter. Piazzetta is also a particularly good spot for vegetarians, as they keep the pots to cook vegetarian dishes separate from those used for cooking meat. Perfect too for kids who love this sharp, up-front food.

Open 12.30pm-10.30pm Mon-Sun (winter hours 5pm-10.30pm Tue-Sun). Closed Xmas. Average Price: lunch £-££ dinner £-£££. Visa, Access.

THE KINSALE GOOD FOOD CIRCLE

Tel: (021) 774026

The Kinsale Good Food Circle is a collection of its many restaurateurs, who publish a leaflet called 'Kinsale à la Carte', and club together to run a Gourmet Festival each autumn.

OYSTERHAVEN

RESTAURANT
THE OYSTERCATCHER RESTAURANT ➡

Oysterhaven Tel: (021) 770822 Sylvia & Bill Patterson

You could be forgiven for feeling a pang of trepidation when you first see the Oystercatcher Restaurant.

Its complete and utter cuteness — a necklace of spangly coloured lights hanging just under the lip of the roof, the gently arcing white-faced cottage lamp-lit at the windows, its ideal location at the crown of the road in this serene fold of the Cork countryside — promises something altogether too perfect, and you fear the reality cannot possibly live up to the first impression.

But, walk inside and the simplicity of the design, the lack of anything contrived or unnecessary in the layout of the single room, and one is reassured. On the tables, tall gobletty glasses spell out their seriousness of purpose, and the happy sound of whisking and whirring that falls out from the swing doors which hide the kitchen banishes any fears, any trepidation. Bill and Sylvia Patterson's Oystercatcher is a well-considered, considerate place, a quiet culinary adventure.

The dinner menu — there is no à la carte selection aside from the broad range of choices on the table d'hôte — reassures even further, concentrating more on describing the source of the ingredients than on dithering with daft culinary details. An obvious starter like Parma Ham is underscored by an organic, rather than a conventionally grown, Galia melon. Inagh goat's cheese — grilled on a bed of salad leaves — is explained as coming from County Clare. Salmon, with a fennel sauce, is from the Atlantic, duck breast from the Landes, the Gruyère which wraps an escalope of veal is from West Cork, venison is local.

This respect for plainness of design and clarity of description ends as soon as the food appears, however, for Bill Patterson enjoys painting a picture on a plate. A Trio of Rock Oysters on a bed of Angel Hair Pasta topped with a Raspberry Sauce is infernally pyrotechnical, and will have both a scattering of green salad leaves and a confetti of shredded, deep-fried onion in the middle of the big black plate. Yet the dish will impress most with its cleanness of taste, the oyster still perfectly sea-salty, the Medusa-like strands of pasta a tangle of mild flavours, the raspberry sauce limber and fresh, barely sweet. A similarly cosmopolitan dish, Hot Smoked Wild Irish Salmon on a Blini with Leek Sauce, features thickly-cut slices of Ummera salmon served on blinis of ethereal finesse, a leek sauce picking up an echo of the greenness from the accompanying salad.

The grandness of the food in The Oystercatcher comes as much, however, from its comforting succour as it does from the high notes you expect from smoked salmon and oysters, venison and duck. Marinated Local Venison on a Pepper Sauce is judiciously sweet and tender, Breast of Landes Duck with a Herb and Sherry Vinegar Sauce is simple and assured, effortlessly understated. Desserts like Prunes in Armagnac with Vanilla Ice-Cream or Crème Brûlée are true to their nature, prepared according to classic strictures. Energetic tipplers and culinary enthusiasts may like to know that, if they find there is still red wine in the bottle when dessert comes around, The Oystercatcher features about half a dozen savoury desserts, including Scotch Woodcock, a voluptuous marriage of scrambled eggs cooked with anchovies and served on toast.

The wine list is a discriminating crusade of fine wines from every continent, with even a red wine from Germany made by the enigmatic Rainer Lingenfelder and a pair of deeply unfashionable Greek wines. The service is perfect, never intruding on the intimately romantic ambience of the restaurant, and the whole experience is blissful, balmy.

Open 7pm-9.15pm Mon-Sun, May-Sept. Closed Nov-Apr, but available for private parties during this time with 24 hours notice, min 4 people. Closed Xmas, also Tue & Thur in Winter, and the month of Jan. Average Price: dinner: ££££. Visa, Access. Recommended for Vegetarians if notice is given. Follow signs for Oysterhaven, and the restaurant is just on your left before you go over the bridge into the village.

ROSSCARBERY

ROSSCARBERY RECIPES

Rosscarbery Tel: (023) 48407 Gillian Boazman

Like any pioneer, Gill Boazman likes to invent and to innovate, and it is in these experiments that one often finds she creates the most exciting and delicious tastes. Recently, her new venison sausages and her venison pie have offered delightfully full and agreeable tastes, not too gamey, the pie perfect for a quick-grabbed snack when you are in the car and hunger-struck.

Her smoked beef sausage, perhaps sliced thinly then scattered over a warm salad of steamed potatoes onto which spring onions have been scattered and olive oil drizzled, is a delightful food for lunch or a comforting supper. The standard pork pies and sausages are consistently enjoyable, though some may crave the more active seasoning which you find in the lovely spinach sausage, one of the best barbecue foods you will find. Joined on the fire by some spicy Rosscarbery barbecue spare ribs, you need only beer and bread for the perfect outdoor feast.

Rosscarbery Recipes' pies and sausages are found in shops and supermarkets throughout south and west Cork and occasionally further afield.

TIMOLEAGUE

PUB FOOD
DILLON'S

Timoleague, Bandon Tel: (023) 46390 Isabelle Dillon

Though it has leapt through the hoops of various owners over the last few years, its focus changing from café with booze, then to boozer with food, and now back again to its stylish, funky origins, Dillon's has always been local and lovely, and the recent decision to use food cooked in the local, lovely Lettercollum House is a smart move. Choose a plate of Anthony Creswell's smoked salmon, maybe some pork terrine or stuffed mussels, have a pint of Guinness, follow up with a slice of tarte tatin and you will wonder when you last enjoyed a lunch so profoundly, simply tasteful.

Food served noon-10pm. Closed Tues. Average Price: meal ££. No credit cards.

RESTAURANT & INDEPENDENT HOSTEL
LETTERCOLLUM HOUSE ➡

Timoleague Tel: (023) 46251 Con McLoughlin

They pride themselves in Lettercollum on the democratic air they can engender amongst their guests, the ideal of back-packers at one table beside BMW drivers at another in the dining room, and hostellers in their dorms just down the hall from the families in the family rooms. And with proper justification. One Sunday lunch, on a fine September day, there were tables of wrinkly old folk beside tables lined up with toddlers, babies in carry-tots, quartets of the chattering classes, local families relaxing in the afternoon balm of the dining room and, just to complete the picture, outside there was a stretched Mercedes limousine with a be-hatted chauffeur, while inside the extended family who occupied it were getting on delightedly with the business of a birthday party. When it came to the time to sing 'Happy Birthday To You', the entire room picked up the tune after a bar or two, as if we had all known each other all our lives.

If the atmosphere is mighty, then so is the food. When Seamus O'Connell worked here, he and Con McLoughlin made a great team, the sparks of one offset by the steadiness of the other. Since Seamus went off to open the Ivory Tower in Cork city, Con McLoughlin's culinary confidence has increased by leaps and bounds, and his food now is as sure tasting and individual as you will find. Having the benefit of a walled garden which gives him most of the organic vegetables and herbs he needs underpins the confident flavours which the food offers, for this is a true cuisine paysanne: a courgette soup is peppery and reviving, a salad composé bright with garden trueness, roast leg of lamb is sweet and fresh garlic and tarragon are perfect bedfellows for it, a daube of beef is soulful and perfect. The small details you want for a Sunday lunch — crisp roast spuds, spoonful desserts, teasingly aromatic coffee — are all done perfectly, and at the end you can only conclude that they are not charging half enough for such taste-addled food. Lettercollum is fabulous for families — feed the kids in the hostel kitchen, put them to bed then you eat downstairs with no need to worry about babysitters or driving — and perfect for anyone, whether you travel by Shank's Mare or stretch limo.

Open 7.30pm-9.30pm Mon-Sat, 1.30pm-3pm Sun (Sun evenings high season only). Closed weekdays mid-Nov-mid-March. Average Prices: ££-£££. Access, Visa. Recommended for Vegetarians. Lettercollum is just outside Timoleague, and clearly signposted.

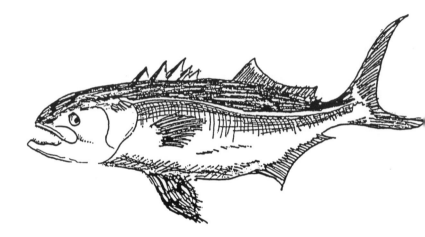

SMOKED SALMON
UMMERA SMOKED PRODUCTS ★

Ummera House, Timoleague Tel: (023) 46187 Fax: 46419 Anthony Creswell

The secret of smoked salmon, the secret which explains our reverence for it, our appreciation and expectation of it, our willingness to leave it well alone and to enjoy it with no more than a squidge of lemon and a slice of bread, our tolerance of its steep price — lies in the fact that it is so pleasurable, so simply pleasurable, to eat this unctuous, mildly viscous, powerfully understated delicacy.

The qualities of serenity of taste and subtlety of taste and sophistication of taste which we prize are never better represented than by Anthony Creswell's precious salmon. Mr Creswell uses only wild salmon, for the farmed fish has none of the strength of musculature or suppleness of texture which the wild environment gifts to the fish. It is then gently smoked to both add the complexity of smoke to the flavour — there are more than 200 active components in smoke — and to enhance the natural oils and sweet, abiding satisfaction of the fish itself.

Ummera smoked salmon is so good, so true in flavour, so sybaritic and satisfying, that the first day you eat a slice is assuredly one of the best days of your life. Anthony Creswell's smoked salmon sets the benchmark for smoked fish in Ireland, and his sweetly smoked eels and smoked chickens are likewise pre-eminent, pristine in their purity of flavour.

The house is the first entrance on the right, over the hill, after the Protestant graveyard in Timoleague.

Ummera operate a splendid and speedy mail order service to all parts of the world.

THE FAR WEST PENINSULAS

BANTRY AND THE SHEEP'S HEAD PENINSULA

AHAKISTA

JAPANESE EATING HOUSE
SHIRO JAPANESE DINNER HOUSE ➡
Ahakista Tel: (027) 67030 Kei and Werner Pilz
There are only two tables in The Shiro Japanese Dinner House, each in separate rooms and each available only to a single party each evening, there is only Kei and her husband Werner, and their food is quite extraordinary, something that demands the realm of the sexual vocabulary to express adequately the pleasure it gives. Here, an ideal of heightened, almost narcotic delight is orchestrated by Kei Pilz by means of a sinuous procession of dishes, each of them separate but, ultimately, sympathetic. Culinary alchemy in The Shiro is conceived as a broad canvas, with a final sense of satisfaction arising only at the conclusion of a meal.

With every delicious morsel parcelled exquisitely, the procession parades food that is a delight to the eye — the filigree fans of tempura served on a wooden board, tenderly carved vegetables, a brown Windsorish sui-mono with tofu and cabbage greens hidden in the soup — a delight to the palate — smoky tea-leaved sea weed as part of Azuke-Bachi, supple sashimi of mackerel, salmon and squid — and, through the course of the evening, it seems to motivate and arouse, and ultimately exhaust, every sense in the body.

Open 7pm-9pm Tue-Sat. Closed Xmas and Jan. Average Price: dinner ££££££. Visa, Access, Amex, Diners (payment by credit card incurs an additional charge of 5%). Recommended for Vegetarians. Signposted from the Cork-Bantry road and from the village of Durrus.

BAR
THE TIN PUB
Ahakista, Tom Whitty
If dinner in The Shiro can seem like an out-take from 'The Wizard of Oz', this unreconstructed corrugated-iron bar just across the road is an essential part of the surreal nature of the evening and, no less, an essential part of a loitering drive through Ahakista and down to the single lonely road at the bottom of the Sheep's Head Peninsula.

CASTLETOWNSHEND

FISH SMOKER
WOODCOCK SMOKERY
Gortbreac Tel: (028) 36232 Sally Barnes
Sally Barnes's fish is to be seen sporadically here and there, and is to be snatched up when you do see it, for it has a deep, wide aura of smokiness asserting itself alongside the fine fish Mrs Barnes uses.

BALLYLICKEY

RESTAURANT
TRA AMICI

Dromkeal, Coomhola Road Tel: (027) 50235 Fax: 50958 Sean Vail

Sean Vail talks modestly about his cooking. 'I guess a way to describe it would be "Occasion Cooking"', he says. 'Italians would cook these type of dishes on special occasions: gnocchi is something the family sits down and makes for something like a wedding, or for Easter'.

Whilst this explanation signals the general direction of the Italian food Mr Vail cooks, it does little to suggest the heights of sublimity to which his cooking can ascend. The real key to his work may lie in the admission that, 'We look at the restaurant as an extension of our home: I would treat people in the dining room the same as if I were entertaining someone in my house'.

The food in Tra Amici looks, superficially, simple: Spaghetti al Pesto, Carpaccio all' Albese, Pollo alla Cacciatora, the familiar dishes we associate with Italian cuisine, but Vail cooks them the way an Italian would cook them at home in Italy, achieving, on occasion, nothing less than a transcendent, mysterious magic.

His Spaghetti al Pesto is the perfect alliance of soft noodles and a sauce which sinuously elides its subtle basil and cheese tastes with the pasta. The tastes are simple, correct, sympathetic, and they are to be found throughout a meal: Vermicelli with clams, soft thimbles of gnocchi with a red sauce, delicate veal that disappears in the mouth, a sublime baked cheesecake.

Everything in Tra Amici amounts to an 'episode for the senses', to quote the great Italian cook and writer Marcella Hazan again. Be warned: one episode is never enough. You will wish to make Tra Amici into a long running series.

Open 7pm-11.30pm Mon-Sat. Closed Xmas and Mar, weekends only off season. Average Price: £££. Visa, Access. Recommended for Vegetarians. Signposted at the Ballylickey Bridge.

HANDMADE KNIVES
HAND CRAFTED KNIVES

Ballylickey Tel: (027) 50032 Rory Conner

'I read an article about knifemaking and took a fancy to it', says Rory Conner of his introduction to the world of hand-crafted knives. 'My first attempts were terrible, disastrous! But I read everything, anything I could get my hands on and bombarded American knife makers with letters, got a few more scars and improved'. Today, Mr Conner's craft is as far removed from the familiar mass production of cooking and eating implements as one could imagine. This is knife-making as art.

Everything he makes is done to order — there is a minimum three month waiting list — and the process is uniquely personal. 'There's one or two people I know', says Rory 'who collect knives, and their wives don't even know how many knives they have. They ring up in quiet voices and say "Look, the wife's going away, can you have it ready in six weeks?", or they say, "Can you send it to my friend, in case she comes back early!", I'm not kidding!'.

The process of ordering a knife from Rory is quite painstaking, with drawings and silhouettes swapped back and forward until the customer is happy with the shape, the

length, the type of wood, the weight. 'Then we start grinding, hours and hours of grinding'.

The knives are made from a stainless steel that is specially manufactured for knife making. For the handles he uses a range of different materials and decorates the knife with a hand-carved illustration.

For the kitchen he makes a cook's knife, an oyster knife, a cheese knife, a paring knife, steak knives, a carving set as well as knives made to order.

Such work is not cheap, of course, but given the sheer amount of labour involved, and the beautiful results, prices are reasonable. If you do splash out, then do bear in mind Rory's tips for good knife maintenance: 'The main thing is don't store them in a drawer higgledy-piggledy, don't leave them in water overnight. Store them upright in a block: on a magnetic rack the knives become magnetised themselves and if there are any metal filings in the kitchen the knives will pick those up. And don't put them in a dishwasher, it's too hot'.

Rory's workshop is part of the entrance to Sea View Hotel: just take the fork to the right.

RESTAURANT AND ACCOMMODATION
LARCHWOOD HOUSE
Pearson's Bridge, nr Ballylickey Tel: (027) 66181 Sheila Vaughan

Larchwood is, first and foremost, a family home. Unusually for a family home, however, it just happens to have a restaurant, and happens to have four rooms upstairs for guests. The lounge, then, is also the sitting room, whilst the dining room is simply a larger than usual family dining room, with various tables arrayed around the walls, some with a splendid view of the splendid garden.

Sheila Vaughan is an expert cook and a well-crafted skill runs right through her kitchen work, producing elegant terrines, baked avocado, lamb's liver with orange and Dubonnet as starters, soups which are fresh and flavoursome, then crisp sorbets. The principal distinction of main courses, whether one chooses fish or meat, is not only their persuasive fulsomeness, but the fulsomely enormous portions: dinner at Larchwood amounts to a feast, a feast which the richly sinful desserts bring to a rousing climax.

If you object to any manner of a domestic atmosphere when dining out, then Larchwood is unlikely to appeal. But, if the thought of only having to climb upstairs to bed after a boozy dinner sounds like just the sort of intensive relaxation you feel you need, then Larchwood, in its unlikely way, may furnish what you crave.

Open from 6.30pm. Closed Xmas. Average Price: dinner £££ B&B £££-££££. Visa, Access, Diners.
Signposted from the Ballylickey/Glengarriff road.

FOOD EMPORIUM
MANNING'S EMPORIUM ★
Ballylickey Tel: (027) 50456 Val Manning

Val Manning's famous Emporium hibernates during the winter. After his second Food Fair in December — a quiet day of good crack and polite wine swigging — the slow days of wintertime see the shop batten down for the duration.

Then, come Easter, and the arrival of the Goat's milk cheeses and the beginning of the herbs and the Irish vegetables, and Val and his staff set about the spring cleaning with a vengeance: rub-a-dub, scrub-a-dub into the wee small hours, and out of its quiet cocoon this brilliant butterfly of enthusiasm, fine food and boundless hospitality comes into its own.

The best way to get the measure of Manning's is simply to loiter around it for as long as you can, looking at this, deciding to buy that, having a taste of this cheese or that cheese or whatever. That way, listening to the greetings and the gossip, you realise that Manning's is less like a conventional shop and more like an unconventional drinks party: everyone in here is a friend and at any minute you are likely to be introduced to someone new, someone nice.

Someone wrote to us once and, in the course of a eulogy about West Cork, praised Val Manning for being 'an excellent host'. For this is what Mr Manning is. Host to his customers. Host to the carefully chosen, carefully nurtured foods he sells. Host to a vision of the shopkeeper as a focus for a community in which he plays a vital part. Host, above all, to enthusiasm for, and devotion to, good food.

Open 9am-9pm Mon-Sun (longer hours in the summer, shorter hours in the winter, but like all good country shops everything is a bit flexible).

HERBS AND HERB PATES
MEADOWSWEET HERBS
Ballylickey Tel: (027) 66024

Jeff and Jenny Startup are not just fine herb growers — you will find their excellent herbs and herb mixtures in neat little plastic bags in a variety of shops in the area — but they also make unusual and unusually good vegetarian pâtés, found in shops in little tubs with a Meadowsweet label stuck on the top. Hazel nut and Sage, Peanut and Parsley, Mushroom and Mixed Herb are just some of the ingenious concoctions Jeff works on devotedly, but each time you meet him there is some new experiment, some new confection of herbs and pulses from which to fashion a perfect picnic, a fail-safe starter.

ORGANIC GROWER
PAUL SCHULTZ ➡
Ardnageehy Beg, Bantry Tel: (027) 51158

Paul Schultz's work is a brilliant example of the diversity which organic methods of agriculture promote, and a testament to his own devilishly hard work. He grows anything, everything, all of it on a mere few acres just outside Bantry and it is inevitably perfectly delicious: swollen courgette flowers, bright sweet peas, tender little courgettes, floury potatoes. His vegetables, found for the most part in Manning's Emporium and the Supervalu in Bantry, can also be bought from the farm and visitors are most welcome, especially if they want to pitch in, grab a spade and learn about organic farming the real way, the hard way.

Telephone for directions. The farm is a few miles west of Bantry.

RESTAURANT AND HOTEL
SEA VIEW HOUSE HOTEL
Ballylickey Tel: (027) 50073 Fax: 51555 Kathleen O'Sullivan

The attention and kindness of the staff is the secret that makes Sea View so charming. 'I thought they were going to give me a big hug when I walked in', said a friend, and if you did indeed get a big hug it wouldn't seem unusual.

The food these huggable youngsters bring to the table, both at breakfast and, especially, at dinner, is so delicious, so buttery and creamy, that you forget your concern for artery and waistline: never mind comfort food, these dishes transport you all the way back to the womb.

People come to Kathleen O'Sullivan's charmingly innocent hotel to have a good time, to celebrate the special events and days of their lives, and they celebrate them with gusto, with determination to wring the best possible memories from the day that is in it. The staff, those huggable folk, are as determined as you that you should have the best possible time.

Open for dinner and Sun lunch, bar food 12.30pm-2.30pm, afternoon tea. Closed mid Nov-mid Mar. Average Price: dinner £££ B&B ££££-£££££. Visa, Access, Amex. Signposted on the N71 as you drive into Ballylickey.

BANTRY

CAFÉ
5A CAFÉ
5a Barrack Street
A laid-back, inexpensive little vegetarian café, where Cookie dreams up contenting soups, good breads (which can be bought to take away) and good salads. The buzz, from the assortment of intriguing odds and sods who hang out here, is always good.
Open 9am-5.30pm Mon-Sat

PIZZERIA
LA FAMILIA
Main Street Tel: (027) 51195
A bright-eyed pizza restaurant, with good, simple pizza breads, pizzas and uncomplicated pasta dishes.
Particularly child-friendly, and kids mop up the sharp and sweet tastes with gusto, but also nice for suppertime food, whether you want supper at noon or midnight.
Open 11.30am-1am Mon-Thurs, 11.30am-3am Fri-Sun. Average Price: pizza and pasta £. No Credit Cards.

WHOLEFOOD SHOP
ESSENTIAL FOODS
Main Street Tel: (027) 61171 (home) Alan Dare
You need to get here early in the morning on the days when the organic vegetables arrive, for the early risers of Bantry make determined efforts to snap up the pick of the vegetables in Alan Dare's shop.

It's a good practice, therefore, to introduce yourself to the proprietor and his cohorts and to find out what is expected, and when. That way, they may be persuaded to hold back some bright tubs of purslane for you, some crisp-as-altarcloth leeks and lettuces, some muddied Cara or Scarlet Pimpernel spuds.

Mr Dare has been slowly improving the shop, ever since he opened, so there is usually some nice surprise in store in the store.

Open 10.30am-5pm (closed lunch 1pm-2pm) Mon-Sat

PUBS AND PUB FOOD

THERE IS A CERTAIN, distinct wildness about Bantry, a certain acceptance of weirdness and waywardness, and nothing better exemplifies this than The Anchor Bar. The interior enjoys a Breughelian gloom, which is mysteriously appealing, and the daft, enigmatic signs and scrawls which decorate every wall add up to a screwball semaphore. If you want to take the pulse of this strange, strange town, a bevy in The Anchor Bar will tilt you straight into its bloodstream.

The Snug, facing the harbour, can seem almost shocking the first time you wander in, for tree trunks and arcing branches sprout from the walls and burrow into the ceiling with hallucinatory energy. You will notice, however, that the regulars, perched on high stools at the bar, leaning into steaming plates of food, have long ceased to pass any remark on this Daliesque dreamscape. As soon as you have ordered lunch from the short, simple menus they prepare each day: breadcrumbed fish, roasted lamb, boiled bacon, with scoops of spuds, soft mashed carrots and easy-going cabbage, the moment you are sipping from a glass of Murphy's — the water in Bantry, for some reason, is not good, and alcohol is a much sounder bet — you will pass no remark on the decorations either, for you will be too busy passing happy remarks on the simple, satisfying food.

Ma Barry's, a nice, narrow old bar, with dried goods still sold alongside the booze and fags, has a cute little snug just inside the front door, wherein it is particularly pleasing to take the waters. While just out of town Emily Pettit's The Brown Pub is a friendly country pub, all exposed stone and bare wood, which serves decent seafood summer lunches.

THE ANCHOR BAR
New Street, Bantry Tel: (027) 50012

THE BROWN PUB
Kealkil Tel: (027) 66147

MA BARRY'S
New Street, Bantry

THE SNUG
The Quay, Bantry Tel: (027) 50057

DURRUS

FARMHOUSE CHEESE
DURRUS FARMHOUSE CHEESE ★
Coomkeen Tel: (027) 61100 Jeffa Gill

The secret strength of Jeffa Gill's cheese lies with its subtlety and its confident but gradual exposition of flavours. Find one of the rounds in peak condition — the outside dusty white like a Bakewell tart, the top mottled like a cooling fruit gratin, the cheese moderately tall and with enough surface to allow the tastes inside to conjoin — and the traces of clean mustard and field mushroom, followed then by apples and pears come creeping into the taste buds as the cheese is eaten. The backdrop for this splash of flavours is a subtle creaminess on which everything rests, but the wizardry of Durrus lies in keeping this lactic energy contained, using it as a carrier for the fruit and savoury notes which a good cheese delivers.

The cheese is also a delight to eat as the texture, whilst being yielding, doesn't simply evaporate in the mouth: the slight resistance as you chew develops the flavours, then the milkiness comes in, almost as an aftertaste. And, every so often, there is a delicious surprise. Another cheesemaker served us some Durrus for lunch one day, and spoke confidently of finding the scent of strawberries sunk deep in the cheese. Somewhat sceptical, we tried the cheese, which would have been about five weeks old and, sure enough, floating around deep in the structure was a precise scent of strawberries: sweet and ever-so slightly bitter. We wished we had a good bottle of Burgundy to follow up the fruitiness; Durrus is an unusually good cheese to pair with wine: a Country Wine at lunchtime, a claret for supper.

Perhaps it is the fact that she only ever uses morning milk that allows Jeffa Gill to achieve this subtlety, but it is very pleasing, as pleasing as the fact that Durrus has been perhaps the most steadily improving of the Irish farmhouse cheeses over the last few years. Some of the cheeses are now aged in a building proximate to sea water and these are especially exciting, but every Durrus bears the signature of painstaking, personal care, personal attention.

The farm is two and a half miles up Coomkeen hill: take the right fork in Durrus village, turn right at the Church of Ireland, drive straight until you see the sign, then look for the marked entrance.

RESTAURANT
BLAIR'S COVE RESTAURANT
Durrus Tel: (027) 61127 Philippe & Sabine De Mey

Philippe De Mey runs a disciplined dining theatre in the beautiful big barn that is Blair's

Cove, and perhaps the best way to get the best out of an evening in the Cove is to choose something from amongst the grilled meats which they produce on the beautiful, wood-fired grill which flickers and flames away at the head of the dining room. The natural fire and alluring odour of wood smoke which the grill gives to racks of lamb and hanks of beef is irresistible.

Ally this with a hungry raid on the great monument of an hors d'oeuvre table for a selection of pâtés, some smoked and marinated fish, maybe a clean soupçon of pickled vegetables, follow with ripe local cheeses with crisp cumin biscuits, finish with some well-made chocolate mousse, and it is all too easy to build a fine meal. In the vaguely gothic ambience, the vaguely gothic roasts, grills, pickles and puddings are just right.

Open 7.30pm-9.30pm Tues-Sat (Mon in Jul & Aug). Closed Nov-Mar. Average Price: dinner: ££££. Visa, Access. One-and-a-half miles from Durrus on the Durrus-Goleen/Barleycove road.

GLENGARRIFF AND THE BEARA PENINSULA

ALLIHIES

ARTICHOKES
ALLIHIES GLOBE ARTICHOKE CO-OPERATIVE
Reentrisk Tel: (027) 73025 Tony Lowes
This is the perfect Co-Op, for it is run by one man, Tony Lowes, and thus concord and harmony reign. All you need in order to get the best out of Allihies — modestly described by Mr Lowes as 'the globe artichoke capital of Ireland' — is to climb out of the car, grab a knife and start cutting some artichokes. Tony also sells the crown sections of the plants through the post.

Follow the signs on the right hand side of the road as you drive from Allihies to Eyeries.

EYERIES

FARMHOUSE CHEESE
MILLEENS
Eyeries Tel: (027) 74079 Veronica and Norman Steele
Veronica Steele's Milleens was the first of the Irish farmhouse cheeses, and it will forever hold a special place in the hearts of many for originating what has turned out to be one of the most wonderful parts of Ireland's food renaissance over the last fifteen years.

The cheese itself has come a long way in that time, changing from something with run-away softness and a charged lactic ooziness into a more conventional, rather more sober cheese. On occasion, one can find a Milleens with the old characteristics and the true nature of the Vacherin style to which it is often compared — apparently these can often be found in the Neal's Yard cheese shop in Covent Garden in London — and when you come across one of these the cheese is simply unforgettable.

Telephone first if you want to buy cheese from the farm, and to get directions as finding it is tricky: you turn left at the graveyard then take the second on the right.

THE SCHULL PENINSULA

BALLYDEHOB

RESTAURANT
ANNIE'S
Main Street Tel: (028) 37292 Annie Barry
Annie Barry has the best, the nicest, manner of any restaurant owner in the country. Her pacific nature with kids is legendary — though Mrs Barry herself is too modest to agree with this — but she works the spell on adult kids with the same surreptitious ease, and quickly has you goo-goo with anticipation for the treat that is dinner in Annie's.

The restaurant is just a single room with tables in multiples of pairs, nice and bright in summertime if you choose an early evening dinner. Mr Barry doesn't try to do too much — and doesn't need to do too much — to coax the very best from his good ingredients. The most preparation a piece of Sally Barnes's super smoked salmon ever needs is a squidge of lemon; with scallops as big and fat and coral-clawed as these a cream and white wine sauce may almost seem superfluous, but the sauce will be generous and precise, as generous and precise as an apricot sauce around a piece of finely roasted duck. The cooking may be light in execution, but it is deep in savour. Right down to the very simple things — some luscious boiled spuds which you gobble up with the appetite of someone who has been hacking turf all day long: their secret, says the waitress, is that they have been cooked in chicken stock — Annie's gets it right. The temperament of this little place never changes, and never needs to, for who would tamper with a classic.

Open 12.30pm-2.30pm, 6.30pm-10pm Tue-Sat. Closed Oct and limited hours off-season. Average Price: lunch ££ dinner £££. Visa, Access. In the centre of Ballydehob.

PUB
LEVIS'S
Main Street. Julia Levis
This timeless, quiet pub might remind you of an Irish dancehall from the 1960s. On the right side, lined along the wall, is the bar, with its masculine bottles arraigned on shelves, the whole lot facing across to the left wall, where a spread of feminine groceries sit contentedly staring across the dancehall flatness of the floor at the boozy male counter. It's a delightfully innocent yin and yang arrangement that may have you wondering whether the pint of Murphy's will ever get up and ask the packet of Rich Tea to dance, and the Ms Levis's themselves delightfully complement the elemental simplicity. 'Been here long?' a visitor asks. 'All my life' replies Julia with the assurance of experience. 'And my mother before me' she adds, for good measure. Evenings in Annie's restaurant usually begin here, but Levis's lovely pub has its own, intuitive, menu.

WHOLEFOOD SHOP
HUDSON'S WHOLEFOODS
Main Street Tel: (028) 37211 Gillian Hudson
Gillian Hudson's shop combines the local with the international: dried herbs from all parts of the globe, and fresh herbs grown by west Cork organic growers. Sea weeds from Japan,

and some which is locally collected: West Cork wakame and kombu as well as dilisk and carrageen. Cheeses come from the next door villages of Schull, from where Bill Hogan brings country butter along with his Gabriel, Desmond, Raclette and the rare Mizen, in effect a vegetarian parmesan, and there is some of Jeffa Gill's cheese from Durrus. There is real ice-cream, Cork-made tofu — both fresh and fermented — local juices, and flour from the south east and from further fields. The noticeboard outside the shop is always a fascinating bricolage of the wild and the weird.

Open 10am-6pm Mon-Sat (closed lunch 1.30pm-2.30pm)

DUNBEACON

GOAT'S CHEESE
DUNBEACON GOAT'S CHEESE
Dunbeacon, Tel: (027) 61025 Francie Bainbridge

A solitary goose sulks at the entrance to the Bainbridge's house and farm. Unusually for west Cork, he's not interested in socialising with the rest of the gaggle, preferring to keep himself to himself.

The Bainbridge's back garden is made up of a series of pens sloping down in the foothills of Mount Gabriel. In one there's the rest of the geese, in another there are little piglets, a third has the goat, another has ducks. All are happy to make a holy show of the mountain side, digging up, pulling through, mucking in.

The cheese produced on this happy farm is a soft, lightly pressed goat's cheese that teams superbly with the white sourdough rolls from Adele's in nearby Schull.

Cheese can be bought from the farm at all times, as long as there is somebody there.

GOLEEN

FISH SMOKER
CHRIS JEPSON
Harbour Smoke House, Ballydevlin Tel: (028) 35283 Chris Jepson

The salmon smoked by Chris Jepson is distinctive on account of its pale baby-pink colour, but there is nothing subdued about its taste which is persistent and well balanced. All the fish he smokes is wild and can be found in the locality. Chris is also the man responsible for smoking Gubbeen cheese, and his expertise has contributed to the most delicious smoked cheese in Ireland.

RESTAURANT
HERON'S COVE RESTAURANT
Goleen Harbour Tel: (028) 35225 Sue Hill

There are indeed herons in the Cove, but whether or not you are ornithologically minded, it is worth travelling down the peninsula to Heron's Cove to eat in Sue Hill's informal restaurant, and to stay in one of the bedrooms overlooking the harbour. Best of all, perhaps, if the weather is fine, to sit outside on the verandah and watch the small implosions from the diving birds. Chinese-style crab claws might be on the menu, huge stonehenge wedges of claw with ginger, garlic and chilli. A cheese plate could offer Durrus, or Carrigbyrne and the bread with which to mop everything will be home-made, a brown soda or marjoram-flavoured scones. In the evening the seafood theme continues, when you can choose lobster from their tank. Unusually, and effectively, you can also choose your wine by looking through their racks, rather than searching a wine list, helping you to identify bottle and vintage by its label.

Flexible opening times based around lunch between noon and 3pm, dinner 6.30pm-9.45pm. Morning coffee and afternoon tea also available. Reservations only during the winter months. Average Price: lunch ££ dinner £££ B&B £££. Visa, Access, Amex, Diners. Heron's Cove is well signposted from Goleen.

SCHULL

RESTAURANT
LA COQUILLE

Main Street Tel: (028) 28642 Jane & Jean-Michel Cahier
Both the menu and the wine list in Jean-Michel Cahier's restaurant are demurely mute and uninformative in that droll French way of doing things. Scallops with garlic butter. Smoked salmon. Monkfish with green and red peppers. Rack of lamb. Fillet of steak. Tarte tatin. Ice-cream.
This lack of elaboration suits M. Cahier's way of doing things, for his food is just as he describes it, unencumbered by frivolity or needless elaboration. With shellfish, he will extract the natural sweetness in cooking and then concoct a suitable sauce, perhaps the narcotic alliance of brandy and cream with scallops, or something smooth and herby for a feuilleté of seafood. With fresh fish, his sense of simplicity is perfect and fillets of john dory, or whatever has been landed in the harbour that day, are cooked just so, retaining vigour and freshness which his use of herbs agreeably accentuates. Cahier is an assured cook, so assured, indeed, that he has no need to be verbose or gimmicky, whether he is assembling toothy moules marinière as a starter or a super-duper tarte tatin for dessert. He simply lets the ingredients and his professional transformation of them do all the talking.

Open 7.30pm-9.30pm Tue-Sat. Closed 3 weeks Feb. Average Price: dinner £££. Visa, Access. On the main street in Schull, near the entrance to the harbour.

BISTRO
PITCHERS

Unit 3, The Fastnet Residence, Main Street Tel: (028) 28623 Gabrielle and Francesca Byrne
Pitchers is a small, street-side room filled with gingham and candle-topped tables, the walls lined with irresistible abstractions in vivid Baconesque colours. While the work hanging on the walls, much of it Gabrielle's own, is reason enough to call into Pitchers, the food is reason enough to sit down and eat: light and light-hearted, even a terrine of chicken seems bubbly — perhaps it's the melon purée on which it rests which teases it so effectively. A salad composée might use walnut oil and team it with brie cheese, and using stir frying and quick roasting means that main courses continue this dashing volatility. Gabrielle and Francesca have come to cooking through the instinct to be creative and artistic, rather than through strict college training, and their lack of any formal

instruction, and their lack of any formality, means the room quickly catches fire with a dinner party festivity and gaiety.

Open 7pm-9.30pm Mon-Sat (Wed-Sat in winter). Closed Xmas period and the month of Feb. Average Price: £££. Visa, Access. Recommended for Vegetarians. Centre of Schull

HOME BAKERY & COFFEE SHOP
ADELE'S ➥

Main Street Tel: (028) 28459 Adele Connor

Just as Adele's is someplace that is ever youthful, so you will be stolen back to your short-trousered days the instant you bite into something creamy and over-the-top in this cosy café, and exhale then with adolescent delight at the indulgent sweetness of this fine baking. A bite of a chunky meat pastie can seem an evocation of simpler days, when your Mammy was there to save you from your own stupidity, some tea and a jammy scone a comfort you might have enjoyed when school was over and you were at the kitchen table. This is the secret of Adele's: the baking is utterly expert — that crumbly, rich carrot cake, that testy and tingling lemon cake, those soft sourdough rolls — but it is also very maternal, very involving, very pleasureful. You don't admire the craft, for it is not there to be congratulated on how clever it is, it is there just to make you feel good. Adele's is an enclave of domestic peace, somewhere to gather yourself together, somewhere to take on board the comfort of food.

Open shop and café open 9.30am-7pm, restaurant open 7pm-10.30pm Tue-Sat, 11am-7pm Sun. Closed Dec-Easter. Average Price: café £ restaurant ££ B&B £££. No Credit Cards. Recommended for Vegetarians. On the main street in Schull, at the top of the hill.

DELICATESSEN & BAKERY
THE COURTYARD ★

Main Street Tel: (028) 28390 Dennis & Finola Quinlan

Here is a Courtyard story.

Bill Hogan, local cheesemaker, tells Dennis Quinlan that he is making enormous new cheeses called Mizen. They weigh forty five kilos, they take two years to mature, and in circumference they are simply huge. 'I'm afraid they won't fit into your cheese cooler', says Bill. 'No bother', says Dennis. 'We'll get a bigger cooler', Later, Bill Hogan mentions to Finola that Dennis has said that they will get a bigger cooler just to accommodate the new Mizens. 'Oh, we will', says Finola.

This sense of encouragement, this sense of excitement, lies behind everything the Quinlan's do in The Courtyard. The shop reveals a simple truth about them: they love good things, and they want to sell them. This makes The Courtyard a true cornucopia, for it is packed to the rafters with the finest Irish foods, many of which have to do little more than travel a few miles from up or down the road, for this area is rich in fine things, some of which have to do no more than be carried in from the back, for Jackie Bennett bakes stoic, sweet loaves, kneaded by hand, out in the bakery.

As if this wasn't enough, the food served in the bar and in the café is terrific: beautiful and bounteous ploughman's lunches with a posse of farmhouse cheeses and soft bread to soak up some Murphy's, crisp salad leaves with melting vol-au-vents, buttery doorstops of sandwiches. All these good things, all this good work, all under one roof.

Shop open 9.30am-6pm, bar food available 10am-7pm Mon-Sat (food available until 4.45pm off season)

PUB FOOD
THE BUNRATTY INN

Main Street Tel: (028) 28341
Very popular for the up-front pub food they serve, but also a nice joint in which to pass the time by partaking of alcoholic substances.
Food served noon-4pm Mon-Sun

FISH SHOP
NORMANDY IRELAND

Tel: (028) 28599/28638 Xavier
This fish shop is right down on the pier in Schull which augers well for freshness. Whole fish and fillets — wild salmon, turbot, hake, brill, pollack, ray and ling — are sold as well as clever cuts like monk and ray cheeks. Shellfish are processed as well as sold in their shells.
Open 10am-6pm Mon-Fri, 10am-3pm Sat (with much more limited hours in winter).

FARMHOUSE CHEESE
GUBBEEN ★

Gubbeen House Tel: (028) 28231 Giana and Tom Ferguson
The progress of Tom and Giana Ferguson's Gubbeen cheese, from the early days when West Cork chee-makers were regarded one and all as radical fringe hippy throwbacks, and

when folk were deeply suspicious of anything artisan, on through the hoops and vicissitudes of the business of being a small food producer, and on then into popular acceptance, is a parallel of the development of Ireland's food culture during the last decade.

Gubbeen was central amongst the farmhouse cheeses in marking a break from the uniformity of mass produced food which so seduced the country during the 1960s and '70s, and in stating that here was a food which could stand comparison with the most celebrated foods made anywhere in the world. Not only that, but the cheese made a positive feature of the characteristics of the local climate, the local grass, the local milk, and stated that these were an integral element of good food. Local, pure, hand-made. It may seem strange now, but those notions were considered passé only a decade ago, when the bright future beckoned us on into a bland and monotonous diet.

The Fergusons drew on their own resources when making the cheese, for it reflects their own determination and intelligence, their discrimination and affection for natural things. You might compare it to a pont l'eveque, except that such comparisons are by now largely redundant when one discusses Irish cheeses, for they are their own thing, they speak of their own place. The skills in curing which bring out the bloom of a Gubbeen, the skills of the cheese-smoker which Chris Jepson contributes to the smoked Gubbeen, exploit the benefits of dairy science, yet at bottom they remain instinctive, natural.

And that is the key to Gubbeen, and to all the Irish cheeses, and the increasing hunger of people in Ireland and elsewhere to seek out and enjoy these tastes, these skills, and to regard these foods as a vital part of eating and living well, speaks volumes for the contribution which the cheesemakers, and especially the Fergusons, have made to our food culture. They are the poets of the food world.

Gubbeen and Smoked Gubbeen are available throughout the country.

FARMHOUSE CHEESE
WEST CORK NATURAL CHEESE ★

Ardmanagh Tel: (028) 28593 Bill Hogan & Sean Ferry

On a cheesemaking day, Bill Hogan's blue-painted cheesemaking room seems to contain all the excitement and promise of a railway station in the early morning. There is the hiss of steam from the ancient and beautiful boiler, the gurgle of pipes as water heats up, the sense of a beginning, a journey beginning.

And this is no idle emotion, for each of the cheeses made by Bill and Sean have a lengthy road to travel: some of the Desmond cheeses will be ready in six months, some of the Gabriel cheeses will take nine months, but the newest cheeses which they have been making here —Mizen cheeses weighing no less than 45 kilogrammes — will start out on a long journey, for they will not be mature for at least two years. 'They are promises at the horizon of what could happen in Ireland', says Mr Hogan, who learnt his skills in both Switzerland and Costa Rica, way up in the mountains, making thermophilic cheeses that age slowly, patiently. 'We are dedicated to our own obsessions', he adds, and one would need to be, for making super-hard cheeses of this nature is terrifyingly hard work. The heat as the milk is warmed, the grain-like elusiveness of the curd as it is stirred, the sheer physical strength required to lift such a volume of curd and then to set it inside a wheel as it is shaped is enormous, exhausting.

But every bit as enormous is the reward. Take a slice of aged Gabriel and the mouth is assailed by scents and tastes as sweet as pineapple, a sort of volatile super-sugar, and as fine-edged as walnut. A small Mizen is buttery, lush, calling out for a glass of champagne, a Desmond more powerful, a perfect match for a floral wine from Alsace. It is in their synthesis of maturity and freshness that the West Cork Natural Cheeses leave most others standing, for they don't become mere blunderbusses as they age, but instead acquire a subtlety, a persistence that puts one in mind of fine Burgundy: power with finesse. 'My teacher Joseph Durbach described these cheeses as "stored-up sunshine"', says Bill Hogan, and their encapsulation of summer meadows, rich milk, sun-filled days warms the soul when you eat them.

RESTAURANT
THE RESTAURANT IN BLUE
Tel: (028) 28305 Burvill & Chris
The Restaurant in Blue is found amongst a handsome collection of buildings, just outside Schull on the road to Goleen, Burvill and Chris are thoughtful hosts, keen to do their best to accommodate and to please.

Open 7am-late Mon-Fri (limited hours in winter — closed Mon & Tue and sometimes Wed, closed Jan).
Average Price: dinner £££. Visa, Access.

SKIBBEREEN AND THE BALTIMORE PENINSULA

BALTIMORE

CHEZ YOUEN

Baltimore Tel: (028) 20136 Youen Jacob

Youen Jacob's cooking is popular in a lighthearted way, but deeply understood and deeply sunk in the culture of serious cuisine.

It is the sauces which give away his easy affinity with his craft. An emulsion of mayonnaise in which to dunk your shellfish platter. Cream with green peppercorns for roasted beef. A hollandaise of angelic lightness under a fillet of salmon. Simple food, perfectly done, and at lunchtime the fish and shellfish and sauces marry so well with a bottle of Muscadet that you might just forget that there is any work to be done. When you get around to eating some tarte tatin, the best tarte tatin in your life, you wish the crumbly, intensity could last forever.

The music is always good, the atmosphere unpretentiousness, and there is fun to be had.

Open for lunch and dinner Wed-Mon. Closed Nov-Jan with limited opening times around Xmas and New Year.

Average Price: lunch £££-££££ dinner £££-£££££. Access, Visa, Diners, Amex. In centre of Baltimore, overlooking the bay.

SKIBBEREEN

SHOP
THE KITCHEN GARDEN

North Street Tel: (028) 22342

Jenny Mass's shop is one of the most pristine and polished you will find anywhere. The window is dressed with a cornucopia of fresh vegetables, while inside every requisite and necessity proffers itself to you with wanton energy. Packets of pulses are arranged standing to attention. Fruits and veg are as much of a decoration as a do-consider. Herbs and spices are parade ground perfect, and the wheels and truckles of cheese, the fresh golden butter, the dark brown chorizos or the thin packets of Westphalian ham are anticipatory and salivatory.

Open 9am-8pm Mon-Sat

SHOP
FIELD'S

26 Main Street Tel: (028) 21400 J.J. Field

There is always some manner of a surprise waiting for you in Field's. Fresh ducklings plucked and perched in the cooler. Bright hyssop standing guard with a mass of other gingerly vigorous herbs just as you walk into the shop. Some decent wine at a decent price to go perfectly with all the other culinary paraphernalia you have assembled for dinner. Though one could call J.J. Field's shop a supermarket — it has trolleys and miles of aisles and folk in white coats to point you in the direction of whatsoever you might want — it is still nothing so much as a great big local store. The chatter of the locals as they line up at the butchery stall or the cakes and bakes or the wet fish; the unflustered queues at the checkouts as the girls speed the goods through with a word of gossip; the feeling that everyone knows everyone else, or at least will come to know them sometime soon, none of this spells out the modern, anonymous supermarket. And Field's also shows its sense of locality in its support for locally produced foods: pies from Rosscarbery, puds from Clonakilty, salads from Leap, vegetables grown locally and organically. It's a happy shop, a happy place, a happy space, a market that is undoubtedly super.

Open 9am-6.30pm Mon-Sat ('till 7pm Fri)

FISH STALL
NADINE'S FISH STALL

The Bridge, Skibbereen Tel: (028) 22734

A visit to Nadine's impresses and encourages the appetite, not just because the fish always looks spanking fresh, but because Nadine will use her Gallic shopkeeping skill to arrange the fillets, the steaks and the whole fish as if they were set to be entered in an aquatic beauty contest.

Slivers of small sole will lie in a pillow of fillets. Bright-eyed John Dory will perch one against the other, sharply outlined as a carving on an Etruscan bowl. Planks of ling will lie flat and coated with salt crystals. Tails of monkfish will be reflectively purple and white in a chain. In the tank, dark lobsters and granite-grey oysters will lie under bags of black and brown mussels. It is all a splendid theatre.

Perched on the bridge in Skibbereen, with water always flowing underneath, Nadine's has a home that is poetically appropriate, the perfect place to buy a fishy, a wee wee bonny fishy.

Open 9am-6pm Tue-Fri (Sat in summertime), closed 1pm-2pm for lunch.

O'BRIEN'S OFF LICENCE

29 Main Street, Skibbereen Tel: (028) 21772

Generously and rather broadmindedly, O'Brien's nice little shop sells not only a decent selection of decent bottles of wine and crates of cans of beer, it also sells home brew kits for folk who want to make their own concoctions, a curious case of a shop drinking the hand that feeds it. They also have lots of pipe smoking paraphernalia, cute Swiss army knives, sherries and ginger wine for maiden aunts and bottles of De Kuyper gin with its life-enhancing message engraved on the side of the handsome green bottle: 'He who De Kuyper nightly takes, soundly sleeps and fit awakes'.

Open 9am-8pm Mon-Sat, limited hours on Sun.

ACCOMMODATION
GABRIEL COTTAGE

Smorane Tel: (028) 22521 Suzanne Dark & Dominic Lee

Somewhat better known as Irish Peddlers, Dominic and Suzanne organise the dream of the gleam of the open road seen from the saddle of a bike. If you wish to escape from it all and slow down to a human pace, head here for a cycling holiday.

You stay in either the restored stone barn or in the house itself, in rooms that are sugar-sweet nice. Suzanne and Dominic describe their rooms as reflecting 'our love of simple country style', but this undersings the dreamy, cosy, out-of-it-all nature of the rooms, and the dapper perfection of the farmhouse.

You will get to know the house because super meals — vegetarian meals — are served around the big old table at the end of a hard day hacking the roads of West Cork, and staunch breakfasts will set you off at a fast pedal in the morning.

Open for dinner for guests. Closed Oct-Apr (other times by arrangement). Average Price: dinner ££-£££ B&B £££. Visa, Access. Recommended for Vegetarians (it helps if Vegans give notice). Cycling holidays include 3 evening meals, cycle hire, loan of waterproofs and route planning. On the Clonakilty/Skibbereen road, a mile or so east of Skibb.

HERBS
WEST CORK HERB FARM
Church Cross, Skibbereen Tel: (028) 22299 Rosarie O'Byrne

A sign on the main road from Skibbereen to Ballydehob points you to the West Cork Herb Farm, and when you turn off the road you drive into an enclave of good things. The O'Byrnes mastermind this essential organisation with the dynamism and determination, and quiet achievement, that has always signalled their work, painstakingly restoring this collection of houses, organising a shop, laying out the grounds, and selling vibrant and lovable herbs of every hue and colour.

There's a race to buy their honey, their bees are feasting on borage and thyme when other hives have to content themselves with ivy, and their daughter's special recipe for Clara's cooked pesto sauce is something they are all rightfully proud of.

Open 10am-6.30pm Mon-Sat, 12.30pm-6.30pm Sun. (Winter hours noon-5.30pm Mon-Sun).

THE ISLANDS OF WEST CORK

RESTAURANT
HEIR ISLAND RESTAURANT ➡

Island Cottage, Heir Island Tel: (028) 38102 John Desmond & Ellmary Fenton

Island Cottage represents such an almost impossible dream, something so utterly unlikely and obstinately awkward, that it had to be doomed to success.

If you wanted to do something unlikely, something awkward, how about this. Open a small restaurant. On an island, which means that your customers, having made their way down to the far reaches of West Cork, must also make a boat journey across. And then, just to complete things, offer only one set menu each evening: no choice, apart from whether you would like your salad before or after some Gubbeen cheese. In doing this, you are breaking almost every rule of modern cooking, which states that your premises must be accessible, and so must your food.

But the inaccessibility of Heir Island has proven to be the rock of its success. For one thing, the boat journey across is so entrancing that you find yourself talking in Moon-in-June couplets even before you have hit the island: the sky, the sea, the instant comradeship with the other diners. This is a Fred and Ginger affair, a Cary Grant and Joan Fontaine special.

And as for the inaccesibilty of the food, there are important precedents for John Desmond's stubborn refusal to cook a broad menu. Alice Waters in San Francisco's famed Chez Panisse restaurant offers only one dinner menu each evening, predicated upon what foods are in season and to hand. In London, Sally Clarke does the same. The only important rule about restaurant cooking is that it should be good, and on this Mr Desmond scores handsomely. Skill and sympathy are bedfellows in his work, so much so that on one visit here the entire congregation of eaters broke into spontaneous applause when he shyly peeked his head out of the kitchen. His style owes a lot to French imprimaturs, but a love of rustic richness is also at play.

We sat down one morning, after a visit to Island Cottage, to write and describe the evening. The prose that gushed out was so embarrassingly purple, so toxic with exaggeration that it was worthy only of perfumed notepaper. It took, fully, four or five days before we had calmed down enough in order to try to achieve some balance, some critical perspective.

Abandon all rationality, ye who take the boat to Heir Island.

Open Mon-Sun (ask details of boat times). Closed Nov-Apr. Average Price: £££. Boatman charges approx. £3 per head. No Credit Cards. The best boat to get leaves from Cunnamore. Driving from Skibbereen to Ballydehob, turn left at Church Cross (signposted to Heir Island). Keep going until the road ends at the Cunnamore car park.

ICE-CREAM AND GOAT HERDING COURSES
CLEIRE GOAT'S CHEESE

Clare Island, Skibbereen Tel: (028) 39126 Ed Harper

Ed Harper teaches courses in goat husbandry, as well as making his ever-popular goat's ice-cream for island day trippers. He's on the island during the summer months only, and no trip to Clare made during the season should be made without seeking him out.

COUNTY KERRY

THE MOST SINGULAR THING ABOUT KERRY, aside perhaps from the petulant but not unpleasing pride of the locals, is the character of the light that washes over the county. At times it can seem to be purest monochrome, with sheets of celluloid-silver light dissecting the hob-black tones that cover the hills. Then, with a sweep of wind that is announced by a canon-fire rumble through the valleys, it will change to become peat-dark and gun-metal grey, and the hills will appear to be backlit, like some stage set or a post-modern painted landscape. The sea will dance with threatening dark washes devoid of colour, a lick of white foam fringing the waves, whilst on the land the light will fade to softer, natural shades.

It is an uncanny theatre of non-colours, and you try to explain away the curiousness of it all by reference to how far west the county is slung, how deeply sunk in the Atlantic ocean so much of it is. But this won't, somehow, convince you that the weird and singular quality of the light isn't just another aspect of the mysticism which can seem so readily believable in County Kerry. The soft mists with the promising threat of what hides behind them, the swirling fogs that further innoculate the light, the sense that a prospect of simple abandonment could lie just around the corner. You might find yourself here and just decide to stay, simple as that.

But if the character of the light in Kerry seems subdued, refracted, the character of the locals is distinctly unalloyed. They are an intensely self-regarding people, happy with themselves and with no need of your own or anyone else's approbation, thanks all the same. In The Kingdom, as they call it, every man and every woman is a king.

THE DINGLE PENINSULA

DINGLE TOWN

You might look out of your bedroom window at six in the morning, take a peek down John Street, and see a flock of sheep being driven up the road. Later in the morning, a horse will pull a trailer up the same street, in the opposite direction, with a farmer sitting easily on the back and a couple of milk churns beside himself. Where else, then, will you be but in Dingle?

Dingle always feels like a seasidey town, whatever the time of year. There is no sense of the ocean ever presenting anything of a threat, no real sense that wintertime will tumble down from the enclosing mountains and engulf the town with cold and closedown. The incline of the streets and their intimate scale, the bright innocence of the buildings, gives a slightly unreal, almost a surreal, softness to this tiny place. Best of all, Dingle is a town that feels it is in exactly the right place. Whether you drive eastwards down the peninsula past Inch Strand, or come south over the Connor Pass, Dingle always looks like a refuge, a haven, somewhere to fine heart's-ease.

RESTAURANT
BEGINISH RESTAURANT
Green Street Tel: (066) 51588 John & Pat Moore

Pat Moore may not be just such a young woman these days, but the energy, enthusiasm and devotion which she brings to her cooking is not just youthful, it is positively adolescent. Fall to talking about books and cooks, after a delicious dinner on a warm summer's evening in the conservatory at the back of the Beginish, and the volubility, the adrenalin comes rushing out. 'Have you seen this one?' she asks, carting out the latest super-text from a super-chef such as Bernard Loiseau, still in its original French, and there are many questions about this book or that and then this restaurant and that. Mrs Moore, wisely, is a well-travelled cook and on her travels she and her husband eat.

You can tell this in her food, which is hungrily inquisitive, full of those little gestures which announce, quietly, the improvisations and experimentations of a cook who wants to learn more and more. One of the greatest errors made by many chefs is their disinterest in the work of their peers. Mrs Moore has not only eaten their food, she is a perceptive critic of the work of even the most luminary chefs, and she knows how to assimilate the strengths of others into her cooking, and how to avoid their shortcomings.

Where this comes most actively to play is in her appreciation for flavour, and the need to maintain the integral flavour of an ingredient whilst contrasting or comforting it with an apposite sauce. Starters such as some splendid crab meat will combine simply with a chive mayonnaise, whilst tender pinky prawns will have a sharply spiced mayo to play against. A fillet of turbot will sit on a scrumptous bed of potato purée with a clean, lean chive sauce circling the dish, whilst roasted john dory will have a dazzlingly colourful brunoise of vegetables tapestried all around the dish with a creamy mustard sauce perfectly accenting the freshness and liveliness of the fish. Tastes are very positive and happy, and the sense of balance in the main courses is instinctively judged.

You could come down slow and happy from high points such as these, but desserts are another ace card of the Beginish: a rhubarb soufflé tart so shockingly light as to beggar belief, and home made ice-creams that are childishly scoffable. The wine list is generously good, with a fine selection of half-bottles and some clarets and some Italian wines, such as the groaning-with-fruit Italians Sassicaia and Tignanello, at excellent prices.

Open 6pm-9.30pm Tue-Sun. Closed Dec-mid Mar. Average Price: dinner £££-££££. Visa, Access, Amex, Diners. Almost opposite the Catholic church in Dingle town.

RESTAURANT WITH ROOMS
DOYLE'S SEAFOOD RESTAURANT
John Street Tel: (066) 51174 John & Stella Doyle

John and Stella Doyle's restaurant has an international reputation, so it may come as a surprise to those who visit for the first time to see just what an informal place Doyle's Seafood Restaurant actually is: flagged floors, back-to-the-wall seating, an easily understated décor and an absence of any fussiness in either the food or the service, the perfect surroundings for a pint of stout and some shellfish. In this dining room the

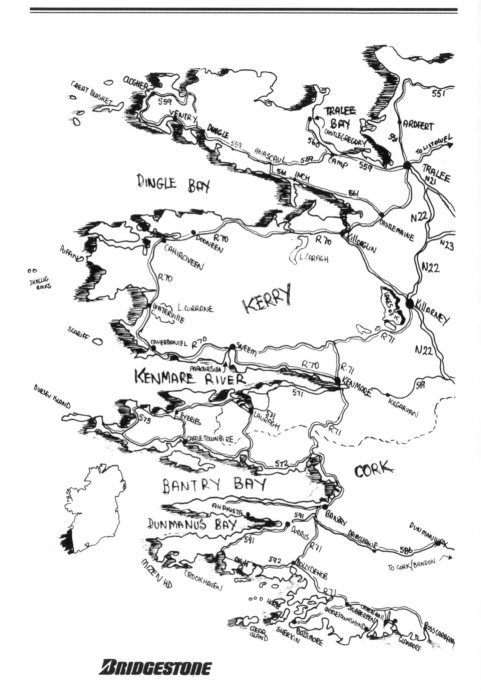

strengths of Doyle's — good bread, good house wines by the half-litre jug, efficiency — seem perfectly appropriate.

This functionalism is counterpointed by the fine, svelte good taste of the six rooms in Doyle's Townhouse, which adjoins the restaurant. The rooms have the confidence of good taste, with well-chosen, clever, useful design, the touch of something done well, done just right, and a comfortable night will be happily rounded off by a fine breakfast in which the delicious homemade sausages pair off with some heavenly black pudding.

Open from 6.30pm Mon-Sat. Closed mid Nov-mid Mar. Average Price: dinner £££-££££. Visa, Access, Diners. Dingle town centre.

CAFÉ & BOOKSHOP
AN CAFE LITEARTHA
Dykegate Street Tel: (066) 51388 Seoirse O Luasa
One of Dingle's two splendid bookshops-cum-cafés.

Open 9am-5.30pm Mon-Sat

BUTCHER
CURRAN'S VICTUALLERS
Green Street Tel: (066) 51398 Noreen Curran
'What is the secret of your legendary smoked bacon?', you ask Noreen Curran, and Noreen Curran will tell you, straight off, 'There's no secret'.

But there is, of course, and the secret is care. Careful handling of the loin to begin, for it is dried and left to hang overnight, and then careful smoking over oak chips and shavings — in a little shed out back of the shop — by Michael the butcher. The result is a smoked bacon intensely charged with an oaky, supple oiliness that is a joy to cook and to eat, and it is best eaten with some of Noreen's legendary black pudding. Noreen calls the pudding 'cake', an apposite name for it is shaped like a sponge cake, it is moist and tender like a sponge cake and a slice first thing in the morning will likely convince you that it must be your birthday, for this is assuredly a treat.

There are two Curran's butchers on Green Street: Curran's Victualler's is the one lower down, closer to the harbour.

Open 8am-7pm Mon-Sat (from 9am Sat)

RESTAURANT, BAR, BOOKSHOP & CAFÉ
THE ISLANDMAN
Main Street Tel: (066) 51803 Karl Frolich
The Islandman is a supersmart quartet of temptations. The bar is continental in character and perfect for a glass of wine first thing, an aperitif before dinner or a digestif last thing at night. The café is ideal for good apple pie and coffee at eleven, maybe a chocolat just before bed, or a sandwich at lunchtime. The restaurant produces contenting, simple food at most times of the day, and the book shop diverts your gaze with neatly arranged titles that summon your attention. It is a brilliant combination of functions, all of them carried out in an atmospheric series of rooms whose considered design is accented by fastidious housekeeping.

Open 9am-11pm Mon-Sun during the season (more limited hours in winter). Average Price: meals £-££. Visa, Access. Dingle town centre.

ALSO OF INTEREST

FENTON'S, Green Street Tel: (066) 51209 Pat Fenton. Seafood and mountain lamb in a friendly and appealing space Open 12.30pm-3pm, 6pm-11pm. Closed Nov-Apr. Average Price: lunch ££ dinner £££. Visa, Access, Amex, Diners.

THE HALF DOOR, John Street Tel: (066) 51600 Mick Casey. Pleasant, low-key restaurant with seafood orientated menu. Open noon-2pm, 6pm-11pm. Closed Nov-Mar. Average Price: lunch ££ dinner £££. Visa, Access, Diners.

GARVEY'S BUTCHERS, Holy Ground, Dingle Tel: (066) 51397 Tom Garvey Late in the year, try Garvey's as a source for Kerry mountain lamb. 'Better than anywhere else', they say. Of course, they say that in Connemara too. Open 9am-7pm Mon-Thurs, 9am-9pm Fri & Sat, 9am-1pm Sun.

THE OLD STONE HOUSE B&B, Cliddaun Tel: (066) 59882 Michael and Becky O'Connor's cosy little cottage is a good base, and their extraordinary fund of knowledge about the peninsula is a boon to travellers. Open all year, including Xmas. Average Price: B&B £££. Visa, Access

KILQUANE

SMOKED SALMON AND SHELLFISH
DINGLE BAY SHELLFISH

Kilquane, Ballydavid Tel (066) 55183 Ted Browne

Ted Browne is a passionate man: passionate about the preparation of good food and passionate about the enjoyment of good food. But the secret passion which makes the fish and shellfish he prepares so spectacularly good is the rigorous orthodoxy which underlies his work. Like few other food producers or processors, Browne is a trained chef, and it is the chef's obsessive demand for improvement which drives his efforts. He doesn't view his smoked salmon or his cooked crab claws and crab meat as something to simply be

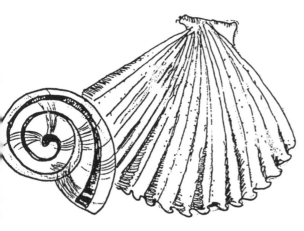

prepared and then shifted out around the country. Instead, like any good cook, Browne sees his own stamp, his own signature, on every parcel of Dingle Bay shellfish that is driven away from Kilquane.

And then, there is the obsessive experimentation, the tinkering, tinkering with foods to make them better, more accessible, with no loss of integrity, no loss of signature. There is the bisque which has been in development for years and which will, surely, make its way into the marketplace one of these days, or the clever cake of smoked salmon which is assembled from salmon trimmings. Ted Browne has that hungry energy, that hungry creativity, which animates the very best people who work with food, and Dingle Bay Shellfish is every bit as personal and precious as the most considered presentation of the very best chef.

Ted Browne's crab and smoked salmon is available in many of the pubs and restaurants in and around Dingle.

THE RING OF KERRY

BLACKWATER

FARMHOUSE CHEESE
CAPPAROE GOAT'S CHEESE

Greenane, Blackwater The Hensel Family

The Hensel family make a deliciously rich and unctuous soft goat's cheese, which they pack into jars and cover with a darkly yellow organic olive oil. If you find it, don't miss it, for the richness and purity of the flavour is totally distinctive, as is the neat hand-script which they use on the label to describe the cheese.

You can often buy the cheese in The Pantry in Kenmare, otherwise ask locally for 'The Bicycling Germans'.

CAHIRCIVEEN

RESTAURANT
THE OLD SCHOOLHOUSE

Knockeens, Cahirciveen Tel: (0667) 2426 Ann O'Kane

There is much thoughtfulness about the Old Schoolhouse, and they do work hard to please as much as they can in this easy-going, good time place.

Open 11am-9pm Mon-Sun. Closed Nov-Mar. Average Price: lunch ££ dinner £££. Visa, Access, Diners.

CAHERDANIEL

RESTAURANT
LOAVES AND FISHES

Caherdaniel Tel: (0667) 5273 Helen Mullane & Armel White

They are a good twosome, Helen Mullane and her man Armel White. She sets the tone of Loaves and Fishes at just that right combination of unabashed holiday happiness — the small and intimate room with candlelit tables, the comforting crooners on the stereo — while he takes care of the culinary ambience — busy sounds of whisking and slicing and sizzling can be heard from the kitchen, and the aromas of something brewing or reducing drift out to set the appetite up for the evening.

Together, they deliver a splendid confection in Loaves and Fishes, making this one of those places which you dream about finding when you are travelling or touring or just plain loafing around. Armel White's food is deeply flavoured and his aim with combinations is to find a new fusion of tastes, so smoked salmon will be grilled and have some warame scattered on top, quail's eggs may be poached in red wine, prawns will be scampied, some roast duck set off by a sharp blackcurrant sauce. But whatever diversities he chooses, he is able to make the dish work, and with some simple but ruddy vegetables and fine desserts, you find this food is extremely enjoyable to eat. In the context of the romantic and carefree calm of the restaurant, it is just the food you wanted. Prices are splendidly modest, and just another part of this charming miracle.

Open 6pm-9.30pm Tue-Sun, Closed end Sept-Easter. Average Price: dinner £££. Visa, Access. Caherdaniel is on the Ring of Kerry about 45 mins from Kenmare.

KENMARE

RESTAURANT
THE OLD BANK HOUSE
Main Street Tel & Fax: (064) 41589 Matthew d'Arcy

Matt d'Arcy has been best known over the last years as the head chef in the illustrious Park Hotel. The attraction of this happy town must be strong, for Mr d'Arcy has moved no further than just up the street to open The Old Bank House.

His new premises may be simpler than the grandeur of The Park, but the strengths of d'Arcy's cooking, strong flavours, impressive technical command of his craft and a flair for complicating and combining, are every bit as evident here as before.

His love of variation and complication is everywhere: in starters such as smoked salmon with a cucumber and dill vinaigrette, or duck liver mousse with caramelised oranges, in main courses like salmon with noodles and a curry flavoured sauce, or chicken and salmon with a prawn sauce, in desserts like a timbale of mango parfait with a fruit coulis, or a tuile of honey and lavender ice-cream. This is very classic and yet very modern food, the product of a long apprenticeship and a lot of learning. In the modest dining room, in the company of a good bottle from the wine list, it is fun to enjoy it all.

Open 6pm-11pm Mon-Sun (closed Sun off season). Closed Xmas. Average Price: dinner £££. Visa, Access. At the top end of Main Street.

WHOLEFOOD SHOP
THE PANTRY
30 Henry Street Tel: (064) 31320

A useful shop for hunting down local foods.

RESTAURANT
PACKIE'S ➥
Henry Street Tel: (064) 41508 Maura Foley

They are a well-informed people, Kerry people. Mention the name of Maura Foley to them and a clever, knowledgeable mien sets into their faces, motivated mainly, one reckons, by a firm sense of pride.

Kerry people know that Mrs Foley is a brilliant cook. They know that she is one of the best cooks anywhere in the country. And, of course, here she is cooking in Kerry, in The Kingdom itself. Wouldn't you be proud to have Maura cooking on your stomping ground?, is what the look says. And you agree, but add that the trip to Kenmare to eat Maura Foley's food is one of the most worthwhile, pleasure-promising and well-rewarded trips you can make.

This a happy, up-for-it place to eat, with great staff, great prices and a wonderful bistro buzz. Simple foods cooked in here seem almost a revelation, their taste is so real, so true. Sole meuniere. Crab claws. Vanilla ice-cream. You name it, and you will scarcely be able to remember when you last ate it so good. It was a desire to simplify her food and to cut prices which led Maura Foley to begin this smashing venture, and this foresight reveals the same stroke of simple genius that you find in her cooking.

Open 5.30pm-10pm Mon-Sat. Closed end Dec-end Feb. Average Price: dinner ££-£££. Visa, Access.

COUNTRY HOUSE HOTEL
THE PARK HOTEL
Kenmare Tel: (064) 41200 Francis Brennan

If one were to hold a poll of hoteliers to find the hoteliers' hotelier, no one would lay a bet with you that the winner would not be Francis Brennan. Mr Brennan is, quite simply, the very personification, the very essence, of the hotelier. His skills are so effortless and so graceful that you can't imagine that he ever actually learnt them. Far more likely, you reckon, that he was born this way, popped from the womb with this integral and instinctive grasp of how to run an hotel to the very highest standards, and then some.

It is Francis Brennan who personifies and motivates The Park Hotel, articulates its thoughtfulness and appositeness, ensures that the food is correct, that the rooms are perfect, makes it the place it is, makes it like no other place.

Restaurant Open 1pm-2pm, 7pm-8.45pm Mon-Sun. Closed mid Nov-Xmas (open for Xmas period) early Jan-Easter. Average Price: lunch £££ dinner £££££. Visa, Access, Diners, Amex. At the top of the slopes of the village of Kenmare, The Park is well signposted.

BISTRO
THE PURPLE HEATHER BISTRO
Henry St Tel: (064) 41016 The Foley family

A few doors down from the Foley family's Packie's restaurant, and motivated by the same concern for thoughtful, good food.

Open noon-6.30pm Mon-Sat. Closed Xmas. Average Price: lunch ££. Visa, Access.

HOTEL
SHEEN FALLS LODGE
Kenmare Tel: (064) 41600 Fergus Moore

Sheen Falls Lodge plights its troth, unambiguously, at high rolling, free-spending travellers with a taste for restrained décor and lavish food. You might find yourself dining alongside visiting foreign royalty in the La Cascade Restaurant but, if you do, don't worry: they will be too discreet to effect to recognise you.

Fergus Moore's cooking is luxurious in design and execution, updating super-duper foods such as foie gras by means of the vogueish use of balsamic vinegar, or allying smoked duck breast with deep fried haricots.

The ideal he pursues is that of a principal ingredient allied to a sympathetic staple and a rich sauce seen with dishes such as duck with roasted garlic and Sloe gin essence, or turbot and john dory on braised leeks with a chive butter sauce. Desserts are equally lavish: hot chocolate soufflé with a pistachio and white chocolate ice-cream, Ceylon tea parfait with cinnamon biscuits and a lime caramel glaze.

Many will relish this unapologetically lush style of food, just as they will relish the hotel's unapologetically lush style of decoration.

Open 7.30pm-9.30pm Mon-Sun. Closed early Jan-mid Mar. Average Price: dinner £££££. Visa, Access, Amex, Diners. One kilometre outside Kenmare on the Glengarriff road.

THE REST OF KERRY

LAURAGH

SHELLFISH
PAUL, DOT & TERRY HAYNES
Glandore Lake, Lauragh Tel: (064) 83110
Paul, Dot and Terry dive to the depths to seize the riches of the seabed: oysters, clams, mussels, lobster, sea urchins, you name it and they will be able to get it. They supply local hotels and restaurants and make the lengthy trip to Ballymaloe House in east Cork every Friday, just in time for the buffet preparation which opens Friday's dinner.

Drive through Lauragh village, and on your left you will see an old ESSO sign and a signpost for Glandore Lake. Follow the road and the Haynes' house is the first you come to on the lake shore.

KILLARNEY

RESTAURANT
THE STRAWBERRY TREE ➤
24 Plunkett Street Tel: (064) 32688 Evan Doyle
In Evan Doyle's lovely restaurant you can eat the tastes of the future, and boy, do they taste good. Mr Doyle has always been the most perspicacious of proprietors, always running the restaurants he has been associated with in pursuit of an ideal of good food rather than mere profit. In The Strawberryt Tree, which has now moved upstairs and sits over and above the sweet little Yer Man's Pub, Doyle has managed to achieve an ambition of sourcing all the food for his restaurant from local organic and artisan producers.

So, there will be venison from that dazzlingly talented butcher Armin Weise from down the road in Fossa, the organic vegetables from Jo Barth are imported in from County Cork, a job Mr Doyle undertakes himself. There is free range beef from Thady Crowley, and free range duck and chicken from Barry's farm. Pat Spillane from just down the street and around the corner supplies fresh fish and shellfish, and everything, but everything, has the stamp and signature of its supplier on it: on the menu are the written guarantees from them all, their determination to supply the best and nothing but.

'Real Foods' is what they call it, and the results are truly sublime. Corned beef comes parcelled up in a pouch of cabbage with a parsley sauce inside, making for a memorable and joyful surprise. When they have it on the menu the fillet of beef is chocolate-rich and deep in flavour. This is a daring and wholly admirable move, for in chasing down the tastes of the future Mr Doyle has had to revert to the methods of the past. This ingenuity and foresight makes this charming, intimate restaurant even more valuable. The staff, incidentally, are amongst the very best in the country.

Open 6pm-10pm Mon-Sun (Sun nights high season only). Lunch available in the bar downstairs. Closed Dec-Mar. Average Price: dinner £££. Visa, Access, Amex, Diners.

RESTAURANT
GABY'S RESTAURANT
17 High Street Tel: (064) 32519 Geert & Marie Maes

Gaby's has moved a little bit further up the street from its old location, but nothing has changed with Gert Maes' cooking. In a town full of froth and flotsam, this man is a serious cook, and Gaby's is just the sort of unserious restaurant you desperately want to find in Killarney. The restaurant is almost a café in style, with design and furnishings that are unpretentious and intrinsically Continental. The cooking, meantime, concentrates on Mr Maes' confident skill with fish and shellfish, and you can choose anything, from an impressive shellfish platter, maybe black sole in a cream sauce, some smoked mackerel pâté or hot smoked trout, right through to their own secret way of preparing lobster fresh from the tank, and things will be done right, just right.

It is reassuring to note that the availability of dishes is always subject to the success, or lack of success, of the local fleets. So pray for good weather.

Open 12.30pm-2.30pm Tue-Sat, 6pm-10pm Mon-Sat. Closed mid Dec-mid Mar. Average Price: lunch £££ dinner £££. Visa, Access, Amex, Diners

FOSSA

SAUSAGE MAKER AND CHARCUTIER
CONTINENTAL SAUSAGES ★
Fossa Tel: (064) 33069 K.A.Weise and Ann Myers

In the hands of a quiet man like Armin Weise, the business of the butcher becomes art. He takes a raw product, applies to it creativity and articulation, and transforms it from something ordinary to something out-of-the-ordinary. 'There are so many things you can do', says Mr Weise in his tram-car-quick English. 'It's just the imagination'.

His imagination burns bright and brilliant. A section of smoked kassler will be wrapped around a tumbril of broccoli which is set in aspic, creating an extraordinary cross-section of colours when the meat is sliced: jade jewels of vegetables in the centre with a bracelet of tender meat on the outside. Cooked hams and meats are disassembled and then reassembled with the panache of never-built Soviet Constructivist architecture, glorious pile-high confections that seem to belong more to the fantasy of a Dali-esque dream than to the solid simplicities of charcuterie.

There are blood sausages marbled with lardons, cured venison which looks as supple and tender as a side of smoked salmon, dark red beef marinating in a lush assortment of twenty or more spices, all of these on a counter which is a dolly-mixture concoction of colours and shapes. Abandon any attempt at self-restraint when you walk in, and prepare to fill the freezer.

Signposted from Fossa. Open 8am-8pm in the summer, often 7 days. Winter 8am-6pm Tues-Fri, 8am-1pm Sat.

KILLORGLIN

RESTAURANT
NICK'S RESTAURANT
Lower Bridge Street Tel: (066) 61219 Nicholas Foley
Crowds and crowds of carousers flock to this cheerful pub in the hilly town of Killorglin, meaning that Nick's enjoys the celebratory atmosphere of a Friday night wedding whether or not it is actually an early Tuesday evening or maybe just a wet Wednesday.

The food accentuates the simplicity and festivity of the place, bumper Saturday night specials like rack of lamb, fillets of fish in creamy sauces and simple, superb steaks from Kerry cattle.and several drinks to begin in the bar, as you listen to the whooping choruses on the piano, is imperative even before you consider ordering anything to eat.

Open noon-3pm for bar food, 6pm-10pm restaurant Mon-Sun. Closed Nov-Easter. Average Price: lunch ££ dinner £££. Access, Visa, Amex, Diners. Half way up the hill on the road coming from Tralee or Killarney.

FARMHOUSE CHEESE
WILMA'S KILLORGLIN FARMHOUSE CHEESE
Ardmoniel, Killorglin Tel: (066) 61402 Wilma Silvius
Found in local shops and beginning to make its way further afield, Wilma's is a rich and buttery gouda-style cheese, with nice traces of peppery sharpness. Do look out in particular for the cheese sold marked as 'mature', for then the meld and blend of flavours are at their best.

You will find the cheese for sale in the Continental Sausages shop in Fossa.

MILLTOWN

BUTCHER
BURKE'S
Bridge Street, Milltown Tel: (066) 67345 Mary Burke
It was her smoked bacon which first brought us to Mary Burke's shop in Milltown, but we soon realised that it was not just the fine, lightly toasty bacon which was good. Everything Mrs Burke sells is characteristic in taste, true in flavour — spring lamb's liver, home-cooked hams — just as sweet and charming as the lady herself, which is some amount of sweetness and charm.

Open 8am-7pm Mon-Sat ('from 9am Sat)

TRALEE

FARMHOUSE CHEESE
KERRY FARMHOUSE CHEESE
Coolnaleen Tel: (068) 40245 Sheila Broderick
Sheila Broderick's cheddar-style cheeses are earthy and agrestic, whether the plain Kerry cheese or those flavoured with a variety of ingredients. The plain cheese suits a fair bit of age to get the very best out of it, so it can be a good idea to buy from the farm.
Thirteen miles along the Tralee-Listowel Road you will see a sign for Lixnaw. Take the road on the right, go up the hill, past two houses opposite one another. The Brodericks' is the next painted entrance on the right. Cheese is sold from the house, or you can buy it in O'Connor's delicatessen in Listowel.

WHOLEFOOD RESTAURANT
ROOTS RESTAURANT
76 Boherbue Tel: (066) 22665 Ruth O'Quigley
A few little tables in a little room, with nicely satisfying wholefoods cooked by Ruth.
Open 10.30am-5.30pm Mon-Sat

TUOSIST

FARMHOUSE CHEESE AND HOME-PREPARED TAKEAWAY FOOD
OLD ARDAGH
The White House, Tuosist Tel: (064) 84500 Lisette & Peter Kal
Lisette Kal discovered the recipe for their Old Ardagh cheese in a Dutch cheese cookery book, but this is not, in fact, a Dutch recipe. Rather, the recipe was that for a cheese made by Irish monks in Ardagh, who would no doubt be glad that the tradition still survives. It's a semi-hard goat's cheese that matures to pefection. Aside from cheese the Kals must be the dream ticket for the holidaymaker's perfect holiday, the perfect food for the evening meal in your caravan or cottage. They make up seafood takeaways that are as far removed from your average seaside fish and chips as it is possible to get. The seafood platter places mussels, smoked sea trout, prawns, shrimp and sea trout pâté beside a Cognac sauce and serves it with home-made brown bread. They also make mussels in garlic butter, scallops in a creamy seafood sauce, and a salad of smoked sea trout with a fresh herb sauce. You can also buy fresh and smoked sea trout, smoked salmon and shrimp. Another option is a special three-course meal of prawn cocktail, pizza and cassata ice-cream. For the curious Peter will take trips out on his boat to teach the art of shrimping as well as going to see the seals and Lisette's original paintings are for sale at the house — she also takes commissions to paint people's house and garden. And finally, the wondrous Speculaas, the rich Christmas sweetmeat which must be eaten all year, is a concoction of spices and handmade marzipan, and is just one of the sweets and desserts Lisette makes along with hand-made chocolates, jams, cheesecake and birthday cakes made to order.
The Kals' cheese is on the cheeseboard at both the Park and Sheen Falls and you can buy it and the chocolates and Speculaas at Val Mannings Emporium in Ballylickey, County Cork. In Kenmare the Pantry sells their cheese, O'Sheas sell the chocolates. Otherwise you can order direct from the house. Everything is incredibly reasonably priced.

COUNTY LIMERICK

I T TENDS TO GET A BIT OF STICK, DOES LIMERICK. Public perception of the city is of somewhere with relatively little to offer, and there can be no doubt that at times it can seem charmless, cussed. The county, likewise, is not somewhere which tends to excite people to sing its praises spontaneously.

And yet there is magnificent coastline here, and Limerick city has been working hard to beautify itself, especially to make a feature of the River Shannon which cuts a stylish swathe through it.

And there can be surprises in the county — the heart-stunning charm of Adare, for example, which has a claim to be the prettiest village in the country, the cloistered charm of parts of the city, the smooth sloth of the coast. But Limerick needs a sense of itself and a sense of standards, it needs to realise that in food terms it is not just competing with itself but with everywhere else. Ireland's food culture is moving on, moving on. Limerick has no option but to move on with it

ABBEYFEALE

FISHMONGER
DALY'S FRESH FISH
Abbeyfeale Tel: (068)31974 Michael Daly
A pristinely-kept shop selling spanking fresh fish.
Open 9.30am-6pm Tues-Wed, 8.30am-6pm Thurs-Fri, 10am-3pm Sat

ADARE

RESTAURANT
THE MUSTARD SEED
Adare Tel: (061) 396451 Dan Mullane
Perhaps it is the nearby presence of much-hyped and expensive hotels — from time to time staffed by superstar chefs — which keeps both the food and the staff in the Mustard Seed on their proverbial toes, but this is a restaurant that manages to charm and to please, manages to achieve that balance of thoughtfulness and expertise which characterises a happy, hungry restaurant.

Dan Mullane has held onto that sense of excitement and creativity which restaurateurs all too often and all too quickly trade in for cynicism and indifference. Mr Mullane is too busy to have time for these vices, however, and his lovely little restaurant reverberates with a motivated and urgent excitement which is quite thrilling all on its own.

While the food in the Mustard Seed is often spoken of as representing 'New Irish Cooking', it still retains an earthiness and instinctive sense of comfort. There can be exciting creations with dishes such as mallard, shark, perhaps sea weed, maybe sweet-and-sour rabbit, but there will also be pan-fried salmon, escalope of veal, rack of fine Limerick lamb. Mr Mullane still likes to have his fun with these staples however: duck with beetroot and mint, or maybe hazel nut oil; blue cheese stuffed into the veal. Desserts may tread a

VENISON

THE DEER, LIKE THE MAJESTIC GOOSE, fails to thrive when subjected to late twentieth century techniques of intensive farming. Instead the fallow, red and sika deer of Ireland benefit from the clean grazing grounds to be found in the Irish midlands.

They are a graceful animal and easy to romanticise, but the reasons which have led to an increase in the numbers of deer which you find in Ireland are economic, rather than romantic. EC milk quotas have led many farmers in Ireland to look for an alternative product, a food that was not surplus in the European Community. Venison, thanks to its modern appeal as a low-fat food and the fact that it wasn't subject to a quota system, was the food which suggested itself.

Government grants followed and, in tune with the general spirit of cosseting farmers in this country, support groups to act and advise on marketing and distribution have been established, including the Irish Venison Co-Op in Limerick.

But venison production in Limerick pre-dates this latest economic push. In 1989 Jonathan Sykes and his wife Betty published 'The Irish Venison Cookbook' under their own imprint, based on their own researches, for the Sykes farmed venison here at Springfield Castle

in Dromcollogher from before the modern systems began. The meat from their and other herds can now be found throughout the country, used to make venison sausages in O'Flynn's butcher's in Cork and by Gill Boazman of Roscarberry Recipes, being made into winter-friendly pâtés or cured and smoked venison from Armin Weise in Kerry, cropping up on restaurant menus here and there.

JONATHAN & BETTY SYKES
Springfield Castle Tel: (063) 83162

IRISH VENISON CO-OP
Limerick Food Centre, Raheen Tel: (061) 301212 Kay Caball

more expected route, but they will enjoy quirky creativity and true flavours.

The quality of the ingredients used in the restaurant is excellent, service is astute and free of any nonsense, and the dining rooms perfect little havens of relaxation. The Mustard Seed may have celebrated neighbours who tend to target the top dollar, but it is to the Mustard Seed that the smart money makes its way when in Adare.

Open 7pm-10pm Tue-Sat. Closed Xmas and Feb. Average Price: dinner £££. Visa, Access, Amex, Diners. In the centre of Adare village.

CRATLOE

SHEEP'S CHEESE
CRATLOE HILLS

Cratloe Tel: (061) 87185 Sean & Deirdre Fitzgerald

The best known Cratloe is a pale-white sheep's milk cheese which, unusually perhaps, is made in a shape reminiscent of a blancmange dessert.

Whilst it is subtle and light in flavour, do try to seek out that cheese, in the shape of a small curling iron or a small gouda, which the Fitzgeralds age for a longer period of time. With a caramel brown coat and a harder, leaner consistency, this Cratloe develops a much greater spread of flavour and shows sheep's milk at its best.

HOSPITAL

CASTLE FARM GOAT'S CHEESE

Hospital Tel: (061) 83496 Catherine Corkery

This milk-white goat's milk cheese uses pasteurised milk, and comes wrapped in a pill-box bright plastic coat. Fresh and cottage cheese and some vegetarian cheeses are also available.

KILMALLOCK

FARMHOUSE CHEESE
GLEN-O-SHEEN

Ballinacourty, Kilmallock Tel: (063) 86140 Matthew & Margaret O'Brien

Glen-o-Sheen must be one of the last unpasteurised cheddars to be made and sold in these islands. You see it in shops in handsome tall truckles of up to 30lbs in weight.

Do be patient with it: the buttery, buttercup yellow cheese is at its best after many months of ageing, when the milkiness first of all subsides a little, but then reappears as a rich, buttery melt.

Take the road to Kilfinnan from Kilmallock, and when you come to the townland of Glenroe, Glen-o-Sheen is signposted both on the road and at the farm.

LIMERICK

RESTAURANT
RESTAURANT DE LA FONTAINE
12 Upper Griffin Street Tel: (061) 414461 Alain Bras-White
The unusual layout of this restaurant gives it a bar area which, it seems, has been imported from a French bistro and which is as big as the dining room.

Perhaps this is appropriate, because the best thing about this restaurant is its lengthy and changing wine list, a clever and expansive selection of good wines which the waiter expounds on with a confident knowledge, even if it turns out that he hasn't, in fact, got the half bottle of this-or-that which you chose.

No matter, there are many others to select.

The food comes from that noble tradition of French bistro, hunky terrines or delicate and effete crab concoctions, the classic combination of lamb and haricot beans.

Prices, alas, leave any bistro far behind, and when you do fork out for a speciality such as a freshly cooked foie gras and it comes then ringed with iceberg lettuce that has been shredded with a knife, and triangles of toasted sliced pan bread, you wonder why they went to so much effort with the liver.

Open 12.30pm-2.30pm Mon-Fri, 7pm-10pm Mon-Sat. Closed Xmas. Average Price: dinner £££-££££. Visa, Access.

PRODUCER'S MARKET
LIMERICK SATURDAY MARKET
The Limerick market is an ambling sprawl of cars and carts, stalls and set-ups which snakes around the city first thing on Saturday morning.

Best things to look out for are bakes and preserves, and maybe some good tufty carrots or other root vegetables. Kilshanny farmhouse cheese makes its way down from Lahinch and mingles with the other artisan products.

Do be warned that the Market, which is near the town centre, is amazingly difficult to find, even if you have been there before, and it is usually necessary to ask directions, possibly — indeed probably — three or four times.

FISHMONGER
RENE CUSACK LTD
Dock Road Tel: (061) 317566 Rene Cusack
A great big warehouse of a building houses a small stall at the front which sells good fresh fish and some fine smoked salmon.

Open 8.30am-5.30pm Mon & Tue, 8am-5.30pm Wed & Fri, 8am-4pm Sat

WHOLEFOOD SHOP
EATS OF EDEN
Spaight's Shopping Centre Tel: (061) 419400 Nancy Flexman & Rita O'Mahony
Not just the familiar paraphernalia of a wholefood shop, but good also for organic vegetables, breads and other local foods.

Open 9am-6pm Mon-Fri, 9am-6.30pm Sat

COOKED FOOD AND DELICATESSEN
IVAN'S
Caherdavin, Limerick Tel: (061) 455766 Ivan Cremins
'This is a shop that does everything' says Ivan Cremins. The shop has an instore bakery, a deli counter and a sandwich bar. The breads are conventional soda plus breads flavoured with walnuts and oatmeal. The deli counter sells the Abbey Burren jams made from apricot and almond, apple and cinnamon, some farmhouse cheeses, particularly Cooleeney from Mrs Cremins home-county of Tipp, plus hand-made cooked foods and salads.
Open 7am-11.30pm Mon-Sun

ALSO OF INTEREST
THE SHANNON BASKET OF GOOD FOOD, Limerick Food Centre, Raheen Tel: (061) 301212 Kay Caball
As a subsidiary of the Irish Venison Co-Op, the Shannon Basket has been set up to promote and distribute some of the artisan produce of the area, both to the catering trade as well as to good specialist shops. Products include free-range Fermore Venison smoked by Armin Weise in Kerry and organic lamb and kid meat from the Burren hills; shellfish from Redbank Seafoods, smoked fish from Peter Curtin's Burren Smokehouse; the wonderful Inagh and Cooleeney cheese from Clare and Tipperary respectively, as well as two cheeses from Kerry: Wilma's gouda cheeses from Killorglin and the cheddar cheeses from Kerry Farmhouse Cheese made by Sheila Broderick. Glen-o-Sheen, Limerick's own mature, unpasteurised cheddar cheese and the Castle Farm Goat's cheese, also from Limerick, are also part of the group.

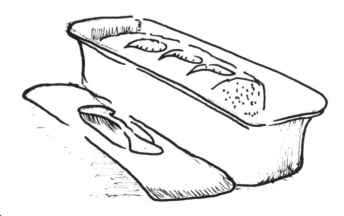

COUNTY TIPPERARY

I N I WENT AND WAS PRESENTED TO HERSELF and the family as one who had ridden ever so far to see Knocknagow. There were some hot griddle cakes on the table, brown on the crust, and white as driven snow inside until the yellow butter melted on them under the hospitable efforts of one of the girls, while the mother cooked rashers and eggs. I was, in real truth, homerically hungry, and I did homeric justice to the feast'.

Thus the cycling traveller William Bulfin recounts a supper in County Tipperary in the home of a farmer who insisted he come in to eat and then insisted he stay the night. Bulfin's book, 'Rambles In Eirinn' was published in 1907 and is a terrific hoot, though Mr Bulfin — a man revealed by his photograph in the book ('Taken in Buenos Aires after his return from the Pampas') as being of the handlebar moustache and starched collar persuasion — did not intend to be amusing.

What Mr Bulfin did get right was the generous nature of the people of Tipp — we, too, have eaten the griddle scones and the rashers and eggs — and that much has not changed. The accent, the manner, the mores of the county and its people are steady-going, easy to get on with, easy to like.

CAHIR

ORGANIC FARMER
BALLYBRADO HOUSE
Cahir Tel: (052) 66206 Joseph Finke

Joseph Finke grows and gathers wheat, oats and rye from his own fields and the fields of other organic farmers, and distributes the flour and the oatmeal throughout the country under the Ballybrado label. He also rears beef and lamb, slaughters it and butchers it locally, and you can occasionally find it in some Dublin supermarkets.

The Ballybrado operation is a visionary adventure, for it is organic farming practiced on a fairly large scale, rather than the conventional man-wife-dog-and-three-acres set up which is so commonplace. Mr Finke's work offers a vision where organic farming is the norm, and not something left-field or alternative. Indeed, the efficiency and independence of the Ballybrado operation demonstrates that we should regard so-called 'conventional' farming as something illogical and, these days, effectively nonsensical.

Ballybrado flour is widely available

CASHEL

RESTAURANT
CHEZ HANS
Cashel Tel: (062) 61177 Hans Peter Matthias

Hans Peter Matthias' superb operation will shortly be celebrating a quarter century in business, and it is testament to this man's hard work and acute professionalism that his restaurant — splendidly housed in an old church — feels just as modern as some funky place in Dublin's left bank.

Partly this is because the ambience of Chez Hans is so timeless. It may have been a church at one time, but nowadays this svelte operation buzzes with the motivation and energy of a brasserie. Waiters and waitresses glide and scoot around the tables, ferrying food to famished folk who drive long distances to Cashel to enjoy the unique buzz of the place.

And they come for the food also, for the cooking is true and accomplished, with a basis of French styling sharpened by a fondness for strong flavours and seasonings and a sturdy grasp of how to utilise Irish ingredients to present them at their best. Portions of whatever you choose — be it fish or shellfish, meat or game, something creamy or something chilly for dessert — are hugely generous, indeed perhaps slightly too much so. But, when the mood is good and the food is good, you do want to take your time and linger awhile.

Open 6.30pm-10pm Tue-Sat. Closed Xmas and 3 weeks in Jan. Average Price: dinner £££. Visa, Access. Just beside the Rock of Cashel, and clearly signposted from the Dublin-Cork road.

RESTAURANT
THE SPEARMAN
Main Street Tel: (062) 61143 The Spearman family
As an on-the-road stop between Dublin and Cork, The Spearman is a godsend, for service is speedy and the restaurant is a calm space in which to loosen up and stretch the legs. The food is zappy with flavour, with soups especially good and fish dishes light and perfect, just what you need to get the engine started again.

Open 12.30pm-3pm, 6.30pm-9.30pm. Closed Xmas. Average Price: lunch ££ dinner £££. Visa, Access.

CLOGHEEN

FARMHOUSE CHEESE
BAYLOUGH CHEESE
Mount Anglesby, Clogheen Tel: (052) 65275 Dick & Anne Keating
The Keatings' territorial-type cheeses are buttery and gentle in flavour, blessed with the aromatic scents of flora which their good pastures gift to their milk. They have often been compared to a good Cheshire cheese, and whilst the consistency of the cheeses is vaguely Cheshireish, the tastes are stronger and more lactic than you will find in an English cheese. Baylough is usually sold when still very young, but as they are wrapped in black and yellow plastic coats they are easy to age, and then the flavours mellow and intensify, and call out for a good glass of red wine.

The farm is just outside the village of Clogheen. Ring for accurate directions. Much of the cheese is sold in Peter Ward's shop in Nenagh.

CLONMEL

MARKET, SHOP AND RESTAURANT
THE CLONMEL ORGANIC MARKET AND THE HONEY POT
14 Abbey Street Tel: (052) 21457
On Thursdays and Fridays the lucky citizens of Clonmel are treated to the joyous sights and zestful smells of an organic market, replete with all manner of vegetables, each in

numerous varieties. One Friday in September there were no less than four types of potato, four types of apples, two types of beans, as well as onions, shallots, garlic, tomatoes and cherry tomatoes, Swiss chard, cabbages and cheese. Everything is symbol standard organic or, indeed, of biodynamic standard.

The Honey Pot operates as a wholefood shop and restaurant throughout the week, so go for their lovely potato nests, where hats of mashed potato are stuffed with carrot, marrow, celery and broccoli, in a tomato sauce, served with an excellent potato salad and a crisp tomato and onion salad.

Market 10am to 6pm on Thursdays and Fridays

FETHARD

FARMHOUSE CHEESE
CASHEL BLUE

Beechmount, Fethard Tel: (052) 31151 Jane & Louis Grubb

Jane and Louis Grubb's Cashel Blue is now so famous that, along with Veronica Steele's Milleens, it is effectively synonymous with the Irish farmhouse cheese movement. Like Milleens, it has a mighty reputation abroad, and at home it is the second-biggest selling farmhouse cheese.

Like any good cheese, it is temperamental, and needs careful handling to allow the blue veining to seep through the curd and saturate every inch of the cheese with salty, potent tastes. You find it reaches this ideal state at about three and a half months old, and if you can arrange to get a cheese at this age it should promise flavours and satisfactions that are almost addictive. At Christmastime, of course, a Cashel Blue is almost de rigueur, so to get the best try to order a cheese from the farm and arrange for it to hit its peak on the happy day.

NENAGH

DELICATESSEN AND COFFEE BAR
COUNTRY CHOICE ★

25 Kenyon Street Tel: (067) 32596 Peter Ward

If you went into Peter Ward's shop looking to buy a particular farmhouse cheese and the man himself said something like 'Well, I'm not sure that that one is quite ready yet, but there is a lovely cheese here that is just right, do you think you might like to try that?', you wouldn't think to yourself: why doesn't he give me what I want?

No, instead you will think: If Peter Ward says it is not ready, it is not ready, and if Peter Ward says this one is ready, is at its best, then that is the one to buy.

Mr Ward, though he would be too modest to admit it, is an Irish affineur, a cheese expert, a man who can tell just by feeling and smelling a cheese whether it is ready to be cut and served and sold. His feeling is quite instinctual, but deadly accurate, and his instinct for good food, for things served at their best, is the animus of this wonderful shop. The hams he bakes himself to be sold by the slice are terrific, the goods on the shelves are splendid, the coffee shop in the back is great for a snack, great for lunch, and invaluable if you are travelling anywhere near to Nenagh and need a break from driving and some food to sustain you. And his professionalism and dedication give Country Choice a marvellously motivated atmosphere: it is fun to shop here, fun to allow yourself to be persuaded that the cheese you wanted is not ready and to enjoy the delight of trying something unexpected. The shop, by the way, is particularly excellent for sourcing high quality foods for Christmas baking.

Open 9.30am-6.30pm Mon-Sat

MUSTARDS & SALAD DRESSINGS
LAKESHORE FOODS
Coolbawn Tel: (067) 22094 Hilary Henry
Hilary Henry is a determined woman. Meet her and you will be in no doubt that if Mrs Henry has a plan, some new venture, some new mustard or condiment or dressing which she wants to create, then that mustard or whatever will be created, will be invented, and will then be sold tirelessly and professionally at food fairs throughout the country. The Lakeshore foods are splendid things: faultlessly made, very alluring and pleasing, and very individual and artisan.

Lakeshore mustards and dressings are available throughout the country.

ROSCREA

ABBEY STONEGROUND WHOLEMEAL FLOUR
Mount Saint Joseph Abbey Tel: (0505) 21711
'Milled for the Cistercian Monks of Mount St Joseph Abbey, Roscrea' announces the bright blue and white two kilo bags in which Abbey Stoneground is sold and, as if this monastic seal of approval wasn't enough, the label, reassuringly, also states; 'Ingredients: Wheat'. The brothers themselves use the flour to bake splendidly sensual bread, which you can buy from the Abbey and the guesthouse.

The flour is available in shops throughout the country.

THURLES

FARMHOUSE CHEESE
COOLEENEY CHEESE ➡
Cooleeney House, Moyne, Thurles Tel: (0504) 45112 Breda Maher
Get one of Breda Maher's camemberts when it is at its creamy, oozy best and you get one of the finest foods you can buy in Ireland. The rich pastures and boggy depth of the land in this part of Tipperary allow Mrs Maher to make one of the most effulgent, lurid, and insolently powerful cheeses in Ireland, something so good you would walk a country mile in the rain to eat it again.

How do you get a Cooleeney in this state? Well, if you have the confidence of a fine affineur such as Peter Ward in Nenagh or Val Manning in Ballylickey, then you can simply ask them to hold a cheese for you until it is richly mature — the ideal is to get a cheese which effectively needs a spoon in order to be eaten. If you don't have the good fortune to know a good shopkeeper, then buy the small Cooleeneys, the ones in the ash boxes, when they are right at their sell-by date, and then hold on to them for a few days.

Otherwise, travel to the farm and pick up one yourself — this, of course, is the awkward but ideal thing to do. Then, take it home, treat it gently, and the reward will repay any effort necessary to find the cheese in perfect condition. Cooleeney is like good Burgundy or rare truffles: haunting, but extra-delicate. Get it once when it is perfect, and you will chase that perfection for the rest of your days.

Cooleeney House is about three miles off the main N7 Dublin-Cork road. Take the turning opposite Mary Willie's Roadhouse, you'll be turning right if you're heading south towards Cork. Go straight for three miles, and you will see Cooleeney House right in front of you when you reach the end of the road. Always telephone first to check the availability of cheese.

COUNTY WATERFORD

I N 'THE WAY THAT I WENT', Robert Lloyd Praeger wrote of Waterford and its coast: 'I have lingered over the Waterford coast, because it is known to very few, and is well worthy of being known better. Those who love the maritime scenery of Devonshire will find here an Irish analogue: a high coast — mostly of volcanic rocks it is true, not Devonian, but with Old Red Sandstone at each end — flowery slopes, lofty cliffs and stacks and pinnacled islets with colonies of seabirds of many kinds, as well as Choughs, Peregrins, Raven; and an illimitable sea extending to the southward'.

It is this illimitable sea that cannot be escaped when you are in Waterford. The one hundred and twenty five miles of coastline, still largely known to very few, serves to always underscore and emphasise the huge power and presence of the ocean, the illimitable power of water.

BALLYMACARBRY

ORGANIC PORK, SAUSAGES, KID, BEEF AND VEGETABLES
VICKY HESLOP
Tooracurragh, Ballymacarbry Tel: (052) 36304 Vicky Heslop
Vicky Heslop is one of the longest established organic growers in Ireland, but her caramel-coloured pork always manages to surprise you afresh with its intensity of flavour, its goodness. One bite of this and you'll never be able to go back to conventionally farmed pigs.

You can buy Vicky's pork — sold by the joint as well as by the side — at her farm, and she also sells bacon and sausages. The bacon is cured for her by Rudd's up in Offaly and — all too occasionally — you can find her pork loin made into Kassler by Ed Hick in Sallynoggin in Dublin.

Vicky also grows vegetables organically and supplies them to nearby guesthouse Hanora's Cottage.

Telephone for directions. You can buy Vicky's meat and her organic vegetables from the farm. Hanora's Cottage, Tel: (052) 36134 Owen Wall.

CAPPOQUIN

SHEEP'S CHEESE
KNOCKALARA IRISH SHEEP'S CHEESE
Cappoquin Tel: (024) 96326 Wolfgang & Agnes Schliebitz
If it is the handsome label drawn by Agnes Schliebitz which first draws your eye towards Knockalara — a beautiful pencil drawing of mummy sheep, daddy sheep and baby sheep — it will be the clean, refreshing, almost lemony taste of this sheep's milk cheese which will draw you back.

Fresh, limber, and filled with bright flavours, with a little ageing the curdiness of the cheese begins to bind together, knitting together the sharp, cool tastes. When young, it works beautifully in a summer green salad, much better than any imported feta cheese, and marrying perfectly with olive oil dressings. Wolfgang also imports some German wines, including some interesting red wines which are rarely seen.

The cheese is available in good delicatessens. As the farm is difficult to find, if you wish to visit it is necessary to telephone first for directions.

CHEEKPOINT

PUB FOOD
MCALPIN'S SUIR INN
Cheekpoint Tel: (051) 82182/82220

On a warmish Wednesday evening in May, a Thursday in August when the sun is still bright outside, a Friday evening at anytime of the year, the happy regulars who pack out McAlpin's Suir Inn sit themselves down on the benches around the walls, exhale with pleasure and wait for the good, familiar grub which has brought them down to far-flung Cheekpoint to come wheeling out of the kitchen. They know what they like, they like what they know, and they know they will get what they like and what they know everytime. This is one of the happiest dining places to be found anywhere in the country.

In fact, McAlpin's attracts such devotion that the behaviour of the regulars is rather like the carry on you get at a religious service. The slightly hushed whispering before the ritual commences, the automatic calls and responses — 'What would you like?', 'Pint of Guinness, jug of white wine, one fish pie and a prawns in garlic butter, then two lemon syllabubs', 'Pie and a prawns here?', 'Yes, thanks', 'Syllabubs?', 'Here, please' — then the pealing notes of pleasure as a sense of good grace suffuses, and you realise there won't be a sermon this evening. They do good works in McAlpin's, good works indeed, and you leave, definitely, in peace.

Open 6.45pm-9.30pm Tues-Sat, pub open from 6pm. Down at the harbour in Cheekpoint.

DUNGARVAN

FARMHOUSE CHEESE
RING FARMHOUSE CHEESE
Gortnadiha House, Ring Tel: (058) 46142 Eileen and Tom Harty

Tom and Eileen Harty's cheese is as up-front and no-nonsense as the couple themselves. A spicy, tongue-coating brew that fills the mouth with clean mineral tastes that reside along with the sharp, lactic tension of the cheese, you will find that you will need something tough and tannic to drink with this handsome effort, easily recognisable in its great big orange-coated truckles. Something from the Rhone Valley or a New World Shiraz is probably called for, something that has a length of taste that lasts as long as the cheese itself, for Ring has a concentration of flavour that persists and persists.

Gortnadiha House is just off the N25, a couple of miles west of Dungarvan, and the cheese can be bought from the farm. Telephone to arrange an appointment and to get precise instructions on how to find the farm.

DUNMORE EAST

PUB SERVING FOOD
THE SHIP
Dunmore East Tel: (051) 83141 D&L Prendiville

Dunmore East is a picture-postcard-perfect place with a handsome port and lots and lots of holidaymakers during the season. If you find yourself amidst the lots and lots of holidaymakers and the fishermen, then follow the smart money to The Ship where the food, served in a simple restaurant which is an adjunct of the bar, is effectively tasty and especially appealing during the hot summertime days, as you worry about your sunburn.

Open 7pm-10pm Mon-Sun, 12.30pm-2pm Sun. Check opening hours off season. Closed Xmas. Average Price: dinner £££ lunch ££. Visa, Access.

KNOCKANORE

FARMHOUSE CHEESE
KNOCKANORE CHEESE
Ballyneety, Knockanore Tel: (024) 97275 Eamonn Lonergan

Eamonn makes plain, herbed and smoked cheeses from cow's milk, in a Port-Salut style. Knockanore is the younger version, Ballyneety the more aged, and perhaps more interesting, version.

The cheeses are widely available.

WATERFORD

DELICATESSEN
CHAPMAN'S DELICATESSEN
61 The Quay Tel: (051) 74938/76200 Mr Prendergast

Home-made fudge and mascarpone, soured cream and liquid glucose, country butter and

BASKETS

WALKING ONE HOT, sun-bright day through one of the many narrow, stone-wall lined paths in the smallest island of the Arans, we came upon Tómas Griffin Tom, a striking septuagenarian, sitting on a wall plaiting long lengths of sally rods that shot up in the air all around him before his nimble fingers weaved and subdued the slender shoots into gracefully articulate warps of wood.

His cute strategy of cutting such a vivid profile — somewhere between a Cheshire cat and a mischievous pixie — worked wonders on us visitors: called over and engaged in chat and banter with Tom and his sister, we were speedily sold no fewer than four baskets on the spot, each gnarled turban of nimble branches weaved into a shape very peculiar to the islands.

Sadly, those who make baskets on the Aran Islands are few, and they are ageing, so the tradition of basket-making in this corner of Ireland is threatened by old age and youthful indifference.

Happily, basket-making is still a thriving craft in other parts of the country and, if other shops follow the example of Val Manning's Emporium in Ballylickey and use handsome wicker, instead of monotonous wire, as shopping baskets, then this graceful, tactile, craft will continue to thrive.

Willows for basket-making are usually cut during the winter, before the sap rises. This produces a rod with little pith which makes it flexible enough to plait. Willows love water, so if you buy a hand-made basket, leave it out in the rain occasionally for a soft soaking, in soft rain, will prolong its life.

The willow basket featured on our cover was made by Norbert Platz in Co Cork, and the willow was grown in Co Waterford.

BASKET MAKERS

NORBERT PLATZ
Ballymurphy, Innishannon, Co Cork Tel: (021) 885548

JOE HOGAN
Caoladoreacht, Loch Na Fuaighe, Seanafearachain, Finney, Co Galway

ALISTAIR SIMMON
Upper Moyra, Falcarragh, Co Donegal

TOMAS GRIFFIN TOM
Tom, Inis Oirr, Co Galway

hand-made sausages, farmhouse cheeses and wholefoods, crystallised fruit and fresh-ground coffee, preserves and breads. Chapman's is a super shop, full of foods for cooks and bakers, full of the foods of the area as well as select stuff from the rest of the globe.

At the back of the shop there is a café, Chapman's Pantry, which sells soups, good sarnies, pies and quiches, with teas and coffees.

Open 9am-6pm Mon-Thur, 9am-9pm Fri, 9am-6pm Sat. Pantry open from 8am-6pm Mon-Sat.

RESTAURANT
DWYER'S OF MARY STREET
5 Mary Street Tel: (051) 77478 Martin Dwyer

Martin Dwyer likes to cook, and it shows. Lettuce and sorrel soup, monkfish in a herb crust with tapenade, garlic prawns in a rosti nest, are just some of the signature dishes of

a cook who walks that line between food which keeps his own interest maintained by presenting a culinary challenge and by introducing new foods and new tastes, and yet can manage to make this food seem comforting and accessible to a somewhat cautious clientele.

Dwyer has built a rapport with his audience over the last few years, and this has meant he is able to bring them along with him, gradually getting more involved and exciting, whilst always cooking in a style that is considerate and honest. The restaurant itself is a molly-coddling sort of space, and the combination of motherly service, soft music and good food may propel you towards a proposal, even if it is just to suggest you walk arm in arm along the riverfront after dinner.

Open 6pm-10pm Mon-Sat. Closed Xmas. Average Price: dinner £££. Visa, Access, Amex. Waterford town centre, near the bridge.

WHOLEFOOD SHOP
FULL OF BEANS
9 George's Court Ian & Sonia McLellan
Look out for the local Dunmore East Yogurt if shopping in Ian and Sonia's nifty little wholefood shop, where you can also find organic vegetables, good oils and pulses, breads and whatnots.

RESTAURANT & GUESTHOUSE
PRENDIVILLE'S RESTAURANT & GUESTHOUSE
Cork Road Tel: (051) 78851 Paula Prendiville
The rooms in Prendiville's are simple affairs, their lack of ostentation counterpointed by Paula Prendiville's cooking, which enjoys a measure of involvement and complication, but manages to hang on to distinct feminine susceptibility. The dining room is almost suburban in style, but cosy and welcoming, especially for the ferry-disgorged traveller.

Open 12.30pm-2.15pm, 6.30pm-9.30pm Mon-Fri, 6.30pm-9.30pm Sat. Closed Xmas. Average Price: dinner £££. Visa, Access, Amex. On the way out of Waterford on the N25 in the direction of Cork.

RESTAURANT, HOTEL AND COUNTRY CLUB
WATERFORD CASTLE
The Island, Ballinakill Tel: (051) 78203
Though Waterford Castle looks like to be somewhere that demands a Rolex, a Roller and a roll of folding stuff before you make your way on the ferry over to the island, this bourgeois paradise should not blind the inquisitive to the fact that the food and the wines here are worthy of anyone's attention and, if you choose carefully, you can enjoy superb food and brilliant wines without having to mortgage the house.

Paul McCluskey's cooking is innovative but thoughtful: smoked quail and duck with fennel and baby corn, veal with prunes, salmon rolled in oatmeal on a ginger sauce, lemon sole on a grapefruit butter sauce, excellent vegetarian pastas.

This is intelligent cooking that benefits greatly from impeccable ingredients, and the short ferry journey across, and the panelled dining room, add to the sense of fun and romance.

Open 12.30pm-2pm, 7pm-10pm Mon-Sun (Sun 'till 9pm). Open for Xmas. Average Price: lunch £££ dinner ££££. Visa, Access, Amex. Recommended for Vegetarians. Some three miles outside the town, and well signposted on the Dunmore East road.

ULSTER

BRIDGESTONE

COUNTY CAVAN

CAVAN CAN OFTEN SEEM SOMEWHERE slightly indeterminate, unsure whether it belongs as part of Ulster — there is undoubtedly some of the plain-speaking and some of the wildness of the Ulster character at play — or if it belongs to its neighbour Connaught — there are crisp lakes and something of the raw elementalism of the western counties here, though spiritually Cavan is not a western place — or whether some of the characteristics of Leinster hold sway — that plain but proud nature which you find a little bit further east.

What is distinctive, however, is the self-deprecating sense of humour, and the way in which it acts almost as a private joke amongst the locals, for this is a self-contained and contented place. And the lakes have an almost odious power, the massive complex of the Erne system that lies west of Cavan town possessing a gripping threat, the ability to make the land seem as nothing more than islands, a place where water holds sway.

BELTURBET

FARMHOUSE CHEESE
CORLEGGY FARMHOUSE GOAT'S CHEESE ★

Corleggy, Belturbet Tel: (049) 22219 Silke & Michael Cropp

It is impossible to divorce the happy and instinctive tastes of Silke Cropp's Corleggy goat's milk cheeses from the environment where they are made. On a small farm just outside Belturbet, with the River Erne speeding lazily past down at the bottom of the pastures, Michael and Silke keep a small herd of goats who pasture on land which has never been sprayed, meaning that Corleggy cheeses carry the Organic symbol.

The farm has a great sense of integrity and individuality to it: the porky pigs in one field who are fed on the whey left over after cheesemaking, the kids who help out and drive the goats into their pens at milking time, the smell of herbs which is so pervasive, the happy huddle of outhouses and the cheeseroom, the cutesy-pie cottage in which the Cropp family live. It seems like Beatrix Potter country, it seems like The Farm That Time Forgot, but here it is in County Cavan and, thanks to Silke, here it is producing one of the most distinctive and typical cheeses you can find.

Corleggy is made with a vegetarian rennet and sea salt, and the taste is fresh and unalloyed, very precise and clean, perfect with a glass of claret after dinner but also surprisingly good to cook with.

Silke also makes a cow's cheese in the winter season, and there are soft goat's cheeses preserved in oil, these often decorated with borage and other flowers, for Mrs Cropp has an artist's spontaneous grasp of colour and appearance, and other soft goat's cheeses sold in little crottins. All of them are subtle but very pure in flavour, allowing tastes to emerge and unfold cautiously as you eat them, but it is the pillars of Corleggy which are the perfect product of this perfect farm. Dubliners can buy the cheeses at the fortnightly Dublin Food Co-Op, but the farm is distinctly worth a visit, just to see a protean vision of an organic farm, and to take away with you a memory that will taste good for years.

In Belturbet take the road beside the cinema - it is the road on the right as you come into town by the N3 from Cavan - which runs down to the River Erne, then at the bridge turn left and continue for about one-and-a-half miles until you see the sign saying 'Corleggy Cheese'. Visitors are welcome to the farm to buy cheese and vegetables and to see the farm itself - groups should ring beforehand to arrange a visit.

CAVAN

RESTAURANT
THE OLDE PRIORY RESTAURANT
Main Street Tel: (049) 61898 Samuel and Marie Schwab
The heartiness one expects of a County Cavan menu is shown in full strength in The Olde Priory: a full page of various steaks, a full page of various lamb dishes, a page of pork preparations and one of brochettes, before a pair of fish options and a solo production for vegetarians. It can seem all too obvious, but Samuel Schwab is a confident cook and his meat dishes are well-achieved and redolent with flavour.

There is also a small pizza menu, you can order a meat fondue for two persons, and the wine list actually contains some wines from Switzerland which they import themselves: Dôle Du Valais Les Raccards — Dôle is a blend of the Pinot Noir and Gamay grapes — and Johannisberg Du Valais, Vent D'Est — the Johannisberg better known perhaps as the Sylvaner grape.

Open 12.30pm-10pm Tue-Sat, 6pm-10pm Sun. Closed Xmas. Average Price: lunch £ dinner £-£££. Visa, Access. At the Cathedral end of Main Street in Cavan town.

CLOVER HILL

THE OLD POST INN
Clover Hill Tel: (047) 55266 Seamus McArdle
A surprising number of houses throughout Ireland are not connected to the mains electricity supply and in these outposts you will often find a throw back to a past era: the inexplicably romantic gas lighting. Rather like steam trains, this lighting gives to those that fall within its narrow arc a warm knot in the tummy.

The Old Post Inn — obviously — needs electricity, but, as part of the pretty renovation and

transformation of this country post office into country restaurant with rooms, still uses gas lighting to give the dining room an atmosphere which haunts the folk memory of those who dine here.

A good option on the menu is always pork, the restaurant uses the pigs reared by Silke Cropp, fed on the whey of Corleggy cheese. It's also a good on-the-road stop — or indeed stopover, there are en suite bedrooms upstairs — on the road between Dublin and Donegal.

Open 11am-10pm Mon-Sun (dinner à la carte menu starting from 6pm). Open for Xmas. Average Price: lunch ££ dinner £££. Visa, Access, Amex, Diners. Five miles north of Cavan on the Clones road.

CROSSDONEY

B&B
LISNAMANDRA HOUSE
Crossdoney Tel: (049) 37196 Bert & Iris Neill
Bert and Iris Neill's house, just south of the complex of lakes, is famed principally for the gargantuan breakfasts they offer to the sodden fishermen, healthy walkers and holidaymakers who make their way here — the list of options is as long as a telephone directory but a lot more interesting — but they deserve their fame every bit as much for the spontaneous charm which they gift to the house.

Open May-Oct. No evening meals (suppers and flask-filling offered). Average Price: B&B £££. No Credit Cards. Lisnamandra House is clearly signposted on the Crossdoney Road leading from Cavan town.

MILLTOWN

COOK
FRED MÜLLER
Tirliffin, Milltown Tel: (049) 34260 Fred Müller
Quite how one might describe Fred Müller's operation is a process that stretches the boundaries of conventional classification. It's not a B&B, though he can arrange a bed in a local cottage if you don't fancy the trawl back home, and at night these lakes are spooky, mean. It's not a restaurant, either, for the cooking and eating takes place in Fred's house, and you eat in his dining room. There may be certain parallels with places you might have tried in France, but otherwise nothing suggests the experience of dining chez Fred. It may not be to everyone's taste, but adventurers may appreciate the extraordinary uniqueness of it all.

His cooking reflects the zest of a man who belongs to that tiny band of cooks whom we might call hunter-gatherers: dinner free-associates with ingredients that have been fished or hunted in the wild, or reared by hand by artisans. Influences in the cooking come from Fred's travels in all parts of the world. A meal can be truly epicurian, satisfying the senses with extraordinary tastes and textures.

Open for bookings only. Average Price: ££££. No Credit Cards. Coming from Cavan town you find the cottage by turning left twice: however, it is not quite as simple as that, so ring to make arrangements to be guided from Butlersbridge.

VIRGINIA

FARMHOUSE CHEESE
RYEFIELD FOODS

Ryefield House Tel: (049) 47416 Anne & John Brodie

The energy of the Brodies is only miraculous. At home all week long working the farm, milking the cows to make the orange-coloured and black plastic-clad Ryefield, a sweet and understated territorial cheese which can be compared to a good cheddar, they scoot up the N2 and down to Dublin at the weekends to run splendid stalls at both the Mother Redcap's and Blackrock markets.

Here, alongside their own cheeses in both the matured and fresh styles and the Boilie cheese, soft little balls of cheese preserved in oil which is their latest addition, they sell many of the other farmhouse cheeses and a host of other foods which Anne organises and collects and coaxes out of her neighbours. At Christmas time a visit to the Ryefield stalls reveals the magnificent panoply of Cavan farmhouse foods: plum puds laced with liquor, fruit-packed Christmas cakes, newly baked biscuits and breads and cakes, hand-made fudge and other sweets, jars of carefully prepared preserves, the whole lot of it exploding out of Anne's stall and brimful of good cheer, just like Anne and John themselves.

Ryefield cheeses are sold in two weekend markets in Dublin, at Mother Redcap's and in the Blackrock market. See entry for Ryefield Foods in the Dublin chapter.

ALSO OF INTEREST

CASEY'S STEAK BAR, Ballinagh, Tel: (049) 37105 Noel and Rita. 'The steaks are good and £10 buys a big one, fully garnished with onions, mushrooms and potatoes' is the feedback concerning Casey's Steak Bar. Open 10.30am-10pm

COUNTY DONEGAL

I N DONEGAL, IN WINTERTIME, THE ROADS AND TREES UNITE in their boot-black, bible-black starkness, an ancient bog oak darkness that covers over the sea and gives the small fields a feeling of utter, aching loneliness.

Driving through the valleys, the roads feel like nothing more than intrusions into a wicked landscape, crawling apologetically through animate nature, snaking low as a snake while the mountains maintain a snarlful eye as you run a gauntlet through them, past ferns as torchy red as the young Maureen O'Hara's hair.

That lazy wind will rush straight through you and into your bones, should you decide to take a walk on some of the northern beaches, and the villages quietly close in on themselves, dim lights humming all day in dim houses. Outside the light is cold as that line from T. S. Eliot's 'The Waste Land': 'I will show you fear in a handful of dust'.

Summer scatters all this gloom and introversion, and one then thinks of Eliot again: 'Yet with these April sunsets, that somehow recall/My buried life, and Paris in the Spring/I feel immeasurably at peace, and find the world/To be wonderful and youthful, after all'.

Nowhere else offers the intense brilliance of a sunset in Donegal, and not even the peachy light that settles over the River Liffey in Dublin late in the day can compete with the lurid volumes of russet and rouge light that annoint the county. The harshness and starkness is repelled, the place seems habitable again, though not bounteous, for Donegal never seems a place of riches, of abundance. Instead, you understand that the good things of life are hard-won here, and that winning them makes the people tough, hard.

BRUCKLESS

RESTAURANT WITH ROOMS
CASTLEMURRAY HOUSE

Dunkineely Tel: (073) 37022 Thierry Delcros

You can take a Frenchman out of France, but you can't take the Frenchness out of a Frenchman's cooking. Up here, in the wilds of Donegal, in a cosy restaurant with rooms, Thierry Delcros creates a little oasis of French cuisine every evening, an oasis whose popularity has been spreading like wildfire. Castlemurray has become a very cultish place, particularly amongst Northerners who can scoot across to here in no time whatsoever.

The menu, like so many in France, is appositely dumb: onion soup; prawns with garlic butter; duck pâté salad. Then roast stuffed chicks; hunter's plate; crispy lobster. Then crème caramel, or ices and cakes with cassis or somesuch. Familiar food, of course.

But there is a wonderful surprise in store. The menu is no more than a grammar of terms, and doesn't even hint at the compulsive, adorable tastes which M. Delcros can conjure from his own skill and good Donegal ingredients, many of them produced by local bio-dynamic farmer, Thomas Becht. The duck pâté salad, for example, will be a slice of the meat served on toast, but the sweet jelly which enfolds the slice will be serene and perfect, a maelstrom of slowly rendered flavours. The profiteroles stuffed with crab meat, served with a soupçon of spicy tomato confit and a gently sympathetic sauce, will have you doolalley with delight.

The crispy lobster, served portioned and in a pillow of filo pastry, is a great dish, a demonstration of exacting culinary control, whilst the stuffed chicks marry wonderfully with pommes boulangere and crisp red cabbage. Above all, this is gloriously French food, a virtuoso demonstration of how Irish foods and French skills are perfect platefellows.

Desserts are as heavenly with flavour as everything else: the crisp bite of cassis in an ice, the yielding milkiness of a brûlée or a caramel. The dining room has some of the most entrancing views you will find anywhere and, giddy with booze and with the pleasure points pulsing, you tumble off to a cosy bedroom on a culinary high.

In the morning, breakfast is especially fine, for M. Delcros has fully got to grips with the Irish breakfast of bacon and eggs and gives it a sharply realised European tweaking. Book early. Likely, you will book often.

Open 7pm-9.30pm ('till 10pm Sat and Sun) Mon-Sun. Closed Xmas and Mon-Wed off season. Average Price: dinner £££. Visa, Access. Signposted just after the village of Dunkineely, heading west out of Donegal town.

OYSTERS & SWEATERS
TRAUDE SLAUGHTER
Darny, Bruckless Tel: (073) 37232

The combination of oysters and sweaters seems curious but appropriate, the armour-clad mollusc with its determination not to be prised apart, counterpointed by a softly enfolding gansy with which to wrap yourself up in.

Traude Slaughter sells both, and you can buy either a sea-salty Pacific oyster or an autumn-hued hand-knitted jumper by firstly following the quirky signs and turning off the road and down the lane just before you come into Bruckless, travelling west from Donegal town.

Follow the signs on the left side just before Bruckless.

BUNDORAN

RESTAURANT
CONROY'S GERMAN-IRISH CLUB
Seafront Tel: (072) 41280 Mike Conroy

Conroy's German-Irish club has the decorative splendour of a run-down diner in an out-of-season holiday town at the end of yet another bad year.

Don't let appearances put you off. You are here for two of the great luxuries of life. You are here to begin with the Guinness and then begin the beguine with some of Conroy's smoked salmon.

Mike Conroy, an octogenarian with terrifying reserves of energy and a wicked wit, smokes it himself and uses the shavings from oak coffins to provide the smoke for his delicate, limpid, luridly fine fish. Simply take this fish to some brown bread, sip stout in between times, and you will be in heaven without the responsibility of arranging for a full coffin to get there. The salmon can be sent anywhere on the face of the earth, but if you can leave the restaurant without a surfboard-sized fillet of the stuff under your arm your friends will not thank you for having done so, and may not remain your friends for much longer.

The safest bet with the main courses is to ask Mike's wife to shove some buttered fillet of fresh fish under the grill for a couple of minutes and to get it out to you as quickly as possible. The waitresses are wonderful and bi-lingually brilliant, so you can ask in either

German or English — probably even Irish — just how a German-Irish club ever found itself in Bundoran.
Open 6pm-10pm Tue-Sun. Closed Xmas. Average Price: dinner ££. No Credit Cards. You can buy the smoked salmon from the restaurant.

BURTONPORT

PUB FOOD
THE LOBSTER POT
Burtonport Tel: (075) 42012 Gerard O'Donnell
A snack menu is served in The Lobster Pot during the day, but after six pm some above-average bar food with some decent fish and shellfish is available at pretty modest prices until 9.30pm.
Open for food 6pm-9.30pm Mon-Sun. Closed Xmas. Average Price: dinner £££. No Credit Cards. The pub is down near the port.

DONEGAL

WHOLEFOOD SHOP
SIMPLE SIMON
Anderson's Yard, The Diamond Tel: (073) 22687 Andrew Cape
Andrew Cape's shop continues to expand like hard wood: slowly, painstakingly, but solidly. There is now a regular supply of organic vegetables which are exported northwards from County Leitrim, there are farmhouse cheeses, good natural yogurt and a well made carrot cake. In the front of the shop there is an area selling Traidcraft goods, and the air of quiet co-operation which the shop enjoys is always delightful.
Open 9.30am-6pm Mon-Sat. Signposted in The Diamond

PUB FOOD
STELLA'S SALAD BAR, MCGROARTY'S PUB
The Diamond Tel: (073) 21049
This is one of few pubs which makes a conscious effort to cook something original and creative. Stella is in charge of the food in this friendly boozer and her stir-fried vegetables, wrapped up in a pouch of pitta bread, are a delight, the soups are warming against the chill of a Donegal morning, her main dishes simple and trustworthy.

FAHAN

RESTAURANT
RESTAURANT ST JOHN'S
Fahan Tel: (077) 60289 Reggie Ryan
Reggie Ryan and his chef Phil McAfee have been in control since Restaurant St. John opened in 1980, and whilst their joint operation is as seamless as any you will find, it has

never become soulless. St. John still has a sharp, buzzy feel to it, and there is considerable motivation evident, a considerable desire that the customer should have a good time and leave the restaurant happy.The food has evolved slowly over the years — it could be described as old-fashioned, if it had any truck with fashion in the first place — but the central thesis of recognisable cuts of fowl and meat, a good selection of fish and plentiful vegetables follows the 'If it ain't broke, don't fix it' command. Familiarities such as duck liver pâté, beef with a Chasseur sauce, roast duckling with orange, lamb with gooseberry and mint jelly, brill with a lemon butter, carrageen moss, show the sort of food the devoted clientele expect from St. John. That clientele also enjoy a splendid, very keenly priced wine list, and the suburban styling of the dining rooms and the bar area completes the agelessly conservative attraction of St. John.

Open 6pm-10pm Tue-Sun. Closed Xmas. Average Price: dinner £££. Visa, Access, Amex, Diners. Clearly signposted in Fahan village.

GLENCOLUMBKILLE

TEA ROOMS AND FOOD SHOP
GLENCOLUMBKILLE FOLK VILLAGE
Tel: (073) 30017 Christina Daly
The tea rooms in the Glencolumbkille folk village are a welcome haven for decent tea and Guinness loaf or home-made soup and sandwiches. In the shebeen behind the tea rooms you can buy wine made from seaweed and other unlikely ingredients, and dilisk is also available in its raw form. Jars of butterscotch and a mouth-tingling fudge should have the children bawling happily in half an hour's time.

Open from 10am-6pm, Mon-Sat, noon-6pm Sun. Closed end Sept-Easter. Average Price: meals £. Visa, Access.

GLENTIES

BIO-DYNAMIC FARMER
THOMAS BECHT
Dorrian, Glenties Tel: (075) 51286
It is rare to hear farmers praised by their peers, but we've heard much praise from other farmers, as well as customers, of Thomas Becht's careful work on his mixed farm in Glenties. For his labours he has earned both the Organic Trust symbol, and the hard-fought Demeter symbol of Bio-Dynamic farming. Both lamb and beef are available to buy from the farm. If you want to buy fresh cuts you have to buy a minimum of a quarter of a lamb, but smaller cuts are sometimes available frozen. Also for sale at the farm are vegetables in their season, and some dairy produce: farm country butter, milk and cheese. Cow's milk is made into a semi-hard cheese, and the milk from the goats is sold as a fresh cheese. You can buy Mr Becht's butter in Simple Simon in Donegal town, and wizard chef Thierry Delcros uses much of the Becht produce in his restaurant, Castlemurray House.

There are no official opening times to buy produce, and there's usually someone there to help you. But it's always a good idea to telephone first.

GREENCASTLE

BAR AND RESTAURANT
KEALY'S SEAFOOD BAR

Tel: (077) 81010 James & Tricia Kealy

Kealy's is a curious phenomenon. From the outside it is merely an unprepossessing bar in the unprepossessing port of Greencastle, with little to suggest the good cooking that goes on here. Yet by word of mouth and despite its stupendously out-of-the-way location way, way up north, its fame has progressed to range far and wide. 'Do you know that place in Greencastle, that's great', says the man in Belfast whom you met just five minutes before for the first time.

No matter, he is off and reminiscing fondly to a total stranger about this little place off in the hinterland of nowhere. It is the simplicity that people like, aside from the clever cooking and the fact of finding locally landed fish on a local menu — the appropriate food in the appropriate setting.

Open 12.30pm-5pm, 7pm-9pm Tue-Sun. Closed Xmas. Average Price: lunch and snack menu £-££ dinner ££-£££. Visa, Access, Amex, Diners. Opposite the pier.

KERRYKEEL

ACCOMMODATION
KNOCKALLA FARM

Ballynashannagh Tel: (074) 59105 Tim Spalding

Way, way up the gorgeous Fanad peninsula but adroitly adjacent to the road is Knockalla, a farm announced by the happy field of vegetables which stretches enticingly out in front of it. Knockalla offers Bed and Breakfast and also evening meals, specialising in wholefoods and using their own organic produce — the owners themselves are vegetarian. Fanad is one of the most alluringly seductive of the Donegal peninsulas, and touring it offers endless delights and diversions.

Open all year. Average Price: dinner £££ B&B £££. No Credit Cards.

LETTERKENNY

RESTAURANT
CAROLINA HOUSE

Loughnagin Tel: (074) 22480 Mary and Charles Prendergast

Though Carolina House is sveltly modern, Mary Prendergast's orientation is towards the verities of Irish cooking, a direction abetted by her Ballymaloe Cookery School background, and supplemented by her devotion to fine ingredients.

Open 7.30pm-9.30pm Tues-Sat. Closed Xmas. Average Price: dinner £££. Visa, Access, Diners. Carolina House is just off the Derry to Ramelton road, near the golf course.

COUNTRY HOUSE
CASTLEGROVE HOUSE
Letterkenny Tel: (074) 51118
Though principally a guest house, with big, comfortable bedrooms painted in relaxed dark hues, Castlegrove also operates as a restaurant, with both ravenous residents and hungry locals making their way here in search of huge helpings of food. The menu is expansive and maybe a little too much so: it is perhaps wisest to stick with some grilled meat to accompany a good baked potato and a decent bottle of red wine to make up a good dinner, though desserts are well realised.

Open for dinner for guests. Closed Xmas and Feb. Average Price: dinner £££ B&B ££££-£££££. Visa, Access, Amex. Between the two roundabouts in Letterkenny, you will see the sign for the house.

FISHMONGER
SEAFRESH
6a Railway Road Tel: (074) 26118 Michael Boyce
It is an unmissable irony of life in Donegal that whilst the county has some of the busiest fishing ports in Western Europe, there is a stunning paucity of good fish shops. Seafresh, however, is a well-stocked fish shop selling john dory, brill, monkfish, oysters, mussels and other available wetfish and crustacea.

Open 9am-6pm Mon-Sat

LOUGH ESKE

COUNTRY HOUSE
ARDNAMONA HOUSE & GARDENS
Lough Eske Tel: (073) 22650 Amabel & Kieran Clarke
Ardnamona House has one of the oldest collections of tree rhododendrons in Ireland, and whilst their multifarious multiplicity may be of absorbing interest to botanists and the plus-twos crowd, their effect, swooping and drooping all around the gardens of Ardnamona, is to create an atmosphere somewhere between the petrified forest and the enchanted forest. Amabel and Kieran Clarke's house sits fast in the wrap of these eccentric trees, and their bloom of colour in summer is matched by the shocking russet vividness of the ferns in the winter. You can walk and drive around and about the lake and feel you are miles from anywhere remotely civilised: in fact, Donegal town, with its somewhat less serene charms, is about ten minutes away.

There are five rooms in the house, south facing and brightly pastelly, and a self-catering

cottage in the rear yard which can sleep four. Ms Clarke used to cook professionally, an assurance at dinner time for the traveller in County Donegal, which remains somewhere largely denuded of good food.

You may find, however, that the 100 acres of Ardnamona and its frontage onto the lough is as much as you will want to explore.

Open for dinner if pre-booked. Closed Xmas. Average Price: dinner £££ B&B ££££. Visa, Access. Follow signs to Harvey's Point, the house is two miles further down that road.

RATHMULLAN

COUNTRY HOUSE
RATHMULLAN HOUSE
Rathmullan, Letterkenny Tel: (074) 58188/58117 Fax: (074) 58200 The Wheeler family
Still loved for its Sunday lunches, Rathmullan House remains a giant part of local life. The lunch begins with a buffet of hors d'oeuvres, seafoods, salads, pâtés and terrines. 'We are not a grand manor' say the Wheelers in their brochure blurb, 'just a friendly and informal country house which celebrates a part era of gentility and good taste'.

Open 7.30pm-8.45pm Mon-Sun, Sun lunch 1pm-2pm. Closed Dec-Feb. Average Price: lunch £££ dinner ££££ B&B £££££. Visa, Access, Amex, Diners. Turn right after the bridge in Ramelton to Rathmullan. Hotel is on outskirts of village to the north.

RAMELTON

RESTAURANT
HOUSE ON THE BRAE
Ramelton Tel: (074) 51240 Donal Hanley
Donal Hanley's food may be somewhat dinner-partyish but there are sweet little creativities to be enjoyed on the encouragingly adroit menu: marinated peppers stuffed with home-made herb ricotta, for example, to precede some chunky, grilled noisettes of lamb before chocolate ice-cream with raspberries and coffee round out a simple dinner. The House is lushly decorated with Pompeiian frescoes of flowers, fruit, birds and whatnot, framed in strong ochre and green, courtesy of painter Larry Colter.

Open winter: 7pm-10pm Fri & Sat, summer 7pm-10pm Thurs-Sat (enquire about Sun opening times). Closed Xmas. Average Price: dinner £££. Visa, Access. Turn right at the river as you enter the village of Ramelton, then take the right fork up the hill.

COUNTY MONAGHAN

HILTON PARK IS A SEDUCTIVE PLACE. In appearance there is much of the fierce arrogance of old money about this monolith, much of the decisive moral certainty one imagines Samuel Madden possessed when he bought the house in 1734. But in fact Hilton is chalumeau calm, a palette for Johnny and Lucy Madden to assemble the gallimaufry of country house gestures, pitching them together to create a canvas of sheer pleasure.

The house offers vast Princess-and-the-Pea beds, yawning big baths, halls, landings and rooms painted in roaring red and deep greens that come alive with splendour when the evening sun rushes through the windows. A dining room of classical elegance is counterpointed by a downstairs breakfast room of ruddy efficacy. In total, this array of features makes for a house which is a paragon of desirability. 'For me, that place is perfection', a recent visitor — unasked — volunteered.

Johnny and Lucy Madden supply the artistry and the ingenuity which make Hilton what it is, but their work would be nothing without the devoted persistence that underlies their efforts. Lucy Madden's food reveals a cook with an instinctive feel for ingredients, many of them coming from her own organic garden and she has the skill to make food expressive and volatile: no moribund beef and spuds here, instead that fillet of beef will match with a perfect bearnaise that will match the sharp clean sweetness of garden asparagus, following an antipasti of roasted peppers and before some salad and farmhouse cheese and fresh fruit. She is a hungry cook, hungry to experiment, hungry to invent, with an autodidact's devotion to learning that is being gradually put to use in the book of potato recipes she is writing. Johnny Madden himself has just the right sort of nonchalance, not to mention celebrated skills in the kitchen himself at breakfast time, to match this big pile, preventing it from seeming even remotely fossilised, gifting it with a young sense of humour.

HILTON PARK

Scotshouse Tel: (047) 56007 Fax: 56033 Johnny and Lucy Madden
Open for dinner for residents only (except groups and individuals by arrangement). Closed Oct-Easter. Average Price: dinner £££ B&B £££££. Visa, Access. Three miles out of Clones on the L46 to Ballyhaise. Open April-Sept

NORTHERN IRELAND

SUBURBANISATION HAS SOFTENED the social culture of Northern Ireland over the last two decades. It has softened the hungry heart that used to beat in proud cities such as Belfast or Derry and redistributed the residents of these big towns outwards, to places whose souls pulse with the disassembled unease of Edge Cities, strewn with yellow sodium light. If you left Ulster twenty-five years ago and returned tomorrow, you would find the development of the Province to have been unambiguously schizophrenic: alongside places and attitudes which have changed not a jot, there is change, utter change, in every respect.

In parallel with this relentless development, a slow trickle of culinary suburbanisation has softened the food culture of this mercurial sextet of counties.

The modern suburban ethos of eating in the North revolves around convenience and taste-simulation as opposed to creativity and culinary veracity. Ease of preparation is the drug which seduces, seduces those who were weaned on good food, the true and simple good food which underpinned the North for so long: sprightly fadge, good champ, floury Comber spuds in the late summer, soft soda bread, honest butter. The social act of cooking which produced the stoic, peasant cuisine of Northern Ireland is now too little valued and the dishes themselves are often little more than historical symbols.

In truth this process has been going on for decades, ever since the United Kingdom adopted a cheap food policy after the second world war, and the North fell in behind. The collectivist spirit which prevailed then for decades saw no virtue in individuality. Mass production led to mass market foods, chasing any artisans out of the food world. This has led, steadily, to a food culture which is for the most part homogenised, where shopping is done in supermarkets whose miles of aisles offer little or nothing of interest to the discriminating shopper — the person who prizes individuality, character, signature — and led to restaurants and cafés content to offer adulterated tastes, and thus able to offer nothing to the diner in search of personality and the pleasure of culinary creativity.

But there is, happily, a paradoxical edge to this often unhappy picture. Here and there in the North, often in unlikely places, there are individuals whose work is filled with the thrill of creativity and careful choice, whose dedication is daunting, whose abilities and skills are world class. Perhaps it is because they are faced with such a monstrous volume of indifference and indifferent food that their work has such a resonant sharpness, a triumphant sense of opposition, the stubborn refusal to knuckle under.

These individuals are truly remarkable for, without the safety net of an appreciative and critical food culture, they determinedly follow their own heads, determinedly do the things they do with only their own sense of self-criticism to guide them.

And one finds, happily, an echo of this stubbornness in the resilient and upfront character of the Northerners themselves, their gentleness spiced with grit, their suburban circumstances failing to undermine their sense of shared community, their timeless hunger for the good times, for good things. For, in spite of the obvious divisions of the Province, the citizens of Northern Ireland are united by their love of this cautious place and, while things change all around them, often they themselves can seem to be perfectly changeless.

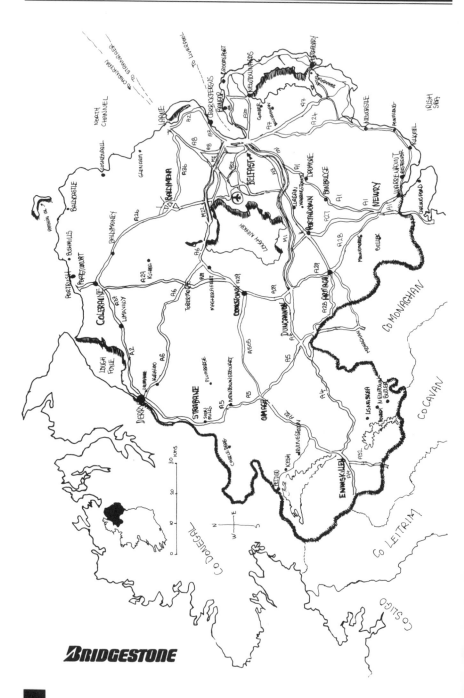

BRIDGESTONE

COUNTY ANTRIM

BALLYCASTLE

BUTCHER'S SHOP AND RESTAURANT
WYSNER MEATS
18 Ann Street Tel: (02657) 62372 Roland & Jackie Wysner
August is the month for Ballycastle, the time when the population swells with blow-ins from Belfast who take themselves up to the north coast for holiday time. Despite its doubtful charms, the town has managed to cling on to an identity as a resort where you can enjoy time out, and its air of relaxation hits a peak on the last day of the month when the Ould Lammas Fair takes over the place, and bus loads of day trippers and car loads of the cautiously curious add to the dizzying numbers of folk wandering around aimlessly and pleasurably.

The town is unusual in Ireland in as much as its best known foods are celebrated in song. 'The Ould Lammas Fair' is a frankly lascivious hymn to dulse, the dark salty seaweed they like to chew in the North, yellow-man, a vile sticky honeycomb concoction, and to Mary

BALLYMENA CHINESE RESTAURANTS

THE SCORES OF CHINESE RESTAURANTS and take-aways which fuel the seemingly insatiable desire for stir-fried rice and chicken chow mein amongst the people of Northern Ireland are, with occasional exceptions, indistinguishable one from the other. Their décor is firmly locked back in the 1970s, when dodgy taste met laminate and velour in a migraine-making crash. Their menus are unchanging testaments to a severely compromised style of Chinese cooking, and their principal function is to fuel their customers with slick, soulless nosh. Ballymena, for some reason, bucks this trend, with both the Manley and The Water Margin capable of creating interesting, thoughtful Chinese food, some of it delightfully surprising. It's best to choose from amongst the speciality dishes of both places, and necessary to ask the staff to give you the real thing.

MANLEY
State Cinema Arcade, 70a Ballymoney Road Tel: (0266) 48967
Open noon-2pm, 5.30pm-11.30pm Mon-Sun. Closed Xmas. Average Price: lunch £ dinner ££.= Visa, Access, Amex. Opposite the Adair Arms Hotel.

THE WATER MARGIN
8 Cullybackey Road Tel: (0266) 652320
Open noon-2pm, 5.30pm-11.30pm Mon-Sun. Closed Xmas. Average Price: lunch £ dinner ££. Visa, Access, Amex. Visible as you drive into town from the Portglenone direction.

Ann, whom the singer remembers in a line of unconcealed eroticism:
> *'But the scene that haunts my memory is kissing Mary Ann,*
> *Her pouting lips all sticky from eating yellow-man'.*

They sell neither dulse nor yellow-man in Wysner's butcher's shop, but it is true to say that this splendid establishment is as much a part of the culture of the town as the Ould Lammas Fair itself. The sausages — compared by some to the immortal Hafner's sausages of Dublin, and perhaps with justification — the splendid black pudding and the many other preparations will have your lips pouting, first with anticipation, later with pleasure.

Open 8am-6pm (Half day Wed in summer, winter closed Wed). Restaurant open 8am-5pm Mon-Thur, 8am-9pm Fri-Sat. (8am-10pm 7 days during high summer). Centre of Ballycastle.

BELFAST

For many years the ethos which Belfast espoused, and the ambience it exuded, was resolutely Victorian. Hard work, a strong sense of self-help and social propriety and a spirit of self-denial — abetted of course by the right of every man and woman to go on the occasional binge — directed the citizens of this once-handsome city.

In recent years, however, Belfast has loosened up, and the citizens have begun to find the attractions of fashion and contemporary cultures to suit their tastes. Where once there was little other than a sense of just-controlled wildness masquerading as the social culture, the city and its people seem more confident nowadays, more European. Their extraordinary resilience and their devoted love of their birthplace has not diminished a jot, but they have been sliding off the shackles of moribund morality quietly and quickly. This stylishness, and the energetic social jizz, makes the city as cooly fascinating as ever.

BELFAST RESTAURANTS

ANTICA ROMA

67/69 Botanic Avenue BT7 Tel: (0232) 311121 Tony Mura

Antica Roma is where Italy meets Hollywood. You could come here just for the surreal indulgence of the décor and the ecstatic energy of the diners, but the food, happily, is not just hype or spectacle. Specialist Italian restaurants have been signalling the death of trattoria food for some years now, and Antica Roma shows that even in these great big Italian joints, tratt grub is passé.

AR has not completely discarded the curious meandering of Italian food followed in Ireland for the last half century, however. Here, in the Irish way, pastas begin the meal and are served in generous starter portions, before you move on to main courses of fish, fowl and meat and finish with desserts. But, if their cucina creativa style is slightly tempered by the expectations of their customers, a little exoticism can allow for some fine food: a tactfully zappy spaghetti with baby squid, excellent pepperdelle with seafood, and balanced with ageless classics like lamb cutlets, you can easily assemble an excellent dinner. The wine list has some dry, cussedly fruity Sicilian wines which are rarely seen, the service is splendid, prices are keen and the atmosphere, particularly at the weekend, is a subdued riot.

Open 6pm-10.45pm Mon-Sat. Closed Xmas week, 12 Jul. Average Price: dinner £££. Visa, Access, Amex.

Half way up Botanic Avenue, just up from Shaftesbury Square.

MANOR HOUSE

47 Donegal Pass BT7 Tel: (0232) 238755 Tony Wong

The Manor House may have the most God-awful location of any restaurant in the country — smack opposite an intensely fortified police station on a road replete with speed barriers — but the zingy, flavour-filled Cantonese food you can enjoy in here makes it worthwhile to stroll down this godforsaken pass.

The restaurant is a standard laminate-and-lacquer array of rooms, and whilst you can of course opt for familiar Chinese food, the real fun happens when you to put them to their mark and put yourself on the culinary edge. Order the unusual dishes — fish head, duck's web — ask for them to be done in the real style with lots of chillies, and then enjoy the energy and excitement of this confident Chinese cooking. Their dish of eel with roasted belly of pork, for example, presents these unlikely flavours as perfectly complementary, the pork sticky and sweet, the eel sinuous and oily, your glass of Chardonnay the perfect complement. This sort of adventure allows you to get the best from the Manor House, and to find some of the best Chinese food in the North.

Open noon-midnight. Closed Xmas week. Average Price: lunch ££ dinner £££. Visa, Access. Recommended for Vegetarians (full menu available with advance notice). Donegal Pass runs off Shaftesbury Square.

NICK'S WAREHOUSE ➡

35/39 Hill Street BT1 Tel: (0232) 439690 Nick & Cathy Price

Years ago, Nick Price used to cook in a restaurant and pub called Daft Eddie's on Sketrick Island, on Strangford Lough. Simple stuff, really: a collection of roasts, a smattering of salads, good for Sunday lunch, super after-sail nosh. The food was as effective and happy an assault on the taste buds as you could imagine. In little or no time, Price had gifted to Daft Eddie's an almost mythic status: back in the bad old days of Ulster food, his was cooking that kept a close and fastidious eye on matters as obvious as freshness, motivation, concern.

Years later, and several moves on from Sketrick, Nick Price is still cooking, and cooking as well as ever. His food is always approachable and always correct, and in Nick's Warehouse he has a funky, lean, dining space which suits the spirited effectiveness of his work.

Take a simple dinner: a mussel soup borrowed from Gerry Galvin's book 'The Drimcong Food Affair' will be sea-salty and chewy-delicious. A pair of lamb chops have a honey and ginger sauce that ties in the light odours of the Pacific Rim with fine sweet Ulster meat. A bowl of crisply fried potatoes, a selection of fresh vegetables, then finish with some blackcurrant cheesecake. Simple stuff, and you would happily eat it every night of your life, when such fine and clever attention has been paid to matters as abstract as freshness, motivation, concern.

Nothing much has changed with the way Nick Price cooks, and nothing needs to. He manages to offer a more intricate menu in the Warehouse, but no matter what you eat, the essential truths remain: the true taste of monkfish and crab allied with chilli and soy: an easy-going boudin blanc with a splash of apple sauce: the utter wit of his notes on the wine list almost as much of a pleasure as the plonk you eventually choose. Anyone could try to do this sort of thing — providing super food in a super space — but no one else could do it with the grace, good sense and good humour that Nick and Cathy Price can.

Open 11.30am-11pm for drinks and coffees, food available wine bar: noon-3pm, restaurant: noon-3pm, 6pm-9pm Tue-Sat, Mon lunch noon-3pm and open 'till 5pm for drinks and coffees. Closed Xmas. Average price Wine Bar: ££ Restaurant: £££. Visa, Access (note: card purchases under £10 subject to 50p surcharge). Recommended for Vegetarians. Hill Street is near the University of Ulster in the centre of Belfast.

ROSCOFF ★

7 Lesley House, Shaftesbury Square, BT2 Tel: (0232) 331532 Paul & Jeanne Rankin

You need a welter of great confidence to serve a cuisine which uses understatement as an integral part of its appeal. Maybe, after a couple of decades in a kitchen seeking out the essentials of flavour, you could pull off a meal which begins with marinated olives and simple bread, then proceeds to a dish of herb risotto with lobster, cooked in a plain broth

BISTROS

THIS COSY LITTLE TRIO OF BISTROS are almost conjoined together in that triangle of busy nightlife between Great Victoria Street, the Dublin Road and Bradbury Place. They are friendly, noisy places, filled usually with friendly, noisy people, but don't for a minute imagine that they try to replicate anything of the true character of a bistro, aside from the friendliness and the noise. Belfast's bistros are closer in style to those establishments popularised in the U.K. by Pierre Levicky, the sort of joints that offer lunch for a fiver. You can get lunch in a couple of these places for a fiver: lentil soup that once nodded across the street at a passing lentil, then chicken legs provençale, the dish as authentically French as Peter Mayle. So don't be tempted by the prices, but do, once in a while, allow yourself to be dragged along after a drinking session has begun, then slurp up yards of plonk and use the grub as a fortifier against the booze.

LA BELLE EPOQUE
61-63 Dublin Road BT2 Tel: (0232) 323244
Open noon-3pm, 6pm-11.30pm. Average Price: lunch ££ dinner £££. Visa, Access.

LA BOHEME
103 Gt Victoria Street BT2 Tel: (0232) 240666
Open noon-3pm, 6pm-11.30pm Mon-Fri, 6pm-11.30pm Sat. Open for Xmas. Average Price: lunch ££ dinner £££. Visa, Access.

CHEZ DELBART/FROGITIES
10 Bradbury Place BT7 Tel: (0232) 238020
Open 5.30pm-midnight Mon-Sat, 5pm-9.30pm Sun. Closed Xmas. Average Price: dinner £££.

to allow the freshness of the herbs to speak out and garnished with thin slices of the pink flesh, a flourish of lobster tail and dots of roe. Then, some squab, with grilled Paris mushrooms and noodles of light pasta piled up in the shape of a fez. Dessert is honey and pine nut ice cream, served in snap cigars with sharp, marinated plums that have the rear-jaw shuddering.

Perfect, perfect, a whirlpool of suborned control, a meal whose coincidence of confidence and culinary savvy speaks volumes about the kitchen that can prepare it. At the end of a lifetime cooking you would be happy to get this close to the ideal of an ideal. In Roscoff, as stylish and cool an eating space as you will find anywhere in the country, Paul and Jeanne Rankin offer this instinctual, artistic food with a minimum of fuss and self-consciousness, with a maximum of concentration on achieving a hard-held vision of the pleasures which food should offer. That they are able to concoct a cuisine of such depth after such a relatively short period of time is little short of miraculous.

Paul Rankin's cooking strives towards presenting a series of delicately and precisely realised tastes, thereby creating a momentum and a rhythm to a meal which arouses and placates, stimulates and satisfies.

Best of all, his food is disciplined and his considerable skills are never wasted on fashionable concoctions or experiments.

Open 12.15pm-2.15pm Mon-Fri, 6.30pm-10.30pm Mon-Sat. Closed Xmas, 12 Jul and some bank holidays. Average Price: lunch £££ dinner £££. Amex, Visa, Access. Recommended for Vegetarians. On Belfast's 'Golden Mile' leading from the city centre to the university.

FISH AND CHIPS

LONG'S FISH RESTAURANT

39 Athol Street, BT12 Tel: (0232) 321848 Walter Titterington

'Terrible weather', says the lady serving you your chips and cod in Long's loveably ancient chip shop and restaurant. Terrible indeed, you agree. 'But at least we don't get any earthquakes', she says, 'Nor hurricanes'. It must be the splendid fish and chips they make in Mr Titterington's shop, that can make such optimists of them.

Open 11.45am-6pm, Mon-Fri. Closed Xmas. Average Pricce: £. No Credit Cards. Athol Street is behind the bingo hall on Gt Victoria Street.

BELFAST RESTAURANTS

THE ASHOKA, 363/365 Lisburn Road BT9 Tel: (0232) 660362 Decently achieved Indian food in an enjoyably lively place. Open noon-1.45pm Mon-Fri, 5.30pm-11.30pm Mon-Sat (10pm Sun). Average Price: lunch ££ dinner £££. Visa, Access. Good Vegetarian choice.

BANANAS, 4 Clarence Street, BT2 Tel: (0232) 339999 Laminated menus, T-shirted ambience. Open noon-3pm, 5pm-11pm Mon-Fri, 5pm-11pm Sat. Closed Xmas. Average Price: £££. Visa, Access, Amex.

BELFAST CASTLE, Antrim Road, BT15 Tel: (0232) 776925 Food available all day in either the bistro or the restaurant. Spectacular views across the city. Open for coffee from 11am, lunch 12.30pm-3pm, dinner 5.30pm-10pm Mon-Sat, 12.15pm-3pm Sun. Average Price: lunch £-££, dinner ££-£££. Visa, Access, Amex.

BENGAL BRASSERIE, 339 Ormeau Road BT7 Tel: (0232) 640099 Open noon-2pm, 5.30pm-11.15pm (Sun 10.15pm). Closed Xmas. Average Price: lunch £-££ dinner £££. Visa, Access. Good Vegetarian choice.

FRIAR'S BUSH, 159 Stranmillis Road, BT9 Tel: (0232) 669824 Old-style cooking. Open noon-2.30pm, 7pm-10pm Tue-Fri, 7pm-10pm Sat. Closed Xmas. Average Price: lunch £, dinner £££. Visa, Access.

RESTAURANT 44, 44 Bedford Street, BT2 Tel: (0232) 244844 Long-established, a recent change of ownership may create a new lease of energy. Open noon-3pm, 6pm-11pm Mon-Fri, 6pm-11pm Sat. Closed Xmas. Average Price: lunch £££ dinner £££. Visa, Access, Amex.

STRAND, 12 Stranmillis Road, BT9 Tel: (0232) 682266 Popular, enduring, familiar. Open noon-11pm Mon-Sat, noon-10pm Sun. Closed Xmas. Average Price: lunch £££ dinner £££. Visa, Access, Amex.

VILLA ITALIA, 39 University Road, BT7 Tel: (0232) 328356 Generates the longest queues of any eaterie in the city. Open noon-2.30pm, 5pm-11.30pm Mon-Fri, 4pm-11.30pm Sat, 4pm-10.30pm Sun. Closed Xmas. Average Price: lunch £-££ dinner ££-£££. Visa, Access, Amex. Good Vegetarian choice.

WELCOME CHINESE RESTAURANT, 22 Stranmillis Road, BT9 Tel: (0232) 681359 One of the better Chinese restaurants amongst the dozens which Belfast offers. Open noon-2pm, 5pm-11.30pm Mon-Fri, 5pm-midnight Sat, 5pm-11.30pm Sun. Closed Xmas. Average Price: lunch £££ dinner £££. Visa, Access, Amex.

PUBS

CROWN LIQUOR SALOON

46 Great Victoria Street, BT2

Not so much a pub as an institution, both for drinking and for the perusal of a grievously hallucinatory interior design. Having a drink in here on a Friday evening at five-thirty will explain the drive, energy and bonhomie of the people of Belfast quicker than any sociological treatise or front-line reportage by a visiting American writer.

THE ROTTERDAM BAR

Pilot Street

Students of architecture may come here to marvel at how this building manages to stay erect — its weird location makes it seem as though it is being used as a prop in a Wim Wender's movie — students of design may appreciate the ancient distillery mirrors, students of music may appreciate the nightly bands, but students of whisky will be most at home in The Rotterdam, for the range of malts and specialist hootches in Chris Roddy's bar is spectacular. At about five o'clock on a summer evening, sunlight distilling through the windows, and a glass of 36 year old Old Comber in your mitt, you may feel you have intruded upon the secret of existence.

THE MORNING STAR

17 Pottinger's Entry, off Anne Street, BT1

The range of food offered by the Morning Star is almost as diverse as the customers who pack themselves around the bar. Two polite gentlemen, discussing a barmitzvah in Vancouver, toy with spiced herring, whilst regulars munching 'the biggest steak in Belfast', calculate their losses on the racing results broadcast on the TV over their heads. Professional types move to the culinary edge with Chicken Piri Piri and everybody loves the home-made pies, the liver and onions and the chips.

What makes the Morning Star particularly unusual as a city centre pub is its changing fish menu: salmon with tomato salsa, monkfish studded with garlic, a giant bowl of mussels or plainly served Cuan oysters, an enjoyably diverse choice.

BELFAST SHOPS

CHINESE SUPERMARKET

ASIA SUPERMARKET ➡

189 Ormeau Road, Belfast BT1 Tel: (0232) 326396 Mrs Pau

Krupuk udang from Indonesia. Long grain rice from Mississippi. Electric rice cookers from Japan. Sea moss fish paste from Middlesex. Under a single, capacious roof, the Asia Supermarket is a splendid bazaar of the bizarre and the commonplace. A place where agar agar sits beside salad cream in an ever-bustling warehouse of Asian essentials.

Hand-made dim sum await your steamers, fresh fruit and vegetables could be long long beans, watermelon, or perhaps four types of Chinese greens: choi sum, kai lau, bak choi or kai chi, each with its individual flower, mustardy taste and healthy green goodness even in the dragging chill of an Ulster spring. In the freezer counters crab toes, oysters, Pacific prawns and even a large grass carp are just visible through opaque frozen bags. Fresh foods include duck and muscly free-range chicken while the non-perishable shelves are filled with joss sticks and shoes, china bowls with gaudy plastic serving spoons, woks and bamboo steamers. The staff are giggly and friendly, making cracks as their customers dodge around the boxes being wheeled in and out as part of the wholesale business which runs side by side with the shop.

Open 10am-7pm Mon-Sun

THE TOP OF THE LISBURN ROAD

IT WOULD BE IMPOSSIBLE to live in Belfast and to live without frequent trips to the wonderful collection of good food shops found near the top of the Lisburn Road. Quite why and how these thoughtful, individual, characterful shops have gathered themselves together in such a small space is a mystery. But the mystery is of secondary importance to the thankful fact that they do exist and the fact that their proximity one to the other makes life so easy for the hungrily curious resident.

New to the area is Cargoes, where a fine sense of discrimination abounds from the careful selection of olive oils, to the handmade pasta, to the very tabletops in this café-delicatessen. The oils come mostly from Italy, imported to these isles by the Camisa family, as well as from Spain and Portugal. The tables are reminiscent of a Paris bistro with their aluminium tops on which to drink fine cups of strong coffee. A range of more than sixty cheeses mix good Parmesan with the best of the Irish farmhouse varieties, and everything underpins Rhada and her partners' desire to find food from 'small family companies'. Cargoes also offer outside catering and ready made freezer foods and desserts.

Arcadia, meanwhile — another deli with a treasure trove atmosphere — continues to thrive, as does nearby Coffey's, a typically competent Belfast butcher, which is also useful for unusual cuts and species of meat, game and fowl.

La Poissonnerie describes itself as a 'fish delicatessen' and, indeed, not only is it an excellent fish shop, selling bright fillets and steaks, but Patrice Bonargent also keeps a splendid cooked fish counter with marinated salmon, stuffed mussels, fish stews and a delicious 'fish roast' — fillets wrapped around a garlic flavoured butter, ready to do nothing with other than bung in a hot oven.

Almost opposite the fish shop June's Cakeshop's cakes and breads — soft pancakes, triangles of soda, potato cake circles and wheaten wedges — are a good example of the North's particular

FISHMONGER
EWING'S
124 Shankill Road BT13 Tel: (0232) 381120 Walter Ewing
An enduring and endearing little shop selling 'white' and 'brown' fillets, pickled herrings and pickled eggs.
Open 9:30-5:00, Tues-Sat

baking culture. The breads and cakes up here are soft and welcoming, hinging perfectly to the Ulster fry, or the cup of tea. Mullholand's has the edge over other greengrocers by offering oyster mushrooms, local organic foods, seasonal berries and imported exotics. A little further down the road, Eatwell treads an expert line between the conventions of the standard wholefood shop and the imprimatur of the decent deli: good yogurts and creams, good sandwiches, good fruit and veg. Service everywhere is plain wonderful.

CARGOES
613 Lisburn Road BT9 Tel: (0232) 665451 Rhada Patterson
Open 9.30am-6pm Mon-Sat

ARCADIA
378 Lisburn Road BT9 Tel: (0232) 666779 Willie Brown
Open 7.30am-6pm Mon-Sat

COFFEY'S
380 Lisburn Road BT9 Tel: (0232) 666292 Mr Armstrong
Open 8am-6pm Mon-Thurs, 7.30am-6pm Fri & Sat

LA POISSONNERIE
Lisburn Road BT9 Tel: (0232) 669903 Patrice Bonargent
Open 8am-5.30pm Tue-Sat

JUNE'S CAKE SHOP
376 Lisburn Road BT9 Tel: (0232) 668886 June Henning
Open 7.30am-5.30pm Mon-Sat

MULHOLLAND'S
382 Lisburn Road BT9 Tel: (0232) 381920 Jack Whiteman
Open 9am-6pm Mon-Sat

EATWELL
413 Lisburn Road BT9 Tel: (0323) 664362
Open 8.30am-6pm Mon-Sat

KITCHENWARE & CAFÉ

EQUINOX

32 Howard Street, BT1 Tel: (0232) 230089 Mr & Mrs Gilbert

Embarking on a caffeine crash course to find the finest cup of coffee in the country would throw up many delights, many disappointments, and few better cups of potently dark nectar than the coffee served in the café at the rear of Equinox.

Served in a thrillingly expensive Rosenthal little cup, the espresso here has the suppleness of deep roast and the energy of high altitude. Two sips, and the body is restored, the brain pulses clear, the blood rushes and rushes. It is a private, orgiastic excursion into the centre of one of life's great pleasures, a selfish culinary cocoon that lasts but a few seconds, and those few seconds are long enough.

In Equinox they annotate this joy with cool sounds, gorgeous croissants, assured cream cheese and smoked salmon bagels, splendid apple juices selected by variety, and other moderne dishes such as Tuscan bean soup. Even before this swish and inspired venture, Equinox kitchenware was an essential, albeit costly, necessity of life, but the café has turned it into a bedfellow.

Open Shop: 9.30am-5.30pm Mon-Sat ('till 9pm Thurs); Café: 9.30am-5pm Mon-Sat ('till 8pm Thurs)

SUPERMARKET

SUPERMAC

Newtownbreda Shopping Centre, Saintfield Road, BT8 Tel: (0232) 491176

Supermac scores over the droves of other Ulster supermarkets simply by virtue of the relaxed ambience, agreeable human scale and user-friendly staff who keep the oldest supermarket in Belfast ever youthful. In particular, the bread and cheese counters and the section devoted to specialist foods are invaluable, but it's always pleasurable to find yourself wheeling a wire trolley around this capacious space.

Open 8am-9pm Mon-Sat. At the top of the Saintfield Road, right on Belfast's A55 Outer Ring.

FISHMONGER

SAWERS

Unit 7, Fountain Centre BT1 Tel: (0232) 322021 Mr Graham

A small shop which is stocked to the rafters with each and every manner of comestible: outside there is an array of fruit and vegetables, including organically grown vegetables, then straight inside the door is a decent fish counter with an array of crustacea and, as you march along, you meet first a cooked meat counter and, at the back, a good cheese counter with a small but select brace of Irish farmhouse cheeses. In between there are certain surprises, and patient staff to assist you through the maze of makes and models.

Open 9am-5.30pm Mon-Sat

BELFAST WINE MERCHANTS

THE BELFAST WINE COMPANY

130 Stranmillis Road, BT9 Tel: (0232) 381760

Though the Belfast Wine Company has cashed in some of its singularity, and taken a turn down market in an attempt to broaden its cheaper and mid-priced range, it is still an attractive shop, with some classy clarets and the occasional offer worth being snapped up as you make your way home.

Open 11.30am-9pm Mon-Wed, 9.30am-9pm Thurs-Sat. Left hand side as you drive up the Stranmillis Road away from the city.

DIRECT WINE SHIPMENTS

5/7 Corporation Square, BT1 Tel: (0232) 238700 Kevin & Kieran McAlindon
Whilst brand new bridges dissect the air above and around it, Messrs McAlindon's shop stands still in its quiet, time-ignoring way. An echoey, arcane and splendid place to buy the fruit of the vine, they have everything from Tokaji Aszu to Tempranillo, and service is helpful and informed.

Open 9.15am-6.30pm Mon-Fri ('till 8pm Thurs), 10am-5pm Sat. Near to the car ferry port in Belfast's docks area.

THE WINE GALLERY

Boucher Road, BT12 Tel: (0232) 231231 Rory McNally
This is a small, enthusiastic and friendly wine shop, set fast on the busy main strip of Boucher Road and featuring a small but attractive array of wines.

Open 9.30am-7pm Mon-Sat

BUSHMILLS

RESTAURANT WITH ROOMS
AUBERGE DE SENEIRL

28 Ballyclough Road Tel: (02657) 41536 Barbara Defres
The Auberge can seem a somewhat surreal experience in the context of the North, with its menus in gothic script and the curious, introverted atmosphere of the small dining room. In provincial France it would not seem anything like so strange, for the concept of opening a dining room for the public in a converted house, or, indeed, in a converted schoolhouse, as this is, is relatively commonplace in areas like the Dordogne.
But, near Bushmills, this strangeness is pleasing, and Barbara Defres' cooking, with its understated but closely understood idea of simple French food, is unexpected and enjoyable. Mrs Defres sticks to classic fare — smoked trout with horseradish, goat cheese on croûtons, poached chicken with a tarragon sauce, Barbary duck, pastry creams and gateaux for dessert — and with the small wine list and the quiet service it makes for a nice space. There are also five bedrooms in the house, not to mention a swimming pool for those who, having plunged in, may want to plunge in some more.

Open 7pm-9pm Tue-Sat. Closed Xmas. Average Price: dinner £££-££££ B&B £££££ Amex. The Auberge is signposted from the B67 and the B147

DISTILLERY
OLD BUSHMILLS DISTILLERY

Bushmills Tel: (02657) 31521
Highly organised and highly entertaining tours of the classic and handsome Bushmills Distillery — the oldest licensed distillery in the world — take place regularly during the

day. At the end of a trudge around tuns and stills, there is the promise of a shot of the hard stuff to sip as you ponder the romantic concept of 'The Angels' Share', that portion of spirit in the barrel which evaporates each year to succour the spirit world.

Open 10am-noon, 2pm-4pm Mon-Thur, 10am-noon Fri. No reservations necessary except for groups.

GLENARM

SALMON FARM
NORTHERN SALMON COMPANY

Glenarm Tel: (0574) 841691 Dr Brian Scott

'I couldn't tell you how delicate they are', says Brian Scott of his salmon, his face acquiring the expression of a patient and exasperated parent, 'I mean, you just have to look at them crossly on a Monday morning and they flip over and die on you'.

Glenarm is blessed with a perfect site. 'The tide out there runs like a river, between Torr Head and The Mull of Kintyre. Our tide runs 2 knots. The fish love it. By about mid-July our fish — transferred around the same time and around the same size as other people's — are about half the size. The reason is, I think, because they're spending so much energy swimming against the tide. But once they get to about 150 grams, the opposite happens. They're now big enough that this is just good exercise and they just put the weight on, and that puts on the muscle texture, so by Christmas our fish are bigger than other people's'. This strong tide also means that any problem with sea lice and fish faeces are dealt with naturally. Glenarm salmon are also stocked conservatively: 'We put the number of fish in a pen that we're going to harvest out of it, we don't double or triple it and then reduce the number. When they are fully grown they are then at the maximum stocking density and at that point they would be between 12 and 14kgs per cubic metre of water inside the pens. That compares with up to 20kgs in Scotland and up to 30kgs in Norway. The fish are happy'.

The happy fish also like the small variation in water temperature in the Glenarm Bay — if temperatures get high then the fish become stressed — and the Glenarm company closes the circle on nature by their feeding practices.

'The basic raw materials are a replica of what they eat in the wild, you must also incorporate a pigment in the diet because there is a pigment in the wild diet. The choice then is between using the pigment which exists in the wild, which we do, or to use an artificial pigment', says Scott. 'Now what we use is manufactured, but it is nature identical. It's very expensive, we spend £40 or £50 a ton extra, which is a lot extra on feed bills, but it gives you something that is as close to nature as possible'.

Brian Scott mentions this ideal, replicating the elements of nature which the salmon encounters in the wild, a great deal. He is unhappy with the public perception of fish farming as a bandwagon of cowboys who have no ambitions other than to make a financial killing. 'Ironically, a lot of the people who were involved in the business at the beginning were marine biologists, ecologists, people who loved the environment, people who were looking for a job that would get them out into the wilds, and the challenge of learning about and working with this wild animal was so fascinating', he says.

In Glenarm, Scott chose a path which sees fish farming as an integral part of a community. 'I realised this was the way I wanted to do it, very local, I wanted my investors

BELINDA HILL'S COLD POACHED SALMON

THIS CLASSIC LUNCH PARTY RECIPE comes from Belinda Hill, who lives in Malahide, County Dublin and whom we met doing a Marcella Hazan course. Mrs Hazan, had she the luck to eat it, would appreciate the purity and subtlety of this now-overlooked masterpiece.

Put the cleaned salmon (or salmon trout) in a fish kettle and almost cover it with cold water. Add a handful of salt, about 12 black peppercorns, a few leaves of lemonbalm if you have it, and a handful of parsley and then either 5 fluid ounces of white wine or a lemon — half of its juice squeezed out into the water and two quarters in with the fish.

Bring gently to a good simmer, then count to thirty, (helpful to count in thousands, ie one thousand, two thousand and so on). Slam the lid on tightly, remove from the heat, and leave overnight to cool.

'If the salmon was a big one' says Belinda, 'I would count to forty'.

Next day, remove the salmon from the liquid, remove the skin and garnish. Belinda serves it with a home-made lemon mayonnaise.

to be local, very committed and to bring something else to the project besides money: local know-how, experience, expertise, contacts, you name it and that's the way it's worked out'.

But is it worth it, this expensive and problematic business of man trying to build the components of nature simply to produce something that we can find naturally in the wild? For Brian Scott, it is the acceptance of Glenarm salmon as a top class culinary product which gives him satisfaction. 'It was only when chefs I respect, top class chefs in England started getting on the phone, and Billingsgate wholesalers called me up and said "We're coming to see you, your fish are very good" and Albert Roux rang me up and said "Can I come and see you, I've been using these fish and they're very good". Then we realised we had something'.

Fresh and smoked salmon are for sale at the shop on the pier in Glenarm. Factory shop open 9am-5pm, Mon-Fri, 2pm-6pm Sat-Sun

LISBURN

FOOD EMPORIUM
GREEN'S FOOD FARE

23 Bow Street Tel: (0846) 662124/662641

This friendly rigmarole of a shop is little different from many standard supermarkets, but the fruit and vegetable section is always good and there is a small corner of speciality foods which may well contain some small, essential ingredient you desperately need.

Open 9am-5.30pm Mon-Wed, 9am-9pm Thurs, 8.30am-9pm Fri, 8.30am-5.30pm Sat

NEWTOWNABBEY

JAPANESE RESTAURANT
THE GINGER TREE
29 Ballyrobert Road Tel: (0232) 848176 Shotaro Obana
Ulster's only Japanese restaurant plays a wonderful trick on the first time visitor, for inside this big house, from the road nothing more unusual than a substantial farmer's dwelling, is an austerely minimalist dining room with Japanese prints, lean dark furnishings and a wooden floor. Unusually, they puncture this contemplative and attractive space with inappropriate Western pop music, and this leavening of the atmosphere is echoed by Shotaro Obana's cooking, which despite its pure and traditional direction is rather more user-friendly than the food served in Japanese restaurants in the south of Ireland. Nevertheless, by choosing carefully, perhaps opting for one of the Taste of Japan menus and enjoying sashimi with green mustard, or kabayaki, the grilled Lough Neagh eel, there are splendid tastes to be enjoyed. Prices are keen, both for lunch and dinner.
Open noon-2.30pm Mon-Fri, 7pm-10pm Mon-Sat. Closed Xmas and 12, 13 Jul. Average Price: lunch ££ dinner £££. Visa, Access, Amex. Leave the M2 at the Glengormley junction, take the sign for Corr's Corner. At the next roundabout take the sign for Ballyclare, the restaurant is 2 miles further, on the right hand side.

ORGANIC FARMER
JOHN HOEY
Shandon, Mallusk Tel: (0232) 832433 John Hoey
With his bookish appearance and clubbable clothes, you could easily imagine John Hoey as a youthful don or someone who does something or other in the Jockey Club or a solicitor's firm. Instead this quiet, thoughtful man is one of the major producers of organic food in the North, supplying his delicious herbs and vegetables direct to restaurants — the improvement in eating standards in Belfast owes a lot to Hoey and his close relationship with restaurateurs — and to certain shops. Like any good grower, his range is broad and diverse and dictated, happily, by the seasons.

PORTGLENONE

FLOUR & COMPOST
OUR LADY OF BETHLEHEM ABBEY
Portglenone Tel: (0266) 821473 Father Jim Conlon
Father Jim is something of a modest media star when he isn't out on the farm fiddling with the Bishop's Hat. If this sounds vaguely disrespectful, rest assured that the Hat is, in fact, an anaerobic digester, a splendid machine which not only heats the monastery — and thereby the shop and the tea rooms and the guesthouse which they also run — it also eventually produces the excellent Abbeygrow and Dungstead composts which the brothers sell. Their Abbeycorn wholewheat flour and porridge oats are resonant, reliable foods, blessing you with goodness.
Craft Shop (Tel: 0266 821754) Open 9.30am-5.30pm Mon-Sat, 1.30pm-5.30pm Sun (closed lunch hour 12.30pm-1.30pm) The monastery is just on the edge of the town and is clearly signposted from the road. The flour is also available in many supermarkets, the compost in many garden centres.

PORTRUSH

FARMHOUSE ACCOMMODATION
MADDYBENNY FARM HOUSE
18 Maddybenny Park Tel: (0265) 823394 Rosemary White

Rosemary White's breakfast presents an agonising drama of multiple choice. Before you head off to sleep you need to fill in the breakfast menu to give them some idea of what you want to eat.

First of all, the porridge. You can have it your way or The Maddybenny Way. The Maddybenny Way is to serve the grains with runny honey, either Drambuie or Irish Mist, and lashings of cream. You'll have it The Maddybenny Way.

Then, the agony of decision continues. Which main dish will it be? The Ulster Fry, with soda and fadge? Kipper fillets poached in lemon juice and dill? Trout braised in lemon butter, then served with smoked bacon and mushrooms? Maybe a smoked haddock ramekin? Or lamb's kidneys? Boiled eggs? Scrambled eggs?

You could flunk the responsibility, of course, and just content yourself with the fresh soda bread and toast, the handmade jams and marmalades, the country butter, a clatter of cups of Earl Grey, or maybe some hot chocolate. But, once the choice is made, sleep will be bound to be sound with plenty to look forward to when you wake.

Open all year except Xmas. Average Price: B&B £££. No Credit Cards. Off the A29, on the outskirts of Portrush.

RESTAURANT & WINE BAR
RAMORE
The Harbour Tel: (0265) 824313 (Wine Bar: 823444) George McAlpin

The re-invention of the Ramore into a more informal dining space, with the kitchen fully open to view and a set of bar chairs at the counter, has lightened the atmosphere of this most swish of dining rooms, set high up in the harbour at Portrush.

The paraphernalia of a working kitchen — the brigade of whisks, the tumbling tresses of garlic, the bottles of oil, the dog-eared texts, are all on happy exhibition along with their white-clad employers who intersect with one another with the sure-footedness of dancers. It's a charming entertainment, right down to the concerned attention devoted to a side of beef as it is quietly prepared for cooking.

In parallel with the reinvented renovation, George McAlpin's cooking has shifted its concentration away from an obsessively detailed French style, bringing on board more of the vogueish influences of the pacific Rim: Japan, San Francisco, Thailand, Indonesia, with considered borrowings from the Mediterranean.

This lighter, light-hearted, style is delivered with confident aplomb. To begin, a quintet of tempura prawns fanned around a big white plate, their crisp, ochre batter offset by the bright playfulness of finely diced peppers tucked under a trio of Mexican tostados, a quiet dish of tagliatelle with a slurpy Roquefort sauce and shards of bacon. Then, some monkfish with utterly splendid local scallops, lightly coated in breadcrumbs and their saline succulence perfectly captured by quick frying, and some char-grilled chicken with the sharpness of red onions and the sweetness of sun-dried tomatoes for annotation. Seasonal vegetables are summer-crisp, a garlicky purée of spuds babyful delicious, desserts of serene lemon tart and a cracking praline ice cream perfectly delivered. The staff are super, the wine list short and clever, breads are excellent, the whole organisation devoted to delivering a good time. At the next table, a lady who drinks a single glass of white wine begins with a lovingly teased up prawn cocktail, moves on to steak and finishes with a dish of ice cream. She is as happy as a sandboy.

Open Wine Bar: noon-2pm, 5pm-11pm Mon-Sun; Restaurant 7pm-10pm Tue-Sat. Closed Xmas and Restaurant closes 2 weeks in Mar. Average Price: restaurant dinner ££££ wine bar lunch ££. Visa, Access (no cards in wine bar).(Rest. needs advance notice). On the harbour in Portrush.

TEMPLEPATRICK

FARM SHOP
DUNADRY FARM GATE
Templepatrick Tel: (08494) 32074 Brian Crawford

Brian Crawford sells humanely reared beef, veal and pork, as well as some fowl and game, usually by the half or quarter carcass. Meat is sold blast frozen, bagged and labelled.

At the Templepatrick roundabout, take the Antrim turnoff. Drive until you come to the Bridge and turn right. If you're coming from the Antrim direction take the first left after the hotel. The turnoff is just adjacent to the river. Then take the first left (after about half a mile) and the farmhouse is the first on the right about half a mile further on. Always telephone first to make sure someone is there to open the shop.

TOOMEBRIDGE

EELS
LOUGH NEAGH FISHERMEN'S CO-OPERATIVE SOCIETY
Toomebridge BT41 3SB Tel: (0648) 50618 Pat Close

'I love eel. Sometimes I think it is my favourite fish. It is delicate, but rich; it falls neatly from the bone; grilled to golden brown and flecked with dark crustiness from a charcoal fire, it makes the best of all picnic food; stewed in red wine, cushioned with onions and mushrooms, bordered with triangles of fried bread, it is the meal for cold nights in autumn; smoked and cut into elegant fillets, it starts a wedding feast or a Christmas Eve dinner with style and confidence'.

Thus the wonderful Jane Grigson, writing on eel in her 'Fish Book' and singing the praises of this mysterious, elegant, poetic fish no more than it deserves, for everything about the eel is picturesque, demanding, alluring. Alas, Northerners have no time for it, and the brown and silver eels which they fish here at Toomebridge are almost all exported to mainland Europe, though some of the local Chinese community buy them, and they can occasionally be found on the menus of Japanese restaurants, matched with a tart kabayaki sauce. They are relatively simple to cook, with a good recipe book like Mrs Grigson's to hand, and eating them offers us, as the late Mrs Grigson writes, 'the occasion for rejoicing'.

Telephone for more details if you want to buy eels. The Co-Op is just on the left before the bridge.

COUNTY DOWN

COUNTY DOWN WEARS ITS CREEDS ON ITS SLEEVES. On the Gold Coast, the slick name for that strip of valuable property which runs east of Belfast, the belief in Mammon is trumpeted loud: vodka and Volvos, golf clubs and gin and tonics, affairs of the heart, the good life in bourgeois livery. But south of here, there is another kind of fundamentalism, which sounds itself off no less loudly. From Comber on south, down through the drive-through villages of Saintfield, Crossgar, sullen Downpatrick, telegraph poles will be ticker-taped with short, sharp notices, sound-bites of theological certainty. 'Saved? Lost?' they ask, and you may, at least, be able to answer the last with a definite 'Yes', for this is a confusing part of the country. Everywhere, there are exhortations urging to know ye the way of the Lord, suggesting you appreciate the sacrifice of the Son of God. There are modest halls — but of course they are modest — with optimistic extensions and signs to placate you, stating that the church is still available to those not yet saved.

BANGOR

OFF LICENCE
THE AVA
132 Main Street Tel: (0247) 465490 The Hillen Brothers

'If there's anything you want us to get special, anything you find when you're away on holiday and you want it when you get back, then we will try to get it for you. Just give us a few days, and we'll try', said the kind lady behind the counter to the gentleman who confessed that he was making his first visit to The Ava. Like the others of us who have maybe been in here dozens of times, he likely imagined he had stumbled upon an Aladdin's Cave of good drinks and hospitable service, for The Ava has that personality and personability which singles out certain shops and makes them worthwhile. The Hillen brothers try hard, and always try hard, and their sense of service and self-criticism means that the shop is steadily getting better, steadily adding more interesting spirits to an already enormous range, steadily adding new designer beers culled from all corners of the globe, working to expand their selection of wines and to line up and list Antipodean superstars, East European replicas of West European varietals, California classics, classy clarets. Unlike a true wine shop, they don't concentrate their direction on certain growers, or stray much beyond the most acclaimed names of the wine world, but there is still much here to delight, still yards of bottles to demand the attention of your credit card. The unselfconscious helpfulness of the staff lifts The Ava high above the norm of off licences in the North, so it can be pleasurable simply to browse, pleasurable to inquire about the chance of securing a bottle of some obscure ouzo or little known country wine or once-sampled Russian vodka, pleasurable to simply buy something good.

Open 9.30am-9pm Mon-Sat. Bangor town centre, opposite the Post Office.

RESTAURANT
THE BACK-STREET CAFÉ
14 Queen's Parade Tel: (0247) 453990 Peter Barfoot

'The exterior has the feel of the entrance to an air raid shelter', was how a friend described the appearance of the Back Street Café, whilst another remembered the lane down which you walk to find the Café as a place where you scarpered for 'Kissin', pissin' and fightin''.

That laneway, The Vennel, now pays host not to snogging youngsters on a Saturday night scrape, but instead to hordes of the eating classes, their bottles of wine slung into plastic bags, their feisty hopes for Saturday night answered — with verve and certainty — by the splendid food of the Back Street Café.

Pay no attention to the grotty lane or the grim exterior. Inside, the Café is a swarth of warm ochre colours on rough plastered walls with an assortment of amiably useless art for sale. The kitchen is open-plan, the waiting staff cool and confident in their work, and Peter Barfoot's cooking is the final delightful trump in this unlikely but essential place.

The daily menu does not neglect the conventional preferences of the North Down diner — lambs' kidneys, sirloin steak, saddle of lamb with rosemary and garlic — but whilst the kidneys get a conventional Dijon mustard sauce, the steak teams up with an unusual beurre de cepe and the lamb enjoys a rich Madeira demi-glace. This is the astute culinary intelligence at play in the Café: this food will not frighten anyone at first glance, but there are so many enjoyable twists, turns and revisions at work that the conventional is transmuted to the sublime. Char-grilled smoked salmon is lush and oilsome, and a smooth sun-dried tomato dressing the perfect foil. Turbot has a smoked garlic beurre blanc that combines subtlety with stunning satisfaction, Calvados and roast baby pears are used to cut the warm cream sauce of roast pork, chives to freshen the beurre blanc served with tiny queen scallops. The confidence extends through to fine desserts: bitingly rich summer pudding, smooth vanilla terrine, excellent goosegog and elderflower ice-creams, and one can forgive a tiramisu that is comprehensively wrong, for it has nothing whatsoever to do with tiramisu.

Come ten o'clock, the music has been switched off and those wide-jawed Ulster accents are beginning to settle into pulsing overdrive, filling the room with relaxed laughter, creating the most perfect Saturday night atmosphere imaginable, the cooking and the crack inspiring everyone to their inspired best.

Open 7.30pm-9.30pm Tue-Sat. Closed 10 days in Jul and Xmas. Average Price: dinner £££. Visa, Access.
The Vennel is a laneway leading off Queen's Parade.

BUTCHER
DAVID BURNS ➡
112 Abbey Street Tel: (0247) 270073 David Burns

We need to borrow a term from the world of wine to best describe the excellent meats which David Burns sells in his sparkling shop, for what characterises his meat is its typicity, its ability to represent the true and distinctive nature of itself.

His lamb is soft and sweet, delicately herby, the fat crisp and oily, lightly salty in flavour thanks to its Ards Peninsula grazing grounds. His beef has that impactful resonance of taste which speaks of careful, generous care towards the animal and attentive, respectful treatment in the slaughterhouse, resulting in food that satisfies with its balance of complex tastes, its simultaneous offering of earthiness and ethereality. His pork enjoys a subtle, intense mouth-feel, a close-grained compactness that has you salivating to simmer it with red wine and a clatter of fennel seeds. His sausages have that sparky, fatty sense of youthful delight that rouses the child in you. Everything, indeed, offers the tastes you want: you expect meat to taste like this, to gift you with these taste sensations, and where so often these days one is disappointed by the texture and taste of meat, David Burns's produce never lets you down. Each thing, each type, is typical, true, superb.

This is all due to the man himself, a devoted campaigner on behalf of good quality meat, a man with astute political skills. His efforts are complemented by a genteel staff of startling efficiency whose skills in the arts of butchering and shopkeeping peal with professionalism.

Open 7am-5.30pm Mon-Wed, 7am-1pm Thur, 6am-5.30pm Fri. Far end of Abbey Street.

WINE WAREHOUSE
STEWARTS' WORLD OF WINE
116 Clandeboye Road Tel: (0247) 466909 Paul Abraham
Although the range of wines and spirits on sale in the Stewarts' Warehouse is attractive, the capacious barn which encloses them has all the charm of an after-the-match football ground. Airless, fluorescent-lit, with a jumble of cases piled on top of each other and a cold corner for beers, this is somewhere to go purely to see if there is anything at decent value and then to buy in bulk. And there are occasional bargains — a decent Saint-Veran selling for under four quid was a recent steal — but the Pile-It-High, Sell-It-Cheap ambience rather dilutes the pleasure of buying a good bottle, so visits here should be confined to those occasions when you are forced into throwing a big party and inviting a lot of people you don't much care for.

Open 9.30am-9pm Mon-Sat. At the top of the Clandeboye Road, past the football stadium, just off the Bangor ring road.

COMBER

HERB FARM
THE HERB FARM
Cockle Point Cottage, 31 Ringneill Road Tel: (0238) 541992 Margaret McShane & Bill Franklin
Margaret and Bill supply fresh herbs, some vegetables and flowers to restaurateurs, grown in their 'high-rise' conservatory, known locally as Franklin's Folly.

CROSSGAR

WINE MERCHANT
JAMES NICHOLSON ★
27A Killyleagh Street Tel: (0396) 830091 Fax: (0396) 830028 Jim & Elspeth Nicholson
Of all the bizarre locations where people who work in food and drink in Ireland contrive to locate themselves perhaps Jim Nicholson's wine shop takes the biscuit for the bizarrest. His beautiful shop, elegantly lit like a French couture house, bright and light like a West

Coast conservatory, calm and mellifluous as a country draper's, is in Crossgar.

As a village Crossgar has the deadly dull feel of someplace that knows, deep down, that it is Nowheresville Incarnate. In conservative County Down, where you would safely reckon that people still talk about the 'demon drink', the very idea of opening a shop which sells the greatest wines of the world seems to be the purest form of madness. Admirable madness, of course. But mad, all the same.

Yet Jim and Elspeth Nicholson's shop has a trade which is currently increasing at a rate of 40% each year. They have managed not only to survive, but to veritably thrive in this apparently hostile environment.

They have done this not only through the selection of wines sold, but also through careful thought of the design of the shop itself and through the excellent tastings and events which they organise. For right down even to the quality of paper on which they print their list, Jim and Elspeth Nicholson do things right.

The distinctiveness which invades every part of the business, the sense of choice dictated by quality, tumbles resplendently over into the wines he sells. In this regard, Jim Nicholson's philosophy is simple.

'We always try to deal with families who are involved in their own businesses', he says. 'Literally every business that we have been involved with has been a family concern'.

And a list of the names of the great winemakers whose wine Nicholson sells reveals men with a headstrong, hands-on bent for both quality and personality: Aimé Guibert of Mas de Daumas Gassac, Henry Ryman of Chateau la Jaubertie, Gaston Huet from the Loire valley, Gerard Jaboulet and Etienne Guigal from the Rhône valley, Esme Johnston from Bordeaux, Paul Croser from Australia, Kevin Judd from New Zealand, Rainer Lingenfelder from Germany, the Bergqvist family from Portugal, Serge Hochar from the Lebanon. Who would not drive to Crossgar, to the Heart of Nowhere, to cull a case from this stellar line up?

Open 10am-7pm (shop), 9am-5pm (office). Killyleagh Street runs off the centre of Crossgar. Delivery free throughout the north for a minimum order of one case.

DONAGHADEE

ICE-CREAM PARLOUR
THE CABIN
32 New Street, Tel: (0247) 883598
The Cabin is the original, and still the best, place to eat hand-made ice-cream. With its clean, unsophisticated shelves and old-fashioned counter, its jars of boiled sweets and a kindly lady to take your money, it is a slice of commerce that time forgot: frozen as perfectly as the crystals of milk in the ice-cream itself.

The gentle, white-coated old gentleman who makes it makes vanilla flavoured ice-cream, and that is that, though you can decide to stick a chocolate flake into it should you be less of a purist.

Why is it so good? Because the innocence and mothers' milk goodness which ice-cream portends is made real here, reminding you of times when you were so much younger, and had cuts on your knees and ice-cream on your chin.

Open 11am-6.30pm Mon-Wed, 11am-9pm Fri-Sun. (Closed Thurs).

DROMORE

FARMHOUSE CHEESE
CAORA & DRUMILLER CHEESE
15 Leapoges Road Tel: (0846) 692211 John & Mary McBride
Although John and Mary McBride pasteurise the sheep's milk they use to make both Caora and Drumiller cheeses, these pale, pale white log and feta cheeses still have the well tuned, slightly sharp and very cleansing pleasure which a sheep's milk cheese gifts to a salad — for which the Drumiller, particularly, is an invaluable asset. The Drumiller Greek-style yogurt is a deliciously real and satisfying transformation of the milk, splendid for cooking classic dishes such as Broad Beans and Yogurt, to garnish a moussaka, or to off-set a bowl of sweet summer berries.

DUNDRUM

PUB & RESTAURANT
THE BUCK'S HEAD INN
Dundrum Village Tel: (039675) 868/859 Craig & Maureen Griffith
Billowing lobelia interspersed with fuscia dangling from the window boxes, teams of white haired grannies with pleated checks and cardies arriving with their kids and grand-kids, give a clue to the fact that the Buck's Head is less a pub than a restaurant meets country tea rooms. Three menus, fish, open sandwich and vegetarian are printed on different blackboards. So options range from gratin of Cuan oysters, grilled under a quilt of emmental cheese, home made hamburgers or pakoras with a sweet and sour sauce. A new extension will mean that guests can sit under a conservatory cover and the beer garden at the back is actually a garden rather than the more usual conciliatory yard of outside space.
Open 12.30pm-2.30pm (lunch), 5.30pm-7pm (high tea), 7pm-9pm dinner Mon-Sat. 12.30pm-2.30pm (lunch), 5.30pm-8.30pm (high tea) Sun. Closed Xmas. Average Price: meals ££. Visa, Access. Recommended for Vegetarians. In the centre of Dundrum village.

GROOMSPORT

RESTAURANT
ADELBODEN LODGE
Donaghadee Road Tel: (0247) 464288 Fax: (0247) 270053 Margaret & Dennis Waterworth
Dennis Waterworth saw a description of his wife in these words of Henry Ford, so much so that he had a plaque made for the restaurant quoting: 'You can do anything if you have enthusiasm. Enthusiasm is the yeast that makes your hopes rise to the stars, is the sparkle in your eyes, the swing in your gait, the grip of your hand, the irresistible surge of will and energy to execute your ideas. Enthusiasts are fighters. They have fortitude. They have staying quality. Enthusiasm is at the bottom of all progress. With it there is accomplishment. Without it there are only alibis.'
The Adelboden is a wonderfully motivated restaurant. The Waterworths and their staff

keep it bubbling along — enthusiastically! — for twelve hours a day offering first a lunch menu, then afternoon tea, then high tea and finally dinner. Vegetarians get their own full pasta, rice or crêpe menu. The plain eaters of North Down can have steak, a real beef burger or battered cod with home-made chips. Culinary dare-devils can choose their own sauces for fish or pasta and the verity of Margaret Waterworth's cooking is immensely pleasing to all tastes at all times of day.

Open noon-midnight Tue-Sat. Closed Xmas. Average Price: ££-£££. Visa, Access, Amex. Recommended for Vegetarians. Signposted on the coast road to Donaghadee, just outside Groomsport.

HELEN'S BAY

RESTAURANT
DEANE'S ON THE SQUARE
Station Square Tel: (0247) 852841/273155 Haydn & Michael Deane
There are interesting and amusing influences visibly at work in Deane's On The Square. The semi-revealed kitchen harkens to a bistro ambience and the happy sounds of sizzle-sizzle that extrude from it serve to puncture the cloistered atmosphere of this manifest old station building, as do the picturesque but vaguely nervous waiters with their manes of pony-tails. The copy of Ian McAndrew's 'Fish Cookery' which generously sits on the window ledge signals the direction of Michael Deane's cookery: a fondness for the pyrotechnics of preparation and elaboration, the robust use of colour on a plate as crisp carrots intersect with bushy green broccoli, all interleaved around pillows of salmon with baby scallops or coins of lamb sitting astride a splendidly clever turban of potato purée finished off with a crisp grated potato cake.

These are valuable moves away from the suburban signatures which other aspects of Deane's curtsey to for the benefit of their clientele: the dull music, the obvious wine list, the crowded little bar downstairs, the severely-trimmed prices. But the confidence that will come with extra experience should see Deane's settle down and relax a little more, allowing the waiting staff to be as brassy about the food as they should be, for there are good tastes here — a fine duck terrine set off with carefully placed summer salad leaves and an appropriate walnut dressing, the shellfish sauce around a seafood sausage, softly poached pears with a bitingly intense blackcurrant sorbet — and it is a fun place.

Open 7pm-10pm Tues-Sat, 12.30pm-3pm Sun. Closed 2 weeks Jan. Average Price: £££. Visa, Access. The restaurant overlooks the station platform in Helen's Bay. Look for the newly-restored tower.

HILLSBOROUGH

BAR & RESTAURANT
THE HILLSIDE
21 Main Street Tel: (0846) 682765
An appropriately picturesque pub in the sloping village of Hillsborough, the Hillside Bar serves crowd-pleasing bar snacks for around a fiver.

Open noon-2.30pm (lunch), 3pm-8pm (bar snacks), 7pm-9pm dinner. Closed Xmas. Average Price: £-££. Visa, Access. Hillsborough town centre.

HOLYWOOD

BISTRO
IONA BISTRO

27 Church Road Tel: (0232) 425655 Bartjan Brave

The Iona Bistro is a fail-safe. You bring along your own bottles of wine, sit on the steep stairs quaffing your plonk as you wait for a table, and then enjoy not only the rushy familiarity of a true bistro — gingham table cloths, candles stuffed into wine bottles, waiters who rush around the place, the hum of conversation, the steady backbeat of well-chosen music — but also food that is packed with true tastes. The blackboards offer a trio of starters and main dishes, with an unannounced vegetarian choice always available, and then probably a quartet of desserts, and no matter what you choose, the food in the Iona has always been distinguished by both simplicity and voluble, lively tastes.

An excellent grained mustard dressing picks up a straightforward salad of avocado and melon, a cauliflower and cheese soup is rich and warming, the peanut sauce on a lamb kebab well-realised. Salmon will be lightly grilled and served with a serene cucumber sauce, lamb adorned with gracious tastes of rosemary, a vegetarian stir-fry shaken up with a good cashew nut sauce. With fried potatoes and crisp salad leaves, it's relaxed, welcoming, astute food, completely familiar, of course, but the verve and pleasure of these true tastes mean you could eat this food every night and never tire of it.

Open 6.30pm-midnight Mon-Sat. Closed Xmas. Average Price: £££. No Credit Cards. Recommended for Vegetarians. Holywood town centre, up the stairs over the Iona Wholefood Shop.

SPECIALIST SHOP
THE IONA

27 Church Road Tel: (0232) 428597 Heidi Brave

The Iona shop combines food and crafts, and both sections display a selective and clear-visioned mind at work. The selection of organically-grown vegetables is small but always pristine — flootery rocket leaves, tiny courgettes, small bursts of seasonality in the shape of beans and peas, fresh new spuds, crunchy apples — the breads are wholesomely efficacious, though perhaps a little worthy and old-fashioned, and all the essential ingredients to usher forth good cooking from soup to nuts are handsomely displayed and alluring. The crafts, likewise, are must-have, must-buy beautiful.

Open 9.15am-5.30pm Mon-Sat. Holywood town centre.

RESTAURANT
SANTÉ

30 High Street Tel: (0232) 428880 Bartjan Brave

Whilst the layout of Santé cannot count as its greatest asset, creating certain awkward and stranded spaces, the understated cooking is a modest, well-understood pleasure.

Each dish has a good feel and the necessary balance to make it work, so a cream of celery soup will have the firm sweetness of celery and the background of a good chicken stock, a goat's cheese salad will be daisy-chain circled by purslane and chervil, roasted peppers and baked courgette, the tastes melding and mixing sympathetically. Puy lentils are cooked in a classic style, with lardons of bacon and a little cream, and come sitting under a grilled breast of chicken, the result a good mix of colours and flavours. Roast pork with polenta has the yellow staple sliced into half moons, and the loin of pork roasted. This is quiet, softly-spoken cooking, and this, just as much as the real flavours, is a pleasure. The variety of menus offered during the day allow one to pick and choose with ease, and Santé is a friendly space, easygoing.

Open 12.30pm-2.30pm, 6.30pm-10.30pm Tue-Sun (no lunch Sat, Sun 'till 9pm). Closed Xmas, 12 July. Average Price: lunch £££, snack menu £-££, dinner £££. Access, Visa. Recommended for Vegetarians. In the centre of Holywood

CAFÉ AND CRAFT SHOP
THE BAY TREE
Audley Court Tel: (0232) 426414 Rosalind MacNeice
The cute little dining room in The Bay Tree nestles at the back of a cave of hand-thrown crockery and hand-threaded wicker baskets, a light, bright rinkydink of small tables that promises relaxation and fondly regarded food the second you walk in. Sue Farmer's cinnamon scones and her sinfully rich carrot cake with its coxcomb of crushed nuts on top are vital staples for morning coffee or afternoon tea, and her lunch menus enjoy a quiet creativity, with vegetarian dishes like mushroom and broccoli croustade or a spicy peanut chicken offering a clever divertissement from crowd-pleasers such as cod Florentine. 'We don't serve any padding', says Ms Farmer, and nor do they: the bread is good, the salads crisp and fresh, and the affable feminine ambience makes The Bay Tree quite charming.

Open 10am-4.30pm, Mon-Sat. Set back from the street amidst a courtyard of shops.

DELICATESSEN
PANINI
25 Church Road Tel: (0232) 427774 Tony McNeil
Panini appears almost as an outpost of Antonio Carluccio's culinary empire, with the media-cuddly Italian's pastas, mushrooms, sauces, books and whatnot displayed everywhere throughout this attractive space, their packagings alluring, their prices expensive. Otherwise, Tony McNeil's shop combines a variety of Italianate leanings, with a tiny coffee bar with a scattering of seats at the far end, a healthy cold counter with good cheeses, cooked and smoked meats, prepared salads and pâtés, a selection of Deli France and other part-baked breads, and staples such as oils, vinegars, teas and coffees

Open 7am-6pm Mon-Sat. Holywood town centre.

ORGANIC GROWER
HOLYWOOD ORGANIC FOODS
23 Seaview Terrace Tel: (0232) 423063 John McCormick
Saturday mornings find John McCormick in the big barn which doubles as an Organic Farm Shop on the Clandeboye estate, a couple of miles out of Holywood, a couple of miles out of Bangor, surrounded by a clatter of tables with his organic produce laid out on top. There will be purply beets, soil-covered spuds, green broad beans, boxes of eggs, sharp red tomatoes, tightly-knotted heads of Little Gem and Sierra lettuces. The location seems an apposite and appropriate spot to buy his fine produce: the tactility of the wood and the logged trees outside adding to the earthiness of the experience. Like the other principal organic growers in the North, John Hoey of Shandon and David Hawthorn of Derry, John

McCormick's influence as a grower is much greater in impact than the modest size of his operation might suggest, simply because the produce of these growers is in such demand from smart restaurateurs and decent shops. It is thus easily accessible and not overpriced, for in a typical piece of Northern understatement they don't make a song and dance about it all. They just get on with the business of growing and distributing their glorious foods.

The Clandeboye shop is open on Saturday mornings and signposted from the road.

MOIRA

BUTCHER
MCCARTNEY'S FAMILY BUTCHER ➡

56/58 Main Street Tel: (0846) 611422 George McCartney

What is most impressive about George McCartney's shop is not just the superspeed efficiency of the staff as they attend to the infernally awkward requests you make upon them — 'Could you please label the eight types of sausages I've bought, and cut me just two slices of the baked ham and a slice of black pudding, no two slices, and some pie,

which one now? that one and that's all, no wait, I want some silverside and will that freeze well do you think?'.

It's not even the daunting excellence of the meat they sell: the celebrated sausages, of course, in all their multifarious porky glory, the splendid beef and texel lamb, the lovely meat pies and puddings.

No, George McCartney's secret is consistency. Come in here week in and week out, year in and year out, eat your way through every sausage and cut of meat, through every preparation for the freezer and fridge and oven and grill and barbecue, and you will never be disappointed by a single thing. Work your way slowly through the two dozen or more types of sausage, and each will be as good as the other. Indeed, you will only ever be delighted by every single thing, for George McCartney respects his métier, respects his customers, respects his profession, and this respect, then, is reciprocated by the long queues of folk who snake through the shop, people who have come from each and every direction because they know they will get what they want, and know that it will be right. But with so much goodness on offer, so much to experiment with and enjoy, it is agonisingly difficult to make up your mind. Just as well the staff are all super-efficient, and patient.

Open 8am-5.30pm Tue-Fri, 7am-5.30pm Sat

NEWRY

BAKERY
ARTHUR MCCANN LTD
Victoria Bakery, Castle Street Tel: (0693) 2076 Christopher McCann
McCann's brack is available in local shops, including the petrol station shops at the border. The portercake is widely distributed in tourist shops.

NEWTOWNARDS

RESTAURANT
THE GASLAMP
47 Court Street Tel: (0247) 811225 Elizabeth & Chris Crow
The Gaslamp is the kind of place where you could order steak au poivre 'Well done' and no-one would reproach you or regard you as old fashioned. It's that kind of restaurant: unshowy, unconcerned about the fads and fashions of food, concerned more to facilitate the conservative demands of its customers by offering them hugely generous portions of the straightforward foods they want to eat when they eat out. So, there will be Cumberland sauce with pâté, sumptuous fillets of fish such as turbot or hake, curiosities such as Cuan oysters wrapped in smoked salmon, alongside the steaks and the supremes of chicken. For many locals it is a favoured, favourite place, somewhere to head to confident that you will get exactly what you want, exactly the way you want it.
Open 6.30pm-10pm Tues-Sat, 12.30pm-3.30pm Sun. Always open for bookings, including Xmas day and New Year. Average Price: dinner £££. Visa, Access, Amex. The Gaslamp is in the centre of Newtownards, about one hundred yards from the Old Priory building.

SHOP
HOMEGROWN
66B East Street Tel: (0247) 818318 Trevor & Margaret White

This busy, confident little shop is a treasure, simply because it is filled with foods that you both want and need. Lots of different types of onions, good garlic, in-season marrows, four or five varieties of potato, loads of good quality soft fruits and strangenesses such as mangoes, beans of all hue, salads which sit spanking fresh in their bowls, cooked meats that have a genuine, satisfying edge to their taste. Its location — right bang in the middle of a sullen housing estate — makes it a little awkward to find, but interestingly adds an ironic delight to the pleasure of being able to find here the foods you want, the foods you need.

Open 8am-5.30pm Mon-Sat. At the top end of the town, and hard to find.

PORTAFERRY

RESTAURANT AND HOTEL
THE PORTAFERRY HOTEL
10 The Strand Tel: (02477) 28231

Perhaps it is the old-fashioned nature of the Portaferry Hotel which is the attraction for its acolytes and adherents. Best in the area for bar snacks after you've disembarked from the ferry.

Open lunch 12.30pm-3pm, 'light bite menu' 3.30pm-5pm, high tea 5.30pm-7pm, dinner from 7pm. Closed Xmas. Average Price: meals ££-£££ B&B £££££. Visa, Access, Amex. Facing the harbour.

WARINGSTOWN

RESTAURANT
THE GRANGE
Mill Hill, Main Street Tel: (0762) 881989 The Lynn Brothers

It is its sofas that have made The Grange famous. Guests, who find themselves sitting comfortably in each cushioned grip, grasping gin and tonics and nibbling crispy things, show a noted reluctance to make their way downstairs to the restaurant. But when they do they find the menu reads like a well-thumbed copy of Larousse Gastronomique, and is as comforting as the armchairs they have left behind.

Open 12.30pm-2pm, 7.30pm-10pm Tue-Sat. 12.30pm-3pm Sun. Closed 1 week Jul. Average Price: lunch £££ dinner £££. No cards. Waringstown is signposted from Lurgan and the restaurant is near the centre of the village.

ALSO OF INTEREST
THE BARN RESTAURANT, 120 Monlough Road, Saintfield BT24 7EU Tel: (0238) 510396. Recently taken over, the restaurant furnishings and gardens will need painstaking refurbishment and redecoration. But as the cooking is good, there is much hope that The Barn will once again join the ranks of Ulster's leading restaurants.

COUNTY FERMANAGH

The QUIET BEAUTY AND MOURNFULLY LOVELY SUNSETS of the Fermanagh lakelands might have been the foundation of a roaringly vibrant tourism culture, had political matters in the North been simpler over the last twenty five years. The soulful pleasures of land and water in this part of Northern Ireland are intense: softly misted mornings of chiffon white, painterly evenings with Rothko-deep oranges and reds strung across the sky in an abiding communion of colours.

But the involvement and influence of outsiders has been minimal, and culinary matters have remained old-fashioned, with certain mavericks quietly working and thriving at what they do best, a gentle-hearted collusion between cooking and companionability.

BELLANALECK

RESTAURANT
THE SHEELIN
Bellanaleck Tel: (0365) 348232
The Sheelin is probably as well known for the brown bread and the brown bread mixture sold in shops throughout Ulster as it is for the popular and familiar food it produces for its devotees.

Open Summer: 10am-6pm Mon-Tues, 10am-9.30pm Wed-Sat, 12.30pm-9.30pm Sun. Winter: 10am-6pm Mon-Thur, until 9.30pm Fri-Sat. Closed Xmas. Average Price: lunch ££ dinner £££. Visa, Access, Amex. Just of the A509.

ENNISKILLEN

RESTAURANT
FRANCO'S
Queen Elizabeth Road Tel: (0365) 324424 The Sweeney Family
Bring a light-hearted mood to Franco's, maybe sometime late on a weekend night, and the jeans 'n' t-shirts, the waxy candles, the funky music and the fun food ambience will seem just perfect. They base their forays into Italian food firmly around pasta and pizza, with myriad manifestations of each métier on offer, but there are also many fish dishes

amongst their specialities and the occasional clever concoction intrudes from time to time amongst the daily specials.

Open noon-11.30pm Mon-Tues, 'till 1am Wed-Sat, 5pm-11pm Sun. Closed Xmas. Average Price: lunch ££ dinner £££. Amex. Walk down the hill behind the town hall and Franco's is on your left.

PUB WITH FOOD
MELVIN HOUSE AND BAR
1 Townhall Street Tel: (0365) 322040
The Blake family have run Melvin House for five decades now, and their pub lunches — steaks, grilled trout, entrecote cuts of pork or beef and real chips — are a staple of the town.

Open 9.30am-6pm Mon-Thurs, 'till 9.30pm Fri, 'till 10pm Sat. No food served Wed evening or Sun. Closed Xmas. Average Price: lunch £ dinner £££. Visa, Access.

IRVINESTOWN

RESTAURANT
THE HOLLANDER
5 Main Street Tel: (03656) 21231 Jim, Margaret & Stephen Holland
'We try to cater for all' declare the trio of Hollands — Jim in the bar, Margaret and Stephen in the kitchen — and their generous sized menu gushes with Saturday night certainties: rump steak, sirloin steak, T-bone steak, fillet steak; garlic sauce, pepper sauce, Chasseur sauce and the bumper production that is the Symphony of Seafood: a fillet of lemon sole, topped with a fillet of salmon, topped with a fillet of sole, topped with large prawns, topped with 'our special sauce'.

These generous dishes are complemented by generous enthusiasm — 'Our head chef Stephen's following two seafood specials are very strongly recommended', trumpets the menu proudly — for the Hollands do their very best to cater for carnivores and vegetarians, young and old, parties and wedding groups, solo diners and courting couples.

Open 11.30am-2pm Mon-Sat, 5.30pm-11pm Mon-Sat, 6.30pm-10pm Sun. Closed Xmas and Mon & Tue Oct-Jun. Average Price: lunch ££ dinner £££ wine bar snacks £. Visa, Access. On the main street in Irvinestown.

LISNARICK

RESTAURANT
THE CEDARS
Castle Archdale, Drumall Tel: (036 56) 21493 Wesley Robinson
Wesley Robinson trained as a butcher before turning to the restaurant business, and his thoroughgoing appreciation of good meat makes The Cedars someplace to take advantage of good beef, beef which is resonant with the subtle but deep and long-lasting tastes which signal an animal which has been properly cared for. You can get a truly blue steak here, if you have the nerve, with the meat shown a hot pan for a matter of mere seconds, but the restaurant doesn't confine itself to carnivores, and whilst the cooking is modest and familiar it is carefully and thoughtfully achieved and the domestic ambience of the house

itself is charming. The Cedars is a particularly good stop if you are boating on the lakes.
Open 6pm-9.30pm Wed-Sat, 5.30pm-9.30pm Sun. Closed Xmas. Average Price: dinner £££. Visa, Access.
Just outside Lisnarick village on the Enniskillen to Kesh road (which is also the main Donegal-Dublin road).

LISNASKEA

BUTCHER
L. H. RICHARDSON
Main Street Tel: (0365) 721263 Adrian Richardson
Adrian Richardson is a passionate advocate in the cause of pure beef, an intelligent
butcher who sources his meat with meticulous attention to detail and who even finishes
the pasturing of his meat himself when it is possible. Mindful of the vicissitudes which
attend so much meat production these days, Mr Richardson has gone back to the safe and
secure old ways — buying locally from trusted farmers, bringing great skill to the business
of butchering and hanging of the meat — in order to be able to sell meat which vindicates
his concern and expresses his skill.
Open 8.30am-6pm Mon-Sat. Closed all day Thurs.

COUNTY LONDONDERRY

DERRY IS A SELF-MYTHOLOGISING SORT OF PLACE, confident about its charms and confident about itself, in the same way you might find in Donegal or Kerry. Even in John Hewitt's topographical poem 'Ulster Names', the poet hits a sauntering stride when the city arrives:

You whisper Derry. Beyond the walls
and the crashing boom and the coiling smoke,
I follow that freedom which beckons and calls
to Colmcille tall in his grave of oak
raising his voice for the rhyming oak.

People here, you feel, believe that they are keepers of a true flame. Strangers might wonder what locals make such a fuss about, but the city has a spontaneity and friendliness which are instantly affecting and infectious, and the countryside has a quiet lilt to it, an easy sense of itself.

COLERAINE

RESTAURANT & COUNTRY HOUSE
MACDUFF'S
Blackheath House, 112 Killeague Road, Blackhill Tel: (0265) 868433 Joseph & Margaret Erwin
Macduff's is the cellar restaurant of Blackheath House, a handsome, quietly unimposing Georgian rectory. Margaret Erwin's cooking is friendly and accessible, with the benefit of almost two decades of experience behind it. The house has six comfortably thoughtful rooms for those who are touring or who wish simply to make a proper night of it.
Open 7.30pm-9.30pm Tue-Sat (7 days Jul & Aug). Closed Xmas. Average Price: dinner £££ B&B ££££. Visa, Access. Just off the A29, seven miles south of Coleraine, four miles north of Garvagh.

DERRY

HOTEL/RESTAURANT
BEECH HILL COUNTRY HOUSE HOTEL ➥
32 Ardmore Road, Derry Tel: (0504) 49279 Fax: 45366 Seamus Donnelly
Quite how Noel McMeel manages to so confidently stride that danger zone, wherein a cook must satisfy the conservative demands of his customers and at the same time create food which inspires his own imagination, is one of the most intriguing questions in the world of Irish food.

Just look, for example, at what McMeel will do with something as timeworn, and theoretically uninspiring, as a breast of chicken. Firstly, he gets a good bird that has a touch of farmyard firmness in its texture. Then, he makes a fresh, surreptitious basil sauce for underneath a bed of poppy seed tagliatelli which the breast, sliced across the centre, rests upon. The pasta, made to a very eggy mixture which echoes Raymond Blanc's soft, moist French style, gives the dish not just a bland counterpoint to the chicken and the sauce, but synthesises its rich taste with the other ingredients. The dish is so effective at furnishing alliances of tastes and giving sensual pleasure that it achieves a measure of transcendence.

This delicately achieved fusion of ingredients and cultures jumps out from the menu: a tongue-caressing soup of courgettes; a filo parcel of mushrooms on a bed of lentils served with a mild curry sauce; a seafood sausage sitting on softly stewed baby leeks with a prawn sauce all around; a glorious confit of duck — flinty with dark tastes but light and supple in texture — comes with pickled red cabbage and a clean green peppercorn sauce.

But, however he manages it, his successful achievement of dishes which combine tried and trusted favourite tastes with forays into modern styling and technique is nothing but a joy, and it has been possible to see, on return visits to Beech Hill, that he has begun to transcend the lessons learnt at the hands of other fine chefs — a love of colourful complexity borrowed from Ian McAndrew, a love of earthy flavours brought from Paul Rankin — and has begun to sign dishes with his own signature.

Not only that, indeed, for in McMeel's absence the kitchen can produce food which has all the elements which you associate with his work: gracefulness, strength of flavour and a dazzling capacity to invent. You don't expect food of this order in an hotel, and to find it in the romantic and innocent dining room in Beech Hill is a joy.

But can he bake a cherry pie? He can, and he can bake a rich, soft plum pudding with a thin brandy sauce or a lissom series of chocolate mousses that are ethereal confections. Derry just does not know how lucky it is to have this young man cooking such fine food a mile outside the city.

Open 7am-10am, 12.30pm-2.30pm, 6.30pm-10pm Mon-Sun. Closed Xmas. Average Price: breakfast £-££ lunch £££ dinner £££. Visa, Access, Amex. Beech Hill is signposted from the A2, just past Drumahoe as you come into Derry on the main Belfast road.

KILLALOO

ORGANIC FARMER
BRACKFIELD FARM
Killaloo Tel: (0504) 301243 David Hawthorne
David Hawthorne supplies his organic lamb and vegetables to local restaurants, but callers to the farm can also buy meat provided they can cope with a complete carcass. Telephone for more details.

The back lane of the farm runs down beside the Killaloo primary school.

LIMAVADY

COUNTRY HOUSE
DRENAGH
Limavady Tel: (05047) 22649 Maj Gen & Mrs P.M. Welch
Drenagh is one of the most highly and most affectionately regarded country houses in the north. People who have stayed here are liable to become veritably rhapsodic when discussing its delights.

These ear-bending confessions rhapsodise not just the house itself, though it is a most imposing and serene mansion house dating from 1835, or indeed even the splendid food and the seriousness with which the cuisine is regarded.

No, what zings the strings of people's hearts is the sense of appropriateness which the house engenders, the Welchs' manner of doing things just right. Many of the country houses in Ireland enjoyed such a rash of prosperity and busyness during the fulsome 1980s that they have adapted less well to the more critical and competitive 1990s. Drenagh is a somewhere that demonstrates the charms of the country house vocation and the country vacation, and shows why it is valuable, and fun.

Open Mar-Nov, dinner for guests only. Average Price: dinner £££, B&B £££££. Visa, Access. On the Limavady/Coleraine road, 1 mile out on the left. Go in via the first gate lodge. There is no sign.

PORTSTEWART

BUTCHER
J.E. TOMS & SONS

45 The Promenade Tel: (026583) 2869

Bangers, burgers and steaks are the staple of the Toms and Sons empire, but happily they take their cue from the other cutting edge charcutiers in the North rather than undiscriminating supermarkets, and the level of skill and enthusiasm at work here, the joie de vivre which one finds in the multitude of meats, is quite infectious. For the droves of caravan-bound holiday makers who trek annually to Portstewart there is a wonderful array and display of meats designed for the barbecue alone, including garlic burgers, Hawaiian style pork sausages, Chinese style pork ribs and stuffed bacon chops.

Open 8am-6pm Mon-Sat. On the seafront.

COUNTY TYRONE

NORAH BROWN IS MODEST ABOUT HER COOKING SKILLS. 'It's just instinct', she says, 'for I have no training. The dishes are just dishes I like to cook'. But would we not all like to be gifted with the instinct that knows that a soupçon of gin will gift the damson sauce accompanying some cheddar pears with a special little secret taste.

We should all like to know that whilst a splash of port may seem to be a strange bedfellow to a redcurrant sauce, in fact the pair together achieve the serenity of a sonata and spur on the delicious pleasure of a dish of chicken Wellington.

In truth, Mrs Brown is right, though far too modest. What is especially enjoyable about her cooking in Grange Lodge Country House is the fact that it has the well-won confidence of the domestic cook, so the dishes have the comfort of simple tastes and simple presentation. At the end of a hard-driving day, the pleasure of sitting down in the small dining room in Grange and eating dinner — chicken terrine baked in the Aga, fisherman's moneybag, where fresh salmon is cooked in a filo parcel — gives joy to both body and soul. This food seems ageless, coming as it does out of the inquisitive nature of a confident cook like Mrs Brown, and coming as it does out of a tradition of serious and accomplished domestic cooking.

Whilst we must regret the decline in domestic cooking skills, a fact that seems most prevalent in the North, Norah Brown's food speaks contentedly of the ages of tradition, where skills and secrets were handed down in a family from mother to daughter, skills that gave cooks easy-handed confidence and the ability to compile and unravel tastes and flavours in a meal.

So, in Grange, dinner wears an easy rhythm, the surprise of some lemony mushrooms flavoured with garlic and bacon giving way to the succulence of a lamb fricassee with a lemon and thyme sauce, before a sticky pudding of sharp lemon roulade ends a meal in quiet triumph, and you are restored, restored to beaming best.

And what do your thoughts turn to the instant dinner is over? To breakfast, no less, and a bowl of porridge that may have already begun its long overnight simmer in the oven. In the morning, it will receive the expert ministrations of Ralph Brown as he first scatters crystals of brown sugar on top, then annotates the soft grains with a generous splash of Bushmills whiskey before a cloak of rich cream melds with the sugar and the hootch. From first mouthful, you are in culinary heaven, the pleasure points in your body reaching some sort of frothy ferment, a ferment maintained by a generous and expert Ulster Fry, and a glass of the local Cumwins apple juice.

There is a downside, however, to this domestic sang-froid. The quality of domestic cooking amongst women such as Norah Brown has meant that the best food in counties such as Tyrone, indeed west of the River Bann, remains largely a domestic affair. Restaurants and hotels in Tyrone cannot hold a candle to the skilful, careful cooking you find in places like Grange Lodge.

Where commercial establishments cook by rote and under threat of profit, women like Mrs Brown cook by instinct abetted by generosity, preserving the sound understanding which gifts their food with character, comfort.

Eating here, you feel you have stumbled on the heartbeat of the county, found out just what it is that makes it tick.

GRANGE LODGE

Grange Road, Dungannon Tel: (08687) 84212 Norah & Ralph Brown
Open for dinner Fri & Sat. Guests only during the week. Closed Xmas. Average Price: dinner £££-££££ B&B
££££. Visa, Access. 1 mile from M1 junction 15. Take A29 to Armagh, then follow signs to Grange.

CUNWIN'S PURE APPLE JUICE

Cornamuckla House, 60 Bush Road, Dungannon Tel: (08687) 24637 B. Cummings

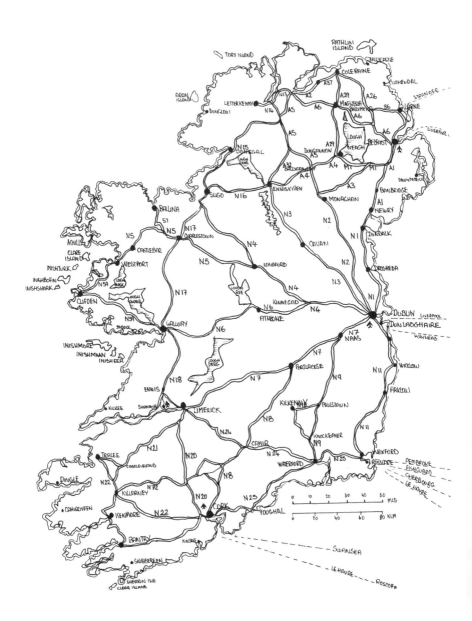

BRIDGESTONE

ARRIVAL AND DEPARTURE

These suggested places to stay and places to eat are chosen on account of their proximity to ferries and airports and, of course, their comfort, suitability, their charm.

PORTS

DUN LAOGHAIRE AND DUBLIN NORTH WALL PORTS

Accommodation:

ANGLESEA TOWN HOUSE 63 Anglesea Road, Ballsbridge, Dublin 4 Tel: 01-683877. Great big breakfasts are one of the favoured features in Sean and Helen Kirrane's comfortable house, convenient for both the North Wall and the Dun Laoghaire ferries.

AVONDALE HOUSE Scribblestown, Castleknock, Co Dublin Tel: 01-386545. Very close to both the North Wall ferry and Dublin airport, Frank and Josie Carroll's house is small, great fun.

CHESTNUT LODGE 2 Vesey Place, Monkstown, Co Dublin Tel: 01-280 7860. Nancy Malone's charming house, and her own charm, make Chestnut one of the nicest places to arrive at, and one of the hardest to leave from.

Restaurants:

ELEPHANT & CASTLE 18 Temple Bar, Dublin 2 Tel: 01-679 3121. The 'no-reservations' policy means one may have to wait for a table, but the E&C's zappy food is perfect for shaking off travel tiredness.

ROLY'S BISTRO 7 Ballsbridge Terrace, Dublin 4 Tel: 01-668 2611. Romantic, good value, but booking beforehand is usually necessary.

ODELL'S 49 Sandycove Road, Dun Laoghaire Tel: 01-284 2188. Convenient to the Dun Laoghaire ferry, the food in Odell's is simple, tasty.

ROSSLARE FERRY

Accommodation:

FURZIESTOWN HOUSE Tacumshane, Co Wexford Tel: 053-31376. For many travellers, Yvonne Pim's house is now a musn't-miss for first and last nights in Ireland. Delicious cooking.

MCMENAMIN'S TOWNHOUSE 2 Auburn Terrace, Wexford, Co Wexford Tel: (053) 46442. Thoughtful, comfortable, professionally run townhouse.

NEWBAY HOUSE Newbay, Co Wexford Tel: 053-42779. Paul and Min Drumm's big pile is one of the friendliest of the country houses.

Restaurant:

EUGENE'S RESTAURANT Ballyedmond, Co Wexford Tel: (054) 89288. A pub, a chipper and a restaurant all run by Eugene & Elizabeth Callaghan. Eugene, believe it or believe it not, is a former Roux Brothers' Young Chef of the year. So expect dazzling food, dazzling pub food and even dazzling fish and chips.

CORK PORT

Accommodation:

GARNISH HOUSE Western Road, Cork City Tel: 021-275111. A model B&B amidst the droves of faceless houses on the Western Road, with Hansi Lucey laying on the charm by the ton.

SEVEN NORTH MALL 7 North Mall, Cork City Tel: 021-397191. A beautiful town house with great views over the river and Angela Hegarty's house also offers excellent value and super breakfasts.

Restaurant and Accommodation:

ISAAC'S HOSTEL 48 MacCurtain Street, Cork City, Hostel Tel: 021-500011. Restaurant Tel: 021-503805.

The food in the Brasserie at front is very pleasing, strong on flavour. The bathrooms in the hostel are clean and clever, the rooms smart, the sheets good, breakfast is fine. Isaac's is closer in style to a pensione than a hostel.

LARNE AND BELFAST PORTS

Accommodation:
ASH ROWAN 12 Windsor Avenue, Belfast BT9 6EE Tel: 0232-661758. Sam and Evelyn Hazlett's house is quiet and comfortable, in a quiet and comfortable part of town.
OAKHILL COUNTRY HOUSE 59 Dunmurray Lane, Belfast Tel: (0232) 610658. May Noble's house is one of the best-regarded places to stay in the city.
Restaurants:
NICK'S WAREHOUSE 35/39 Hill Street, Belfast BT1 Tel: 0232-439690. Friendly, fun, super food and ambience in Nick and Cathy Price's inimitable restaurant and winebar.

AIRPORTS

These suggestions give some ideas for places to eat and places to stay if arriving at one of the local airports in Ireland. If arriving at either Dublin or Belfast airports, then check the entries for those cities in the Ports section.

SLIGO

GLEBE HOUSE Coolaney Road, Collooney, Co Sligo Tel: 071-67787. The bedrooms are simple and straightforward, but Brid Torrades' cooking in the restaurant is an indulgent delight.
TRUFFLES RESTAURANT 11 The Mall, Sligo, Co Sligo Tel: 071-44226. The greatest pizzas to be found anywhere in the country, and a great buzzy atmosphere.

KERRY, FARRANFORE AIRPORT

Dingle:
DOYLE'S TOWNHOUSE AND RESTAURANT John Street, Dingle, Co Kerry Tel: 066-51174. Super rooms in this professional organisation.
BEGINISH RESTAURANT Green Street, Dingle, Co Kerry Tel: 066-51588. Splendid cooking in John and Pat Moore's relaxing restaurant.
Kenmare:
HAWTHORN HOUSE Shelbourne Street, Kenmare, Co Kerry Tel: (064) 41035. A lovely B&B, simple as that.
PACKIE'S RESTAURANT Henry Street, Kenmare, Co Kerry Tel: 064-41508. Maura Foley is one of the most celebrated cooks in Ireland, someone who simply does everything right.

WATERFORD

AHERNE'S SEAFOOD BAR AND ACCOMMODATION 163 North Main Street, Youghal, Co Cork Tel: 024-92424. Great big, comfortable rooms and one of the best fish restaurants in the country

KNOCK

ECHOES RESTAURANT Main Street, Cong, Co Mayo Tel: 092-46059. The place to eat when in Mayo: soulful, sublime food from Siobhan Ryan.
TEMPLE HOUSE Ballymote, Co Sligo Tel: 071-83329. Many people's favourite country house, not too far north of the airport.

GALWAY

MOYCULLEN HOUSE Moycullen, Co Galway Tel: 091-85566. Relaxing, laid-back Arts & Crafts house.

NORMAN VILLA 86 Lwr Salthill, Galway Tel: 091-21131. A small but perfectly beautiful B&B: an aesthete's delight.

SHANNON

BALLYTEIGUE HOUSE Bruree, nr Charleville, Co Limerick Tel: 063-90575. Margaret Johnson's house is a great place to wind down after an Atlantic hop.

FERGUS VIEW KILNABOY, Corofin, Co Clare Tel: 065-27606. Lovely cooking from Mary Kelleher in a cosy farmhouse B&B near to Mullaghmore.

EATING ON THE ROAD

A S YOU TRAVEL THE MAJOR ROADS OF IRELAND, bright signs along the way have hunger-ending boasts such as 'Food Served All Day', 'Fast Food Served Here' or — this one the truckers' favourite — 'Good Food And Plenty Of It'.

These injunctions to break your fast are, in reality, the culinary equivalent of 'Abandon Hope All Ye Who Enter Here'. What you can expect in these places is inferior fuel food: high-protein, highly-seasoned and, usually, highly greasy grub which is lifted from freezer to microwave and which rarely enjoys the benefit of any sort of meaningful culinary intervention.

Often the situation can appear hopeless, with the main thoroughfares nothing but tarmacadamed deserts without an oasis in sight for the discriminating eater. But, take heart. There are good On-The-Road places, and more and more are appearing every year. Just as our national cuisine has been revolutionised in a decade, the same is happening to On-The-Road eateries. If you choose carefully, pleasurable meals and snacks can be found, food with sufficient goodness and soul to compare with happy memories from the Continent or the 'States or further afield. The following are the choicest places to enjoy good food when travelling the major roads in Ireland, and we have also added some places in the major towns which are very suitable for when you arrive or just before you leave, mainly by virtue of having good food and no-nonsense service which allows you to get in and out in decent time.

Many serve fairly simple food, designed to revive flagging spirits and energies, set you back to rights and get you thundering happily off up the road. But, here and there, the efforts of someone to prepare handmade food and to serve it graciously will give a special pleasure.

THE M1/A1 BELFAST-DUBLIN

THE CONTINENTAL MEAT CENTRE Clanbrassil St, Dundalk, County Louth Ann and Alo Putz's fine shop is perfect for making up your own rolls for picnicing in the car as you head north or south: fill them with excellent salamis, or stuff them with liver sausage.

THE CHUCK WAGON nr Swords, County Dublin About 4km north of Swords and signalled by a posse of trucks. Don't let the truckers dissuade you from pulling up and ordering the sausage and bacon sarnie wrapped up in a kerchief of soda bread. 'Do you want onions?' demand the insouciant damsels who man the 'Wagon. You do want the onions, but hold the sauce. Brilliant up-and-at 'em food. Easy parking.

THE ELEPHANT & CASTLE Temple Bar, Dublin The E&C is a good spot if you have to divert into the city, by virtue of the fact that it is easy to find, you can choose either a little or a lot from their menu at any time of the day and — during the day — the service is swift.

THE M2 BELFAST-DERRY

NICK'S WAREHOUSE Hill Street, Belfast BT1 Just before you head off up the M2, Nick Price's Warehouse allows you to scoot just off the connecting road and enjoy something snappy in the downstairs bar. Signposted at the Albert Clock.

THE BEECH HILL HOTEL Drumahoe, County Londonderry It is worthwhile building up an appetite for Noel McMeel's superb cooking, for this man can work up a storm of elegant, graceful, tasteful food: lushly oily confit of duck on a bed of pickled cabbage; gorgeous chicken with a red pepper mousse served with a tarragon cream; dynamic filo of mushrooms with chunky lentils and a creamy curry sauce. Breakfast, lunch and dinner are served. Easy parking.

THE N2 DUBLIN-DERRY

CASEY'S STEAKBAR Ballinagh, County Cavan Good value steaks, with chips and onions, naturally. Just south of Cavan town. Easy parking.

THE OLD POST INN Clover Hill Open from 11am-10pm Mon-Sun, this restaurant and rooms, five miles north of Cavan, gives a pretty and restful diversion without having to turn off the main road. Easy parking.

THE N3 DUBLIN-ENNISKILLEN-DONEGAL

MCGROARTY'S The Diamond, Donegal, County Donegal Stella is in charge of the food in this low-ceilinged pub and she knows what she is at: great soups, good salads, lovely stir-fry-filled pitta bread. Thoughtful, comforting food.

THE N4/N6 DUBLIN-GALWAY

MOTHER HUBBARD'S nr Kinnegad, County Westmeath A few miles east of the wide strip of Kinnegad, John Healy's Mother Hubbard's is probably the dream diner. Formerly a caravan which was decorated with mug shots of third-rate celebrities, it has been Fairy Godmothered into a neon-lit, spruce, friendly place. Clean as a whistle throughout, with trucker food favourites that also appeal to ordinary mortals, it has a telephone, pristine loos with condom machines for both sexes, baby changing room, high chairs and is open early 'till late. Easy parking.

LOCKE'S DISTILLERY Kilbeggan, County Westmeath Home-made bread and cakes.

THE LOFT Kilbeggan, County Westmeath Comforting scoops of mash with their hot specials, friendly service.

THE N7/N8 DUBLIN-CORK

THE AYUMI-YA STEAKHOUSE Baggot Street, Dublin 2 The Ayumi-Ya should be an essential stop for anyone who has to depart the capital — on whatever road — around about lunchtime and wants some energy-packed food to make the miles speed by. If you can eat in, then a bowl of noodles is the perfect fuel food. If you can't, then their take-away Bento Boxes are the most perfect prepared picnics possible: some salted and steamed fish, a little rice, some succulent prawns, nice sweet butter beans, whatever you like.

MORRISSEY'S, Abbeyleix, County Laois The sandwiches and the coffee are what you would expect, but this glorious pub should be on every travellers' itinerary. Have a pint, and embrace the stilled sense of history.

TREACY'S nr Portlaoise, County Laois; A single-storey thatched pub on the left hand side of the road as you head south after Portlaoise. Treacy's is The Trucker's Choice — you will notice it by the long line of trucks parked at the side of the road and in the huge car park — so if you want quickly served, rather obvious food — beef, lamb, spuds — you will get it and you will get lots of it. Easy parking.

THE SPORTSMAN'S INN Cullahill, County Laois For years, under the astute eye of Mrs O'Connell, the Sportsman's reigned supreme, but since her retirement, the ambition of the pub has dimmed and whilst it remains a decent place to grab a bite one can't help but remember the glories of the past. Easy parking.

THE SPEARMAN RESTAURANT Cashel, County Tipperary The Spearman serves perfect fuel food: deep-tasting soups, delicious fish dishes with soulful sauces, mega BLTs, and everything is just what you felt like. Its location at the top end of Cashel town makes it a travellers' must.

LA BIGOUDENNE Crêperie-Restaurant Fermoy, County Cork A charming single-room restaurant and, thanks to the best buckwheat crêpes you will find in the country, La Bigoudenne has delightful food for drivers and passengers. The owners are French and cook their savoury and sweet dishes with loving skill and understated aplomb. Aside from the crêpes, the other food is happy and fortifying. Clean loos and good for changing baby. Open from 12.30pm-10.30pm with a more formal restaurant in the evening starting from 7pm — though they will try to accommodate with simpler meals if you're passing by.

ARBUTUS LODGE Montenotte, Cork Just up the hill and just off the road as you come into town, the lunches in the bar at Arbutus offer good food at good prices. Easy parking.

THE CRAWFORD GALLERY CAFÉ Emmet Place, Cork Either before you set out or just when you arrive, this is one of the quintessential lunch places. One day, a potato and fresh herb soup, then fresh brill with a hollandaise, made for a meal that was little short of wonderful. Great cakes, and excellent for people watching. Open from mid-morning for coffee and on Saturdays for brunch.

THE LONG VALLEY Winthrop Street, Cork This pub may seem like strangeness itself the first time you walk in — weird music, ladies in white coats with operating theatre expressions behind the bar — but those same ladies make the meanest sandwiches in town and pull a soft pint of stout for non-drivers. Do note that, being a pub, they do not welcome children.

THE N7 DUBLIN-LIMERICK

COUNTRY CHOICE Kenyon Street, Nenagh, County Tipperary Peter Ward's lovely shop is one of the best shops in the country, and in the back has a super coffee shop and lunchtime place which is perfect for sandwiches and savouries. Chances are you will spend at least seventeen quid in the shop itself before you finally manage to leave. Easy parking.

IVAN'S Caherdavin, Limerick Ivan Cremins' shop is open from 7am-11.30pm Mon-Sun, and there's sandwiches, breads, cheeses and cooked foods stocking the shelves and counters.

THE N9 DUBLIN-WATERFORD

THE LORD BAGENAL Leighlinbridge, County Carlow James Kehoe's restaurant is famed for its gargantuan and wonderful wine list, but as somewhere near to the main road it is also a good place to stop over, even if you aren't drinking. Usefully, it has climbing frames for kids, or for those with surplus energy. Easy parking.

SHORTIS WONG John Street, Kilkenny, Co Kilkenny A deli where you will find a good sandwich, or maybe some of Chris Wong's super street food which can transport you to the East with just one bite: the lamb murtaback this man makes is sublime. A diversion from the main road, but worth it.

THE N11 DUBLIN-WEXFORD-ROSSLARE

THE STONE OVEN Lower Main Street, Arklow, County Wicklow Good bread and savoury delights signal the chance to improvise a picnic in Egon Frederick's bakery. Easy parking.

EUGENE'S RESTAURANT Ballyedmond, County Wexford Take the R741 to Wexford out of Gorey rather than the main road and in Eugene's you will find not just the best on-the-road food — in restaurant, pub and chipper — but some of the best food in the country. Easy parking.

MICK THE FRYING IRISHMAN Castlebridge, County Wexford Michael Murphy's chipper is quietly legendary. Fish and chips, done right. Easy parking.

THE N15-N17 GALWAY-SLIGO-DONEGAL

GOYA'S Shop Street, Galway, County Galway The place to picnic on luscious cakes and breads. Best of all, buy some of Eamonn McGeough's corned beef in Roche's Stores, bring it here and slide it in between a yeasted white roll, squidge on some mustard and, Heaven!

THE GOURMET PARLOUR Bridge Street, Sligo, County Sligo Catherine and Annette's trâiteur is the best place to assemble a picnic of excellent savoury foods. The sandwiches are salady, sodabready and delightful.

THE OLD STABLES Drumcliff, County Sligo If peering at Yeats' grave should make you peckish, this is a good roadside tea shop during the season. Easy parking.

THE CANAVAUN LOUNGE Cliffony, County Sligo Good on-the-road sandwiches and a more extensive but well realised menu during the summer as you saunter north or south. A very friendly pub indeed. Easy parking.

THE SMUGGLER'S CREEK Rossnowlagh, County Donegal A little bit off the main road, perhaps, but they serve a good cup of tea and offer a great view across the bay for free. Easy parking.

MCGROARTY'S The Diamond, Donegal, County Donegal See the N3 above.

THE N18 LIMERICK-ENNIS-GALWAY

ABBEY MEATS/THE FOOD EMPORIUM Abbey Street, Ennis, County Clare This inventive and inspiring shop is, typically, good for sandwiches, filled rolls and frankfurters.

THE CLOISTER Abbey Street, Ennis, County Clare A nice pub with simple, clean tasting food which is especially enjoyable at lunchtime, a meal which is served well into the afternoon.

MORAN'S OF THE WEIR Kilcolgan, nr Galway, County Galway They serve an extensive menu in Moran's but we have never gotten any further than their celebrated oysters and brown bread, the original on-the-road grub. With a glass of stout, this is the perfect food to get your motor, of whatever nature, up and running. Parking.

THE N20 CORK-LIMERICK

LONGUEVILLE HOUSE Mallow, County Cork For a luxurious lunch in one of the nicest country houses. During the summer you can eat in their gorgeous conservatory and this, with William O'Callaghan's glorious, rigorous food, can make for one of the most sublime culinary experiences. Easy parking.

THE N22 CORK-KILLARNEY-TRALEE

CONTINENTAL SAUSAGES Fossa, nr Killarney, County Kerry Good salamis, sausages and cooked meats, all of them perfect for a picnic, and somewhere to have a cup of tea and some good cake. If lucky, you may even persuade them to slap a handsome hank of beef into a frying pan for you and find yourself having the most delicious dinner. Easy parking.

THE N25 CORK-WATERFORD

THE FARM GATE Coolbawn, Midleton, County Cork A slight detour off the main road but this is a bubbly, lively restaurant with easeful, feminine food, and fronted by a super shop where you can assemble a picnic if you don't want to stop. Easy parking.

AHERNE'S North Main Street, Youghal, County Cork For pub food in the bar which is a mile better than most other pub food you will find, or a more seriously fishy lunch in the restaurant.

THE SHIP Dunmore East, County Waterford A dander off the main road, of course, but if you find yourself in this frothy village, The Ship is the best in the area: friendly, fun food. Make sure to check opening times out of season. If it is early evening time, then do try The Suir Inn at Cheekpoint, also down this way and a good stop for enjoyable food. Easy parking.

CHAPMAN'S PANTRY The Quay, Waterford A fine food shop with a busy café tucked in at the back which is good for snacking.

THE N71 CORK-KENMARE

THE SUGAN Pearse Street, Clonakilty, County Cork Extra care and concern makes for above-average pub food, in a nice friendly boozer on the main street of this lovely village.

FIONNUALA'S ITALIAN RESTAURANT Ashe St, Clonakilty, County Cork The pizzas and pastas are very good, the former particularly suitable for kids.

MOBILE CHIPPER Inishannon, County Cork Just outside the town, after you cross the bridge heading west, there is a Dutchman of exceedingly good cheer who runs a very popular mobile chipper and very conveniently runs it right at the side of the road. For some reason, it is now fenced off, but still accessible. Do try the frikadels. Easy parking.

FIELD'S SUPERMARKET Main Street, Skibbereen, County Cork Good for prepared pies — look out for Gill Boazman's pork and venison pies in particular — and other picnic foods.

ANNIE'S RESTAURANT Ballydehob, County Cork Deliciously reviving food in a charming restaurant. Easy parking.

SEA VIEW HOUSE HOTEL Ballylickey, County Cork Cheerful, maternal food, the sort of creamy, buttery dishes your parents will lap up, with sweetly innocent service in a grand old hotel. Bar food available at lunchtime in the summer. Easy parking.

MANNING'S FOOD EMPORIUM Ballylickey, County Cork Most things you might need for a picnic, especially the cheeses. Easy parking.

THE PURPLE HEATHER Henry Street, Kenmare, County Kerry One part of the Foley family empire, with typically tasteful, fatigue-evaporating food, in a friendly pub.

INDEX

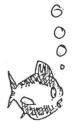

OTHER TITLES FROM ESTRAGON PRESS

The Bridgestone 100 Best Restaurants in Ireland

The most critical up-to-the-minute guide to the finest restaurants in Ireland. Evaluates in depth the most committed, creative and exciting cooks working in Ireland today.
Price: £5.99

"The McKenna's writing style — you might call it emerald prose — one of the finest food reads I've encountered for a long time." Simone Sekers, The Sunday Telegraph.

The Bridgestone 100 Best Places to Stay in Ireland

From simple B&Bs to grand Country Houses, from welcoming Farmhouses to luxurious Hotels, this book finds the best places to stay in Ireland
Price: £5.99

"Essential reading for all travellers...personally and carefully researched by the two authors, established authorities on all that is good in Ireland's food."
Sandy O'Byrne, The Irish Times.

The Bridgestone 100 Best Places to Eat in Dublin

The definitive critical independent guide to the finest meals in Dublin, from pizzerias to the grandest restaurants. Simply the essential guide to the capital city's best food.
Price: £4.99

"The best guide to that charming country." Emily Green, The Independent

The Bridgestone Vegetarian's Guide to Ireland

A comprehensive guide for vegetarians to the finest Irish food, in the style of the award-winning Bridgestone Irish Food Guide. Covering every possible food source, from farms and shops through to restaurants and the best accommodation, this is the definitive guide for vegetarians.
Price: £6.99.

ORDER FORM

All titles in the Bridgestone Series from Estragon Press are available in good book stores nationwide.

If you missed any of the Series or have trouble getting them locally, they can be ordered by post direct from the publisher.

Simply fill out the coupon below, enclosing a cheque or money order for the correct amount (add £1.50 per book for postage and packing), and the relevant title(s) will be dispatched to you immediately. Be sure to fill out your address completely, and to print carefully.

Please send me the following title(s) from the Bridgestone series (please tick):

❏ **The Bridgestone Vegetarian's Guide to Ireland £6.99**
❏ **The Bridgestone 100 Best Restaurants in Ireland £5.99**
❏ **The Bridgestone 100 Best Places to Eat in Dublin £5.99**
❏ **The Bridgestone 100 Best Places to Stay in Ireland £5.99**

I enclose a cheque/money order (delete) for £_____, (including P&P)

Name ....

Address ....

....

....

....

....